# ENERGY AND ENVIRONMENT

*Readings from*
# SCIENTIFIC AMERICAN

# ENERGY AND ENVIRONMENT

*With Commentaries by*
## Raymond Siever
*Harvard University*

W. H. Freeman and Company
*San Francisco*

For Doris, whose queries always helped

Most of the SCIENTIFIC AMERICAN articles in *Energy and Environment* are available as separate Offprints. For a complete list of articles now available as Offprints, write to W. H. Freeman and Company, 660 Market Street, San Francisco, California 94104.

**Library of Congress Cataloging in Publication Data**

Main entry under title:

Energy and environment.

  Bibliography: p.
  Includes index.
  1. Power resources—Addresses, essays, lectures.
2. Fossil fuels—Environmental aspects—Addresses, essays, lectures. 3. Atomic power—Environmental aspects—Addresses, essays, lectures. I. Siever, Raymond. II. Scientific American.
TJ163.24.E53    333.8′2′08    79–21980
ISBN 0–7167–1052–8
ISBN 0–7167–1053–6 pbk.

31,010

Printed in the United States of America

9 8 7 6 5 4 3 2 1

# PREFACE

The energy crisis has produced a bewildering array of both professional and popular books, articles in daily newspapers and slick magazines, novels, and the timely movie "The China Syndrome." This reader brings together thoughtful views of some of the major issues in articles that were selected to give a deeper analysis of a number of different problems; for the ways we use energy and its effect on our environment are many problems, not one. The articles concentrate on choices that we must make over the next two decades, rather than what we should do tomorrow or what we may face a hundred years from now. Because of this emphasis, the focus is on fossil fuels and nuclear power—the forms of energy now in heavy use—and their consequences, rather than on alternative sources such as solar and wind power. These alternatives, particularly solar energy, are still in the early phases of speculation, research, and individual invention; so far they generate an insignificant proportion of the energy used in the world. Thus it is not possible to compare them with more conventional, established forms of energy production. Certainly this does *not* mean that conventional sources are preferable to solar, but that, whatever the reasons for our unfortunate ignoring of these alternatives for so long, they cannot replace oil, coal, and nuclear power before a good many years have passed and we learn what role they are capable of playing.

This reader begins with a general introduction, and each section with an introduction that summarizes the issues raised and shows how the subjects of the articles relate to each other. Each article is preceded by a commentary that outlines its main points, sets a background to the subject, and poses some serious problems that may not have been covered in the article. The introduction to each section should be read before the articles in it. For students who are not familiar with many of the topics, a good procedure might be to read the individual article commentary quickly first, then the article, and then the commentary again more carefully for review.

It is impossible to make a reader of this kind as current as the news of the day. The articles will give the reader a knowledgeable background to understand the news as it happens. For example, in the summer of 1979, President Carter and the U.S. Congress focused on synthetic fuels to replace some of the crude oil the United States imports. The articles in this reader will make clearer how such syntheses are accomplished, and their advantages and disadvantages.

I am indebted to my colleagues and friends—and especially my wife—for the many conversations, the many questions and answers that have been raised in these matters that are so crucial for us all. I was particularly helped by Léo Laporte, who read the manuscript and made many perceptive comments and suggestions. My thanks to Evelyn Stinchfield, capable as always, who typed the manuscript.

*July 1979*                                                                *Raymond Siever*

# CONTENTS

*Note on cross-references:* References to articles included in this book are noted by the title of the article and the page on which it begins; references to articles that are available as Offprints, but are not included here, are noted by the article's title and Offprint number; references to articles published by SCIENTIFIC AMERICAN but which are not available as Offprints, are noted by the title of the article and the month and year of its publication.

ENERGY AND ENVIRONMENT

# GENERAL INTRODUCTION

It is hard to fight the tendency to make a problem go away by pretending it isn't there—or, perhaps worse, merely accommodating to a bad situation rather than trying to change it. Those who knew of the limit to our natural reserves of oil and gas had long warned that there would be an end to the era of abundant, cheap energy. Few listened. The energy "crisis" is almost a decade old as far as general recognition is concerned, yet governments and the people of the world, many of them poorly informed and others distrustful, have not advanced much beyond their thinking of 10 years ago. Some dismiss the problem as nonexistent, the invention of greedy corporations. Others are confident that we will surely find the solution if and when the time comes, with a sublime optimism hardly warranted by what we know.

The dimensions of the energy crisis are now known. The amounts of oil, gas, coal, and uranium ore in the Earth are finite. We know approximately how much of each there is and can guess how much we are likely to discover in the future. We also know how much is recoverable by present methods of mining and extraction and can even predict some improvement in the next two decades. However, we can estimate only on the basis of weak assumptions the increase in demand for energy and the awareness of environmental costs over the next 20 years. Much depends on the future expansion of economies of both developed and developing nations, the economic and political disturbances of those economies, and how well political leaders are able to cope with the hard choices that they and the people they govern must make. However we calculate future demand and production, it is hard to avoid the conclusion that by the year 2000 we will have to substitute other energy sources for a good part of the oil and gas we have been burning profligately for the past decades.

We need to know more about the consequences of the choices we make. We know that we can substitute coal or nuclear power for oil and gas in the near future. We hope, but cannot be sure, that solar energy will be available on a large scale before several decades pass. The world's governments will have to choose patterns of investment (research, planning, money) among these alternatives. As yet, our information is incomplete as to what the choices should be. Some of that information is in the realm of science. We still do not know enough, for a most important example, about the carbon cycle in the atmosphere and the oceans to make completely reliable predictions of the effect of increased fossil-fuel burning on the carbon dioxide content of the atmosphere. We know still less about the effects of increased carbon dioxide on the global climate. We do not yet know enough about movements of underground waters in general to predict with great certainty how much water may pass through a specific formation in which radioactive waste is stored over tens of thousands of years. We cannot ever be "sure" of the answers to these questions beforehand. All we can do is to predict on the basis of present knowledge. How to increase that knowledge so that we become "sure enough" is on our current agenda.

Other questions are technological, demanding new devices and processes. One of the most pressing is the ability of nuclear engineers to run nuclear power plants without accident. But no less urgent are the removal of the sulfur in coal, either before it is burned or from the stacks after burning, and the protection of miners and process workers from diseases incurred during the preparation of fuel for the energy plant. A multitude of such questions are at the center of the costs of environmental management related to energy utilization.

Most of us have faith in our ingenuity and inventiveness in handling such technological problems. It really is true that if we could go to the Moon we can solve some of the technological problems that face us. What we cannot guarantee is that the solutions will be sufficiently cheap to be acceptable. When we sent astronauts to the Moon, cost seemed to be no object; now it is. How to balance economic costs against public-health considerations is a moral and philosophical question that most members of this society have yet to tackle in a meaningful way. Is there a defensible position between counting lives lost as an ordinary part of a cost-benefit analysis and insisting that preserving a single life is worth any cost?

A large number of responsible scientists and engineers have been working hard to define the problems and how we might find solutions to them. In this collection of articles, we see some of the products of their research. They have searched for ways to stretch our existing reserves of fossil fuel and for new ways of generating energy in useful forms. In many of their works, we see the growing recognition that there are choices to be made and that there are environmental costs, for both the existing sources and the new sources we envision.

Most of the articles in this collection are thoughts about the future—how we might cope, plan for development, and project lifestyles and economies. Many of the authors are concerned with the immediate future; others are thinking about the world of their children or grandchildren. It is encouraging that these concerns illuminate their work, for those who see a future are the optimists among us.

The task of choosing this collection was, as it usually is for the compiler, a hard one. Many excellent articles had to be left out for one reason or another. My choice was based on the relation of the article to the main theme, how our future need for energy will depend on the available natural resources, our technological and scientific innovative power, and the care with which we assess the environmental costs of all of the alternatives. Environmental costs are guaged not so much in esthetic losses—the disappearance of wild lands or pristine lakes and rivers—as in terms of the public health. Is the cost of abundant energy to be the health of those who mine the resource, those who prepare it for final use, or the population that may be affected by air or water pollution?

The scope of this book does not permit the inclusion of material on all the alternative sources of energy. One of these is solar energy, fast becoming a more attractive possibility for many of our needs, though not a panacea for at least a few decades. There are many environmental trade-offs for energy use that are not treated in detail in the articles, such as the ways we may be able to clean up sulfur dioxide emissions from the burning of fossil fuels. Nevertheless, I hope that these articles will give some sense of the intense preoccupation with these subjects of an increasing number of thoughtful people from a variety of professional backgrounds.

How we manage these problems will depend in part on the scientific and technical advice government leaders get from their skilled populations. How well those skilled people perform depends on how well society recognizes their vital function and gives them the wherewithal to do their work. How well they are heard depends on the clarity with which they present realistic choices. At the same time, we must recognize that scientists and technologists may have biases and inflexibilities related to the business or governmental world they have lived in for much of their careers. There is a natural tendency, for example, for most nuclear engineers to support nuclear power, just as lifelong outdoors people are willing to suffer a drastic cut in energy to preserve a wilderness area. People from heavily urbanized areas may look at things differently from those in rural communities. All of us are social and political animals, and it is doubtful that our backgrounds can be totally excluded from our choices of what to work on and what choices to push. So a word of caution about experts: They may be looking at only one aspect of a problem that ramifies into many disciplines, only a few of which even the best of us can master.

Decisions about our future are being made every day in our own capital and those of other nations. I hope that those who have read this book will be better able to judge and influence their governments.

# I

# ENERGY:
# THE SOCIETAL SETTING

Why the urgency of the need for energy? Unlike other natural or artificial products, there are no substitutes for energy, only different forms. Though aggregated muscle power of many individuals built the pyramids of Egypt and other great works of the past, power-driven machinery has made possible the agriculture and the production of so many goods and services of modern developed countries. The peoples of the world are becoming aware of that fact, particularly the poorer people, those of the developing countries who want a share of the Earth's wealth. More than that, the possession of energy reserves gives economic and political power, as anyone knows who has watched the formation and actions of the OPEC nations over the past decade.

The goal of energy independence for the United States and other countries is a response to the increasing international strategic importance of energy supplies. Yet such a goal may remain not only impossible but even an unnecessary vision, for energy resources are distributed unevenly around the Earth, and nations will have to share and exchange, perhaps with new rules to govern the barter. The United States was fortunate in having great resources of oil and gas; however, it has used a great deal of those resources and now must increasingly turn to imports. We still have much coal. In contrast, the United Kingdom and parts of Europe, though once gifted with great supplies of coal to power their industrial revolution, have nearly exhausted their coal reserves and must turn to other sources of energy. Mexico is now known to be sitting on great reserves of oil and gas, far too much for that country to use itself in the foreseeable future. Some countries have the uranium ore to power nuclear reactors but little technological capacity to exploit that resource, whereas others, like many European countries, have the means to build reactors but no uranium resources. Most Third World countries—except the Peoples' Republic of China—are poor in both nuclear and fossil fuels. It must be obvious that an international exchange network of energy resources and technology will have to be developed in a way not foreseen and perhaps not foreseeable at this moment.

The articles selected for this section illustrate some of these issues. The first article explores the general relationships between economic development, largely dependent on a supply of abundant energy and other resources, and aspirations of the world's poor for middle-class status. The second article sets out the picture of our world oil reserves, the latest in a series of attempts at defining how much oil there is and, at present and projected rates of production, how soon we will run out. The third article considers the same questions for coal reserves and production. Given the existence of these two major sources, and ideas about how the infant nuclear power industry might correlate supplies of uranium ore and rates of use, we logically come to the fourth article, a consideration of energy policy for one large technologically advanced country, the United States.

# 1

# World Resources and the World Middle Class

## COMMENTARY

The stage is set for our view of the future of energy, resources, and the environment by the question, "What do societies want?" Because we live in a time when societies, from the most highly industrialized to the most primitive, are changing rapidly, it may not be possible to find a common denominator. Nathan Keyfitz proposes a simple answer in terms of consumption: Societies aspire to middle-class patterns of use of goods and services (though the cultural implications of membership in this class vary greatly from one country to another). Dividing the world's population into two classes on the basis of poverty income level, Keyfitz concludes that the rapidity with which portions of the world population are passing from poor to middle class will be outstripped by population increase. This will happen even at a time when the *rate* of increase of population growth may have dropped to zero, for the total world population is nevertheless predicted to reach over 6 billion in the year 2000. The increase in income as people move into the middle class has important consequences. Their consumption increases, and they use much more of the world's resources and energy than they did as part of the poor. Because the world's poor and middle classes are not divided evenly among nations, the developed—the affluent—grow more rapidly in income, and the distance between rich and poor grows.

The gap between aspirations and possibility is worsened by the prospect of an absolute limit to the use and environmental costs of energy and resources. We cannot mandate ever expanded production of goods for consumption, hoping that sooner or later everyone will catch up. Each middle-class person requires from 15 to 30 barrels of oil per year, whereas the poor person makes do with one barrel at most, in the form of kerosene, bus fuel, and fertilizer. Will there be enough for everyone to be middle class? Keyfitz contrasts the "pessimistic" geologists and resource experts, who worry about running out of high-grade ores and oil and gas, with the "optimistic" economists, who are prone to argue that our technological capacity for inventing substitute materials and different paths of technology is unbounded. Whatever the distant future, right now it seems that there is not enough for everyone in the world to have a high level of consumption.

Though one answer may be a decrease in the consumption patterns of the affluent portion of society, consumption as the aspiration of most peoples seems to be the rule, and to deny it means to give a complete reorientation to society. At the time he wrote, Keyfitz pointed to China as an example of a different choice—working toward a relatively uniform division of goods and services throughout the population, the classless society. Yet three years later, at the time of this writing, China—at least the present post-Mao political regime—has opted for a more standard pattern of industrialization, education, and "modernization." This may well lead to the same pattern of consumerism as has evolved in the USSR and other originally revolutionary countries.

In the event that we do not choose to reduce consumption, the burden of enlarging the poor's rate of entry into the middle class would fall to the scientists and technologists, who, it is hoped, will show us how to get more for less. If we cannot steadily maintain a high level of use of our knowledge and ability to make our food, resources, and products more cheaply and with less energy, then we force the world to face reduced consumption, keeping most of the increasing world population poor and blocking their access to the affluence that most now want.

# World Resources and the World Middle Class

by Nathan Keyfitz
July 1976

*Economic development means entry into the high-consumption world middle class. In view of the limits that are set by world resources, only new scientific and technical knowledge can accelerate the rate of entry*

How much economic development is possible? Surely the planet and its materials are finite and not even all its present four billion people can live like Americans, let alone the six or eight billion that on present trends will be alive when a stationary world population is established. Indeed, there is doubt whether the 250 million people expected to populate the U.S. in the year 2000 will be able to live as Americans do today. How far, then, can industrial society spread through the preindustrial world before it reaches a ceiling imposed by space, raw materials and waste disposal?

That is the wrong question to ask, if human knowledge and capacity for substitution and the resilience of economic systems are unbounded, as they may well be. In that case the right question—and certainly a more tractable and pragmatic question—is how *fast* can development progress, whether toward an ultimate limit or not? What rate of technical innovation can be attained, oriented to allow a corresponding rate of expansion of industry, and how many of the world's people will that expansion enable to enter the middle class each year?

Attainment of the middle-class style of life is what constitutes development in countries as widely separated geographically and ideologically as Brazil and the U.S.S.R. In the process peasants gain education, move to cities and adopt urban occupations and urban patterns of expenditure. Changes are involved in people themselves, in where they live, in their kind of work and in the nature of the goods they consume. These changes can be visualized in terms of a definable line, comparable to the poverty line officially drawn in the U.S., across which people aspire to move. The pertinent questions then become: How many people are moving across the line each year, what is their effect on resources, at what rate can resources be expanded by new techniques and therefore what is the size of the window through which the world's poor will climb into the middle class during the remainder of this century and beyond it?

A main issue of development for many of the people of Asia, Africa and Latin America is how to enlarge that window into the middle class. Since, according to a generally accepted view, it is middle-class people who limit their families, the rate of movement into that class helps to determine the level at which the world population can be stabilized, and that level in turn will determine the degree of well-being that can be supported by world resources. And if shortage of resources makes the opening into the middle class as it is presently constituted so narrow that the majority will never be able to pass through it, then the sooner we know this the better. The Chinese rather than the Brazilian-Russian pattern of development may be what people will have to settle for.

The questions I have raised are difficult for many reasons, including the lack of statistical information, uncertainty about the capacity of productive systems to substitute common materials for scarce ones and uncertainty about the directions in which technology will advance. Some data and some pointers are available, however.

Let us begin with population. The world population, according to the United Nations estimates I shall be following, passed the four-billion mark in 1975. It had passed the three-billion mark in 1960. Whereas the last billion was added in 15 years, the first billion had taken from the beginning (one or two million years ago) until 1825. The growth has been far faster than exponential growth at a fixed rate of increase (as with compound interest); instead the rate rose from something like an average of .001 percent per year through the millenniums of prehistory to 1.9 percent through the decade and a half from 1960 to 1975.

Apparently the rate of increase will not rise further. The same 1.9 percent, according to the UN medium variant, will hold until 1990, and by the end of the century the increase will be down to 1.6 percent per year [*see illustration on page 11*]. Other estimates place the peak earlier and make the decline in rate of increase faster. Insofar as the increasing rate of increase constituted a population "explosion," we can draw relief from the fact that we are now down to "only" exponential growth. (This peaking was inevitable because of what mainly caused the rise to begin with: the decline in mortality during infancy and childhood. Mortality improvement after the reproductive ages does not affect increase much and in the long run does not affect it at all. Once the chance that a newborn infant will survive to reproduce itself gets up to about .90, the scope for further rise is limited, and whatever rise takes place will be offset by even a small decline in the birthrate.)

Those who worry about the population explosion can take some comfort in this peaking of the rate of increase, but not very much. Dropping to exponential growth still leaves the world population increasing (on the UN medium variant) by about 75 million per year now, with the annual increment rising to 100 million by the end of the century. And the absolute increase, rather than the rate, seems to be what matters. To feed the present yearly increment requires nearly 20 million tons of additional grain each year, which is more than the Canadian wheat crop and about the same as the crops of Argentina, Australia and Romania taken together. To look after the annual increment of population on even a minimum basis is going to be difficult enough; the real issue, however, is not how many people can live but how many can live well.

Production of most things consumed by the world's people has been increasing at a higher rate than the 1.9 percent per year of population. During the period from 1960 to 1973 meat output increased at 2.8 percent a year, newsprint at 3.7 percent, motor vehicles at 6.8 percent and energy consumption at 4.9 percent, and the rise was similar for many other commodities. These numbers can be taken to mean that on the average mankind is year by year eating better and reading more, becoming more mobile and substituting machine power for the power of human muscles. Such a conclusion would seem to be confirmed by worldwide figures on productive activity or income. For example, adding up the gross domestic products of all countries for 1970 yields a gross world product of $3,219 billion, an average of $881 per head. The total has been going up at nearly 5 percent per year in real terms, that is, after price increases. Even allowing for the 1.9 percent increase in population, we seem to be getting better off individually at about 3 percent per year. Projecting on this basis, real goods per head would double every 23 years; each generation would be twice as well off as the preceding one. To dispose of twice as much wealth as one's parents, four times as much as one's grandparents, surely cannot be regarded as unsatisfactory; the world, such figures seem to show, is moving toward affluence. That conclusion requires substantial qualification.

The division of a total number of dollars by a number of individuals to obtain an average per head has a long tradition; dividing one number by another is an innocent operation and without any necessary implication that everyone obtains the average, and yet it puts thoughts into people's minds. The first thought might be that things are not bad with $881 per head for the entire global population—a conservative conclusion. The second thought might be that things would indeed not be bad if the total was actually divided up—a radical viewpoint that has been voiced often in recent years. Income is an aspect of a way of life, however, and only a trifling part of a way of life is directly transferable.

The fallacy of redivision is encouraged by putting income into terms of money and performing arithmetical division. To say we should divide income so that everyone in the world can have his $881 is to solve a real problem with a verbal or arithmetical trick, because behind the numbers is the fact that Americans live one way and Indians another way. If, starting tomorrow, Americans were all to live like Indians, then their higher incomes would simply disappear. There would be nothing to transfer.

How much is transferable depends on the extent to which Americans could consume like Indians while continuing to produce like Americans. Simon Kuznets and others have pointed out that as soon as one tries to plan a transfer the tight bond between production and consumption frustrates the attempt. For example, the cost of travel to work is called consumption, but if people stopped traveling to work, production would fall to zero. What about the cost of holidays and entertainment, which are elements of consumption but which refresh people for further work? What about nutrition, education and health services? And what about the enjoyment of consumer goods that is the incentive to work and earn? All of these and many other parts of consumption feed back into production. Moreover, to discuss massive transfers of capital would be futile for political reasons even if it were economically practical: the declining U.S. foreign-aid budget shows how unappealing to the major donor this path to world development is.

Because the world population is heterogeneous, no style of life is in fact associated with the world average of $881. Following that average through time leads to the mistaken impression that things are getting better every year and will do so indefinitely. Even a two-way breakdown of the average is a major step toward realism.

Of the total world population of four billion estimated for 1975, 1.13 billion, or nearly 30 percent, live in developed countries. The fraction of the annual increment of population accounted for by those countries is much less, however: only 10 million out of 75 million, or 13 percent. The annual increment in the less developed countries is more than 65 million, and it will rise to 90 million by the end of the century (again on the UN medium estimates). This division of the world into two kinds of countries, rich and poor, or more developed and less developed, has become familiar since World War II. That world 1970 product (or income) of $881 per head is in fact an average of the developed countries' $2,701 and the less developed countries' $208.

Recent fluctuations obscure the long-term rates of increase, but suppose income for the rich and poor countries alike increases at 5 percent per year in the long term. On the population side, suppose the future increase is .5 percent per year among the developed countries and 2.5 percent per year among the less developed. Allowing for these population numbers brings the 5 percent annual gain in total product that was assumed for both down to about 4.5 percent for the developed countries and only 2.5 percent for the less developed ones.

The result is a widening gap between the two groups of countries, an exercise in the mathematics of geometric increase [see illustration on page 12]. Think of the developed countries starting at $2,701 per capita and increasing at 4.5 percent per year in real terms; after 25 years they have risen threefold, to a per capita income of more than $8,000 in 1995. By that time the income per

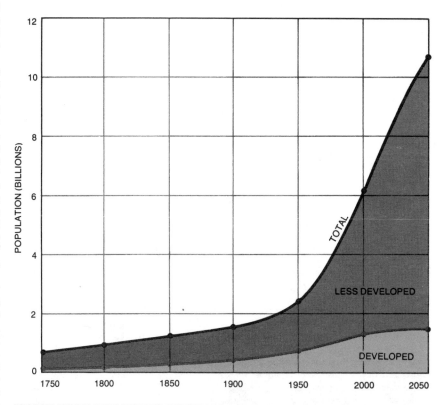

"POPULATION EXPLOSION" CURVE is the result of more-than-exponential growth; the annual rate of increase has itself been rising, most sharply in the past century, largely because of the decline in infant and childhood mortality. In this layer chart the total population (projected to the year 2050 according to the United Nations medium estimate) is given for countries currently classified by the UN as "developed" (light color) and "less developed" (dark color).

head in the less developed countries has not even doubled: their $208 has risen to only $386. By the year 2020 the grandchildren of the present generation will have, in the one set of countries, more than $24,000 per head and in the other countries the still very modest $715—one thirty-fourth as much as the rich, and not yet as much as the 1970 world average!

The calculation shows how a heterogeneous population is bound to develop a widening gap between rich and poor if per capita rates of increase are frozen. I have assumed that all national incomes increase at 5 percent per year. Overall national-income growth is not conspicuously different, on the average, for the poor and the rich countries, and so it is the differences in population growth that are decisive.

To speak of developed and less developed countries is an improvement on treating the world as being homogeneous, but it has been overtaken by the events of the past three years. Where two categories of countries once sufficed, we now find we cannot do with fewer than four.

The shifts in raw-material prices have created resource-rich countries such as Abu Dhabi and Venezuela, whose wealth is comparable to that of the developed countries, which by way of contrast can be called capital-rich. Some countries that were poor have actually been developing, including Singapore, Korea, Taiwan and Hong Kong. Finally there are the many countries that are truly poor, lacking (in relation to their population) both capital and resources. We have, then, the resource-rich countries, the capital-rich countries, the developing countries and the poor countries. Specifically identifying and classifying all cases to provide numbers for population in these groups is not easy. (Indonesia has resources but not enough so that any likely rise in prices would make its 135 million people rich.)

The new categories of resource-rich and developing countries might be defined in such a way that they total 200 million people each; the fact remains that most of the world's people are in countries that have no leverage through either control of capital or control of resources.

No country is homogeneous, however; the poorest countries contain some rich people and the richest contain some poor. Nations and their governments dominate our age so completely that individuals too easily drop out of political as well as statistical view, yet the welfare of governments is not a worthy ultimate objective; it is the people of the poor countries who deserve our concern. And so what follows will deal as directly as possible with people.

The typical poor person and the typical middle-class person are easy to visualize; the first is a peasant in Java, Nigeria, the Brazilian Northeast or elsewhere in Asia, Africa and the Americas; the second is a city dweller in San Francisco, Frankfurt, Leningrad or Tokyo with an office job that puts him well above the poverty line. There are less obvious representatives. Along with the peasant group one should count as poor the wage laborer of Calcutta or the urban unemployed of the U.S. And the middle-class group includes the unionized construction worker, the bus driver, the keypunch operator and the successful farmer in the U.S., Europe, the U.S.S.R. or Japan; that some of these are considered blue-collar is secondary to their earning a middle-class income.

In survey after survey most Americans, when they are asked where they think they belong, place themselves in the middle class. The self-classification by which most Americans tend to call themselves middle-class and Indians tend to call themselves poor accords with the distinction I have made. Most of those called middle-class in the world live in the cities of the rich countries, but some of them live in poor countries and some live in the countryside. The crucial part of the distinction is that middle-class people are in a position to make effective claim to a share of the world's resources that accords with modern living.

With an income measure of welfare, people fall on a continuum and the location of the poverty line is arbitrary. As a country grows richer its standards rise, so that the same fraction of its population may be defined as "poor" even as everyone in the country is becoming better off. In the case of the U.S., however, it has been possible to reach broad agreement on a Social Security Administration definition of poverty based on relatively objective criteria. An average urban family of four, including two children, is said to require $3,700 a year (at 1974 prices) to pay rent, buy clothing and meet basic nutritional needs, and similar levels are set for other types of household.

"Middle class" describes a style of life and can cover not only physical necessities but also such conventional needs as power lawn mowers and winter vacations in Florida. It needs to be specified separately for each culture before one can see how many people enjoy it and what the energy and resource consequences of the enjoyment are. Pending such a study I propose to call middle-class those who are above the equivalent of the U.S. poverty line, wherever they may live. Cultural differences make poverty in one country intrinsically noncomparable with poverty in another country, but they make average money incomes just as noncomparable. The effort to quantify important notions must not be prevented by some degree of qualitative difference; the fraction under the level of consumption represented by the U.S. poverty line is not the definitive way of measuring the world's poor, but it

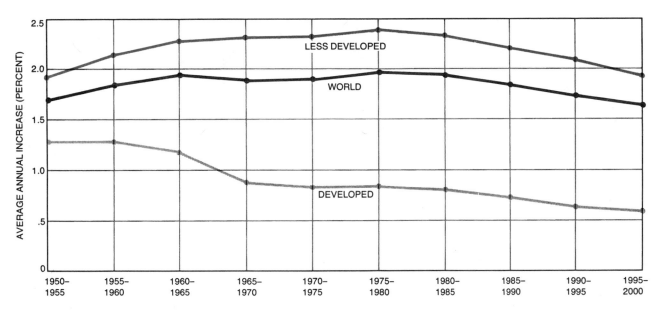

RATE OF INCREASE of population is apparently reaching a peak during the present half decade. The average rate of increase per year is plotted for five-year intervals for the developed (*light color*) and less developed (*dark color*) countries and for the world as a whole (*black*). The rate of increase turned down several decades ago for the developed countries and is expected to do the same thing soon in the less developed countries. The "explosion" is ending, in the sense that the growth of the world population will be less than exponential.

will serve for the moment. In the U.S. that fraction was 11.6 percent in 1974, an increase from 11.1 in 1973 but a decrease from 22.4 in 1959. Of the U.S. population of 210 million in 1973, some 23 million were poor; call the remaining 187 million middle-class. Let us try to find indexes that will provide a corresponding number for other countries.

Passenger cars in use might be taken as roughly proportional to the middle-class, or above-poverty, population. In the U.S. in 1973 the number of passenger cars was 101 million and in the world as a whole it was 233 million, a ratio of 2.3. Insofar as the 233 million passenger cars in the world are being driven and ridden in by a world middle class, we can multiply the U.S. middle class of 187 million by 2.3 and derive a world total of 430 million middle-class people. This number is too low, because automobiles are less a part of daily life even in other affluent countries; we know that trains continue to be used in Europe for much travel that is done in the U.S. by automobile.

Let us try telephones as the indicator. The world total in 1973 was 336 million telephones and the U.S. total was 138 million. On this index the world middle class was 187 million times 336/138, or 455 million. With electric energy as the indicator a similar calculation gives a world middle class of 580 million. Each one of these indicators is surely defective. One can nonetheless hope that their defects are more or less constant over the 20 years or so that I propose to apply them to establish a trend.

A slightly different way of doing the calculation is to take it that modern living requires about four metric tons of crude oil a year for heating, air conditioning and motoring, so that the world output in 1973, 2,774 million tons, could cover the needs of 700 million people. (The calculation is approximate because some poor people do use a little oil and large supplies go to military and other government uses.)

Averaging the several approaches gives a world middle class of 500 million for 1970. What is important is that the corresponding average number—indexed on automobiles, telephones, electric energy, oil and other items—was something like 200 million for 1950. That indicates an average increase of 4.7 percent per year in the world middle class: the workers, and their families, who are integrated into industrial society, utilize its materials as the basis of their jobs and apply their incomes to consume its product. In doing so they have an impact on resources and on the environment. Just how great is the impact of change in status from poor to middle class, particularly compared with the effect of population change?

Raw materials are used by people, and so, if all else is fixed, the drain on resources must be proportional to the number of people. If each year the world population is 1.9 percent larger than it was the year before and nothing else changes, then each year resources are claimed by 1.9 percent more people, and in the course of 37 years we

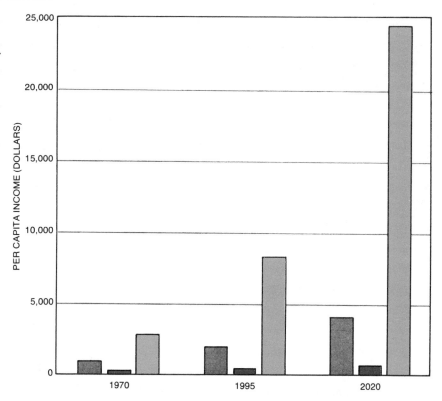

WIDENING GAP between per capita incomes in the developed and in the less developed countries is caused by the more rapid growth of population in poor countries. UN figures for the developed (*light color*) and less developed (*dark color*) countries and for the world as a whole (*gray*) were projected on the assumption that total income will continue to increase at 5 percent per year in both sets of countries but that the population of the developed countries increases at only .5 percent per year while that of less developed countries increases at 2.5 percent.

shall be on the average twice as dense on the land and shall be consuming twice as much iron and other metals and twice as much crude oil. This statement is not true of pollution, where more-than-proportional effects enter. It is true of resources insofar as technology for production and patterns of consumption both remain constant.

Actually they do not remain constant; they exert effects in opposite directions. Technology has been stretching the use of materials. We know how to put the tin on the can more thinly; we can make rubber and fabrics out of coal; we recycle aluminum. The movement, guided by price changes, is always toward less scarce materials. As income goes up, however, per capita consumption increases: more cans are used, albeit each with a thinner layer of tin. Worse still, new materials are invented—detergents, plastics, insecticides—that take a long time to reenter the cycles of nature once we are through with them. It is the net effect of these tendencies that we need to estimate.

One way to get at the net effect of increased consumption per head and of technological improvements is to determine the residual change after population increase is allowed for. Let us try this for energy consumption in the U.S. in 1947 and 1973. The 1947 consumption was 1.21 billion tons of coal equivalent and the 1973 consumption was 2.55 billion. Meanwhile the population rose from 144 million to 210 million. If the

larger population of 1973 had held to the same volume and patterns of consumption and production as the smaller population of 1947, it would have required 1.77 billion tons of coal equivalent. Hence of the total increase of 1.34 billion only .56 billion was due to population growth; the remainder of the increase, .78 billion, was due to affluence. Affluence was more important than population [*see illustration on next page*]. Similar calculations can be made for metals and other materials, for pollution, for the primary caloric content of food, indeed for any kind of impact that can be measured.

As an alternative way of analyzing the consumption of materials, consider that from 1950 to 1970 the part of the world population that was affluent went from 200 million to 500 million: while total population increases at 1.9 percent per year, middle-class high consumers increase at 4.7 percent. Each high consumer requires the equivalent of three-quarters of a ton of grain, whereas the poor get by on a quarter of a ton. (The consequent ratio of land use is less than three to one, because agriculture is more efficient in rich countries.) The middle-class person requires from 15 to 30 barrels of oil, whereas the poor person makes do with one barrel at most in the form of kerosene, bus fuel and fertilizer. The land and energy content of clothing may be in a rich-to-poor ratio intermediate between those for food and for transport. As a kind of average of these several ratios, suppose the

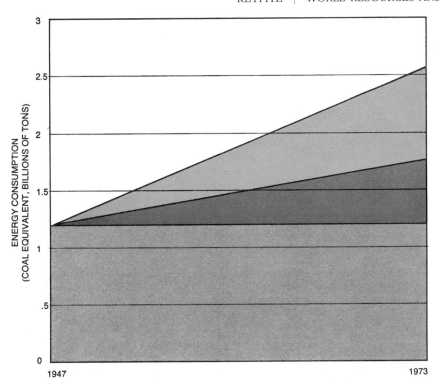

**U.S. ENERGY CONSUMPTION** would have increased from 1.21 billion tons of coal equivalent in 1947 to 1.77 billion tons in 1973 if it had merely kept pace with the rise in population. In fact, however, energy consumption rose to 2.55 billion tons in 1973. The increment (*light color*) due to a rise in per capita consumption stemming from affluence was larger than the increment (*dark color*) attributable to population growth. The same is true of many other materials.

middle-class person has five times as much impact on the material base as the poor person. Then the average person on the high side of the poverty line must be taken as being equivalent to five people on the low side in fuel and metals consumed. In considering impact we therefore calculate as though in 1975 the planet had not four billion people aboard but 6.4 billion. Of these, 3.4 billion were poor and three billion represented the fivefold impact of a world middle class that probably numbered 600 million.

This would make the average total impact of the small middle class on resources somewhat less than that of the large number of the poor. The middle class has been increasing at 4.7 percent per year, however, and the poor less than half as fast. At the growing edge the increase of affluence has much more effect than the increase of population; the movement of people into the middle class has more effect on materials and the environment than the increase in the number of poor people.

Indeed, it has so much effect that if the population explosion is now ending (in the sense that the world rate of increase is peaking at 1.9 percent per year and starting to decline), we now face another explosion. It arises from the arithmetic of combining two exponentials, which is to say two progressions (population growth and middle-class growth) each of which has a fixed ratio.

The effect can be expressed in stylized form by supposing the 1975 population of four billion projected forward in the ratio 1.6 every 25 years (equal to the fixed rate of

1.9 percent per year). Suppose at the same time that the middle class triples every 25 years (equivalent to a fixed 4.5 percent per year), as it did from 1950 to 1975. The poor population is the difference between the resulting numbers. If the people above the poverty line average five times the impact of those below it, then we must add five times the middle class to the number of poor for the total impact. The result is a steadily increasing rate of increase of the impact, from 2.7 percent per year in 1950–1975 to 3.1 percent and then to 3.5 percent[*see illustration on page 33*]. This is based on continuance of 1950–1970 rates of economic development and of population growth. Population growth will slow down, but that will not greatly reduce the impact, which in this illustration would be increasingly due to affluence. Our difficulties in maintaining the population and affluence levels of 1976 suggest that this model will not work. We cannot hope to keep tripling the middle class every 25 years. The main reason is shortage of resources.

Natural resources account for only about 5 percent of the value of goods and services produced in the U.S. and other developed countries. Resources are hence curiously two-sided: extracting them accounts for only a small part of the cost, yet they are the sine qua non of existence, to say nothing of progress. And particular materials do run out. England's Industrial Revolution was in part a response to a firewood crisis: cheap coal was substituted for wood,

which had become scarce and very dear. In America, on the other hand, wood was cheap and labor was dear, so that houses were built of wood rather than stone, which is more labor-intensive. Now timber is dear here also, and masonry and aluminum are substituted in some products. Plastics take the place of paper in packaging. Cultivated southern pine is used for newsprint instead of the limited pine and spruce of the northern forests.

Thus history shows the resilience of the productive system, its ability to substitute commoner materials for scarce ones. Nevertheless, the extrapolation of this capacity must take account of time. Invention, innovation and capital replacement can proceed only at a certain pace. It is this pace of innovation that needs to be studied, since it sets the rate at which industrial society can spread in the face of environmental and resource limitations.

Limits to the spread of industrial society under present technology are suggested by the record of trade in raw materials over the past quarter-century. To take one example, in 1950 the production and consumption of energy were in virtual balance for the developed countries as a whole. Their deficit amounted to less than 4 percent of consumption. By 1973 production in the developed countries had nearly doubled but consumption had far outrun it and the deficit had swollen to a third of consumption.

The story for metals and other resources is not very different. No country, developed or not, has been provided by nature with a greater quantity and variety of mineral and other resources than the U.S. Yet even the U.S. had become a net importer of minerals by the 1920's, and it now imports all its platinum, mica and chromium, 96 percent of its aluminum, 85 percent of its asbestos, 77 percent of its tin and 28 percent of its iron—to select from a long list. Of course, the shortages of some of these minerals are not absolute but are a matter of price. The U.S. could produce all the aluminum it needs from domestic clay, but bauxite from Jamaica is cheaper. Having virtually exhausted the iron ore of the Mesabi Range, the U.S. resorts to lower-grade domestic taconite and to imports, in a proportion determined by prices.

The increase of more than 4 percent per year in the number of middle-class people who have come on the scene is too rapid in that these high consumers have to comb the world for resources, but on the other hand it is much too slow to satisfy the billions of people who are waiting in the wings. Whereas Europe, Japan and the U.S.S.R. have made great gains during the UN Development Decades, most of Asia and Africa are dissatisfied with their progress. Moreover, a realistic calculation would probably show a larger gap between the impact on resources of those who have raised themselves from poverty and that of those who are still poor. The weight of a middle-class person is in many respects more than five times that of a peasant. It is to keep the argument conservative that I suppose the ratio is five times and that the world middle class triples every 25 years.

The combination of these two modest assumptions produces, as we have seen, a surprisingly high measure of impact for the end of the century, by which time the middle class, which was at 600 million in 1975, would increase to 1.8 billion and have the effect of five times that number, or nine billion. The total impact projected to the year 2000 is, then, that of nine billion plus 4.6 billion poor, or 13.6 billion people. This compares with an impact of 6.4 billion for 1975, calculated in the same way. If strains are already apparent in materials and energy, what will happen with a doubling of the rate of consumption?

The accelerating impact that appears from recognition of two categories of people rather than one category is offset in some degree by the decline in the impact per dollar of income once income rises beyond a certain level. People take very high incomes in services rather than in more and more automobiles. Moreover, the relation of impact to income varies from one culture to another, as an anthropologist would point out; an economist would add that the relation can be counted on to change as raw materials, and hence the goods made from them, become scarce and costly compared with less material-intensive forms of consumption. Although the impact on materials may taper off with increased wealth, the impact on air and water may be greater than proportional. There may be thresholds: the air may hold just so much carbon monoxide, a lake just so much fertilizer run-off, without undue effect, but beyond a certain critical point the effect may quickly rise to disaster levels. Such critical points clearly exist in renewable resources. Fishing or cutting timber up to a certain intensity does no damage at all, but continued over-fishing or overcutting can destroy the fish or tree population.

The rate and direction of development of the period 1950–1970, unsatisfactory though it may be in that the absolute number of the poor would continue to increase until well into the 21st century, is still faster than can be sustained on present strategies. The resilience of the economic system, and technical innovation in particular, can be counted on to respond to needs, but only at a certain rate of speed. One can imagine sources of energy, the capacity to dispose of wastes and substitutes for metals all doubling in the century to come, but it is not easy to conceive of such a doubling in the 15 years that would keep the middle class growing at 4.7 percent per year.

To say that civilization will collapse when oil supplies are exhausted, or that we will pollute ourselves out of existence, is to deny all responsiveness and resilience to the productive system. The geologist or resource expert tends to focus on the material and technical process he knows and may be less than imaginative with regard to how a substitute might be found to deal with a shortage. On the other hand, the economist may be too imaginative; he may too readily

suppose substitutes can be found for anything as soon as it becomes scarce. The ensuing debate between pessimistic raw-material experts and optimistic economists has generated whatever knowledge we have on the subject. The middle ground to which both sides are tending is that every barrier that industrial expansion is now meeting can be surmounted by technological advance, but not in an instant. It is not a ceiling on total population and income that we have to deal with but that window. How large can the window be made?

One conclusion to be drawn from the arithmetic I did above is that a projection in terms of ratios is probably wrong in principle; in the face of natural and human limitations the pace of advance may be determined in absolute numbers rather than ratios. If, for example, pollution effects are proportional to fuel burned, then successive absolute increments in fuel consumption

have the same bad effects on the fixed volume of the atmosphere. We should think not of the percent expansion of the middle class but of its absolute increase.

The calculation made in this way starts with the annual growth in world population of 75 million at the present time, gradually increasing to 100 million by the end of the century, and compares that increment with the number annually emerging into the middle class. If the latter went in a straight line from 200 million in 1950 to 500 million in 1970, then the average annual increase was 15 million. My stylized model, wherein industrial society expands through the emergence of people from the peasantry into city jobs as capital expands (while those not yet called remain at their old peasant incomes), goes back ultimately to Adam Smith. This simple application of the Smith model suggests that currently 15 million people join the middle class each year and 60 million join the poor. Even if the middle-

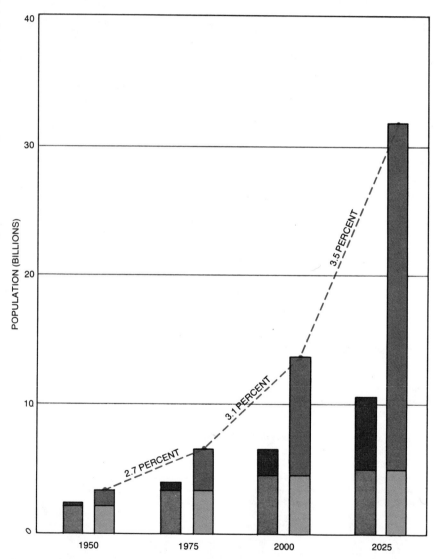

FUTURE IMPACT on world resources is affected by the growth of the middle class, whose members are assumed to consume five times as much as poor people. In population alone the middle class (*dark gray*), increasing at 4.5 percent per year, would eventually be larger than the poor population (*light gray*). When the middle class is multiplied by five, the resulting "consumption population" (*color*) is seen to grow at an annual rate that increases from 2.7 to 3.1 and then to 3.5 percent. World resources are already strained by the 1975 "consumption population."

class increment could rise to 20 million per year, the poor would still be increasing by 80 million per year at the end of the century. This at least is one reasonable extrapolation of the process of development in the postwar period. Other population estimates are lower than the UN's, but accepting them would lead to the same result: the large majority of the new generation will be poor. Therein lies the harm of rapid population growth.

The natural increase of the affluent population will create difficulties in the years ahead even though birthrates are low. Suppose the window is wide enough for 20 million to pass through it each year. Who will they be? The way the world is made, the children of the currently affluent of America, Europe and Japan will have first claim. The U.S.S.R. has found no way of preventing its elite from placing their children in the elite, and neither has the U.S. On the basis of 600 million for the middle class in 1975, a net natural-increase rate of .5 percent means three million children per year in excess of deaths. Apart from children who simply replace their parents or grandparents, of the 20 million net admissions each year three million would be further children of those who have already entered the middle class and 17 million would be new entrants. And these 17 million new entrants would be divided among the poor of the developed countries and those of the less developed countries, with the former having the better chance. Poor people in the poor countries sense that the odds against

them and against their children are great.

All of this, it should be noted, can be seen as a critique not of development but of one particular model of development. The distinction between poor and middle-class represents the Brazilian and the Russian direction but not the Chinese. Whether because of China's special culture or the personality of Mao Tse-tung, both the specialization that equips people for middle-class jobs and the durable structures of industry and administration in which those jobs have their place have been insistently denied there. It is asserted that everyone can do everything, that people ought to take turns working as peasants, driving trucks and being scholars; people need only so much to eat, to wear and to live in, and consumerism beyond that austere minimum is vice, not virtue. Whether this view can spread among other cultures and without a regime of the same type is not clear. There is little present sign of its spreading even to India, let alone to Japan, Europe or America.

Thomas Malthus gave us a land theory of value, Karl Marx a labor theory and development economists since World War II a capital theory. Land, labor and capital are plainly all needed (and to assign priority to any one may be as much an ideological choice as a practical one), but a dynamic factor superimposed on all of them is new scientific and technical knowledge. At many points we need to know more in order even to discover the problems we face: only recently have we found out that insecticides

can be dangerous poisons to organisms other than insects, and that the current worldwide rise in skin cancer may be related to depletion of the ozone layer of the upper atmosphere. Knowledge is needed even to see where the window restricting passage into the middle class is located, and only knowledge can open it wider.

Other ways of widening the window have been suggested. One is to raise the price of the raw materials on whose export some less developed countries depend for foreign exchange. Price increases such as those of the Organization of Petroleum Exporting Countries (OPEC) can have little overall effect, however, on the number of middle-class people in the world (although they have some effect on whether the newly middle-class will speak Spanish or Arabic or English). Who ultimately bears the burden of such price raises is not clear. Some of the burden is carried by poor countries that are not endowed with raw materials; when the repercussions have worked themselves out, India may find it has contributed a higher proportion of its income to Saudi Arabian opulence than the U.S. has. Certainly some U.S. fertilizer that would have gone to India before 1973 now goes to the Middle East; German chemical-plant investments are similarly diverted. The offsetting of oil price rises by French arms sales to Iran has everything to do with national power and little to do with the total distribution of poverty or even the national distribution. The main point is that only a small fraction of the world population is in resource-rich areas.

A second way to help more people escape from poverty might be for those who have already entered the middle class to moderate their consumption. In principle, if one meat eater cuts his consumption, then five grain eaters can increase theirs. If American automobiles were smaller, more metals and fuels would be available for automobiles in Zaïre and Bangla Desh as well as—more immediately—fertilizer plants in those countries. If urban Americans were to live like the equally affluent Swedes, U.S. energy consumption might be halved. The trouble is that goods, as well as jobs that require materials, fit into other social activities in an interlocking scheme that is hard to change; social configurations are as solid a reality as raw materials. After two years of talking conservation, the U.S. consumes as much fossil fuel as ever. Faced with a world shortage of raw materials, every person of goodwill wants to see wasteful practices reduced, but the intrinsic limits on transfers I mentioned at the outset and the enormous inertia stored in producing and spending patterns make reduced consumption an unlikely way for the U.S. to help the poor countries.

Foreign aid and investment along conventional lines are a third possibility, but they have been disappointing. They have aided in the development of some countries (Canada is a striking example), but for various reasons the volume is inadequate to the magnitude of the problem for most of the

**CONSUMPTION AND PRODUCTION** of energy were about balanced in 1950 in the developed countries: they produced the coal, oil, gas and hydropower whose energy they consumed, except for a small shortfall made up by imports from less developed countries. By 1973 rising production had been outstripped by consumption; shortfall amounted to a third of consumption.

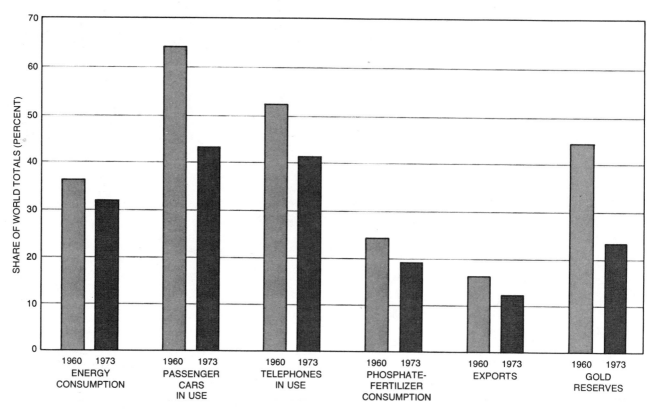

INCREASE IN AFFLUENCE outside the U.S., particularly in Japan and Europe, has reduced the disproportionate U.S. share of energy consumption, durable goods and other indicators of wealth. Movement of more people across the poverty line would extend this effect.

world's population. Even where investment is solidly based in economics some intellectuals argue that it creates dependency, and the politicians of poor countries often respond by expropriation. Ironically the very mention of expropriation is expensive for the poor country because it makes investors demand a higher return.

One can say that better prices for raw materials, reduction of consumption by the rich countries and conventional foreign aid and foreign investment all ought to be pursued, but the experience of the 1950's and the 1960's shows that they will not make a decisive difference in the size of the window through which escape from poverty is sought.

What will make a decisive difference is knowledge: of how to produce amenities with less material, how to substitute materials that are common for those that are scarce, how to get desired results with less energy and how to obtain that energy from renewable sources rather than from fossil fuels. We have seen some results in the past decade. With the advent of integrated circuits, a calculator that cost $1,000 and weighed 40 pounds is now replaced by one that costs $10 and weighs a few ounces. Artificial earth satellites have lowered the cost of communication; they provide television in Indian villages and may ultimately make telephone calls around the world as cheap as local calls. Synthetic polymers have replaced cotton and wool and thus released land. The list of what is still needed is too long to itemize: efficient solar collectors, compact storage batteries to run automobiles on centrally generated power, stronger and cheaper plastics (for automobile bodies, for instance) and so on.

If the time dimension in the implementation of these inventions is crucial, then everything that is done to hasten invention will pay off for the world movement past the poverty line. There are many stages, from pure scientific investigation to the translation of science into technology, to the engineering that makes a production model out of a working prototype and finally on to parts contracting and the assembly line, and each stage takes time. The U.S., once foremost in the speed with which it could convert knowledge into the production of goods, is said to be losing this preeminence; a slowing down would have bad consequences not only for the American competitive position among industrial nations but also for the world escape from poverty. The need is not confined to scientific and engineering knowledge; prompt solutions are also required of many problems in biology and medicine, climatology and geophysics. The technical and social knowledge for birth control is of special importance; whatever the size of the window through which the poor escape into the middle class, the lowering of births will at least bring closer the day when world poverty ceases to increase in absolute amount.

Some part of American research has been directed specifically to labor-intensive devices suited to poor countries, and that line of investigation ought to be encouraged. Even after the Green Revolution, for example, poor countries still have special agricultural problems. Apart from such specific research, the U.S. helps all countries when it develops knowledge that makes its own industry more efficient.

A particular preoccupation of the less developed countries is dependency; even commercial indebtedness is seen as neocolonialism. The technical evolution of the poor countries along lines suited to their own needs will be aided by American expansion of knowledge in that it will widen the choice of techniques available to them. In order that any such American contribution not create commercial indebtedness, it would be advisable to place the new knowledge and inventions in the public domain as the common possession of mankind rather than in patents on which royalties could be drawn.

Both production constraints and environmental constraints limit the growth of the world middle class. The way the U.S. can help to open the window is not through schemes for division of the existing product but by contributing knowledge that will expand the product. Solving production and environmental problems starts at home, but any genuine contribution will have value worldwide. Incentives can be devised to direct technology in environment-saving rather than environment-damaging directions. No one can forecast how much time it will take to solve any one technical problem, let alone the complex of problems, but that time—whatever it may be—will be shortened by a larger and more immediate mobilization of scientific and engineering talent.

# 2

# World Oil Production

## COMMENTARY

More than 30 years ago, M. King Hubbert set out his analysis of the future of fossil fuels—how production of a nonrenewable resource would eventually outstrip the rate of new discoveries, and why there was some urgency in planning for the future of energy. The general picture, remarkably enough, has not changed much since then. More recently, in "The Energy Resources of the Earth" (SCIENTIFIC AMERICAN Offprint 663), Hubbert, a geologist and geophysicist, concentrated on the ultimate resource—how much oil and gas were eventually likely to be found, basing his analysis on geological factors, the history of production in the developed countries, and a geological comparison between unexplored and known regions. In this article, Andrew R. Flower, a statistician and economist, tackles the problem from a somewhat different point of view. Flower focuses on proven reserves—the number of barrels of oil that are reasonably considered to be left in the ground, adjusted for the proportion of recovery, usually about one-third of the total in the ground. Flower's conclusions are much the same as those of Hubbert's earlier analysis.

The author brings us the conclusions of a two-year international study group, the Workshop on Alternative Energy Strategies, composed of people from business, government, and universities in 15 major non-Communist oil-importing countries. He starts with a figure for the total reserves ultimately recoverable, 1.6 trillion barrels, which is in the middle ground of estimates ranging from 1.3 to 2.1 trillion barrels. Then come possible scenarios for how long the reserves will last, assuming two different paths the world may take, a high economic growth rate and high energy prices versus a low growth rate and constant prices. As new oil and gas fields, particularly the giant ones that have always given us the bulk of the oil, become harder and harder to find, and as production from existing fields declines, demand from either growth alternative will eventually exceed supply. Nations will then have to turn to alternative sources of energy or find themselves unable to produce all the goods and services they want, including food. This point will be reached somewhere between 1990 and 2004.

It is hard for many to realize fully that the occasional big discoveries, such as those in Mexico in 1978 and 1979, do not change the picture. They may only change the projections by a few years. In the estimates based on ultimate resources rather than proven reserves, they do not change the picture at all; only a major revolution in the geological theory of oil formation that would lead us to explore rocks and regions hitherto completely ignored would do that. And for the past 100 years, certainly for the past 30 or 40, we have had no influential theories, outrageous or otherwise, that would point in that direction. To hope for a new theory that will bail us out is equivalent to hoping for a repeal of the Law of Conservation of Energy.

Political and economic constraints in the next two decades can alter the situation. If the OPEC nations were to restrict production, even in the face of rising demand, we would come sooner to the time when there will not be enough oil to satisfy world demand. The result of this behavior may not be all bad: It would allow a good deal of oil to remain in the ground for a long time, thus giving a cushion to the shock of a rapid drop in production. Flower does not treat the matter of conservation in this article except to note that strong efforts would be required to reduce demand enough to make any significant difference. Such efforts will have to overcome resistance from many quarters in any country, particularly in the United States, where needless waste is common. The conclusion is inescapable: We must plan now for gradual shifts to other sources of energy and for conservation too. Occasional new discoveries must not be allowed to divert us.

# World Oil Production

by Andrew R. Flower
*March 1978*

*There is only a finite amount of oil and there are
limits to the rate at which it can be recovered.
Sometime before the year 2000 the decreasing supply
of it will fail to meet the increasing demand*

The supply of oil will fail to meet increasing demand before the year 2000. As oil production inevitably levels off and then falls, alternative fuels will have to meet the demand for energy, which will continue to grow in the face of even vigorous attempts at conservation. The oil-importing countries have perhaps as few as five years or perhaps as many as 20 in which to accomplish a transition from dependence on oil to greater reliance on other fossil fuels, on nuclear energy and eventually on renewable energy sources. Because large investments and long lead times are required for developing new energy resources the effort must begin immediately.

These are among the major conclusions of a two-year international study, the Workshop on Alternative Energy Strategies. Some 70 people recruited from business and industry, government and the universities in 15 major non-Communist oil-importing countries came together under the direction of Carroll L. Wilson of the Massachusetts Institute of Technology to study world energy supply and demand, to identify potential problems in satisfying energy requirements and to consider strategies that might solve the problems. (The "world" we considered was the world outside the Communist areas. The U.S.S.R. and China are major producers and consumers of energy, but statistics on their reserves, production, consumption and trade are rough estimates at best and their trade with non-Communist countries does not loom large.) The workshop participants came from the U.S., Canada, Mexico, Venezuela, the United Kingdom, France, West Germany, the Netherlands, Denmark, Sweden, Norway, Finland, Italy, Iran and Japan.

The workshop developed projections of energy supply and demand under var-

ious assumptions, notably concerning economic growth and the price of energy. Two basic scenarios were formulated, one assuming a high economic growth rate and high energy prices and the other a low growth rate and constant prices. The high-growth, high-price scenario assumed that economic growth in the non-Communist world would average 5.2 percent per year between 1976 and 1985 and 4 percent between 1985 and 2000, and that energy prices would remain constant (in real terms) until 1985 and increase 50 percent by 2000. The low-growth, constant-price scenario assumed that economic growth would average 3.4 percent per year until 1985 and then 2.8 percent until 2000, and that real energy prices would remain constant during the entire period.

Within that framework energy-demand forecasts were prepared for the various regions for each fuel and were aggregated to project the total energy demand in 1985 and 2000. In the case of oil, which today meets more than half of the energy needs of industrial societies, the projections suggest that energy-conservation efforts will have some effect, so that the growth in demand will be less than the 6 percent average annual rate between 1960 and 1972. Given high economic growth and high oil prices, the demand for oil was postulated to grow at the rate of 3.6 percent per year until 1985 and at 2.6 percent per year between 1985 and 2000. With low growth and constant prices the projected rates of growth in oil demand were 2.5 percent and then 1.8 percent. These rates established two demand curves for oil. The next task was to consider how long the supply of oil is likely to satisfy those demands. (Although the workshop was concerned primarily with energy prospects up to 2000, the central importance of oil prompted us to consider the pros-

pects for oil reserves and production until the year 2025; projections beyond 2000 are necessarily highly speculative.) In this article I shall tell how the workshop projected estimates of future oil supply and reached its conclusions on the relation of supply and demand.

It is a popular misconception that oil is found in vast underground pools that need only to be pumped dry. Actually oil is found in small spaces in porous rock, somewhat like water in a sponge. It seeps slowly through the porous material until it is trapped by impervious rock, often as a layer between water and gas. The oil is usually under pressure, and a well releases that pressure; the oil flows into the well, where it either rises to the surface (if the pressure in the field is sufficient) or is pumped out. Oil recovery under natural pressure is considered "primary" production, and in the U.S. today such production recovers on the average about 25 percent of the oil in a reservoir. "Secondary" recovery is achieved, in fields where it is feasible, by pumping water or gas into the reservoir to produce more pressure on the oil. "Tertiary" recovery, not yet widely applied, can sometimes be achieved if the viscosity of the oil is lowered so that it flows more easily, either by heating the oil (by injecting steam, for example) or by injecting chemicals into the reservoir. Secondary and tertiary methods have increased recovery in the U.S. from about 25 percent of the oil in place in the 1940's to about 32 percent now. Most of the world's oil is produced from conventional fields by these methods and by the recovery of natural-gas liquids as a by-product of natural gas. The workshop considered only those sources, excluding oil from shale, tar sands and the liquefaction of coal.

The major factors that determine potential oil supply are the amount of proven reserves (oil recoverable from known reserves at current prices and with current technology) and the rate at which those reserves can be exploited. Each field has a potential production rate that depends on the size of the field, its geology and its installed facilities. In general it is impossible to produce more than 10 percent of the recoverable reserves in a field in any one year without reducing the amount of oil that can ultimately be recovered. In some fields the rate may be higher and in others it may be lower, but overall a reserves-to-production ($R/P$) ratio of 10 to 1 is probably the minimum ratio that is feasible for the world's oil reserves. To apply a 10-to-1 $R/P$ ratio globally, however, would be to imply that all known oil fields can simultaneously produce at the maximum rate. The fact is that some fields will always be under development and will not yet be producing oil even though they contribute to the proven-reserves total. A more justifiable estimate of the maximum rate of production from worldwide proven reserves is provided by an $R/P$ ratio of 15 to 1.

What one needs in order to project a basic oil-supply curve is therefore a yearly figure for the remaining proven reserves. That is obtained by adding to the proven reserves of a base year the gross additions to reserves and then subtracting the amount of oil that has been withdrawn from reserves: the cumulative actual production. The maximum potential production from those reserves is determined by dividing the reserves figure by 15. As long as oil demand is less than potential production, actual production by definition equals demand; when demand exceeds potential production, demand is necessarily limited to potential production, which then becomes actual production. The important question is: At what point does an $R/P$ ratio of 15 bring potential production below projected demand? To establish that date we need (having estimated the demand) to determine the proven reserves in a base year and the probable annual rate of gross additions to reserves.

Estimates of proven recoverable reserves are uncertain, and they change from year to year. The workshop analy-

sis was based on figures published at the end of 1975 by *Oil and Gas Journal*, compiled from estimates made by governments and oil companies. Remaining proven reserves were then put at 555 billion barrels, some 80 percent of it in the member nations of the Organization of Petroleum Exporting Countries (OPEC), mostly in the Middle East. Production to date, on the other hand, has been primarily in North America. In all some 846 billion barrels had been discovered in the non-Communist world by 1975, about a third of which had been consumed.

One guide to the rate of discovery in the future is the rate at which proven reserves have been increased in the past. There are two ways to evaluate past discoveries. One can simply compare consecutive year-end published figures or one can backdate the changing and generally increasing estimates of the oil in each field to the year in which the field was discovered. For example, a field discovered in 1960 might initially be estimated to contain a billion barrels of recoverable reserves. Five years later information obtained as the field is devel-

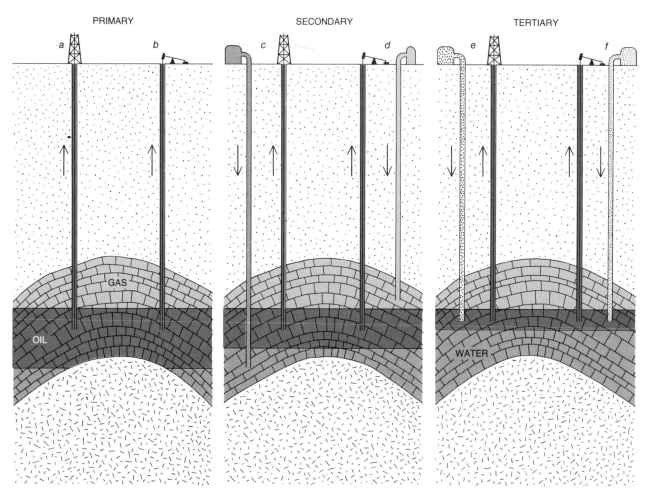

PRIMARY                          SECONDARY                          TERTIARY

OIL IS GENERALLY FOUND under pressure in porous rock, often in a geological structure such as the one shown here. Drilling a well into the oil-bearing stratum releases the pressure, and in primary production the oil flows to the surface (*a*) or is pumped out (*b*). When the natural pressure is too low to bring the oil to the well, secondary recovery may be achieved by pumping water (*c*) or gas (*d*) into the field to increase the pressure. In tertiary recovery the oil's viscosity is lowered by injecting steam, which heats it (*e*), or by injecting a chemical (*f*).

oped or as recovery techniques improve might increase the estimate to 1.2 billion barrels. Comparing year-end estimates attributes the extra .2 billion to 1965; the backdating method attributes the .2 billion to the 1960 discovery.

The year-to-year method emphasizes current changes in the rate of additions to reserves—new estimates for established fields as well as the impact of newly discovered fields [*see upper illustration on opposite page*]. It shows the five-year average (which smoothes out year-to-year fluctuations) rising from about 22 billion barrels per year between 1950 and 1965 to more than 50 billion between 1965 and 1970, when the magnitude of Middle East reserves in fields discovered before 1950 was being recognized. Since 1970 the yearly additions to reserves have been only about 25 billion per year. The backdating method, on the other hand, emphasizes that much of the late-1960's increase was in fields discovered before 1950 [*see lower illustration on page 22*]. It flattens out the 1950-to-1970 rate to an average of about 18 billion barrels per year, with a drop to 15 billion after 1970.

In making estimates for the future it is necessary to consider two different components of gross additions to reserves: first, reserves in genu-inely new discoveries and, second, additions to reserves in fields discovered before 1975, either through reassessment of what they contain or through enhanced ability to recover the oil.

The rate at which genuinely new reserves were added in the past would have been much lower without the discovery of the massive reserves in the Middle East, where about 60 percent of all the non-Communist world's known reserves have been found in a region that measures only some 800 by 500 miles. Might such a prolific oil-bearing region be found again? It is not very likely. Many of the remaining possible areas of the world have already been evaluated by seismic testing or exploratory wells and no evidence of a new Middle East has come to light. New discoveries probably will continue to be made in the Middle East itself, but there the rate at which new reserves are found has already fallen off.

In the Middle East and elsewhere it is in areas that are identified as being most likely to contain large accumulations of oil that exploratory wells will first be drilled, and the discovery rate will decline further as the search moves into less promising areas. At the same time the incentive for exploring will be reduced as the likelihood of finding large fields declines. Although some 30,000 oil fields have been discovered, about 75 percent of the remaining oil lies in a few very large fields, each of which holds more than 500 million barrels of recoverable reserves. Only 240 such fields have been discovered in the past 100 years; there cannot be many more. Yet in hostile environments, such as the North Sea, a field with 500 million recoverable barrels is about the smallest field that can justify the high cost of development. All in all it seems unlikely that genuinely new discoveries will continue to be made at even the rate of 15 billion barrels per year that has been achieved over the past five years.

What about additions to reserves in fields discovered before 1975? The estimation of recoverable reserves has become much more accurate than it was in the 1950's, so that the upward corrections of the past 25 years are not likely to be repeated on anything like the same scale. A more probable source of additions to reserves is the improvement of recovery techniques. Today the average world recovery rate is probably about 30 percent. Each 1 percent increase in the rate will therefore increase recoverable reserves by a thirtieth. Applying such a factor to the proven reserves of 555 billion barrels and to half of the cumulative production of 291 billion barrels (as an indication of reserves not previously considered recoverable) works out to an addition of about 25 billion barrels for each 1 percent increase in the recovery rate. John D. Moody, a petroleum consultant, and Robert E. Geiger of the Mobil Oil Corporation have suggested that the world-wide recovery rate will eventually average 40 percent, which would mean an addition of 250 billion barrels to reserves in currently known fields.

Taking all these factors into account, the workshop based its projections on two different gross-addition rates for the period from 1975 to 2000: 20 billion and 10 billion barrels per year. The higher rate assumes that new discoveries will decline gradually and that enhanced recovery will make a significant contribution, accounting for at least half of the gross additions by 2000. The lower rate assumes a more rapid decrease in the rate of new discoveries and a much smaller yield from enhanced recovery. We assumed that between 2000 and 2025 gross additions would decline gradually to four billion barrels per year (in the high-additions case) or three billion barrels (in the low-additions case) as total discoveries approach the inevitable ceiling: the total ultimately recoverable reserves, which we took to be about 1.6 trillion barrels in the non-Communist areas.

We were now in a position to develop oil-supply profiles for the two demand scenarios I outlined above, one assuming a high rate of economic growth and

PROVEN RESERVES
TOTAL: 658 BILLION BARRELS

| | |
|---|---|
| SAUDI ARABIA | 152 |
| OTHER MIDDLE EAST | 208 |
| OTHER OPEC | 90 |
| NORTH AMERICA | 40 |
| OTHER NON-OPEC | 65 |
| COMMUNIST AREAS | 103 |

CUMULATIVE PRODUCTION
TOTAL: 341 BILLION BARRELS

| | |
|---|---|
| SAUDI ARABIA | 23 |
| OTHER MIDDLE EAST | 61 |
| OTHER OPEC | 55 |
| NORTH AMERICA | 133 |
| OTHER NON-OPEC | 19 |
| COMMUNIST AREAS | 50 |

**WORLD'S REMAINING OIL RESERVES as of the end of 1975 were estimated (*left*) by *Oil and Gas Journal*. Of the total of 658 billion barrels, 555 billion were in the world outside the Communist areas. Note that whereas most of the remaining recoverable reserves were in the Middle East, most of the production of oil up to 1975 (*right*) had been in North America.**

high energy prices and the other assuming a low growth rate and constant prices.

Given high growth and high prices—and also the higher rate of additions to reserves, which is more likely if oil prices are high—production first fails to meet demand in 1997. That is, applying the $R/P$ ratio of 15 to 1 to the recoverable-reserves figure for 1997 yields a potential production in that year of 86 million barrels per day, whereas demand in that year is projected as being 87 million barrels per day. Thereafter, as reserves continue to decrease, the 15-to-1 $R/P$ ratio reduces production to 80 million barrels per day in 2000 and about 30 million in 2025 [*see top illustration on page 24*]. If in this scenario we substitute the lower rate of additions to reserves (which is less likely but certainly possible), production ceases to meet demand in 1990, when it peaks at only 72 million barrels per day. Thereafter it declines to 50 million barrels per day in 2000 and about 20 million in 2025.

Given low growth, constant prices and the low rate of additions to reserves, oil production fails to meet demand in 1994, when production peaks at 66 million barrels per day compared with a projected demand in that year of 66.5 million barrels. Production then falls to 53 million and about 20 million barrels per day in 2000 and 2025 [*see bottom illustration on page 24*]. If, in the face of low growth and constant prices, additions to reserves proceed at the higher rate, production could meet demand until 2004, when production would peak at 81 million barrels per day.

The trouble with the oil-supply profiles I have just described is that they make a somewhat unrealistic assumption: that oil-producing countries will continue to increase their production to keep pace with demand, limited only by an $R/P$ ratio of 15 to 1. In the real world some oil-producing countries outside OPEC may want to reduce their dependence on imported oil and may therefore produce oil at a rate higher than the rate set by a 15-to-1 ratio. More important, the countries that are net oil exporters (in particular the members of OPEC) may restrict production well before the 15-to-1 ratio is reached in an attempt to conserve their reserves. It is therefore necessary to modify the analysis: to look at production in the non-OPEC and the OPEC countries separately.

To consider non-OPEC and OPEC production separately requires an estimate of how future additions to reserves will be divided between the two regions. There are no well-established geological estimates. We assumed that 50 percent of the additions will be in the non-OPEC countries and 50 percent in OPEC, which is to say 10 billion and five

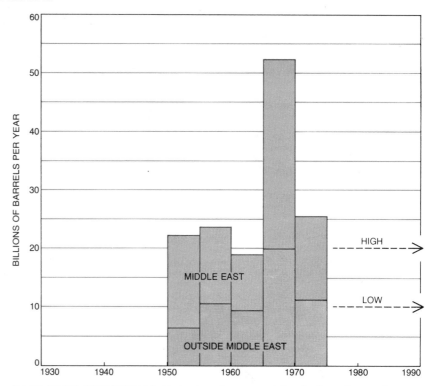

**RATE OF OIL DISCOVERY** in the past can be represented as is shown here: as five-year averages of the annual increase in proven reserves published each year by *Oil and Gas Journal*. Here both new discoveries and reassessments of reserves are credited to the year in which they were made. This method calls attention to the period of the late 1960's, when a major increase in known reserves resulted mainly from new estimates of vast reserves in Middle Eastern fields.

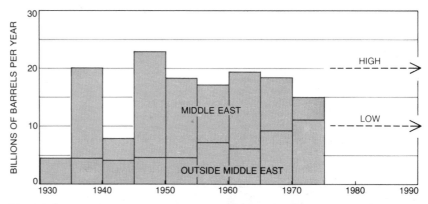

**DISCOVERY RATE LOOKS DIFFERENT** when only new discoveries are credited to the current year, with any revised estimates of the oil in known fields being backdated instead to the year in which each field was originally discovered. Backdating tends to smooth out the five-year fluctuations. In both this chart and the one at the top of the page the broken lines at the right indicate high and low assumptions concerning the future rate of additions to oil reserves.

billion barrels per year for each region on the high-additions assumption and the low-additions assumption respectively. Much of the non-OPEC region is still unexplored and should yield a large proportion of the new discoveries; enhanced recovery will be more important within OPEC, where 80 percent of the known proven reserves are situated.

Each national team participating in the workshop estimated its country's oil production for the period from 1975 to 2000 and similar estimates were developed for the other non-OPEC oil-producing countries. For the period from 2000 to 2025 production in the non-OPEC countries was estimated by the methods outlined above, with the further assumptions that the $R/P$ ratio would tend to decline toward 10 to 1 and that the rate of additions to reserves would also decline [*see upper illustration on page 25*].

Calculating future OPEC production is somewhat more complicated, because different countries have very different producing capabilities, economic interests and policies. What is clear is that to achieve the most optimistic oil-production profile would require OPEC production to reach more than 50 million barrels per day before 1995, which may not be feasible for technological reasons or for reasons of national policy. The currently installed "usable capacity" of the OPEC countries is about 37 million barrels per day, and in many countries the expansion of equipment and infrastructure for producing and transporting oil is unlikely to take place on the scale that would be required. The most telling influence on OPEC production, however, will probably be the insistence of particular countries on extending the life of their reserves by restricting production. Some OPEC governments have already suggested specific limits, which would hold OPEC production to a level some 4.8 million barrels per day below OPEC's usable capacity. Such restrictions are most likely to be imposed by countries that are "low absorbers" of oil revenues—countries, such as Saudi Arabia, Kuwait and Libya, that are earning more oil revenue than they can currently apply to domestic needs. On the other hand, Venezuela and Ecuador have already set a ceiling on production to prolong the flow of oil revenue, even though they are "high absorbers" of such income.

The government-imposed restrictions could have a considerable impact on potential production rates. For exam-ple, the OPEC countries of the Arabian Peninsula alone (Saudi Arabia, Kuwait, Qatar and the United Arab Emirates) have 58 percent of OPEC proven reserves. If an $R/P$ ratio of 15 to 1 were the only constraint, they could today produce oil at the rate of 17.4 billion barrels per year, or 47 million barrels per day, which is about equal to the total non-Communist output. They already have in place a usable capacity of 16.8 million barrels per day. Yet in 1975 they actually produced only 11.3 million barrels per day. And if the restrictions they have suggested might be imposed are in fact imposed, then their production would be held at 12.8 million barrels per day in the future.

Taking account of such constraints as these, we made three different assumptions about ceilings on Arabian Peninsula production, ceilings whose effect would be felt before the 15-to-1 $R/P$ ratio is reached. If government limits are set at or near present production levels, total Arabian Peninsula output would be held to about 13 million barrels per day. If Saudi Arabia allows its production to increase to about 15 million barrels per day (from some nine million barrels in 1977), the Arabian Peninsula's production would be held to 20 million barrels per day. If Saudi Arabia allows its production to rise to 20 million barrels per day, the output of the peninsula would be held to about 25 million barrels per day.

The OPEC countries outside the Arabian Peninsula have a usable capacity of 20.2 million barrels per day; restrictions proposed by three of these countries could limit non-Arabian OPEC production to .8 million barrels per day less than that capacity. Moreover, the reserves of some of these countries are already being reduced rather rapidly, so that any new additions are likely to enable them to maintain production at the present level rather than to increase it significantly. We therefore assumed an ultimate limit of 20 million barrels per day for OPEC production outside the Arabian Peninsula, a limit that takes into account both the physical constraints imposed by diminishing reserves and the formal restrictions that may be imposed by governments.

Adding the non-Arabian 20 million barrels per day to the three projected Arabian Peninsula limits (13, 20 and 25 million barrels per day) yields three assumed maximum figures for potential OPEC production: 33, 40 and 45 million barrels per day. In the revised analysis OPEC production is assumed to rise with demand only until it reaches one of these three limits, to stay at that level as long as the $R/P$ ratio exceeds 15 and then to decline as remaining reserves decline [see lower illustration on page 25].

By combining the estimated produc-

30,000 FIELDS IN ALL

240 FIELDS WITH MORE THAN .5 BILLION BARRELS

15 FIELDS WITH MORE THAN 10 BILLION BARRELS

FOUR LARGEST FIELDS

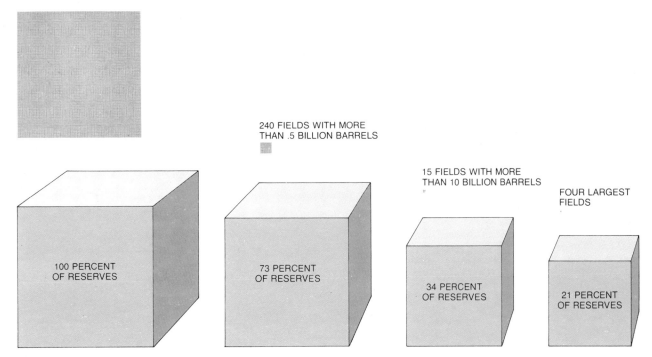

100 PERCENT OF RESERVES

73 PERCENT OF RESERVES

34 PERCENT OF RESERVES

21 PERCENT OF RESERVES

**IMPORTANCE OF LARGE OIL FIELDS is indicated by this illustration, which shows that of the 30,000 fields that have been discovered only 240 contain more than half a billion barrels of recoverable reserves but that those 240 account for 73 percent of the non-Com-munist world's known reserves. Only 15 fields contain more than 10 billion barrels of reserves and those fields account for more than a third of the total. The four largest fields, one in Venezuela and three in the Arabian Peninsula, together contain a fifth of the known reserves.**

tion of the non-OPEC countries with these various assumptions about constrained OPEC production we were able to develop a new and presumably more realistic set of oil-supply curves to set against projected demand [*see illustrations on page 26*]. The impact of the OPEC constraints is clear: production peaks earlier; the gap between supply and demand opens earlier. On the other hand, oil that is kept in the ground in the 1990's helps to maintain reserves and can be produced after 2000, making the decline in production somewhat less precipitous.

Given the high-growth, high-price scenario and the high rate of additions to reserves, for example, the 45-million-barrel OPEC limit moves the peak in the oil supply back to 1989 (compared with 1997 in the unlimited case) and down to 71 million barrels per day (compared with 86 million), but the supply can be maintained near 70 million barrels per day for some 15 years. With OPEC production limited to 33 million barrels per day, demand outruns supply as early as 1981, at only 55 million barrels per day; OPEC continues to produce at the 33-million-barrel level through 2025, however, so that total supply falls off only slowly as non-OPEC production declines.

With demand set by the low-growth scenario and with a low rate of additions to reserves, an OPEC production limit of 40 million barrels per day ordains a peak in supply five years earlier and five million barrels per day lower than in the unlimited case, but again the supply curve is flattened out. If OPEC production is limited to 33 million barrels per day, total supply is constrained to 55 million barrels per day in 1983 and falls off only with declining non-OPEC production until after 2013, when OPEC production finally drops below 33 million barrels.

Are these projections too pessimistic? Some observers might consider our assumptions about gross additions to reserves to be conservative. There have been optimistic estimates that the entire world's ultimately recoverable reserves may be as large as three trillion barrels, which means some 2.4 trillion barrels in the non-Communist areas instead of the 1.6 trillion we took as our central estimate. One basis for the optimistic forecasts is the expectation that new discoveries may be larger than we assumed, particularly in underdeveloped countries that have not yet been subjected to intensive exploration. The other basis is the expectation that major breakthroughs in techniques for secondary and tertiary production will make it possible to recover substantially more oil than we assumed. Neither of these possibilities can be ruled out. What, then, if one supposes that as much as 30 billion

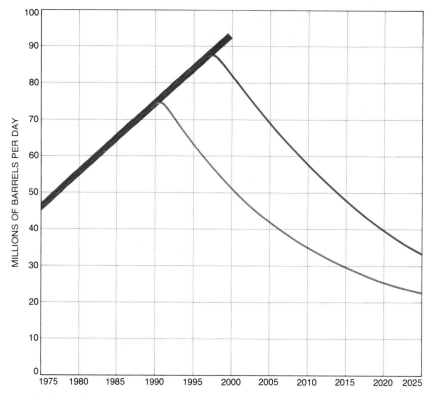

**OIL-SUPPLY PROFILE** was developed by applying a reserves-to-production ($R/P$) ratio of 15 to 1 to projected figures for recoverable reserves. This is the profile according to the high-growth, high-energy-price scenario. Assuming a high rate of additions to reserves (which is more likely if oil prices are high), production (*dark colored curve*) fails to meet demand (*gray*) in 1997. Given a lower rate of additions, production (*light color*) fails to meet demand in 1990.

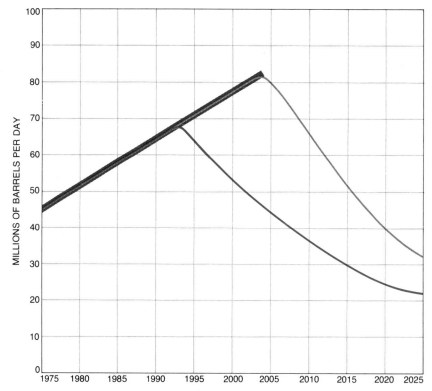

**SIMILAR PROFILE** for low-growth, constant-energy-price scenario shows production (*dark color*) failing to meet demand in 1994, given a low rate of additions to reserves (the more likely situation). If a high rate of additions is assumed, production (*light color*) would meet demand until 2004. Profiles on this page assume that production is not constrained by governments.

barrels per year will be added to proven reserves between 1975 and 2000 rather than 20 billion barrels per year, our high estimate?

If there were no constraints on OPEC production, the 30-billion rate would allow the oil supply to meet potential demand (in the high-growth case) until sometime between 2005 and 2010, when the limiting $R/P$ ratio of 15 to 1 would be reached and production would peak and then decline. As I have shown, however, the level at which OPEC countries are willing to produce oil is more important than the theoretical limit imposed by the $R/P$ ratio. The year in which an OPEC limit of, say, 45 million barrels per day is reached depends on the level of production in non-OPEC countries. Even with a discovery rate outside OPEC of 15 billion barrels per year (half the optimistic 30-billion estimate for the yearly addition to reserves) the OPEC limit would be reached, and would constrain total supply, soon after 1990. By 2000, with OPEC production limited to 45 million barrels per day, total production might be between 75 and 80 million barrels per day.

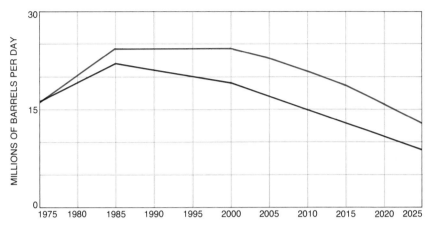

NON-OPEC PRODUCTION is separated from that of the Organization of Petroleum Exporting Countries (OPEC) in order to consider the effects of government limits. Curves show estimated non-OPEC production to 2000, and projections to 2025 assuming declining additions to reserves and declining $R/P$ ratio, for high-growth (color) and low-growth (black) scenarios.

This would be less than 10 million barrels in excess of the figure for total production that we arrived at by assuming a discovery rate of 20 billion barrels per year. And it would still be some 15 million barrels per day below the demand projected for the high-growth scenario. In other words, adopting even the most optimistic estimates of additions to reserves delays the drop in production for only a few years and reduces the gap between supply and demand by only a few million barrels per day.

The future of the oil supply is uncertain, to say the least. The conclusion is clear, however, that the demand for oil in the year 2000 is unlikely to be satisfied by crude oil from conventional sources. Even in the absence of government limits on production, supply will meet demand in 2000 only in the case of the most optimistic assumption about additions to reserves. A more important constraint on production than the actual size of reserves is likely to be the level of production set by producing countries that have large reserves and a limited need for current oil revenue. Limits likely to be set by such members of OPEC will probably cause the oil supply to peak sometime around 1990 at the latest; lower limits could bring the date into the early 1980's.

Although the end of the era of growth in oil supply is probably only 15 years away at the most, it may be followed by 10 years or so of fairly constant production, giving governments and consumers some time in which to make the adjustments that will be necessitated by a real decline in the oil supply. If oil is discovered, or recovery techniques are improved, on a scale greater than can now be foreseen, the effect would be only to delay for a few years—not to obviate— the necessary transition to other fuels. For governments and consumers to allow oil consumption to increase in the fond hope that more oil will somehow turn up is to run the risk that the complex interactions of geology, politics, economic growth and prices will instead dictate a drop in oil production even earlier than we have thought likely, thus increasing the difficulty of adjusting to a world in which oil is scarce.

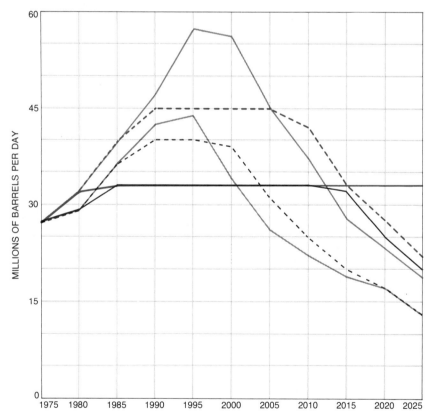

OPEC PRODUCTION is projected on various assumptions about government-imposed limits. For the high-growth scenario with high additions to reserves three curves are shown: government limits constrain production at 33 million barrels per day (solid colored line), or at 45 million barrels (broken colored line), or production is not constrained except by the $R/P$ ratio (light colored line). For the low-growth scenario and low additions to reserves the curves assume that production is held to 33 million barrels per day (black line), or to 40 million barrels (broken black line), or is not constrained (gray). The projections are speculative beyond 2000.

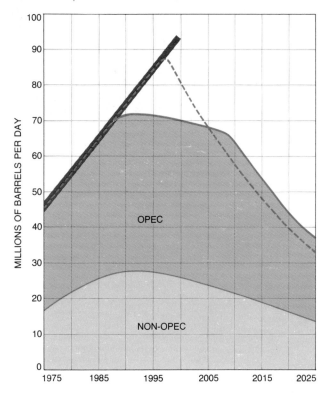

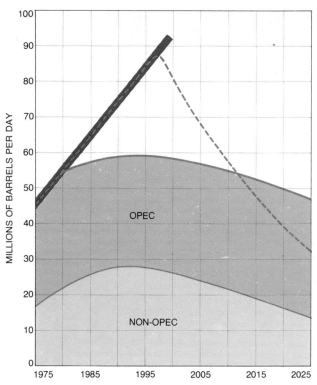

**MORE REALISTIC PROFILES** take into account government limits. These curves are for the high-growth, high-price scenario and a high rate of additions to reserves. Here non-OPEC production is shown combined with OPEC production that is limited to 45 million barrels per day (*left*) and to 33 million barrels per day (*right*) to give total production in the non-Communist areas of the world (*heavy colored line*). In both cases a comparison with the unconstrained total (*broken colored line*) shows that the imposition of government limits would cut supply below demand (*gray line*) sooner (as early as 1981) but that the subsequent fall in oil supply would be less precipitate.

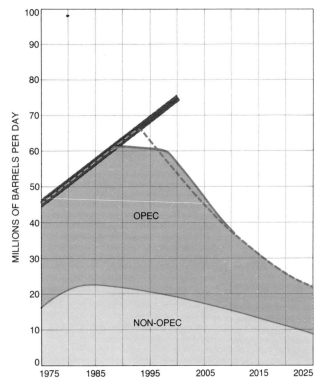

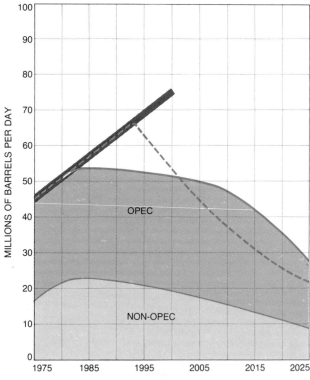

**REALISTIC PROFILE** for the low-growth, constant-price scenario and a low rate of additions to reserves shows similar effects. With OPEC production limited to 40 million barrels per day (*left*) or to 33 million barrels per day (*right*), production fails to meet demand sooner than in the unconstrained case, but later production of reserves that have been conserved keeps supply fairly steady for some time.

# 3

# World Coal Production

## COMMENTARY

Where the previous article on oil production was concerned with our running out of a valuable energy resource, this article by Edward D. Griffith and Alan W. Clarke is about bringing back coal as a dominant energy source, or at least a much more important source than it has been in the past generation. Based on another one of the studies of the Workshop on Alternative Energy Strategies, the point of view expressed by the authors is that coal is abundant and can be exploited to advantage by the United States as supplies of oil and gas diminish. What will be required is a large expansion of facilities for mining, preparing, and transporting the enormous tonnages that will be required. We will also have to invent new ways to use the coal for a variety of purposes other than central power generation, which is now almost the exclusive market for coal in the developed countries. We may have to mine 60 percent more coal than today in the year 2000, say the authors, even if energy demand increases on only a modest scale.

Estimates of the total coal resources available in the world vary, depending primarily on estimates of what reserves are economically recoverable and minable. But all agree that there are vast reserves, enough for at least a hundred years, perhaps many hundreds. Further, these reserves are distributed in the world in a pattern different from that of oil and gas. There are significant, though not enormous, coal resources in Africa, Asia, and South America, in addition to the well-known reserves in Europe and North America. India, for example, a country starved for oil and gas, has approximately 12 billion metric tons of recoverable coal. Australia has expanded its production and supplies a large amount of coal to Japan, a country with few indigenous energy reserves.

The difficulty with Griffith and Clarke's proposal for expanding coal utilization is making it acceptable to the countries that will need to produce and burn coal. Chief among the problems is the amount of air pollution from the large-scale burning of coal, whether from large power plants or from decentralized units, such as small home furnaces (a relic of the past to most people in the United States who grew up after World War II). The most important consideration for public health is sulfur dioxide emissions, which can now be shown to cause a great many premature deaths from a variety of diseases. There is promise for such emissions to be cleaned up more efficiently at considerably less cost than the messy treatment now in use, but we need a major committment to high-quality research and development. If such were to be sponsored by the Department of Energy, it would cost only a small fraction of the enormous sums spent on nuclear power development. The air pollution that cannot be controlled and is potentially a global problem is the carbon dioxide added to the atmosphere by fuel burning. It is possible that we may warm our atmosphere sufficiently to melt the polar ice caps and raise the sea level to the point of drowning most of the world's major centers of population and much of its arable land.

Another hazard of coal mining that is too often overlooked is the danger to miners themselves. Underground coal mining is one of the most hazardous occupations, and many of our best coals lie too deeply buried to be mined by surface methods. Black lung disease and accidents take a high toll of miners' lives each year. Those coals that can be mined by surface methods, particularly those in the western United States, have another drawback—that reclamation of extensively strip-mined tracts may require far more water than is available now for agriculture or grazing. These drawbacks, in comparison with those of nuclear power, will be decisive in how this and other countries choose between the nuclear alternative and the expansion of coal. Perhaps we will choose to use coal as a transition until the problems of nuclear power are overcome.

# World Coal Production

by Edward D. Griffith
and Alan W. Clarke

*January 1979*

*As oil production peaks and declines, substitute energy
sources will be needed on an enormous scale. Coal
could fill a large part of the gap if its production and
use were encouraged by national policies*

Before World War II coal was the world's dominant fuel. Since then it has steadily lost ground to other fuels, and today it supplies only 19 percent of the energy consumed in the non-Communist countries. During the past 20 years, as worldwide oil consumption roughly tripled, coal production remained nearly constant outside the U.S.S.R., China and Poland. In those countries production increased about 30 percent between 1960 and 1977 but still lagged behind total energy consumption. The virtual stagnation of coal consumption in the non-Communist countries reflects the preference of private and industrial consumers for the convenience offered by liquid fuels, natural gas and electricity, together with the growth of oil-specific markets such as transportation and petrochemicals. With the general recognition that world oil production is likely to peak and decline sometime during the next 25 years, nations will be obliged to seek alternative fuels. Once again coal may be called on to sustain industrial production and economic development throughout the world.

Since coal is not as easily extracted, transported and burned as oil and natural gas are, large increases in coal production and utilization will call both for strong incentives and for fundamental changes in attitudes toward coal. Making coal both available and acceptable will require a major expansion of facilities for coal mining, processing, transportation and utilization, together with new technologies for processing, converting and consuming coal. On the most modest projections the U.S. will have to mine about 60 percent more coal in the year 2000 than it does at present. Conceivably it will have to mine three times more. If such an expansion is to take place, serious economic, social and environmental issues related to coal mining and coal burning will have to be resolved.

We shall outline the implications of large-scale coal development as an alternative to liquid fossil fuels, the options that are open and the issues we believe policymakers will have to face over the next 25 years. Our estimates of coal demand and supply are based on the work of a two-year study, the Workshop on Alternative Energy Strategies, carried out under the direction of Carroll L. Wilson of the Massachusetts Institute of Technology. The study involved some 70 specialists recruited from industry, government and universities in 12 energy-consuming countries and three major oil-exporting countries (the U.S., Canada, Britain, France, West Germany, the Netherlands, Denmark, Sweden, Norway, Finland, Italy, Japan, Iran, Mexico and Venezuela).

The Workshop developed a series of energy projections to 1985 and 2000 based on various assumptions about economic growth, energy prices and government policies. The critical conclusion based on those projections was that sooner or later, and probably before the end of the century, oil demand would strain world supply and oil production would level off and decline. A detailed description of the Workshop's oil analysis has appeared in these pages [see "World Oil Production," by Andrew R. Flower; SCIENTIFIC AMERICAN Offprint 930]. In this article we shall consider the possible use of coal as a substitute for oil, the size of the world's coal resources, the outlook for coal demand, potential coal production in various regions of the world and the possible conversion of coal into synthetic fuels.

Although one lump of coal may look very much like another, there are many different grades and qualities, just as there are many different types of crude oil. High grades of coal have a heating value of some 7,000 kilocalories per kilogram (12,600 British thermal units per pound); lower grades have only half or a third as much. One system of classification divides coal into two broad categories: hard coal (anthracite and the various grades of bituminous coal) and soft coal (brown coal and lignite). The ability of different types of coal to form coke when they are heated in the absence of air also varies widely. Since coke for steelmaking is one of coal's major uses, a second important classification divides coals into metallurgical (or coking) coals and thermal (or steam) coals, which are burned to provide either heat or steam for the generation of electric power.

The total world production of all types of coal in 1977 was 3,400 million metric tons, of which hard coal represented 2,500 million metric tons, or about 70 percent. The leading producers of hard coal are the major developed countries. More than 75 percent of the world output is mined by six countries: the U.S., the U.S.S.R., China, Poland, Britain and West Germany. Among the developing countries the only large producer is India. The U.S. accounts for more than half of all the coal mined and consumed by the non-Communist countries. The U.S.S.R. and China each produce roughly 80 percent as much as the U.S.

World production of brown coal and lignite has been increasing slowly, reaching 950 million metric tons in 1977. East Germany is the largest producer, with 250 million tons, followed by the U.S.S.R. with 180 million tons.

Among the non-Communist countries West Germany is by far the largest producer of brown coal and lignite. Because of the lower energy content of such coals they contributed only 4 percent of the world's total primary energy in 1977, compared with 25 percent supplied by hard coal.

In the non-Communist countries the fraction of primary energy derived from coal (93 percent of it hard coal) declined from 33 percent in 1960 to 19 percent in 1976. The use of coal has been falling steadily in all markets except for the generation of electricity, which now accounts for more than 75 percent of the coal consumed in the U.S., 57 percent in western Europe, 18 percent in Japan and 36 percent in all other non-Communist countries.

Unlike crude oil, nearly two-thirds of which is shipped from its country of origin, most coal is consumed in the country where it is mined. In 1976 only 8 percent of the world's hard-coal production (190 million tons) moved in international trade, mostly as coking coal for the steel industry. Japan, with purchases of 50 million tons, half of it from Australia, was the largest importer.

The world's reserves of coal far exceed those of any other fossil fuel and are sufficient to support a massive increase in consumption well into the next century. The World Energy Conference's *Survey of Energy Resources, 1976,* estimates the world's total resources of all ranks of coal to be 11,500 billion metric tons. Of this amount 1,300 billion tons count as known, or measured, reserves. Of this amount in turn 740 billion tons were deemed economically recoverable when the studies of the Workshop on Alternative Energy Strategies were made. Five regions hold 96 percent of the known reserves. North America has 31 percent, the U.S.S.R. and the other countries of eastern Europe 26 percent, western Europe 17 per-

cent, China 15 percent and Australia 6 percent.

Estimates of ultimate recoverability vary from one coalfield to another depending on the accessibility of the coal, which is influenced by such variables as seam thickness and depth and type of terrain. Recovery rates range from 85 to 95 percent in surface mines and from 25 to 70 percent in underground mines.

The Workshop estimate of 740 billion tons of economically recoverable coal includes coal of all ranks. When adjustments are made for the inferior heating value of the lower ranks, the recoverable tonnage comes to about 600 billion tons of hard-coal equivalent, enough for more than 200 years' consumption at current rates. Expressed in terms of oil equivalent, 600 billion tons of hard coal has the energy content of about 3,000 billion barrels, which is four to five times the current estimates of proved reserves of crude oil.

The World Energy Conference esti-

**COAL-CARRYING "UNIT" TRAINS** have been developed to move coal expeditiously at low cost, usually between one mine and one customer, which is most often an electric utility. The trains shuttle back and forth without being uncoupled, acting much like a conveyor belt. The 110-car unit train that appears in this photograph is one of four trains that together deliver 2.6 million tons of coal per year 600 miles from a surface mine of Amax Carbon Products near Gillette, Wyo., to a power station of the Public Service Company of Colorado near Pueblo, Colo. In 1975 such unit trains carried 169 million tons of coal in the U.S., about half of all the coal that was moved by rail.

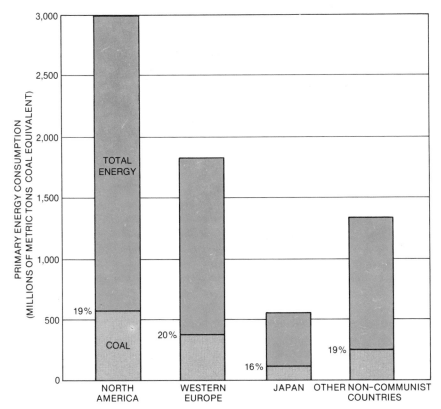

**CONTRIBUTION OF COAL TO PRIMARY ENERGY SUPPLIES** in non-Communist countries averaged about 19 percent in 1976, with little variation among the major regions. In 1960 coal supplied 33 percent of the total energy demand in non-Communist countries and roughly 45 percent in the world as a whole. By 1976 coal's contribution to world energy supplies, including those of the Communist countries, had fallen to about 30 percent. Most of the incremental demand since 1960 has been met by more convenient fossil fuels and nuclear power.

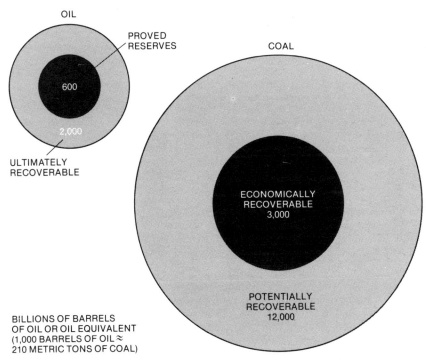

**COMPARISON OF OIL AND COAL RESERVES** shows that the world supply of potentially recoverable coal is equivalent to some 12,000 billion barrels of oil, or six times the estimated reserves of ultimately recoverable oil. The amount of coal that is economically recoverable with today's technology and prices is considerably smaller, equivalent to about 3,000 billion barrels of oil. Even this figure, however, is perhaps five times the proved reserves of oil.

mate of 11,500 billion tons of total world coal resources is equivalent to some 50,000 billion barrels of oil. On the conservative view that on the average 25 percent of the coal is recoverable, a total of 2,500 billion tons of coal, equivalent to 12,000 billion barrels of oil, could ultimately be produced. That is about six times the estimated quantity of the ultimately recoverable oil.

Assessments of world coal resources are less comprehensive than those for oil because exploration for coal has been less wide-ranging and generally less intensive. Many estimates of coal reserves were made when oil was both plentiful and cheap, so that there was little incentive to look for more coal. As interest in coal revives, more reserves are likely to be identified. For example, few of the developing countries have ever had to look for coal. Geology suggests, however, that large areas of the world, including much of the Southern Hemisphere, have a high coal potential.

Australia provides an example of recent coal development. Over the past 20 years geologists have carried out intensive coal explorations, largely inspired by the Japanese need for metallurgical coal. As a result substantial coal reserves have been found in New South Wales and Queensland, and Australia's annual output has been tripled. Measured Australian reserves of bituminous coal are now roughly comparable in energy content to the proved oil reserves of Saudi Arabia. By the same token exploration in southern Africa is now yielding favorable results, indicating that world coal resources may be far greater than has been estimated. Moreover, there are almost certainly major coal deposits offshore; for example, large coal deposits are thought to lie under the North Sea. Such potential coal resources are not included in even the most optimistic estimates of coal reserves.

The true size of the world coal reserve, however, is not a critical value. Known coal resources can support any likely level of exploitation for decades to come. What is in doubt is the willingness and ability of nations to accept large increases in coal production and utilization.

The key to estimating the future role of coal is determining the potential development of coal demand. Large increases in coal production will be realized only if the demand for coal develops and is perceived far enough in advance for the necessary investments in production and transportation to be made. The critical question, then, is whether the demand for coal will continue to stagnate or will rise sharply as the availability of oil declines.

A number of conditions will have to be met before coal can again fill a growing share of the world's energy needs.

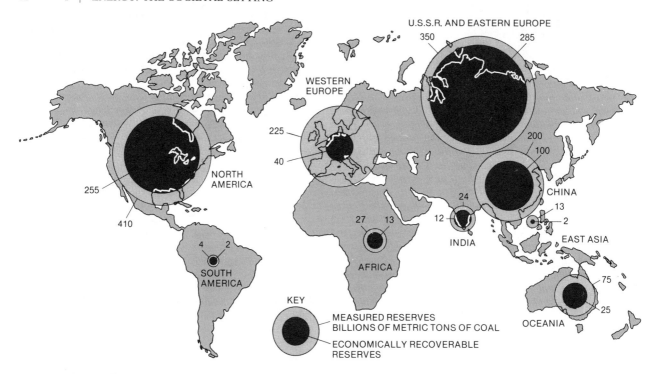

**TOTAL MEASURED RESERVES OF COAL** are 1,300 billion metric tons, of which some 740 billion tons are estimated to be economically recoverable, a 200-year supply at current production rates. (Adjusted for heat content, the 740 billion tons are equivalent to 3,000 billion barrels of oil, the figure given in the bottom illustration on the opposite page.) "Measured reserves" are the quantities of coal in well-surveyed deposits whose extent and quality have been established by adequate sampling. Most of the currently measured coal reserves are located in the Northern Hemisphere, but the rest of the world is likely to increase its share through new exploration for coal deposits.

There must first be a clear recognition that alternatives to oil are needed and that coal is one of the cheapest and most abundant fuels. That implies an awareness of the long-term energy outlook, policy decisions by governments to encourage both the production and the utilization of coal, and public attitudes that make such policies feasible.

There must also be a clear recognition that widespread burning of coal without appropriate controls would pollute the air, with serious consequences for the environment and possibly for the climate. New technologies are being developed to control the emissions of sulfur dioxide and nitrogen oxide from burning coal. Moreover, because the hydrocarbons in coal have a high ratio of carbon to hydrogen the burning of coal yields more carbon dioxide per unit of heat released than does the burning of oil or natural gas. The carbon dioxide content of the atmosphere appears to be rising, and some scientists are concerned about possible effects on the climate. What contribution the combustion of fossil fuels will make to the rise in atmospheric carbon dioxide and what the ultimate consequences will be are not yet known, but the potential for harmful effects must be faced if the burning of coal is to increase greatly. There is need for additional research and development in flue-gas desulfurization, fluidized-bed combustion, chemical coal-cleaning and other techniques for the burning of coal with a minimum of pollution. Govern-

ments must also act to settle debates on clean-air standards and encourage investigation of the long-term effect of fossil-fuel combustion on the earth's atmosphere.

Extensive facilities for mining, transporting and burning coal will also have to be built. The construction of such facilities will call for a huge capital investment and for the development of improved methods for handling coal in clean and convenient ways. Better handling techniques are particularly important to industrial, commercial and domestic consumers, who would otherwise prefer to use oil or gas. Residential and small commercial consumers are not going to return to shoveling coal and ashes. Small-scale fluidized-bed units with automatic stoking and ash removal may someday, however, be practical for heating apartment houses and commercial buildings.

The cost of coal is currently competitive with the cost of oil and natural gas for large consumers, even after allowing for the added costs of coal facilities and pollution control. Energy pricing and tax policies could also be designed to supplement the economic incentive for the use of coal if governments want to encourage such use. Choices between coal and other energy sources will be based on a combination of price, environmental, convenience and other factors that bear on the consumer's perceived self-interest.

In the analysis carried out for the Workshop on Alternative Energy Strategies it was clear that in all cases coal production can be expanded to meet the projected demand for coal. Estimates were made of coal demand in the non-Communist countries consistent with various world economic growth rates (ranging from 3 to 6 percent per year) in combination with energy costs at various prices (ranging from $11.50 to $17.25 in 1975 dollars per barrel of oil or its energy equivalent), with various national energy-policy responses ("vigorous" or "restrained") and with policy emphasis placed either on coal or on nuclear power. The countries included now consume about 70 percent of the world's energy.

The lowest projected demand for coal in the year 2000 is 1,610 million metric tons of hard coal or its equivalent, an increase of only 27 percent over the demand in 1976. The low projection is based on an annual economic growth rate of 3 percent and an energy cost of $11.50 per barrel of oil or its equivalent (the 1975 price) in combination with government policies favoring nuclear development. The highest projected demand, 2,575 million metric tons (an increase of 103 percent over 1976), results from a model in which a 5 percent annual growth rate is combined with an energy cost of $17.25 per barrel of oil or its equivalent (a 50 percent increase over 1975) and policies emphasizing coal more than nuclear power. With the same rate of economic growth and cost of energy but with the emphasis changed in favor of nuclear power the demand for coal still reaches 2,225 million tons, an increase of 75 percent over 1976. On this model the North American demand alone would be 1,035 million tons, an 85 percent increase over 1976.

Since the production of coal can potentially exceed any projected demand, a major issue is the possibility of directly substituting coal for the declining oil-based fuels. Our analyses indicate that an all-out program to substitute abundant coal for limited oil could add from 200 million to 600 million tons to the estimates given above for the demand for coal in the year 2000. For example, in an extreme case the industrial demand for coal in 2000 could be twice the Workshop estimates if coal were substituted for an equivalent amount of oil. Although the degree to which energy consumers will be willing and able to use coal instead of oil is uncertain, these analyses emphasize the potential usefulness of coal as a major substitute for oil. At the same time the magnitude of the changeover that would be required indicates the scale of the difficulties that would be faced in making a major transition from oil to coal.

Individual national governments will have to decide the extent to which they will encourage or discourage the expansion of coal-consuming systems. Since long lead times are needed in shifting away from an energy system dominated by oil, decisions must be made soon if such a shift is to be accomplished before oil becomes scarcer and more expensive than it is today. The choices made in the next few years may set the course for the rest of the century.

On the other side of the coin from demand is the potential supply of coal, realistically estimated on the basis of the resources available for opening new mines and building the needed ancillary facilities. Careful estimates of potential coal production for various models of economic growth, energy price and fuel-policy emphasis were prepared by each of the national groups in the Workshop study. Also undertaken was a special analysis of potential coal production in non-Communist countries not represented in the study group and exports from those countries.

As in the case of the demand estimates, the largest values of potential coal production at the end of the century were elicited by postulating a 5 percent annual economic growth rate, fuel priced at $17.25 per barrel of oil or its equivalent and an energy policy that emphasized coal rather than nuclear power. The projected volume of coal available under these conditions was 3,170 million metric tons, an increase of nearly 150 percent over the 1977 production of 1,280 million tons. The total was arrived at by projecting large increases for North America, the developing countries, Australia and southern Africa. North America was deemed capable of reaching an output of 1,835 million tons, or nearly three times the 1977 tonnage. The lowest projection for coal production from all non-Communist countries in the year 2000 was 2,070 million tons, representing a 62 percent increase over the amount produced in 1977. As we have noted, all the projections of potential production for the year 2000 exceeded by comfortable margins the projected demands for coal made under comparable assumptions of growth rate, energy price and fuel-policy emphasis.

Through the period between 1985 and 2000 western Europe and Japan will be net importers of coal, potentially on a large scale, since their demand will exceed local production. Areas with a substantial potential for exporting coal will be North America, parts of Latin America, southern Africa, South Asia, Australia and certain of the Communist countries. Among the oil-poor developing countries India has the largest potential for producing coal, possibly in the range of 200 million to 250 million tons per year by the end of the century. In several other developing countries with indigenous coal reserves coal could provide a domestic alternative to costly imported oil and a potential source of export revenue. The large coal reserves in China and the U.S.S.R. also make those countries potentially important exporters of coal.

The eventual volume of coal made available for export to Europe and Japan is uncertain because it depends on estimates of indigenous supply and demand for each of the exporting nations. It does appear, however, that international shipments of coal could become a major source of energy for the energy-

WORLD PRODUCTION OF HARD COAL IN 1977 approached 2,500 million tons, an increase of 3.2 percent over the year before and a figure 23 percent higher than the 1960 one. The term hard coal excludes brown coal and lignite, fuels of lower heating value whose production came to about 910 million metric tons in 1977, nearly half of it mined in East Germany and the U.S.S.R. Much of the increase in hard-coal production since 1960 has come in the Communist countries. Total output in non-Communist countries has been between 1.1 billion and 1.2 billion tons throughout the 18-year period. Within this virtually static total there has been a gradual rise in the production of coal in North America, a decline in production in western Europe and Japan and substantial increases in production in southern Africa, Australia and India.

poor industrialized nations and could range up to between 400 million and 900 million metric tons by the year 2000.

The projections of supply and demand made by the Workshop on Alternative Energy Strategies include both steam coal and metallurgical coal. The largest increases available for export will be steam coal. In the long run, however, the distinction between the types of coal may become blurred as new technology makes more types of coal usable for metallurgical purposes.

Coal powered the Industrial Revolution in Europe and North America and was the main industrial and domestic fuel for more than a century. This long history has given rise to a sophisticated coal-production technology. Underground mining, however, is still labor-intensive, particularly in western Europe, and underground-mine coal-production costs are therefore sensitive to wage inflation. Underground mining is also a hazardous occupation, a fact that has led to social and political pressures to enact and enforce strict coal-mining safety and health regulations. One result has been declining labor productivity in underground mines, which is only partly offset by new mining equipment and techniques.

Although underground mining of favorable seams of steam coal and comparatively thin seams of coking coal will remain economically attractive in many areas, significant increases in total coal production will call for a sizable expansion of surface mining. Productivity, or tons of coal per man-day, is typically two or three times higher in surface mines than it is in underground ones. Surface mining, however, has its own problems, most notably the environmental objections to the disturbance of large tracts of land in the course of mining operations and before reclamation of the land.

The environmental, economic and social issues related to coal are potential causes of political conflict in areas of the world that have not experienced large-scale coal mining or coal use. Whether environmental and social opposition will be a constraining factor in the expansion of coal production outside the U.S. remains an open question. In any event the success or failure of U.S. efforts to deal with the issues involved and to meet President Carter's goals for expanded coal utilization (1.2 million short tons per year by 1985) could have an important effect on attitudes toward the development of coal in other countries.

Since the U.S. has half of the world's coal reserves outside the Communist countries and is the largest producer and consumer of coal, its potential for expanded production is important both to itself and to its prospective overseas cus-

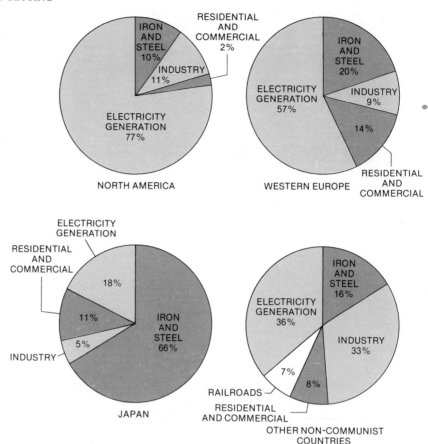

MAJOR MARKETS FOR COAL around the world in 1976 were electric-generating plants and the iron and steel industry. More than three-fourths of the coal consumed in North America was used to generate electricity. In Japan the dominant user of coal was the iron and steel industry. Industrial uses of coal were also significant in developing countries, notably India.

tomers for coal. Projections made for the Workshop indicate that by the end of the century the U.S. could reach an annual production of between 1.1 and two billion metric tons (between 1.2 and 2.2 billion short tons). The low estimate assumes constant real energy prices ($11.50 per barrel of oil or its equivalent) and a policy choice that emphasizes nuclear power as the principal replacement for oil. The high estimate assumes that the real price of energy will rise by 50 percent (to $17.25 per barrel of oil or its equivalent) and that Government policy will encourage the adoption of coal as the principal replacement fuel. In all cases the projections reflect major increases over the 1977 coal production of 695 million short tons.

Although 70 percent of U.S. coal reserves can be reached only by underground mining, it is expected that most new coal production over the next 20 years will come from surface mining in the Western states, particularly on the northern Great Plains. There coal seams are thick, near the surface and under fairly flat land. Western coal typically has a lower heat content per ton than

Eastern coal, but in compensation much of it has a low sulfur content and therefore emits less sulfur dioxide per ton of coal burned.

Widespread surface mining in previously undisturbed areas is opposed by environmental groups and local agricultural interests. There are two principal objections to the extension of surface mining in the Western states: the potential despoliation of large tracts of land and the potentially undesirable social and economic effects in a primarily rural, sparsely populated, agriculturally oriented society of small towns and isolated ranches. Agriculturists are concerned that some of the land currently being grazed by livestock may be ruined for future agricultural purposes and that the water requirements of mining and reclamation may conflict with the needs of farmers. Local residents fear that a large influx of construction workers and miners will tear the social fabric of the small towns. They are worried about noise, dust and accidents resulting from large numbers of coal trains passing through their communities. Such concerns cannot be dismissed.

Large new surface mines are nonethe-

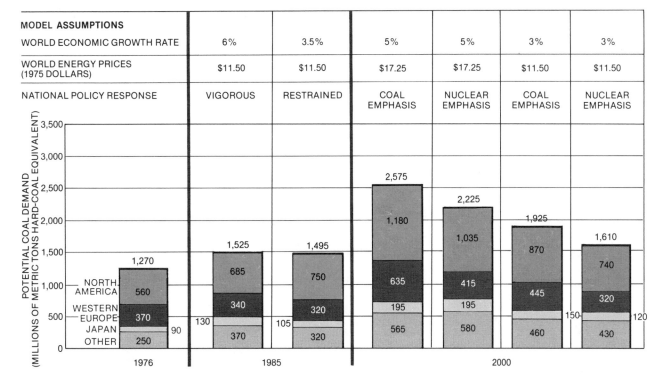

| MODEL ASSUMPTIONS | | | | | | |
|---|---|---|---|---|---|---|
| WORLD ECONOMIC GROWTH RATE | 6% | 3.5% | 5% | 5% | 3% | 3% |
| WORLD ENERGY PRICES (1975 DOLLARS) | $11.50 | $11.50 | $17.25 | $17.25 | $11.50 | $11.50 |
| NATIONAL POLICY RESPONSE | VIGOROUS | RESTRAINED | COAL EMPHASIS | NUCLEAR EMPHASIS | COAL EMPHASIS | NUCLEAR EMPHASIS |

**POTENTIAL COAL DEMAND TO THE YEAR 2000** was estimated by the Workshop on Alternative Energy Strategies, in which the authors participated. The potential demand for the non-Communist countries in 1985 and 2000 is compared here with the actual 1976 demand when various assumptions are made about the world economic growth rate, the world energy price in constant (1975) dollars and the vigor and direction of national policies. In 1975 the world oil price was $11.50 per barrel for Saudi Arabian light crude oil shipped from the Persian Gulf. The largest potential demand in 2000 is projected for a model that assumes an economic growth rate of 5 percent per year, a 50 percent increase in real energy price (to $17.25 per barrel of oil equivalent) and policies that favor coal over nuclear power.

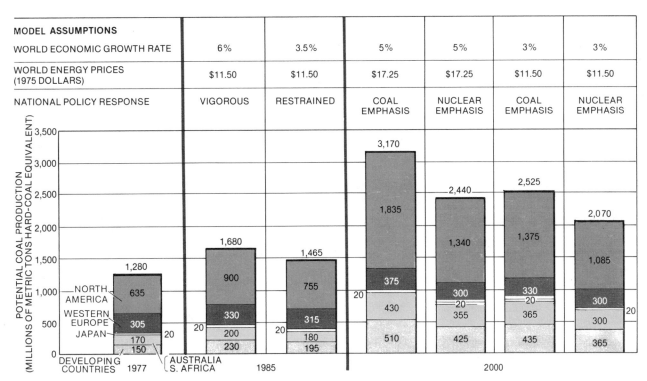

| MODEL ASSUMPTIONS | | | | | | |
|---|---|---|---|---|---|---|
| WORLD ECONOMIC GROWTH RATE | 6% | 3.5% | 5% | 5% | 3% | 3% |
| WORLD ENERGY PRICES (1975 DOLLARS) | $11.50 | $11.50 | $17.25 | $17.25 | $11.50 | $11.50 |
| NATIONAL POLICY RESPONSE | VIGOROUS | RESTRAINED | COAL EMPHASIS | NUCLEAR EMPHASIS | COAL EMPHASIS | NUCLEAR EMPHASIS |

**POTENTIAL COAL PRODUCTION TO THE YEAR 2000** was similarly estimated by the Workshop participants and compared with actual 1977 production. In all models but one (1985, low economic growth rate, constant energy prices, restrained policies) the potential production of coal exceeds the potential demand. With the exception of short-term bottlenecks due to restrained energy policies, the consumption of coal in non-Communist countries should not be constrained by shortages of supply up to the year 2000. Assuming high economic growth, a 50 percent increase in real energy prices and a national emphasis on coal, potential production could reach 3,170 million metric tons by 2000, an increase of almost 150 percent over 1977 production. For North America alone potential production of 1,835 million tons would be an increase of 190 percent over 1977. Increases of 200 percent might be achieved in developing countries.

less being developed in the Powder River basin of Wyoming and Montana. The two states have adopted strict surface-mining regulations stipulating that new mining development must proceed hand in hand with reclamation in order to avoid the kind of despoliation seen in the mountainous coal-mining areas of the eastern U.S. In addition Congress has passed comprehensive legislation to regulate surface-mining activities, to protect water resources and to limit mining in certain areas. Over the next several years the mine operators will be in a position to demonstrate whether they can conduct mining operations acceptably and can rehabilitate disturbed lands effectively. The mining companies are confident it can be done at a cost that is reasonable with respect to the value of the coal produced. If the acceptability of rehabilitation programs is conclusively demonstrated, as it has already been in Europe, environmental issues may recede as a constraint on the future development of coal mines.

Programs are also being evolved at both the Federal and the state levels to help local governments in coal-mining areas plan for (and meet the cost of) expanded social and community services. Apprehension about long rumbling coal trains may eventually be allayed by policies that favor coal-slurry pipelines for moving coal to market or call for the rerouting of some rail lines. Nevertheless, continued opposition to new mines and conflicts over detailed mining regulations, regulatory jurisdiction, royalty sharing, land-use planning, water resources and local government assistance may slow the expansion of Western surface-mining activities. All in all, the uncertainties are so great that the Workshop projections of potential coal production in the year 2000 differ by as much as 500 million metric tons annually, depending on whether or not national policies effectively encourage the development of U.S. coal resources.

The year-2000 projections that embody high estimates of coal production also assume substantial increases in underground mining in the eastern part of the U.S., consistent with the assumed increases in energy prices. For some years the cost of coal mined underground has been rising because of increasingly stringent mine-safety regulations, an associated decline in the productivity of underground mining and a gradual depletion of the most accessible underground reserves. It is impossible to predict whether this trend will continue. The development of Eastern underground coal would, however, stimulate employment and economic activity in parts of the country that have a history of unemployment and underdevelopment. The continued importance of coal mining in the Eastern states seems to be reflected recently in certain Federal pol-

icies favoring Eastern coal. In any case most projections of U.S. coal production predict significant increases not only in the West but also in the East and the Middle West.

The forecast of a rising international trade in coal made by the Workshop on Alternative Energy Strategies implies large increases in coal exports from the U.S. Will the U.S. be willing to accept environmental and social consequences and the depletion of a nonrenewable national resource in order to provide energy for other countries? Good arguments can be advanced for its doing so. For the U.S. coal is not a scarce resource; there-

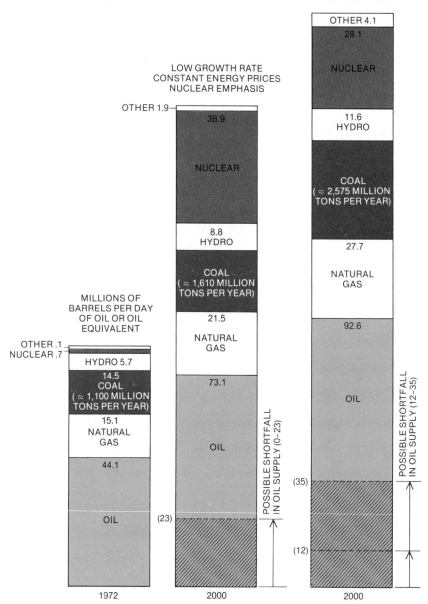

**PROJECTION OF TOTAL ENERGY DEMAND IN THE YEAR 2000,** as estimated by the Workshop, suggests how high the consumption of oil might climb in non-Communist countries if supplies were unlimited. The low-economic-growth, low-energy-demand projection for the year 2000 shows that the appetite for oil might barely be satisfied if new oil discoveries remained high, if the Organization of Petroleum Exporting Countries (OPEC) placed no limits on production, if coal consumption were to increase 50 percent and if a strong emphasis were placed on nuclear energy. A shortfall of up to 23 million barrels per day could arise, however, if discoveries were to falter and OPEC were to impose production limits. In the high-economic-growth, high-energy-demand projection oil shortfalls of between 12 million and 35 million barrels per day are possible. If coal were developed to its full potential of 3,170 million metric tons per year, compared with the expected demand of 2,575 million tons, 600 million tons (equivalent to eight million barrels of oil per day) would be available to relieve shortfall in oil.

fore exporting it to help other countries meet their energy needs, while simultaneously offsetting the high cost of importing oil to the U.S., would seem to be in the broad national interest. Exporting coal would have a positive effect on economic development, employment and the balance of foreign-trade payments. These benefits will not accrue, however, unless three conditions are met. First, the demand for coal exports must be ensured by firm, long-term contracts, based on the buyers' expectation that the coal will be available for export. Second, the environmental and social consequences of expanded coal exports must be made acceptable to the American public. Third, there must be sufficient advance planning to provide for all the facilities that an increase in coal exports will require, particularly the expansion of deep-water ports. Such matters are not yet prominent in the U.S. energy debate. We expect they will be in the 1980's.

Major increases in coal production will call for the construction and operation of a large mining and transportation network to win coal and move it to its markets. Special analyses of mining equipment, transportation facilities, labor and the other resources needed for the rapid expansion of U.S. coal production were prepared for the Workshop. One study conducted by the Bechtel Power Corporation showed that in order to reach an annual production of 2,000 million metric tons of coal at the end of the century the U.S. would need to open 377 new Eastern underground mines, each mine yielding two million tons per year, 75 Eastern surface mines yielding four million tons per year, 232 Western surface mines yielding six million tons per year and eight Western underground mines yielding two million tons per year. The total cost, in 1975 dollars, would be $32 billion. The investment in transportation facilities to carry the coal to consumers would be much higher: $86 billion. That investment would provide 1,400 "unit" railroad trains (trains of about 100 hopper cars each, dedicated solely to carrying coal between the minehead and the consumer), 3,200 conventional railroad trains, 500 large river barges, 9,400 trucks and nine coal-slurry pipelines, each pipeline with a capacity of 25 million tons per year.

The necessary transportation capacity for the bulk of the coal could be provided by either railroad or slurry pipeline or some combination of the two. Railroads are the most suitable where maximum flexibility is required for local transport and small-to-moderate volumes. Slurry pipelines would be the most economic for large and constant volumes over long distances and fixed routes. An extensive railroad network is already in place. The development of slurry pipelines in the U.S., on the other

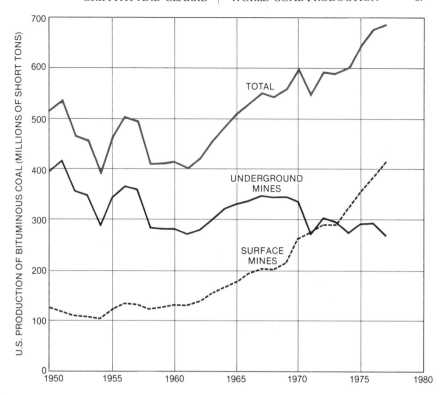

**TOTAL OUTPUT OF U.S. COAL MINES** has increased by less than 3 percent per year since 1954, when production fell to the lowest point since the depression years of the 1930's. Output of underground mines remains below the levels of the early 1950's. In the meantime, however, output of surface mines has climbed by more than 7 percent per year for the past 10 years.

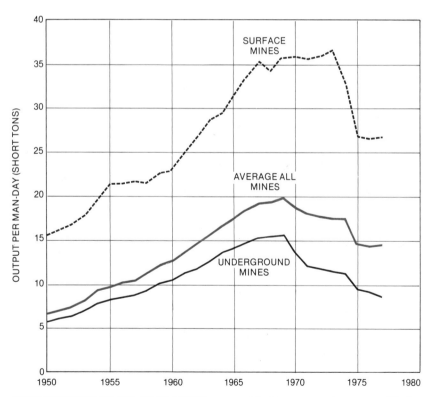

**PRODUCTIVITY OF U.S. COAL MINES,** measured in tons per man-day, rose rapidly between 1950 and 1969. The sharp drop since then has had a number of causes, including new mine-safety and health regulations and, in the case of surface mining, legislation requiring the restoration of the lands disturbed by mining operations. Productivity in the hard-coal mines of Europe, virtually all underground, is much lower than productivity in the U.S.: it is about 2.5 tons per man-day in Britain, about 1.9 tons in France and about 3.8 tons in West Germany.

hand, faces formidable political obstacles that would have to be overcome. Federal legislation to encourage such development has been introduced, but its passage is not yet assured.

The bottleneck most likely to develop in expanding coal exports is seaport facilities. Although the U.S. is already the world's leading exporter of coal (50 million metric tons in 1977), its port facilities are generally inadequate for any substantial expansion of steam-coal exports and have a limited capacity for handling large bulk carriers.

The Workshop concluded that the infrastructure and transportation requirements for a major coal expansion are large but not unattainable in view of the fact that the maximum annual growth rate projected for U.S. coal production is about 6 percent. Nevertheless, even more modest goals will become increasingly hard to achieve if major investments are deferred into the mid-1980's. The industries that provide mining and transportation equipment and resources are capable of doing the job. Clear signals of increased demand are needed, however, to get the necessary expansions under way.

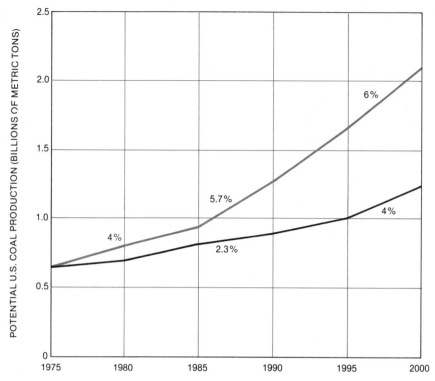

**U.S. COAL PRODUCTION BY THE YEAR 2000** could climb to more than two billion metric tons per year if economic growth rates are high, if world energy prices rise 50 percent above current levels and if Government policies encourage coal production and use. The lower curve shows that potential coal production could be substantially less if growth rates are low and if policies favor nuclear power rather than coal. Percents adjacent to different curve segments indicate average annual growth rates in coal production corresponding to the two models.

Even with an assumed 50 percent increase in the real price of energy ($17.25 per barrel of oil or its equivalent in 1975) and policies to support the development of synthetic fuels the Workshop studies indicate only modest potentials by the year 2000 for the conversion of coal into synthetic gas and oil. The maximum volume of coal-based synthetic fuels in our studies was slightly more than four million barrels per day of oil or its equivalent, with two-thirds of the synthetic gas and most of the synthetic oil being produced in North America. At a typical conversion efficiency of 60 to 70 percent this volume of synthetic fuel would require about 500 million metric tons of coal.

For the U.S., with its large coal reserves, the production of synthetic fuels from coal could be an attractive alternative to rising imports of oil and liquefied natural gas. It would allow consumers to keep their existing oil- and gas-fired equipment, thereby putting the burden of new investment on the energy producers and processors rather than on the distributors and consumers. It would also simplify the control of air pollution by concentrating the utilization of coal in fewer locations. On the other hand, converting coal into other forms of fuel adds to the consumer's cost of energy because of the relatively low efficiency of the conversion process and the high capital cost of the conversion facilities. Synthetic-fuel production requires the mining of larger volumes of coal than direct coal utilization, and if it were pursued in the Western U.S., it would place an additional load on the available resources of water for cooling and for

land reclamation after surface mining.

Unless there are sharp increases in the price of petroleum, synthetic fuels will continue to cost more than natural oil and gas. Because of the high cost of synthetic fuels they will not be developed without vigorous policy support by governments. Eventually the decline of world oil production and the rise of oil prices may cause some major oil-importing regions (particularly North America and possibly western Europe) to begin exploiting their coal resources to produce synthetic oil and gas. Having a synthetic-fuel capability ready in time calls for early policy action to support the demonstration of commercial synthetic-fuel technologies. The lead times are long, and governments would be prudent not to wait for rising oil prices before they undertake to encourage investments in synthetic fuel.

Several major synthetic-fuel projects have already been proposed in the U.S. but will not be viable without Government support in the form of loan guarantees, special pricing arrangements or favorable regulatory treatment. Although some of the projects have preliminary approval from regulatory agencies, the appropriate level of Federal support for synthetic fuels is still being debated in the Department of Energy and in Congress. If favorable Government decisions are made soon, the production of synthetic fuels could be-

gin before 1985 and could reach significant levels by 2000.

Coal is the one fossil fuel likely to remain abundant at relatively low cost for the remainder of this century and well into the next. Therefore it is one of the major replacement fuels available to bridge the gap from the waning era of abundant oil and gas to a future era for which the world must develop alternative energy sources. Coal will be even more important if nations are reluctant, as some are today, to turn strongly to nuclear power. Conversely, decisions to avoid or limit the consumption of coal will increase pressure for the further development of nuclear power and for restrictive energy-conservation measures as alternatives to an unsatisfied demand for oil.

If coal is to serve as such a bridge to a new energy era, governments will soon have to adopt the policies necessary to allow and encourage its expanded utilization. Both public and private investment decisions will be needed to provide funds for opening new mines, building transportation systems including deepwater port facilities and developing the infrastructure for the handling and burning of coal by consumers. Finally, the expanded exploitation of coal will call for satisfactory solutions to the environmental problems associated with the mining and burning of coal, wherever it is done.

# 4

# Energy Policy in the U.S.

## COMMENTARY

The last article in this section, by David J. Rose, puts our choices for energy in perspective and compares the major alternatives, not so much for making the choice right now but as a road map for a far-sighted society. The article was written against the background of the oil embargo of 1973 and President Ford's later urging of U. S. energy independence by 1980. We can be amused by the complete lack of realism of the president's political stance and its time scale; it is now obvious that by the then-targeted year of 1980 our imports will have grown much higher than they were before the 1973 embargo. The imports are reduced only in response to external factors, such as the small reduction in production from Iran and other countries in late 1978 and early 1979 and the restricted amount of gasoline available in the summer of 1979 or, what is really unlikely, a strong move to cut consumption in a presidential election year.

The meat of Rose's article is how we should go about making our decisions. It is clear from his summary of our past actions that we have grossly mismanaged by allowing specific sectors, such as the oil industry or the automobile industry, to proceed, in the virtual absence of any government policy, to maximize corporate gain without regard for the country's future. What government policy existed was devoted to force-feeding an infant nuclear energy industry while ignoring the prudent course—making alternative energy sources reasonable, for instance, by supporting research on making coal a nonpolluting substitute for oil and gas. The energy shortage described by Rose was foreseen much earlier than 1972, when domestic production of crude oil fuels started to fall behind the demand. It was predicted by many as long ago as the late 1940s and 1950s, when on the one hand, all of the oil companies were telling us that there were unlimited supplies, and, on the other, nuclear power advocates were projecting hundreds of nuclear plants around the country by 1980.

In my view, the area where we have had extensive government subsidization and control, the nuclear power industry, illustrates decisions made without real regard for the overall picture. All safety factors were not taken into account adequately. Availability of uranium reserves was not realistically estimated. There was, and is, a general tendency to put all our eggs in one basket—for instance, the concentration on development of the liquid-sodium-cooled breeder reactor. Irreversible choices are made without adequate exploration or preservation of realistic alternatives.

How we will come out in the next decades on the policy decisions posed by Rose, time will tell. It seems clear that the major alternatives in the next 20 years are coal and nuclear power. Though there may well be a strong solar energy option, it is unlikely to be developed adequately before the year 2000. Wind, tidal, and water power are either already developed to the fullest practical extent as major centralized power sources or uneconomical in terms of energy produced versus that expended. The choices between nuclear power and coal are charged with many questions, but safety and public health are at the center of the argument. On the one hand are the deaths attributable to sulfur pollution of the air, accidents in mines, and black lung disease for coal miners; on the other are the dangers of reactor accidents, radioactive and thermal pollution of surface waters from reactors, and the problematic disposal of radioactive waste from nuclear reactors. Perhaps much will be decided by people's preference for facing the dangers of coal that they already know rather than the dangers of nuclear power that are more poorly known, some of them only calculable by complex computer models of what might happen. In comparison, the pollution-free alternative, solar energy, would seem the obvious choice for emphasis by policy makers, but they, too, seem to prefer the known—the conventional energy sources—to the poorly known but potentially abundant source: solar energy.

When Rose's article was written, in late 1973, there was no U. S. energy policy. In mid-1979, there was still none. How long will we wait?

# Energy Policy in the U.S.

by David J. Rose
January 1974

The President's appeal for U.S. energy self-sufficiency
by 1980 cannot be regarded as realistic. The long-range
options that are open to the nation are here considered
in a "taxonomic" approach

Contemplating the energy crisis in their chilly homes this winter and facing an economic turndown stemming from fuel shortages, Americans increasingly wonder where it all went wrong. Had no one foreseen the problems that in retrospect receive so many glib explanations, that now require emergency correction because long-term guidance was lacking and that cannot be truly ameliorated for many years? It should have been obvious to the oil companies, the electric utilities, the automobile industry, Congress, the White House and the universities that without adequate energy an industrial society must throttle down.

The problem is large enough, once it is recognized holistically. The getting, refining, distributing and consuming of fuels account directly for about 10 percent of the nation's economic activity, or about $125 billion per year out of a gross national product approaching $1,300 billion. That is almost equal in dollar value to all of agriculture, food processing and food distribution, activities long recognized as requiring intellectual organization and balance, even to having their own department in the Federal Government. It might therefore seem that the development of a rational, long-range energy policy would be the first order of any nation's business. That the U.S. never had such a policy and is still without one can only be regarded as a major social failure.

In fact, the energy crisis not only was predictable but also was in its general nature predicted. For one thing the petroleum industry is short of domestic refining capacity by about three million barrels per day. Its spokesmen give environmental restrictions on siting as a principal reason. The short-term demand for fuel, however, is well known to be highly inelastic; this means that a small shortage leads to large price increases. Thus not by any collusion but by a little benign neglect the petroleum industry could improve its lot substantially. Compounding the difficulty, and against advice from many sources, the industry has allowed tax credits and other incentives to increase its dependence on overseas refinery capacity. The automobile industry has paid virtually no attention to fuel conservation. The Federal Government has developed little capability to collect data on fuel demand and resources and has been content with petroleum-industry data. Few in decision-making positions in Government or industry paid attention to the scarcity of low-sulfur fuel as they promulgated environmental standards. Federal agencies responsible for developing nonpetroleum fossil fuels (particularly clean fuels from coal, which might have provided not only earlier relief but also competition to petroleum fuels) have been virtually starved while tax funds have been lavished on nuclear reactors. Few universities and public-information groups found it either interesting or rewarding to illuminate the issue. Our present difficulties were largely caused not by ignorance but by irresponsibility.

The President has announced a set of mandatory regulations, effective January 1, designed to reduce consumption of heating oil, gasoline and jet-aircraft fuels by 1.7 million barrels per day, or slightly less than 10 percent of last year's average daily demand. Even with this reduction, the President said, available supplies will still fall 7 percent short of the anticipated demand, so that "additional actions will be necessary." A predicted ultimate shortfall of 17 percent is largely attributed to the oil embargo imposed by the Arab states. As a long-range response to the Arab action the President proposed "Project Independence 1980," which he defined as "a series of plans and goals set to insure that by the end of this decade Americans will not have to rely on any source of energy beyond our own."

Such an ambition seems unachievable without the application of Draconian measures, and probably would be unwise besides. Lack of policy has in effect encouraged substantial foreign dependence. Estimates show that to achieve hemispheric (not domestic) self-sufficiency by 1980 means closing an energy gap of nine million barrels per day. Conceivably this might be achieved by combining the strict conservation of energy with the ruthless exploitation of all the energy resources tappable within the short span of six years. That would mean a sharp curtailment in the booming de-

mand for oil (recently growing at 7 percent per year), the accelerated depletion
of known oil fields, intensified drilling
offshore in the hope of a major strike, the
relaxation (if not the total abandonment) of environmental-quality standards, unrestricted strip-mining and a
wholesale shift from oil and natural gas
to coal, particularly for electric-power
generation. Between now and 1980 it
will be virtually impossible to build
more nuclear-power plants than those
already on the drawing boards. It is also
unrealistic to expect any substantial production of synthetic crude oil from coal
or oil shale by 1980. It is estimated that
to achieve a capacity of five million barrels per day of synthetic oil from these
sources would cost $50 billion and take
eight to 10 years. Solar and geothermal
energy can make no important contribution in the near future. And power from
fusion reactors cannot be expected before the end of the century.

This preamble brings us to the point of
asking what the energy problem is,
instead of only what went wrong. If
there is any excuse for the nation's being
confronted with an energy crisis, it can
be found in the sheer richness of the energy problem. The scale of the problem
is too vast and its time horizons are too
distant for it to fit the customary behavior of the institutions charged (or left)
to deal with energy. For example, industrial rates of economic return lead to
time horizons only five to 10 years hence,
but the problems themselves have a
much longer lifetime, and the rewards
for solving many of them accrue only to
the public at large and not to specific
industries. Thus even if the U.S. could
discern and immediately adopt the wisest set of actions to meet the present
crisis, energy problems would still persist. Some measures and actions now
proposed are part of a continuing series
that, if sensible, will bring gradual progress and improvement but never total
"solutions." Thirty years from now energy will still be a serious topic; only the
details will change.

Analyzing alternative solutions to
technical problems and weighing their
consequences has an increasingly fashionable name: technology assessment.
The term, although useful for naming
the task to be performed, is hardly a
recipe for how to go about the task.
When the problem concerns a subject as
multifaceted as energy, in which technology, economics, resource allocation
and social goals all interact, it becomes
extraordinarily difficult to balance costs
and benefits and reach a national con-

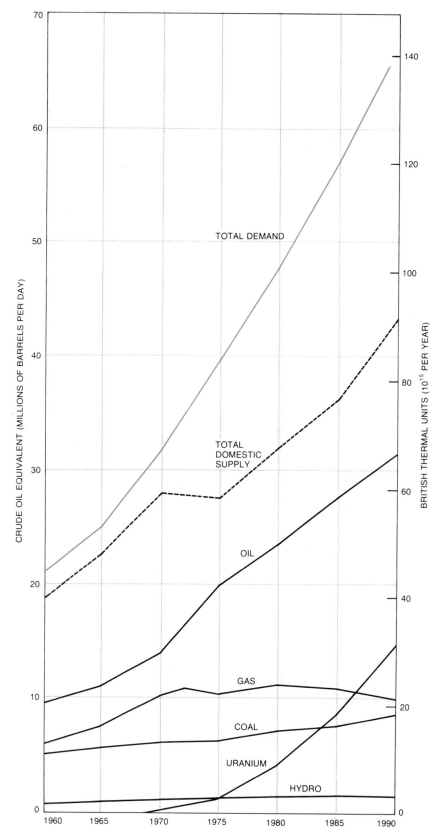

U.S. ENERGY SHORTAGE was clearly predictable at least two years ago when the domestic supply of fuels began for the first time to fall sharply behind the rising total demand
for energy. Domestic production of natural gas and crude oil reached an all-time high in
1972 and has been falling since. The oil and gas curves plotted here include a rising fraction
of imports and, beginning in the late 1970's, limited quantities of synthetic gas and oil from
coal and oil shale. The individual curves for hydroelectric power and fuels add up to yield
total demand. The widening gap between domestic supply and total demand is accounted
for almost entirely by the domestic shortage of oil, as is illustrated on the next page.
(The two illustrations closely follow the projections made by the Shell Oil Company.)

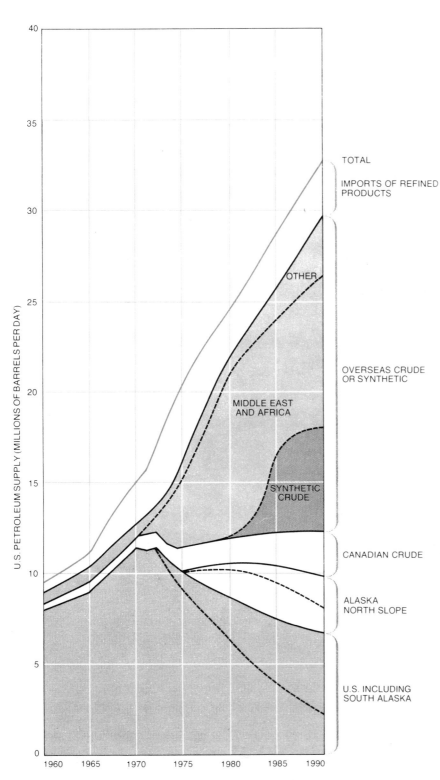

U.S. PETROLEUM SUPPLY (MILLIONS OF BARRELS PER DAY)

TOTAL

IMPORTS OF REFINED PRODUCTS

OTHER

OVERSEAS CRUDE OR SYNTHETIC

MIDDLE EAST AND AFRICA

SYNTHETIC CRUDE

CANADIAN CRUDE

ALASKA NORTH SLOPE

U.S. INCLUDING SOUTH ALASKA

**U.S. DEPENDENCE ON OVERSEAS OIL** cannot be eliminated in the foreseeable future except at what would seem to be prohibitive cost. It is estimated that the U.S. will have to import some 16 million barrels per day of oil from overseas in 1990, of which at least 14 million barrels will originate in the Eastern Hemisphere, chiefly the Middle East and Africa. Just to reduce this figure to eight million barrels per day the U.S. would have to build plants capable of producing six million barrels per day of synthetic crude oil from coal or shale, at an estimated cost exceeding $50 billion. This would be virtually as much oil as the U.S. is expected to pump from all its domestic wells in 1990. The broken lines in the projections for the U.S. and the Alaskan North Slope indicate how even their oil output will fall if there are no further discoveries. The curve for total supply is made up of barrels of varying B.t.u. content, depending on source, hence the total corresponds in B.t.u. content, but not exactly in barrels, to the oil curve in the illustration on the preceding page.

sensus. For one thing, many goals naturally oppose one another, such as cheap coal and minimum land disturbance. It is hard for a partisan of one view, no matter how conscientious, to assess opposing views. At the crudest level, to recognize the validity of an opposing view tends to weaken one's own. More intractable kinds of intellectual imbalance arise when advocates of a particular option attract a band of adherents who, in their overenthusiasm, convert the option into a crusade.

What is needed, among other things, is some overall taxonomy of energy: a listing of the options in a logical hierarchy, so that national debate leads to public illumination and eventually to more satisfactory choices. Unfortunately no unique taxomony exists, but any reasonable one is better than none; one hopes through study of the taxonomy to achieve some degree of insight. Then better decisions will follow. Here I attempt a taxonomy based primarily on technological issues, but it will soon become apparent where and how nontechnical issues enter also, and indeed often dominate the discussion. It will also become apparent that some currently popular ideas lack merit.

The technological discussion proceeds best from the particular to the general. One begins by comparing the simplest technical options (one component with respect to another, say). After that one compares alternative major devices, then alternate strategies for achieving major technical goals and so on, thereby constructing a succession of ever more complex intellectual assemblies. Each higher stage of assessment tends to bring in more and more nontechnological issues, such as environmental cost, resource use or social purpose.

Let us start, then, at a reasonably simple level and choose a topic: Comparison of various nuclear methods for generating nuclear power, arranging the options to produce a structure resembling a mobile, the kind that hangs from a hook on the ceiling [*see upper illustration on page 48*]. The mobile has two main segments: one labeled "Fission" and the other "Fusion." Of these two general routes to nuclear power the latter will probably not be available until after the end of the century. The fission branch of the mobile divides into two subbranches: converters (present technology) and breeders (future technology). Under converters there are two subclasses: light-water reactors and the more advanced high-temperature gas reactors. There are also two subclasses under breeders: the liquid-metal fast-breeder reactor that may be available in the 1980's, and beyond that, perhaps, the gas-cooled fast reactor.

The mobile analogy is useful because it presents specific technological "varieties" as options at the bottom of the structure; at the next higher level the options are between species of devices and at still higher levels the options are among genera, families, orders, classes and phyla. Thus the mobile establishes a taxonomic ordering of alternatives. In making assessments one gives least weight to the individual items at the bottom of the structure and increasingly more weight to options available as one moves upward. As in constructing actual mobiles, one must build the structure and balance the items from the bottom up.

What weights, in development dol-lars, are actually being given to elements in the nuclear-power mobile at the present time? Between fission and fusion the funding ratio is about five to one: $400 million for fission reactors to $80 million for fusion reactors. The ratio is roughly appropriate to the distant time horizon for fusion as well as to its remaining uncertainty. If and when fusion power becomes more certain, it will require more development funds than fission power did; fusion is technologically as far beyond fission as fission was beyond coal-burning.

The principal imbalances appear in the fission program itself. The gas-cooled reactor has been delayed for lack of development funds. The light-water devices were developed either with Federal money (as part of the nuclear-sub-marine program of the Westinghouse Electric Corporation) or with conscious acceptance of initial losses (such as those incurred by the General Electric Company in promoting the boiling-water reactor). The high-temperature gas reactor may actually be safer than the water-cooled reactors, more economical of uranium resources, more efficient (meaning that less waste heat is rejected to the environment) and perhaps even cheaper to build (although not all these advantages are confirmed). Its development lagged because its sponsor, the General Atomic Division of General Dynamics, could not afford to accept losses on the initial units. Now that General Atomic is part of the Gulf Oil Corporation that limitation has been removed; a first reactor nears operation and six more are on order.

A different and more serious imbalance applies to the breeder-reactor program. Its budget of $320 million in the fiscal year 1974 represents a fifth of the total U.S. research and development ex-

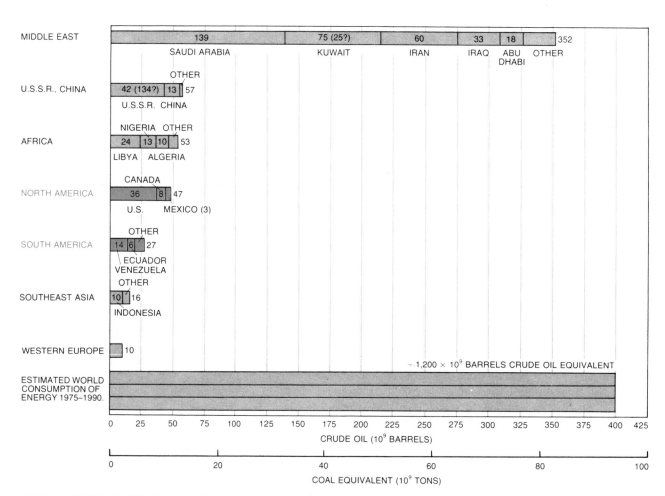

PROVED WORLD RESERVES OF CRUDE OIL total 562 billion barrels, distributed geographically as shown here. More than half of the proved reserve is concentrated in five Middle East states. The U.S.S.R. and China together possess about 10 percent of the total. The entire Western Hemisphere has 13 percent. The estimate for the U.S. includes 10 billion barrels from the North Slope of Alaska. The National Petroleum Council estimated that at the end of 1970 some 385 billion barrels of oil remained to be found on U.S. territory or immediately offshore. This in turn was believed to represent about half of all the oil ultimately discoverable. For the world as a whole N.P.C. estimates that proved reserves can be doubled in the next 15 years. For this reason the estimated total world consumption of energy between 1975 and 1990, equivalent to some 1,200 billion barrels, is not so alarming as might otherwise appear. In fact, natural crude oil will probably be supplying at least 60 percent of the world's total energy demand even in 1990.

penditure on energy and more than a third of the Federal effort. The breeder's chief advantage over present reactors is fuel economy. Whereas present reactors depend on fission of the rare uranium isotope U-235, the breeder can utilize U-238 (99.3 percent of all uranium) by converting it into fissionable plutonium. To be sure, uranium costs will rise appreciably by the end of the century if a breeder reactor is not developed, but since uranium costs are only a small fraction of the total cost, delivered electric-power costs would not rise more than a few percent. Thus a demonstration breeder reactor for the U.S. is less urgently needed than the Atomic Energy Commission, the White House and Congress have maintained. Europe and Japan, far poorer than the U.S. in reserves of fossil fuels and somewhat poorer in uranium, have more urgent reasons than we do to develop all forms of nu-

clear power, including power from breeder reactors.

In addition to pushing the breeder concept faster than the facts warrant, the Government has put virtually all its support behind the liquid-sodium-cooled version, allotting only $1 million per year to Gulf General Atomic's gas-cooled fast breeder. The relative promise of the two concepts is in no such disparate ratio. Still worse, concentration on only one technological device is risky and unwise.

A similar assessment can be made with respect to generating electric power from alternate energy sources. Again the options can be arranged in the form of a mobile [*see lower illustration on page 48*]. Some of the options that have been proposed can be dismissed out of hand. For example, it is easy to calculate that if a low dike were built

around the entire U.S. to harness all the tides, the resulting electric power would only satisfy the needs of a city the size of Boston. To supply the U.S. electric needs by wind power would require windmills 100 meters high spaced a few kilometers apart over the entire country. Most of the suitable hydroelectric sites are already developed. (Hydroelectric generators now account for 10 percent of the U.S. electric-power supply.) It is clear that tides, winds and falling water are not solutions to the nation's energy problem.

The heat of the earth's interior is vast but normal flow of it to the surface is small. It has nonetheless been estimated that subterranean sources of steam and hot water have a potential for supplying about twice as much power as the U.S. currently obtains from hydroelectric sources.

Gaining in popularity is the notion of

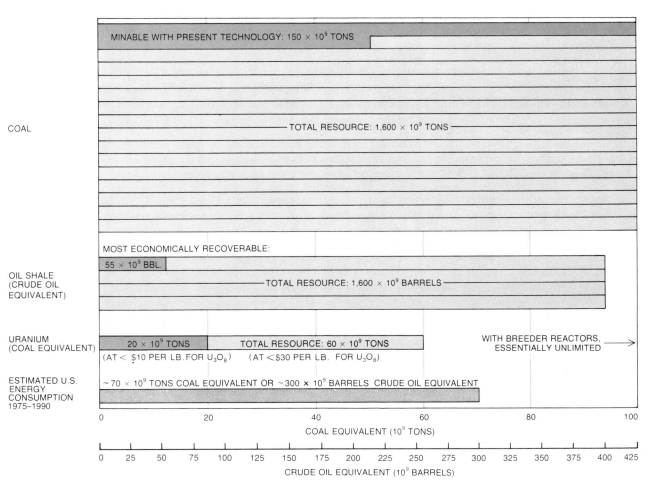

**U.S. RESERVES OF COAL, OIL SHALE, URANIUM** vastly exceed the world's proved reserves of crude oil, as depicted to the same scale on the opposite page. The U.S. coal resource of 1,600 billion tons is defined as half of the coal estimated to be present in beds as thin as 14 inches at depths of up to 4,000 feet. About 10 percent, or 150 billion tons, exists in beds comparable in thickness and depth to those being mined today. The principal deposit of oil shale is in the Green River Formation in Colorado, Utah and

Wyoming. Some 55 billion barrels of shale oil are readily recoverable in seams more than 30 feet thick containing more than 30 gallons of oil per ton. The reserves of uranium are computed on the basis of use in present-day reactors. When breeder reactors are available, the reserve will become essentially limitless. Fuel for fusion, if it ever becomes practical, is likewise limitless. With an enormous effort the U.S. might reduce its energy consumption 10 to 15 percent below the figure represented by the bottom bar.

drilling holes to reach kilometer-size bodies of hot rock that lie anomalously near the surface. There are perhaps 1,000 such bodies in the geologically active western U.S., enough to satisfy the region's power needs for a very long time. The injection of water might both fracture the rock and jack up the strata to facilitate percolation. Steam would be withdrawn through separate exit holes. The idea is not unattractive, but there will be problems. Since hot water dissolves many minerals, it will be hard to keep cooler piping free of mineral deposits. Moreover, percolation channels tend to become enlarged where the flow is greatest, thus leading to large mass flow with poor heat transfer. Such difficulties are well known to the drillers of deep wells.

Solar energy is a different story. It is plentiful and free, but the problem is to collect it efficiently and economically. A million-kilowatt plant, equal in output to the largest conventional generating station, would require a collection area of 100 or more square kilometers, depending on the efficiency of conversion. That might seem to put such options beyond consideration, but a coal-burning plant, obtaining its fuel from strip-mining of coal seams half a meter thick, will cause the same area to be stripped in 25 years. With available technology a solar-energy power plant would cost between five and 10 times as much as a coal- or nuclear-power plant. Advocates believe the cost would fall sharply with suitable engineering development.

The idea of converting solar energy to electric power in space and beaming it down to the earth at microwave frequencies would provide energy around the clock, fair weather and foul. To be economically feasible the cost of available components would have to be reduced by a factor of about 100 and the cost of putting the components in orbit

by a factor of about 10, over and above the economies promised by the space shuttle. Beyond that there is worry about the long-term effect of low-level microwave power on life near the receiving antennas, which would have to cover tens of square kilometers. Meanwhile terrestrial solar energy, including welcome applications of it for domestic space conditioning and water heating, enjoys for the first time some reasonable exploration: $12 million in Federal funds in the fiscal year 1974.

In assessing the available options for generating electric power a corrosive and ill-constructed debate has developed between some vocal advocates and critics of fossil fuels and nuclear fuels. The costs of generating electric power have been rising more sharply than the general price index for two reasons: the dramatically increasing cost of nuclear reactors and the need to use low-sulfur fuels in conventional power plants (or to add sulfur-recovery equipment). Except where low-sulfur coal is plentiful and cheap, nuclear electricity now tends to be cheaper than fossil-fuel electricity. Moreover, the disparity in price will probably increase if air-quality standards force more restrictions on fossil-fuel plants and as clean fossil fuel becomes steadily more expensive.

Several issues enter the discussion, some of them spurious. The clandestine and irresponsible use of nuclear-weapons material is quite unlikely to be prevented by this country's refraining from installing nuclear-power reactors. The core issue is environmental: Which type of power plant is actually, or potentially, more hazardous? It is my opinion that the environmental and epidemiological evidence strongly favors nuclear-power plants. The Atomic Energy Commission has spent more than $1 billion exploring the health and other environmental problems of nuclear energy. Although its

record is not perfect and more remains to be done, a huge amount of information has been made public. The nuclear hazards are fairly well recognized and widely advertised. Principally they are associated with uranium mining and processing, with the normal operation of nuclear plants and fuel-reprocessing facilities, with long-term waste disposal and with accidents.

Conversely, the Department of the Interior, which has cognizance over coal and its technology, has spent hardly anything on the general environmental and epidemiological hazards of burning coal, leaving the problem largely to the Department of Health, Education, and Welfare and the Environmental Protection Agency. Thus the hazards of fossil fuels have been little studied or publicized. The data that do exist show that the total social cost of generating energy with fossil fuels has vastly exceeded the cost associated with nuclear fuels per unit of energy, at least with the environmental and work standards that applied through the 1960's.

For example, Lester Lave and Eugene Seskin of Carnegie-Mellon University and Thomas A. Hodgson of the Cornell Medical College present data implying that the pre-1968 health cost to New Yorkers from unrestricted coal burning in power plants was several thousand deaths per year, plus uncounted nonfatal disabilities of varying severity. Some 50,000 American coal miners are currently disabled with black-lung disease. To these social costs must be added the despoliation of land by strip-mining.

These social costs, which appear to be more than 100 times higher than the equivalent nuclear costs per unit of en-

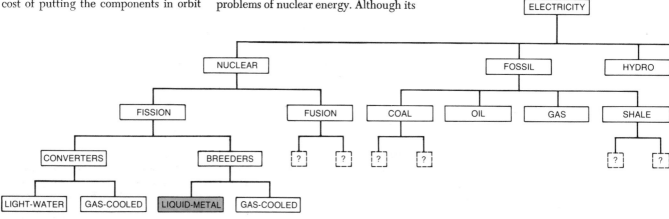

**COMPLETED ENERGY MOBILE is grossly unbalanced. The attention given to energy provision far outweighs the attention to** utilization and conservation. For projects concerned with energy provision the U.S. is currently spending some $1.5 billion per year.

ergy, will no doubt be reduced as environmental standards rise, but the cost of putting fossil fuels on an even environmental footing with nuclear fuels seems prohibitive. Meanwhile debate has concentrated on the more publicized nuclear hazards and has led indirectly to lowered air quality as a result of the construction or retention of fossil-fueled plants. We see here a clear case of unbalanced debate and consequent faulty decisions arising from an initial imbalance in available information. When the public is presented with a balanced picture of the consequences of burning fossil fuel, I feel sure there will be an accelerated movement toward nuclear power and much more caution about relaxing environmental standards during energy shortages.

We now pass to the next level in our hierarchical assessment, the allocation of primary energy resources among users [see upper illustration on page 49]. The electric-utility industry and transportation each take about 25 percent of the nation's fuel supply; another 20 percent is required for space heating and 30 percent is consumed by industry (which also takes about 40 percent of the electric power generated). Here at the level of dividing up the national energy budget it is again fair to ask whether the relative effort to develop better options matches the relative needs.

Again the answer is no, and coal once more serves as a good example. Fossil fuels, in spite of their drawbacks, will be needed for many years, not only for the generation of electric power but also for transportation, for home heating, for industrial purposes and so on. Coal, together with the oil shale of western Colorado and the tar sands of western Canada, is a unique North American reserve of fossil fuels. In a period of ever increasing prices and ever decreasing security the first two are the only resources capable of replacing imported fuels until better and more nearly inexhaustible resources can be rationally developed. The U.S. Geological Survey estimates that the U.S. possesses 1.6 trillion tons of recoverable coal in beds at least 14 inches thick, lying no deeper than 4,000 feet. The total is equivalent to 500 times the total U.S. energy consumption last year and more than 20 times the energy the U.S. will consume between now and 1990 [see illustration on page 45]. Of course, only a fraction of the coal reserve, perhaps no more than a third, is reasonably recoverable with existing technology at acceptable cost.

At present, however, coal provides only 18 percent of the nation's energy needs, a fraction that has dropped with time. (In 1900 coal supplied 70 percent of the nation's energy, and as recently as 1950 it supplied 36 percent.) Most present modes of coal extraction and use have been socially, environmentally and epidemiologically damaging. In this re-spect the technology of coal languishes. Oil shale may be an even worse environmental problem, but these and other difficulties are correctable, in my opinion, if the public has the will to demand correction.

Coal and oil shale (perhaps tar sands too, with the appropriate consideration of Canadian interests) now appear in their proper light: as raw materials for a synthetic-fuel industry that can limit economic and political threats from abroad. The domestic cost of producing low-sulfur crude oil and delivering it to the East Coast of the U.S. has been about $3.75 per barrel (42 gallons) until recently, but now has risen to just above $5. Until last fall approximately the $3.75 price was charged by overseas suppliers, mainly through the operation of the Organization of Petroleum Exporting Countries (OPEC), even though the actual cost of producing and shipping crude oil from the Middle East is only a fraction of that figure.

With the recent outbreak of war in the Middle East the Arab states raised prices substantially, and then several of them cut off supplies to the U.S. Saudi Arabia cut its total exports 20 percent and raised prices to recoup; Libya raised the posted price of her product from $4.604 to $8.925 a barrel. Such prices, of course, can scarcely be maintained under normal conditions. Nevertheless, within the next 10 years the U.S. can expect to be paying $8 or more per barrel (in 1973 dollars) for imported crude oil. Even if the price were to rise no higher, the annual U.S. bill for foreign oil in 1985 could reach $40 billion, if imports rise to the 15 million barrels per day given in some estimates [see illustration on page 43].

Even worse is the threat of eternal political blackmail, which can only be met with determined action by the U.S. One such possibility is establishment of a substantial synthetic-fuel industry. Between now and the early 1980's there would be enough time to develop environmentally acceptable methods for producing oil from coal, and perhaps from oil shale as well, at less than $7 a barrel. At the same time programs now under study will probably lead to the production of clean synthetic natural gas from coal at, say, $1.20 per 1,000 cubic feet, equivalent in energy cost to petroleum at $7 a barrel.

The implementation of such a strategy would be neither cheap nor simple, even if it is a good option. One can ask, "How much syncrude is enough?" and thereby raise a host of other questions. To build the capacity needed to produce five mil-

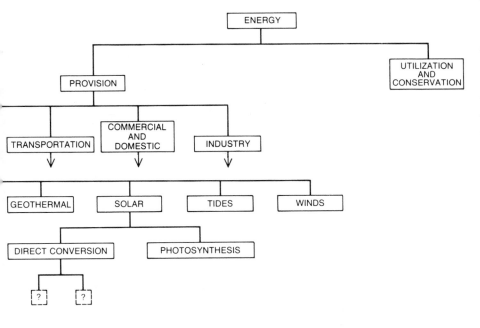

About a fifth of this entire sum is devoted to work on a single mechanism, the liquid-metal fast breeder, which is represented by a single box at the extreme bottom of the mobile.

lion barrels per day (perhaps a third of the projected 1985 imports) would cost about $40 billion. Although that is no more than the U.S. spent in the 1960's on space ventures, its impact on the economy (particularly the construction industry) will be vastly different. Many difficult questions will have to be answered. What will be the impact on the engineering and skilled-labor market? How will other patterns of investment (investment in housing, for example) be affected? What will be the impact on the coal-mining industry? On water resources? What are the alternate strategies? At $7 per barrel how much more petroleum can be produced in the U.S. and its sea-bottom surround? More than 80 percent of the original U.S. petroleum reserve is still in the ground, and more is available with increased effort, but finding and extracting a substantially increased fraction would be very difficult.

International impacts are no less complex. Whether an increased U.S. production capacity would force OPEC prices to remain below $7 per barrel is hard to say, because the U.S. represents only a fraction of the world market. On the other hand, OPEC is not a monolithic structure, and the temptation for one OPEC country to abandon the consortium would be great. If that were sure to happen, the U.S. syncrude industry would have to have been built to stand largely idle. Underpriced by Arabian oil, it would be an economic and political weapon designed by Federal policy not to be used, in the same sense that the Department of Defense builds weapons systems not to be used. Other international questions relate to such matters as whether Western Europe and Japan will remain dependent on the Arab states, will turn to the U.S.S.R. (which is believed to have immense reserves waited to be proved in), or will turn even more to nuclear power. Questions such as these, which are difficult to frame, let alone answer, make the energy problem what it is.

Even if the U.S. does not elect to spend tens of billions on synthetic-oil facilities, coal-extraction technologies call for major improvement. It seems feasible to develop a fully automatic technology for mining coal underground. Where strip-mining remains the method of choice, the land can be properly restored; not doing so is a social problem, not a technological one. In many of the empty regions where coal is strip-mined land sells for not more than $200 per acre, except where coal is present. To reclaim the land properly may cost $5,000 per acre in Appalachia and perhaps $10,000 or more per acre in some Western states, because of the arid climate and the need for long-term care. In contrast, the value of the coal in a two-foot seam in Appalachia may be $40,000 per acre and that in a 50-foot seam in the West may be $1 million per acre. Clearly the reclamation costs are small compared with the sale price of the coal but very large compared with the normal sale price of the land. A social decision, one not based entirely on microeconomics, must be made on the value of the land to the society as a whole.

The preceding assessment applies only to the next 50 or 100 years, certain-

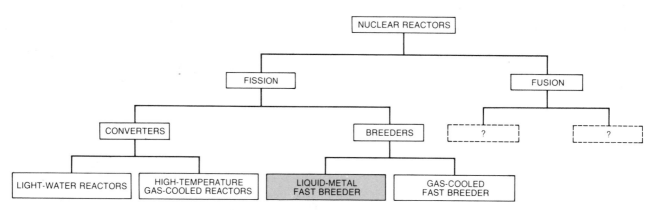

ASSESSMENT MOBILES display in simple, easily grasped form the various technical options available for doing a specific job or reaching a specific goal. Such mobiles are best constructed from the bottom up. A mobile for energy policy might be "assembled," as shown here, by considering first the devices available or potentially available for producing power from nuclear reactions. Light-water reactors have been generating commercial power for 15 years; the first high-temperature gas-cooled reactor is nearing completion. Both are simple converters, that is, they consume the rare uranium isotope U-235. Breeders, now under development, will produce more fissionable material than they consume. The U.S. has budgeted $320 million this fiscal year for development and construction of a liquid-metal fast-breeder demonstration plant. The gas-cooled fast breeder, on the other hand, will receive only $1 million in Federal funds. In the hope of demonstrating the technological feasibility of fusion reactors the U.S. will spend $80 million this fiscal year. Controlled fusion is unlikely to provide significant amounts of electric power before the end of the century.

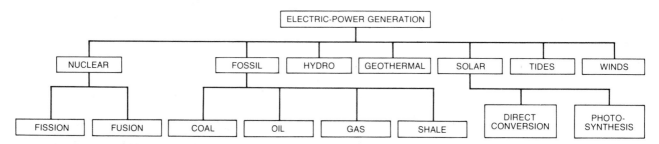

NEXT STEP IN ASSESSMENT leads to a larger mobile that includes sources of energy besides nuclear materials. The actual assessment considers the availability of the source, methods for exploiting it and cost. Tides and winds are readily shown to hold little promise. Geothermal and solar energy are potentially unlimited sources but the technology for exploiting them is rudimentary.

ly not longer. It would be compounding tragedy to convert any large fraction of the domestic coal reserves to liquid or gaseous fuels when coal hydrocarbons are so much more valuable as chemical raw materials. Eventually, as the U.S. and the world switch to energy technologies based on virtually inexhaustible resources—fission, fusion and solar power—coal will no longer be needed as a major fuel source.

I have dwelt on the coal question because it is an excellent example of issues that have deep roots both in technology and in society and that cannot be resolved without serious and simultaneous attention to the consequence of various options. I shall discuss only briefly other issues associated with the allocation of primary energy resources. The U.S. is currently spending about $1.5 billion a year for research and development on new energy options. The total is only about 1.5 percent of the sum that the energy "industry" contributes directly to the gross national product and is thus well below the average research and development expenditure in other technological sectors of the economy. The small scale of the budget for energy research and development is a strong clue to what has gone wrong. Of the $1.5 billion more than half goes toward the provision of electric power, where the options are in the best order. An imbalance arises not because electric-power developments receive too much attention but because other areas have received too little.

We now move to the highest level in this hierarchical assessment of energy: energy provision v. energy utilization and conservation [see lower illustration above]. All the energy provided (the prodigious sum of $1.9 \times 10^{14}$ B.t.u. per day for the U.S., or 11 kilowatts continuously for every person) goes somewhere, and its rational use is only now receiving appreciable attention. The efficiency with which energy is consumed ranges from less than 5 percent for the ordinary incandescent lamp to perhaps 75 percent for a well-maintained home furnace. The automobile engine (particularly since the installation of emission controls) has an efficiency of less than 20 percent. Modern fossil-fuel power plants are more than twice as efficient. On the average probably less than 35 percent of all the B.t.u.'s consumed end up as comfort heat, useful work or visible light. Low as the figure is, it has probably quadrupled since 1900. Up to the present time the allotment of funds for developing more ef-

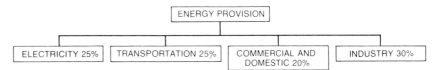

ALLOCATION OF PRIMARY ENERGY RESOURCES is considered at the next higher level of assessment. Generation of electric power, transportation, industry and commercial and domestic consumers take roughly equal shares. In terms of end use the electric energy is divided between industrial, commercial and domestic use, with little for transportation.

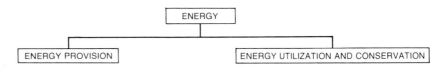

HIGHEST TIER IN MOBILE balances energy provision with energy utilization and conservation. The U.S. neglected the right half of the mobile until the energy crisis arose.

ficient energy converters has been paltry: perhaps a few percent of the total $1.5 billion budget for energy research and development.

The imbalance is beginning to be corrected. For several years a few Federal organizations have quietly and penuriously been studying how energy might be better utilized: the National Bureau of Standards, the Office of Emergency Preparedness and the Oak Ridge National Laboratory. Stimulated by real fuel shortages, their concern has become popular, reinforced by the enthusiasm of the environmentalists and conservationists. An Office of Energy Conservation was established in the Department of the Interior last year, with an annual budget of $6 million.

Some energy-conserving and dollar-saving options are straightforward, easy to apply and have now received attention: lower automobile speed limits, year-round Daylight Saving Time, a reduction in "cosmetic" lighting, lowered thermostats and so on. A less well-known energy-saving option is the use of radial tires, which can reduce gasoline consumption 5 to 10 percent (because of reduced friction between the tire and the road). Other options are easy to envision but more difficult to adopt: lighter automobiles, for example, and commercial buildings designed to achieve comfort with minimum energy consumption.

The study of energy conservation and rational energy utilization has languished for simple reasons. Until now energy has been so plentiful and so cheap that there has been little incentive for people to be frugal. It has not been easy for the individual to perceive that his bargain in energy entailed large costs to the society as a whole. And even when the fact is pointed out to him, the individual rightly sees that any personal

sacrifice he might make has only a minuscule effect in ameliorating an environmental problem. The second big reason for the neglect of energy conservation is that industry is richly rewarded for selling energy and energy-consuming devices.

The various assessment mobiles I have discussed so far can be assembled into one large mobile that includes all the options laid out hierarchically [see illustration on pages 46 and 47]. In this arrangement one can see that utilization and conservation, on the right half of the mobile, merits as much attention and effort as all the options dangling in five tiers on the left half of the mobile. Yet one small line at the bottom left, the liquid-metal breeder reactor, represents an option that will receive $320 million in Federal and private development funds this year: 20 percent of the entire national budget devoted to energy options. What the mobile dramatizes is an embarrassment of blank space, where options are either absent or so poorly formulated that they have received little attention.

Several suggestions for ameliorating future energy difficulties have appeared in this discussion, coming mainly from reflection on new technical options, on conservation methods and on international economic relations. We can see several other strategies being implemented in some measure today. One approach involves a modified laissez faire, leaving parts of the problem to be solved in the marketplace; with increasing scarcity rising prices will bring supply and demand into some kind of balance and less energy will be wasted. To be sure, energy prices have been too low, but overreliance on this approach would work a hardship on many people.

Another strategy is to expand domestic exploration and production of petroleum fuels. The rocks of the continental shelves seem quite similar to the typical sedimentary rocks of the U.S. and Canada, so that they are believed to contain rich petroleum deposits. It is extremely risky to assume, however, that the offshore reserve is adequate to meet an unchecked demand. It should be noted that the much-debated Trans-Alaska pipeline will at its peak carry only two million barrels per day. That amount will not provide much relief from a predicted import requirement of 11 million barrels per day in 1980. Even where an oil field is known to exist it takes from five to seven years to bring it into production. And on the continental shelf off the U.S. eastern seaboard the first hole remains to be drilled; the existence of oil is simply conjectured.

Another strategy that is currently prominent is application of regulatory and other measures to limit energy use: taxes, allocations, rationing and outright bans. The strategy has the advantage that it can be designed for prompt effect. It is the only approach with this feature, and it is therefore invoked in this winter of fuel emergency. We should be aware, however, that such measures generally represent the failure of past policy (or the lack of any policy at all) and that the consequences of stringent regulatory actions are hard to predict. For example, the 1971–1973 controls to combat inflation were a substantial failure. The National Energy Emergency Act sent to Congress on November 21 of last year relies heavily on emergency controls, and it will have little to do with rational long-term energy policy. On the other hand, regulations designed for long-term constructive effect have their place in a coherent energy policy.

One may hope that from some combination of all these possibilities a better energy program will emerge, involving the Federal Government, state governments, industry and other sectors. Clearly the days are gone when parts of the problem could be denied or ignored, as for example when energy conservation and rational energy utilization were ignored by the President's office until the middle of last year.

To choose any particular combination of energy strategies without much thought and analysis would be to compound the difficulties. An adequate national energy policy must of course rise from basic decisions made by or on behalf of the country as a whole, decisions concerning national security, costs, the present and future quality of life and so on. When those decisions have been made, a planner can set down tentative desiderata—not yet firm decisions—about operational strategies. They would include the degree of dependence on foreign oil supplies, environmental standards and the balance between exploitation and conservation of natural resources. Only then can planners arrive at detailed strategies to achieve selected goals: the technology of nuclear power, new types of automobiles and so on. The process is obviously not straightforward; decisions at each level affect conditions both above and below.

These new intellectual and technological thrusts have their organizational counterparts, and the old arrangements for dealing with energy, at least at the Federal level, are being swept away. In general the old ones were not impressive. Federal energy policy consisted mainly of a strong nuclear program (coming from a strong Congressional Joint Committee on Atomic Energy, and a legacy from earlier military programs), a favorable attitude toward petroleum companies (direct U.S. tax credits for foreign royalty payments, depletion allowances and so on), the benign neglect of coal and several fairly successful regional programs (the Tennessee Valley Authority, for example). Technical activities were mainly in the Atomic Energy Commission; some were in the Department of the Interior and some were scattered in other agencies. Regulatory commissions were only partly effective. (For example, the Federal Power Commission set natural-gas prices so low as to simultaneously destroy exploration initiatives and create an insatiable demand.)

All of this is now changing rapidly. It is clear that more central coordination is required than the fragmented energy groups have managed heretofore. The optimum degree of coordination, however, is an important question. Too little can accomplish little; too much can throw the operations of agencies and groups with legitimate energy interests into disarray. At least there is need for the coordination of policy, and Governor John A. Love's former Energy Policy Office seemed to be doing that.

In jettisoning the Love office, the President sought a two-level approach. At the level of preparing technological options he proposed an Energy Research and Development Administration. This was to combine the energy-related activities of the various Federal agencies. The chairman of the Atomic Energy Commission, at the President's request, came up with a $10 billion, five-year program for the development of alternative energy technologies. These proposed expenditures include many projects already planned. At the policy and executive decision level the President proposed a Federal Energy Administration, to be headed by William E. Simon. Arrangements like this could free up to some extent the development of technological options, while giving the executive group freedom to pick and choose and to transcend narrow technical arguments. Congressional bills to implement these measures were introduced in the Congress by Senator Henry M. Jackson and Representative Chet Holifield.

Also at both the technological and policy levels Senator Jackson's own bill (S. 1283) aims at each of these technological and policy functions, through the allocation of $800 million per year of new funds for non-nuclear research, coordinating activities of the AEC, the Department of the Interior, the National Aeronautics and Space Administration and the National Science Foundation.

In the House, meanwhile, Representative Mike McCormack and his Subcommittee on Energy have considered not only a Department of Energy (not far from the President's ERDA-FEA proposal) but also the establishment of an integrated Department of Science and Technology. That is a still broader concept, requiring more public debate.

Whatever the administrative outcome, I personally favor an authority that will decide about rationing (I favor that too) and other short-term measures. Simultaneously such an authority should make a careful assessment of the long-term possibilities before committing the nation to some very expensive acts of commission or omission. The technology of energy conservation, the development (but not yet massive deployment) of new fuels from coal and oil shale, the full environmental costs of various fuel options all deserve careful study—not forgetting the important international repercussions of a change in the fuel-consuming habits of the U.S.

The role of energy is too pervasive and the interests of the participants are too manifold for any expectation that there will be a simple consensus. It can nonetheless be hoped that the national debate will give rise to a better common understanding of the problem. Then some steps can be taken in the direction of probable improvement, and from that new vantage the view ahead will be a little clearer than before.

II

# ENERGY SOURCES:
# WHAT LIES IN
# THE FUTURE?

The articles in the first section of this reader evaluated the existing stocks of our major fossil fuels. In this section, I have selected several articles that have as their central theme the sources of energy usable in our immediate future. The first two articles, on producing oil and gas from coal, discuss the possibilities of dealing advantageously with the fuel resource that is abundant in the world and particularly in the United States. Where one article emphasizes the possibilities for both oil and gas from coal, the other is exclusively concerned with the possibilities of substituting coal gases of various kinds for natural gas supplies.

The other three articles concern the major nonfossil energy source, nuclear power. Since 1944—even earlier for a few nuclear physicists and science fiction writers—the potential of nuclear power has evoked unbounded hope for the future in some and dread of catastrophe in others. Nuclear power only began to be debated in the 1960s; before that it was only a possibility, and few people were aware enough of the coming shortage of oil and gas to be worried. Now that the infant nuclear industry is on the verge of reaching proportions large enough to satisfy an appreciable fraction of our energy needs, the issues are emerging much more dramatically.

As in most debates on public policy related to scientific and technological issues, the public and their leaders, in government and out, have a real problem in deciding which scientists to believe. Perhaps a better way to put it is to ask, in a rational discourse, which scientists have the most compelling arguments of both a scientific and a public policy nature. By now it has become a fact of political life that we cannot, indeed should not, expect scientists to appear as no one else in society—perfectly disinterested, objective experts who accurately pose all the risks and all the benefits. Some of us may still believe in that myth, but anyone who reads or listens to the testimony of a parade of scientists, engineers, economists, and lawyers before congressional committees will quickly realize what the real world is like: a debate between advocates who emphasize, like a good lawyer, the advantages, and ignore or gloss over the disadvantages.

The flavor of this debate can be seen in some of the articles on nuclear power in this section, all written by ardent advocates of a nuclear future. In following sections, some other arguments have the floor. One thing characterizes all the articles: They are all sound, rational arguments. We are asked to choose, not between rational argument versus foolish argument, as some would have us believe, but between different rational arguments. A few years ago, Arthur Kantrowitz, a prominent scientist and corporation head, suggested a court-room for the resolution of scientific questions such as these. Regardless of the merits of his arguments, Readers will make their own judgment on the basis of an incomplete and not always perfectly matched set of advocates. And that is usually the way judgments are made.

# 5

# Oil and Gas from Coal

## COMMENTARY

One way to avoid the major problems in substituting coal, our abundant resource, for oil and gas, our scarce ones, is to convert solid coal into synthetic liquid petroleum and gas products. These together with oil and gas produced from shale oil and tar sands, are the "synfuels," the subject of several crash programs proposed in 1979 by President Carter and members of Congress.

In this article, Neal Cochran shows how coal conversion might be accomplished with some economy and go a long way toward solving the environmental problems of coal use. One major problem is the pollution of the atmosphere by sulfur oxide gases and other toxic and/or radioactive elements in coal. The other is the difficulty and inconvenience of handling a high volume of solid fuel that has to be transported long distances and does not lend itself to decentralized use in small homes, automobiles, and other places. The carbon dioxide that would have been added to the atmosphere by the burning of coal will still be added ultimately as the synthetic oil and gas from coal are burned. The production of noxious gases from the gasification process would have to be avoided, but, as Cochran points out, it is inherently easier to conceive of solutions in a few large chemical processing plants than in the many plants in which coal would be burned. Many of the solid wastes generated would be in the form of inert slags, an advantage in disposal.

There is some cost to conversion in total energy efficiency. Hydrogen for hydrogenating the coal, which is the basic chemical alteration in the conversion into oil and gas fluids, has to be produced at some cost in energy, even though the processes will recycle the hydrogen and use it in a self-contained plant. On the other hand, the ordinary combustion of coal is not a very efficient process for generating electricity either. More advanced evaluation of these processess will have to await the making of a more carefully calculated energy efficiency budget based on some experience with modern large-capacity plants. Without that experience, crash programs have small chance of economic success.

There is little doubt that processes such as those discussed by Cochran will have some place in our future, for regardless of where we get our supplies of energy for large-scale generation of electricity, we will continue to want oil and gas for many decentralized uses—it would be difficult to run automobiles on nuclear fuel and the electric car has drawbacks. We will need these fluids as raw materials for the vital chemical industry that is now based on petroleum. In a sense, we would return to the old coal-tar chemical industry, which produced the first plastic, bakelite.

# Oil and Gas from Coal

by Neal P. Cochran
*May 1976*

*The conversion can be accomplished by several tested processes. The present effort is to combine such processes in a large-scale system that will manufacture the oil and gas at reasonable cost*

For both political and economic reasons it seems clear that sooner or later the U.S. will come to rely much more on coal as a source of energy than it has over the past few decades. Except in large installations such as power stations, however, coal is not the ideal fuel both because it is not fluid and because it usually burns less cleanly than either oil or gas. Moreover, since coal-driven locomotives and ships have almost disappeared from the scene, coal can scarcely serve at all as a fuel for vehicles. Success in exploiting the nation's huge reserves of coal therefore depends on the development of a technology that will convert coal into oil and gas on a large scale. The principles of the technology already exist, as do a number of pilot and demonstration plants where the conversion is being accomplished on a small scale. The problem, then, is to mobilize the financial and industrial resources that are needed to put the technology on a commercial basis.

The fuller exploitation of coal will entail a substantial shift in the economics of energy. For the past decade or so the sources of energy in the U.S. have been predominantly oil and gas (44 and 31 percent respectively), with coal accounting for 21 percent and all other sources, including hydroelectric and nuclear plants, accounting for 4 percent. In contrast, coal accounts for 75 percent of the nation's fossil-fuel resources.

It is also instructive to look at the markets for energy. Industrial and commercial activities take about 40 percent of the energy produced in the country each year, transportation 25 percent, electric utilities 20 percent and homes 15 percent. The direct consumption of coal is virtually ruled out in transportation and seems unlikely to expand much in industrial, commercial and residential markets because of restrictions against air pollution. To reach those markets coal must be converted into oil and gas.

The conversion of coal into gas was an established commercial technology in the U.S. as early as the 1820's. The "gas works" became a familiar feature of cities of the Northeast and the Middle West, manufacturing gas from coal for illumination and cooking. The gashouses disappeared after World War II as natural gas came to be widely distributed by pipeline, and the technology that sufficed then would be inadequate now because the gas it made from coal could not match the heating value of natural gas.

Although the conversion of coal into oil has not been accomplished commercially in the U.S., it was a large-scale operation in Germany during World War II and is being pursued on a substantial scale in South Africa today. The German production of synthetic gasoline from coal reached the level of 12,000 barrels per day, with the largest plant turning out nearly 4,000 barrels per day. The Sasol synthetic-fuel plant in South Africa, which has operated for 20 years, converts coal into more than 300 million cubic feet of gas per day and then converts the gas into liquids that are similar to petroleum. Neither the German undertaking nor the South African one would be considered large by U.S. standards; the German plants at the time of peak production were processing about 600 tons of coal per day, and the input to the Sasol plant is about 3,500 tons per day. The plants envisioned for the U.S. would process upward of 25,000 tons of coal per day, a level of operation to which the German or South African processes cannot be economically adapted.

The amount of work done to study and develop processes for converting coal into oil has tended to rise and fall with estimates of how adequately the known and projected reserves of petroleum would supply the projected markets for gasoline and other petroleum products. Until recently most of the research in the U.S. was done by two agencies of the Department of the Interior: the Bureau of Mines and the Office of Coal Research. Those programs are being continued by the Energy Research and Development Administration (ERDA), which was established in 1975 to coordinate the Government's research and development efforts to make the U.S. independent of foreign energy resources.

Enough work has been done to make it possible to predict the development of a scaled-up technology that can convert coal into oil and gas at prices that are competitive with the current prices of such products in the U.S. In terms of actual cost, of course, oil and gas from coal cannot now compete with crude oil from the Middle East. One should remember, however, that the cost and the price of Middle East crude are not related, as was demonstrated by the embargo and price increases the exporting countries of the Middle East imposed starting in 1973. In many ways those actions may prove to have benefited the U.S., since they could encourage the development of domestic sources of oil and gas and hasten the production of synthetic fuels from coal. The price of coal can be expected to rise with the price of oil, but the price of synthetic oil and gas will decline with respect to the price of the natural product because the capital charges for plants making the synthetic fuels will stabilize.

In the simplest terms the conversion of coal into oil or gas calls for adding hydrogen to the coal. (The ratio of hydrogen atoms to carbon atoms in coal is .8 to 1; in oil it is 1.75 to 1.) The source of the hydrogen is water (as steam). The energy for the process by which hydrogen is separated from water must be obtained from the coal itself if the economics of the conversion technology are to be favorable. The production of hydrogen is a major cost in the conversion of coal into oil.

It follows that every conversion process

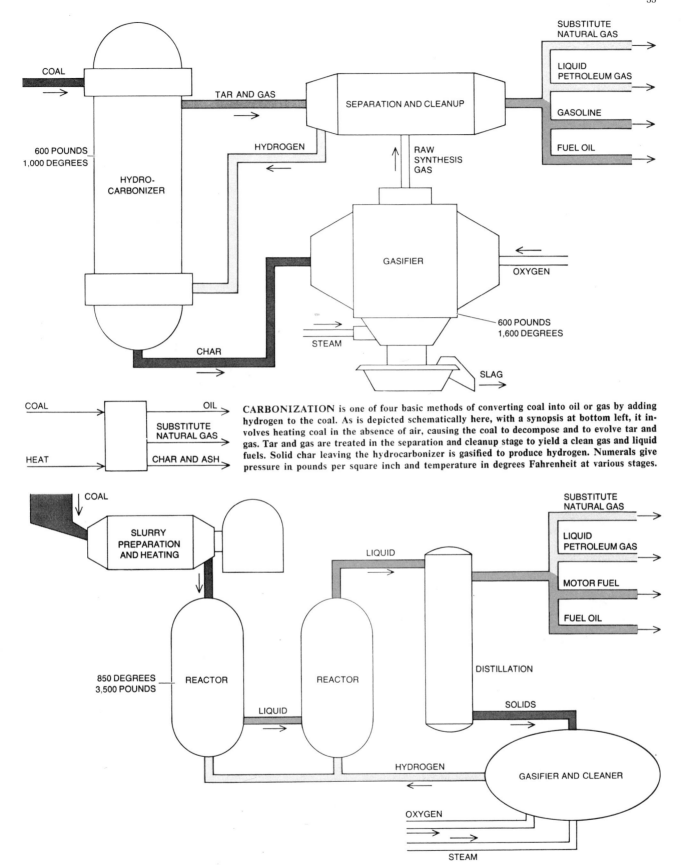

CARBONIZATION is one of four basic methods of converting coal into oil or gas by adding hydrogen to the coal. As is depicted schematically here, with a synopsis at bottom left, it involves heating coal in the absence of air, causing the coal to decompose and to evolve tar and gas. Tar and gas are treated in the separation and cleanup stage to yield a clean gas and liquid fuels. Solid char leaving the hydrocarbonizer is gasified to produce hydrogen. Numerals give pressure in pounds per square inch and temperature in degrees Fahrenheit at various stages.

DIRECT HYDROGENATION of coal is a process that begins with the coal in the form of a slurry. The slurry is fed into a reactor, where it is reacted with hydrogen at high pressure. The reactor usually contains a catalyst, such as cobalt molybdenum, that facilitates the process. After hydrogenation the liquid yielded by the reaction is distilled to remove solids, which are gasified to provide hydrogen for the operation. In this process, as in others, water in the form of steam is the source of the hydrogen that must be added to the coal to convert it into oil and gas.

56

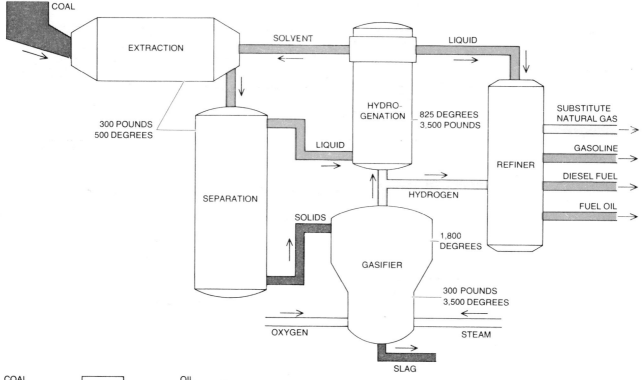

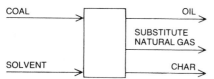

**EXTRACTION PROCESS** for converting coal into oil and gas involves dissolving the coal in a solvent. The hydrogen-donor process, which is one of two methods of extraction, is depicted here. The coal is dissolved by being mixed with the solvent at low pressure. The liquid that results is hydrogenated, yielding both a synthetic crude oil and the solvent for extraction. Since the solvent is rich in hydrogen, it transfers hydrogen to the coal during the extraction process. Part of the coal remains undissolved; it is gasified, as in other processes, to yield hydrogen.

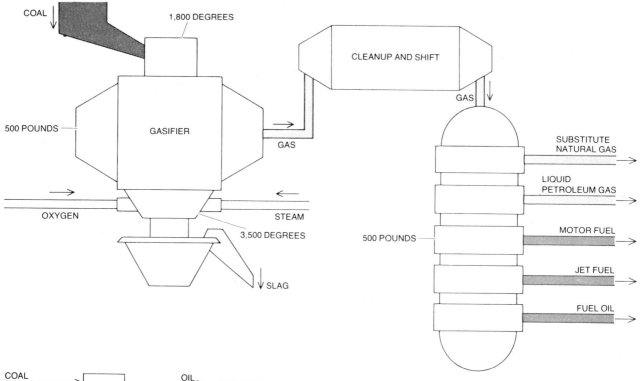

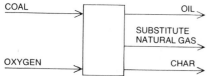

**FISCHER-TROPSCH SYNTHESIS** is the fourth basic method of converting coal to oil and gas. Coal goes into a gasifier, where it is burned in the presence of oxygen and steam. The combustion generates a gas consisting mainly of carbon monoxide and hydrogen. In the cleanup-and-shift stage the gas is purified. Then it is passed over a catalyst, producing not only substitute natural gas of pipeline quality but also a variety of liquid products. Fischer-Tropsch synthesis is employed in a South African plant that processes some 3,500 tons of coal per day.

must involve a gasification step, in which the coal is reacted with steam. The aim is not primarily to get pipeline gas but to make a synthesis gas ($CO + H_2$) that can be modified with more steam ($CO + H_2O \rightarrow CO_2 + H_2$) to obtain more of the hydrogen needed to convert coal into oil and hydrocarbon gas. Moreover, all conversion processes yield a mixture of hydrocarbon gases, including methane ($CH_4$), which is a substitute for natural gas. Since the national economy requires both gas and oil, the aim of a conversion technology should be to conserve the gas generated in the liquefaction of coal and to regard it as a coproduct with the oil.

The simplest of the four basic processes for producing oil from coal is carbonization, which consists in heating coal in the absence of air. The heat causes the coal to decompose, evolving tar and gas and leaving a solid residue (coke). Carbonization has long been employed in making coke. Even though it also yields a liquid and a gas, it is not economically practical for the production of oil because the capital charge for coke ovens is high in relation to the unit cost of the oil produced.

Research is therefore focused on improved carbonization processes. A consortium of companies is developing the COGAS (coal-oil-gas) process, in which carbonization is accomplished in a fluidized bed of coal at comparatively low temperature. The fluidized bed improves the efficiency of decomposition of the coal. The next steps are the combustion of the solid char with air and the reaction of steam with the hot char. Typical products are tar and pipeline gas.

A hydrocarbonization process is the basis of a demonstration plant that will be built in Illinois under a $237-million contract awarded to the Coalcon Company by ERDA. The process yields products ranging from substitute natural gas to a high-quality (low-sulfur) fuel oil by heating coal to about 1,000 degrees Fahrenheit in the presence of hydrogen at a pressure of about 600 pounds per square inch. In the basic carbonization step a moderate hydrogen pressure is established to improve the yield and quality of liquid products (by facilitating the reaction of hydrogen with the products of pyrolysis) and to reduce costs. Material leaving the top of the reactor as a gas is cooled to condense a heavy oil and is then treated to remove sulfur compounds, so that the gas coproduct is clean. The liquid product is distilled to yield a light motor-fuel fraction and a heavy fuel-oil fraction. The gas is distilled at cryogenic (very low) temperature to separate hydrogen, which is recycled to the reactor. The char leaving the reactor is gasified to produce the hydrogen required by the process, and energy for the entire operation is obtained by burning part of the char or the excess gas. The process can be adapted to the recovery of chemicals, but that is not the objective of the present work.

A recent report issued by Coalcon indicates that a full-scale plant would produce the substitute natural gas to sell at a price of $2.40 per million cubic feet. Fuel oil would be priced at $15 per barrel and gasoline at 33 cents per gallon (not including tax). The prices are comparable to current prices charged by producers for natural products and are typical of the prices of synthetic oil and gas.

The second basic conversion process is hydrogenation. It calls for reacting coal with hydrogen at high pressure, usually in the presence of a catalyst. (This was one method employed to convert coal into oil in Germany during World War II.) The coal can be hydrogenated directly by feeding it into a reactor in the form of a slurry. In a system that is being developed for ERDA by Hydrocarbon Research, Inc., the reactor contains a catalyst of cobalt molybdenum, which is kept in motion by the recycling of liquid in the reactor. Intimate contact is achieved between the solid (the catalyst), the liquid (oil) and the gas (hydrogen).

Another system of direct hydrogenation is being investigated by the Pittsburgh Energy Research Center of ERDA. In this system the catalyst bed is fixed, which simplifies the construction of the reactor but complicates the removal of heat and thus the control of the temperature in the reactor. (Recent work seems to indicate that the catalyst is not required.) Control of the temperature in the reactor is crucial in both systems if the formation of carbon and the ultimate plugging of the reactor is to be avoided. The temperature of the reactor also affects the nature and quality of the products.

These systems and other methods of hydrogenation call for a temperature of about 850 degrees F. and pressures ranging from 2,000 to 4,000 pounds per square inch. A lower pressure and a shorter time for reaction limit the reaction between the coal and the hydrogen and favor the production of heavy fuel oil; a higher pressure and a longer time for reaction favor the production of lighter fractions. Following the hydrogenation step the liquid fraction of the product is distilled and decompressed so that solids can be removed. The heaviest oil fraction contains the unreacted solid coal, which must be separated from the liquid. The solid fraction is gasified with additional coal to provide hydrogen for the operation. Direct hydrogenation provides more liquid than any of the other processes discussed here. The selling price of the product will range from $14 to $18 per barrel.

The third basic conversion process is extraction, in which coal is partly or completely dissolved. Two systems are being investigated commercially and in the program of ERDA. They differ in the method of bringing hydrogen to the coal. In the solvent-refined-coal system coal is dissolved in an organic liquid in the presence of hydrogen gas that is under high pressure (about 2,500 pounds per square inch). The process dissolves nearly all the coal and in subsequent steps filters the resulting slurry, distills the liquid fraction to recover solvent and re-forms the coal by cooling. If the starting coal has a high sulfur content (about 3 percent), the remaining solid fuel will contain from .5 to .8 percent sulfur. The products of the system can be improved by further hydrogenation in the presence of a catalyst.

In the hydrogen-donor process coal is dissolved by being mixed with the solvent at a low pressure (about 300 pounds per square inch). The resulting liquid is separated from the undissolved coal and then hydrogenated to obtain a synthetic crude oil and the solvent required for extraction. In other words, the solvent is derived from the process; because it is rich in hydrogen, it transfers hydrogen to the coal during extraction. The hydrogen-donor system has two key features: the extraction process is carried out at low pressure and the hydrogenation step employs a clean feed. In terms of 1975 dollars the selling price of the products of extraction systems is about $2.30 per million cubic feet for the substitute natural gas and $15 per barrel for the oil.

The fourth basic method of liquefying coal is usually called Fischer-Tropsch synthesis, after the German chemists Franz Fischer and Hans Tropsch, who originally developed it. Coal is burned in the presence of oxygen and steam, generating a gas composed mostly of carbon monoxide and hydrogen. The gas is purified and then passed over a catalyst, yielding liquid products ranging from methanol ("wood alcohol") to hydrocarbons of high molecular weight, including waxes and oils. The process can be directed primarily toward the production of motor fuel and substitute natural gas. This process is employed in the Sasol plant to produce waxes, oils, motor fuel and chemicals. It has been estimated that a Fischer-Tropsch plant in the U.S. with the capacity to produce 50,000 barrels per day would be able to sell its output at about $2.25 per million cubic feet of substitute natural gas and $13.05 per barrel (31 cents per gallon) for gasoline.

It is useful to compare the four basic processes in various ways. One is by yield per ton of coal. For carbonization the yield is from one barrel to 1.5 barrels of liquid products and from 4,000 to 5,000 cubic feet of gas products; for direct hydrogenation it is 2.5 to 3.5 barrels and 2,000 to 3,000 cubic feet; for extraction-hydrogenation it is two to three barrels and 3,500 to 4,500 cubic feet, and for Fischer-Tropsch synthesis it is 1.5 to two barrels and 8,000 to 10,000 cubic feet. Another measure is the pressure at which the process operates, since the cost of the equipment rises with the pressure. Carbonization is done at from atmospheric pressure (14.7 pounds per square inch at sea level) to 70 atmospheres, direct hydrogenation at 200 atmospheres, hydrogen-donor extraction at 20 atmospheres followed by hydrogenation at 200 atmospheres and Fischer-Tropsch synthesis at 30 atmospheres. In thermal efficiency the range for carbonization is from 55 to 65 percent, for direct hydrogenation 60 to 65 percent, for the extraction processes 60 to 70 percent and for Fischer-Tropsch synthesis 55 to 70 percent.

Although each of the four basic conversion processes will work by itself, it may be that the most successful commercial operation will be one that involves a combination of processes. Such a plant could be described as a coal refinery. One attractive possibility is a combination of hydrogen-donor extraction and Fischer-Tropsch synthesis. This possibility arises because the synthesis step in the Fischer-Tropsch process proceeds at a pressure of from 350 to 500 pounds per square inch, which is also the range of pressure in the extraction phase of the hydrogen-donor process.

Coupling the extraction and synthesis steps in the low-pressure zone also couples them in the sections of the plant handling coal solids. It is always difficult to handle such solids, and the low-pressure feature therefore simplifies the design of such components as feeders, reactors, piping, pumps, valves and instruments. Low pressure also reduces the cost of the equipment for handling gas.

The steps in a combined process could go as follows [see illustration below]. Coal from the mine, which is treated as an integral part of the plant, is handled directly, with little or no storage. (If oil and gas made from coal are to compete with natural oil and gas supplies, a conversion plant must have a high capacity. Coal-handling is expensive in any case, and the cost rises if the coal has to be put into and withdrawn from a storage pile. Hence it is economical to gear the plant to a large and close supply of coal and to put the coal through the plant at a high rate with minimal storage.)

Leaving the mine, the coal is ground fine and made into a slurry with a solvent that has been produced in the plant and recy-cled. The solvent, a mixture of compounds that are saturated with hydrogen, serves as a source of hydrogen to aid the dissolving of the coal. The slurry of coal and solvent is heated to about 500 degrees F. in a fired heater and then is pumped to the extractor, which can be visualized as two simple agitated tanks. The time the mixture spends in the extractor depends on the feed rate of the plant and the level of slurry maintained in the vessels. With a long residence time the extraction can dissolve more than 90 percent of the coal, but the economics of the process is most favorable when the rate of extraction is between 60 and 75 percent.

The ratio of solvent to coal in this step is about 2 : 1 by weight. Hydrogen can be added to the reactor to enhance the transfer of hydrogen from the solvent to the coal. After extraction the mixture of solvent, liquid extract and undissolved coal is pumped to a filter for separation. The filter, with a diatomaceous earth as the medium, works well

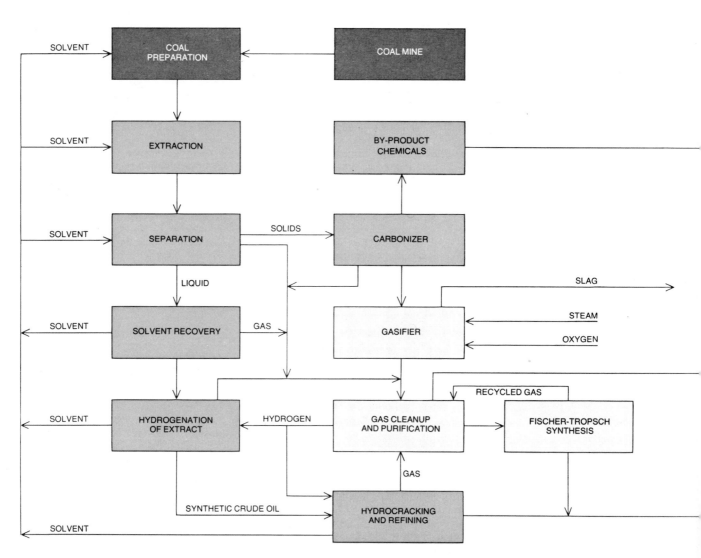

COAL REFINERY as envisioned by the author combines extraction, hydrogenation and Fischer-Tropsch synthesis to yield a large variety of products. Coal moving directly from a nearby mine is ground fine and made into a slurry with a solvent. That is an extraction process. In the next step the liquids and undissolved coal are separated. Solvent is recovered and the remaining liquid is hydrogenated. Solids remaining after extraction go as a sludge to a carbonizer, where the sludge is heated with recycled gas to generate gas and a char. The

for the separation of solids from a liquid that would clog conventional filter cloth.

The filter cake, consisting of undissolved coal and ash-producing minerals, leaves the filter as a wet sludge. The sludge is moved to a fluid-bed carbonizer, where it is heated with recycled gas to recover tar acids and also gases of low molecular weight. Another product of the carbonizer is a solid char similar to the char produced in conventional carbonization. This char serves as a source of energy for the entire process and of hydrogen for the hydrogenation step.

The char is gasified (with oxygen) in a high-temperature, entrained-bed gasifier operating under slag-forming conditions. The gasifier is designed to conserve much of its own waste heat, which is recovered as high-pressure steam. The gasifier also achieves a total utilization of carbon by producing a slag that contains no carbon. Without carbon the slag is inert, which simplifies its disposal as waste.

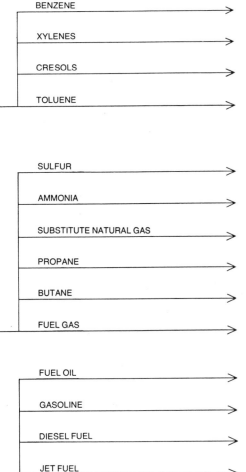

BENZENE

XYLENES

CRESOLS

TOLUENE

SULFUR

AMMONIA

SUBSTITUTE NATURAL GAS

PROPANE

BUTANE

FUEL GAS

FUEL OIL

GASOLINE

DIESEL FUEL

JET FUEL

char is gasified and the gas is purified. The resulting clean gas proceeds to a Fischer-Tropsch step. The liquid extract (*bottom left*) yields a synthetic crude oil that can be refined.

After the gas from the gasifier has passed through the waste-heat recovery system it goes to a purification section of the plant, where acid gases, hydrogen sulfide and carbon dioxide are removed. The ratio of carbon monoxide to hydrogen is adjusted by the addition of hydrogen recovered from gases generated in other processes of the plant. Hydrogen is separated from those gases in a cryogenic separation step. The adjusted char gas then goes to the Fischer-Tropsch synthesis, where it passes over a catalyst. The primary products of this step are naphtha, diesel fuel and premium fuel oil. In addition the synthesis manufactures large quantities of gases of low molecular weight, which become the primary source of substitute natural gas and liquid petroleum gas from the plant.

The liquid extract from the filtration step, representing about 60 percent of the coal brought in from the mine, is distilled to recover solvent, which is employed in extraction and as the wash in the filtration step. Further distillation yields a primary material, the coal extract, which becomes the feed material for the hydrogenation step. Hydrogenation is conducted at a temperature of from 750 to 850 degrees F. and a pressure of about 3,000 pounds per square inch. Both the temperature and the pressure can be varied to alter the proportions of gas and liquid in the product.

The hydrogenated liquid is distilled to make both a solvent fraction, which is recycled, and a synthetic crude oil, which serves as the primary feed for a "cracking" step that yields gasoline. In locations that already have petroleum refineries the synthetic crude oil could be diverted to them. The gasoline produced by cracking would be combined with motor-fuel fractions produced in the Fischer-Tropsch section of the plant.

As I have indicated, a plant making oil and gas from coal must be located at the mine; otherwise the cost of moving from 25,000 to 100,000 tons of coal per day would make the plant uneconomical. Coal varies considerably from one area to another. For example, in the Appalachian region the coal is bituminous and high in volatiles; on the northern Great Plains it is lignite. Energy markets also vary from region to region. The coal refinery I have described, combining extraction, hydrogenation and Fischer-Tropsch synthesis, can be adapted to fit the characteristics of any coal, and the mixture of products can be adjusted to any market. In the Appalachian region the main products might be fuel oil for utility plants and substitute natural gas for residential and commercial consumption. A plant on the northern Great Plains would probably produce a higher proportion of liquids, since they could be transported economically by pipeline.

Suppose such a plant was designed to produce 50,000 barrels per day of liquid products. The plant would require about 25,000 tons of coal per day. The total capi-

tal investment would be about $1.5 billion: $200 million for equipment to mine and prepare coal, $200 million for extraction and separation, $300 million for gasification and synthesis, $100 million for equipment to handle by-products, $200 million for a utilities and services unit, $100 million for the air-separation plant, $250 million for contingencies and $150 million for engineering. Once the plant was operating it would manufacture daily 205 million standard cubic feet of gas, 5,000 barrels of liquid petroleum gas, 40,000 barrels of motor fuels, 5,000 barrels of fuel oil and (as by-products) 500 tons of sulfur and 3,000 tons of slag. The sulfur could be sold or stockpiled; some of the slag could be sold for making concrete blocks and other construction materials, but much of it would have to be returned to the mine as waste.

Twenty plants would produce a million barrels per day of liquid products and 4.1 billion cubic feet of gas. In a year, operating at 90 percent of capacity, the plants would make some 330 million barrels of nonpolluting liquid fuel and 1.353 trillion cubic feet of substitute natural gas. The output would meet about 6 percent of the nation's present demand for energy.

The coal requirement for 20 plants would be 165 million tons per year, which is about 25 percent of the national production of coal in 1975. The U.S. has nearly two trillion tons of recoverable coal. Therefore 100 plants, producing about 30 percent of the nation's energy requirement (stated in terms of consumption in 1975), could be operated for 30 years on approximately 1 percent of the coal resources. In Eastern locations the system would entail a land use of about 10 acres of coal per day.

The total capital investment for this array of plants would be about $30 billion, which is a large figure but a modest one on a national scale. If construction were spread over 10 years, expenditure would be at a maximum of $4 billion per year from the third year through the sixth. Plants could be added at the rate of four per year by increasing the expenditure to $6 billion per year. With this investment and production costs of from $160 to $180 million per year, the output of the plant would sell for $2.10 per million British thermal units to yield a rate of return of 12 percent on a discounted-cash-flow basis. The availability of nonpolluting fuels of high quality at $12.20 per barrel is an attractive alternative to imported oil at steadily rising prices.

To achieve a capacity of a million barrels per day of synthetic fuel calls for a vigorous Government program. Plants would be funded by the Government and operated by industry, which ultimately would buy the successful plants. The creation of a synthetic-oil industry would assure the nation of ample supplies of oil and gas. Moreover, the synthetic fuels would act as a ceiling on the price of crude oil from abroad. At the same time the country would have the assurance that it was no longer dependent on foreign supplies of oil.

# 6

# The Gasification of Coal

## COMMENTARY

In his article, a companion to the preceding one, Harry Perry presents the case for converting coal to gases that will substitute for the natural gases we have been using so heavily for the past 30 years. There are two possible ways of converting coal to more convenient forms, both eliminating the nuisance and difficulty of transporting large quantities of solid fuels. We can convert it to oil, with secondary amounts of gas, or convert all of it to gas. In the latter case, we have a choice between gases of high heat value and those of lower, but perhaps more convenient, heat value.

Whereas conversion of coal to oil is a relatively recent discovery of the twentieth century, as Perry notes, the conversion to gas alone has a longer history going back to the early nineteenth century. Modern processes considerably modify the older methods. Though no large-scale plants have been built to demonstrate the newer processes, there have been a few smaller-scale experiments on two of the better-known processes. Even newer processes, however, are being investigated for possible application. In any conversion of coal to gas, efficiency and economy will have to be compared with those for the synthesis of oils from coal. And both conversions will have to vie with the direct use of coal for electrical power generation. It is difficult to predict at this point which type of conversion of coal will win out, for the best judgment will come only after large-scale plants of each type are built and run for a period of several years. Because of the large capital costs involved, and because the technology for using the products is dependent on the kind of product, we must face the prospect of designing and evaluating total systems with side-by-side operation for a matter of decades. Only then can we decide sensibly whether there is an overwhelming advantage to one or the other. We may even find that the best choice is to keep two systems in parallel, each with its own markets.

At the end of the article, Perry calls attention to another alternative, coal gasification underground. After a long period of desultory investigation in the 1940s, underground gasification was tentatively consigned to a back burner because of the many difficulties involved in maintaining steady underground burning while producing a gas of high enough heat value. In the past year or two, renewed interest in this possibility has resulted from engineers taking new approaches. In particular, they have brought several new techniques to the problems, such as breaking up or "rubbleizing" the coal underground in order to provide better burning. We can expect to hear more of such possibilities in the future.

# The Gasification of Coal

by Harry Perry
March 1974

*This formerly widespread technology, which lost its markets to natural gas and petroleum, is now being reexamined. New methods promise an alternative source of fossil-fuel energy*

Nearly every major city in the eastern U.S. once had its gashouse, where gas was manufactured (usually from coal) for lighting and cooking. The gashouses and the bulky cylindrical storage tanks that stood near them gradually disappeared after World War II as natural gas came to be distributed nationally by pipeline. Now, with both natural gas and petroleum increasingly in short supply, the idea of improving the nation's energy situation by the gasification of coal, which is plentiful, is attracting much interest.

Coal is found in 30 of the 50 states and represents more than 90 percent of the proved reserves of all developed fuels. At the 1972 rate of consumption the proved coal reserves would not be exhausted for some 600 years. Even if coal were the sole source of energy and the total demand for energy rose at the rate of 3.5 percent per year, the proved reserves would last for 47 years and total coal reserves for nearly 75 years.

Natural gas gained its ascendancy because its cost is low and its heating value is high. Like other gas it is clean, easy to distribute and convenient to use. In the years after World War II it therefore became the preferred residential and commercial fuel and also found many industrial applications. For these reasons the consumption of natural gas grew at a rate of 5.4 percent per year between 1947 and 1971, compared with a rate of 3.1 percent per year for the total energy consumption.

Gas made from coal could substitute for natural gas, although the old technology of coal gasification would have to be improved in order to give the product the heating value of natural gas (about 1,030 British thermal units per cubic foot). In addition the unenriched gas made from coal (with heating values of from 125 to 560 B.t.u. per cubic foot) would serve well in a number of industrial applications. It is therefore not surprising that the gasification of coal is being reexamined as a major source of clean energy from domestic resources.

Gas manufactured from coal was first produced in the late 18th century by heating coal in the absence of air. (It was heated by burning part of the coal outside a vessel containing the remainder of the coal; if the coal inside the vessel had been allowed to come in contact with air, it would have burned, forming combustion-product gases rather than gas that could itself be burned later.) The first coal-gas company, which distributed its product for lighting, was chartered in London in 1812; the first U.S. company was chartered in Baltimore in 1816.

In those days the gas was being produced by destructive distillation, that is, by heating the coal to a temperature where it decomposed chemically. The gas produced by the distillation of coal has a heating value of from 475 to 560 B.t.u. per cubic foot, depending on the type of coal and the temperature to which it is heated. A similar type of gas

is produced when coal is carbonized to manufacture coke; frequently coke-oven gas supplemented coal gas when it was locally available and coal gas was in short supply.

In these processes 70 percent or more of the original coal remains as a solid residue, consisting mostly of carbon, that must be sold or otherwise utilized. With coke-oven gas this is no problem, since coke is the major product. With coal the answer lies in going a step beyond distillation to gasification.

Gasification involves not only heating the coal, as in distillation, but also the subsequent reaction of the solid residue with air, oxygen, steam or various mixtures of them. The distillation step releases a certain amount of gas that has a fairly high B.t.u. content because methane ($CH_4$) and other higher hydrocarbons contained in the coal are among the first components to emerge as the coal decomposes. The gasification step produces a gas that is essentially a mixture of hydrogen and carbon monoxide (which has a much lower heating value than the distillation gases do) with some of the gases distilled from the coal. The amount of the distilled gas in the final product varies with the gasification process.

Oxygen is expensive, and so the old gas companies resorted to an alternative process to make a gas that supplemented coal gas and coke-oven gas. The process produced what was known as "blue gas" or "water gas." Anthracite coal from which the fine sizes had been removed, with the large sizes being crushed to an acceptable dimension, was fed to a vessel lined with a refractory material. After the gasifier had been brought up to a suitable temperature the coal (it could also be coke) was blasted with a stream of air and heated further by combustion with oxygen in the air. During the first part of this "blow" period the gas produced was mostly carbon dioxide ($C + O_2 \rightarrow CO_2$), but as the coal or coke in the upper level of the bed grew hotter the reverse reaction ($CO_2 + C \rightarrow CO$) began to go, meaning that carbon monoxide was being produced in increasing amounts. After enough coal or coke had been heated sufficiently the valves controlling the flow of air were closed and other valves were opened to begin the "run" period, in which the hot coal or coke was reacted with steam ($C + H_2O \rightarrow H_2 + CO$). It was a cyclical process, leading to complications in the design and operation of the equipment.

The water gas had a heating value of about 300 B.t.u. per cubic foot compared with the value of from 475 to 560 of coal gas, so that it had to be enriched. The enrichment entailed another cyclical process. The gas made at the end of a run period was hot and contained enough carbon monoxide so that it could be burned to heat refractory bricks enclosed in a "carburettor" vessel. When the bricks were hot enough, the heating gas was shut off and oil was sprayed on the bricks, where the heat caused the oil to be cracked into lighter hydrocarbon products, including methane and propane. The resulting gas, which had a high heating value, was mixed with the gas made during the run period to produce what was known as "carburetted blue gas."

The companies originally sold a coal gas with a heating value of about 550 B.t.u. per cubic foot. Burners were therefore designed to handle a gas of that quality. With burner designs fixed, manufactured gas, no matter how it was produced, was usually adjusted to that heating value. On the introduction of natural gas it became necessary in some areas to produce a gas that could be mixed with natural gas. Fortunately the heating value of the carburetted gas could be controlled to a large extent by adjusting the type and quantity of oil sprayed on the refractory bricks.

Then there was "producer gas," which was even cheaper than carburetted water gas. It had a heating value of from 110 to 160 B.t.u. per cubic foot, which meant that it could not be widely dis-

tributed because the cost would be prohibitive. (Distribution costs account for much of the consumer's bill; even with natural gas the distribution costs in the District of Columbia represent 65 percent of the total delivered cost.) Producer gas served well, however, in industries that required a clean fuel for combustion purposes or a source of heat for manufacturing processes and that could make the gas locally, so that the cost of distribution was small.

Producer gas was made in a continuous process wherein a bed of hot coal or coke was blasted with air or a mixture of steam and air. The final product necessarily contained nitrogen from the air and carbon dioxide resulting from the combustion of carbon with oxygen. The carbon dioxide could be removed, but the nitrogen diluted the heating value of the gas. This disadvantage was unimportant when the gas was burned as an industrial fuel but made it unsuitable as a synthesis gas (hydrogen and mixtures of hydrogen and carbon monoxide employed in making plastics, synthetic fuels and other synthetic products) and for distribution by utility companies.

Starting in about 1850 and continuing until World War II, the technology of making water gas and producer gas was improved steadily in the U.S. After manufactured gas lost its markets in the U.S. the technology was further improved in Europe, where coal was then the only indigenous fuel found in any significant quantity. New processes were investigated, taking advantage of technical advances in other fields such as the development of large-scale oxygen plants, new methods of handling solids in reactions with gas and improved construction materials. At about the time the technology had reached a stage where plants could be installed, however, natural gas was discovered in the North Sea and in North Africa. In addition most of the European nations decided to shift from an economy based on high-cost indigenous coal to one based on what was at the time low-cost imported petroleum. Few coal gasification plants embodying new technology were installed, and interest in further improving the technology flagged.

The two processes that were installed most often in Europe and elsewhere were the Lurgi fixed-bed, pressurized gasifier and the Koppers-Totzek fully entrained, atmospheric gasifier. Both types served mainly to make synthesis gas for the manufacture of ammonia and other synthetic products, although in some places Lurgi plants made a gas

that was distributed as city gas. Neither of these processes meets all the qualifications of an ideal gasification scheme. An ideal process would be a single-stage, continuous operation employing air as the oxidizing medium; it would convert any type of coal into a combustible gas or a synthesis gas that was low in inert constituents.

Although both the Lurgi process and the Koppers-Totzek process are single-stage and continuous, they both rely on oxygen rather than air as the oxidizing medium. The Lurgi gasifier is pressurized, which for most applications of synthesis gas is an economic advantage over processes operating at atmospheric pressure. On the other hand, the Lurgi process requires a sized coal (fines must be removed) and a noncoking or weakly coking coal (because if the bed of coal cokes during gasification, it forms a solid mass that prevents the passage of gas through the bed and brings gasification to a halt), whereas the Koppers-Totzek process will function with any coal.

In the U.S. the renewed interest in coal gasification to produce a substitute for natural gas has led to serious consideration of installing Lurgi or Koppers-Totzek plants. Neither process, however, yields a gas that could substitute for natural gas because it does not have the heating value or the composition required. The gas resulting from each process is basically a mixture of carbon monoxide and hydrogen, plus a certain amount of methane distilled from the coal during heating. Carbon monoxide and hydrogen both have a heating value of 300 B.t.u. per cubic foot—far below the heating value of natural gas. Moreover, local gas companies would not be allowed to distribute such mixtures (although they once were) because carbon monoxide is poisonous and hydrogen is difficult to contain and also has burning characteristics that would require special burners.

Both processes could, however, make a raw synthesis gas that (after purification) could be methanated to yield a gas suitable as a substitute for natural gas. Methanation involves passing the gas over a special nickel catalyst to convert it into almost pure methane, which is what natural gas is. So far, however, the methanation step has not been demonstrated on a commercial scale.

Although research in the U.S. on coal gasification is now centered on making a low-cost synthesis gas from which a substitute for natural gas can be produced, in the near future coal gasifica-

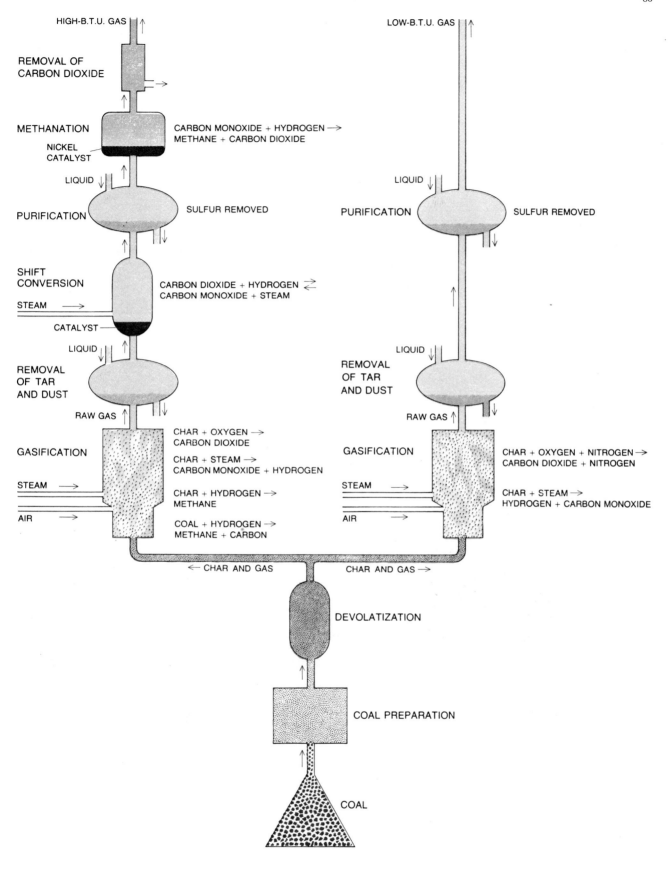

HIGH-B.T.U. GAS

LOW-B.T.U. GAS

REMOVAL OF CARBON DIOXIDE

METHANATION

NICKEL CATALYST

CARBON MONOXIDE + HYDROGEN →
METHANE + CARBON DIOXIDE

LIQUID

PURIFICATION        SULFUR REMOVED

LIQUID

PURIFICATION        SULFUR REMOVED

SHIFT CONVERSION

STEAM →

CARBON DIOXIDE + HYDROGEN ⇌
CARBON MONOXIDE + STEAM

CATALYST

LIQUID

REMOVAL OF TAR AND DUST

LIQUID

REMOVAL OF TAR AND DUST

RAW GAS

RAW GAS

GASIFICATION

STEAM →

AIR →

CHAR + OXYGEN →
CARBON DIOXIDE

CHAR + STEAM →
CARBON MONOXIDE + HYDROGEN

CHAR + HYDROGEN →
METHANE

COAL + HYDROGEN →
METHANE + CARBON

GASIFICATION

STEAM →

AIR →

CHAR + OXYGEN + NITROGEN →
CARBON DIOXIDE + NITROGEN

CHAR + STEAM →
HYDROGEN + CARBON MONOXIDE

← CHAR AND GAS          CHAR AND GAS →

DEVOLATIZATION

COAL PREPARATION

COAL

**STEPS IN COAL GASIFICATION** are charted for two types of gas (*color*). In each case the coal is prepared as necessary and then devolatilized, which entails heating it in the absence of air so that it decomposes chemically, yielding various gases and char. If the objective of the process is a gas with the heating value of natural gas, the steps following devolatilization are as shown at left. The simpler process charted at right yields producer gas, which has a much lower heating value but is suitable as a fuel for a boiler.

tion will also be employed to provide the raw material for the manufacture of other synthetics (alcohols, ketones, waxes and all types of petroleum products) and for the hydrogen required to produce synthetic liquid fuels from coal. (The ratio of carbon to hydrogen is much higher in coal than in oil; coal liquefaction involves producing hydrogen from coal by a gasification process and reacting it with coal so as to increase the hydrogen content of the coal and produce an oil.)

In addition new regulations on the emission of sulfur oxides and the difficulties that have been encountered with stack-scrubbing processes have led to a renewal of interest in producing a low-B.t.u., low-sulfur gas from coal to be burned as a boiler fuel. Most of the early research and development on sulfur oxide control was centered on removing sulfur oxide from the flue gases resulting from the combustion of coal. All the stack-scrubbing processes tested are reported to have been too unreliable for the sustained performance required for utility and industrial boilers, and the costs are much higher than originally anticipated. Two particularly troublesome problems are the large volume of gas that must be treated (making the cost of removal high) and the disposal in an ecologically acceptable manner of the solid waste material that is formed.

If coal is first gasified with air to form a low-B.t.u. gas, the resulting hydrogen sulfide can be removed by proved methods before the gas is burned in the boiler. The volume of raw gas to be treated would be less than half what must be handled when sulfur oxide is removed from flue gas, and no environmentally troublesome by-product would be created. Interest in low-B.t.u. gasification as a means to the control of sulfur oxides has been further stimulated by the possibility that the more advanced processes being developed for producing high-B.t.u. gas could be modified for making low-B.t.u. gas.

Several new methods of coal gasification are being investigated, and two have reached the demonstration stage. Since most of the research has been directed toward producing a substitute for natural gas, all the processes have attempted to retain in the product gas as much as possible of the methane that is released during the early part of the process, when the coal is simply being heated. In this way the overall capital cost and the material requirements per unit of methane are reduced. Retaining methane is also advantageous when a low-B.t.u. boiler gas is made, because the methane makes for a lower cost and a higher quality.

The basic steps required to produce a synthetic natural gas from coal can be described in general terms [see illustration on preceding page]. First the coal is prepared, which entails crushing it to the desired top size, removing fines (if necessary) and extraneous material and drying the coal (if necessary for the subsequent steps). The coal is then either sent to the gasifier or, if it is a coking coal and the process cannot operate with such a coal, pretreated with heat to destroy its coking properties.

The coal is devolatilized, or distilled, either in the gasifier or in a separate vessel. As many of the distillation products as possible are retained to reduce the overall cost of gasification. Since these gases are distilled from the coal during the early part of the process and react more readily with either pure oxygen or the oxygen in the air than the char that is also produced does, the objective of retaining the distilled gases in the finished product requires special provisions to ensure that the gases do not come in contact with the oxygen and steam put into the system subsequently.

For making high-B.t.u. gas most of the processes call for steam, oxygen and either coal or char as the feed materials. The oxygen reacts with part of the carbon to provide heat and raise the temperature high enough for the balance of the carbon to react rapidly with steam to produce a mixture of carbon monoxide and oxygen. If one wanted to sub-

LURGI PROCESS is one of two methods of coal gasification that are available on a commercial scale. It is a pressurized process in which sized coal descending into the gasifier is first dried and then carbonized by reaction with oxygen and steam. In the gasifier's bottom layer the remaining carbon is burned to provide heat for the reactions proceeding above.

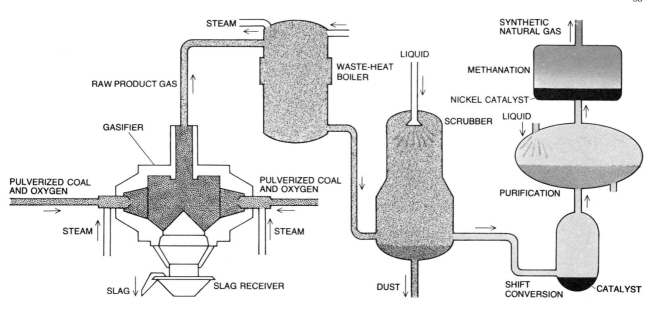

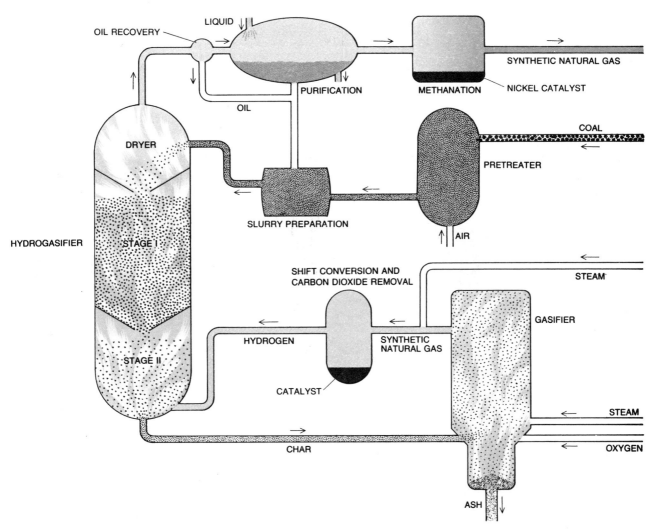

**HYGAS PROCESS** being developed by the Institute of Gas Technology is at the large-pilot-plant stage. Part of the coal put into the gasifier is gasified to form a mixture of carbon monoxide and hydrogen, which after shift conversion is converted to hydrogen. The hydrogen is reacted with coal or char, yielding a product that is largely methane. The gas is subjected to a final methanation reaction to attain a gas of pipeline quality. The HYGAS gasification process operates at high pressure and with a fluidized bed of coal.

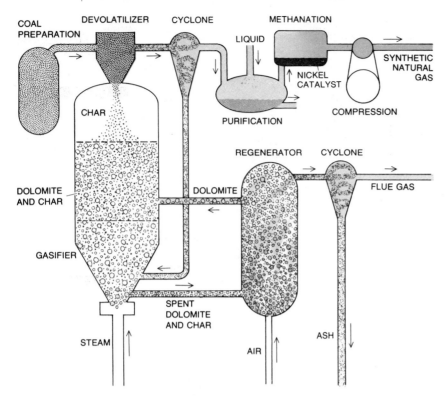

**CARBON DIOXIDE ACCEPTOR PROCESS,** a project of Consolidation Coal Company, is also at the large-pilot-plant stage. Calcined dolomite is circulated through a fluidized bed of lignite char. The dolomite reacts with carbon dioxide produced in initial gasification of coal, liberating enough heat to sustain the carbon-steam reaction. Raw gas produced, containing methane, hydrogen and carbon monoxide, is subjected to a final methanation step.

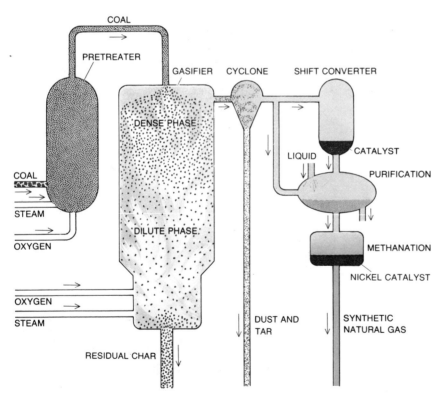

**SYNTHANE PROCESS** of the U.S. Bureau of Mines is at the small-pilot-plant stage. It is designed to produce a synthetic gas that would serve as a substitute for natural gas. Coal is pretreated to destroy its caking properties, carbonized in the dense phase of the gasifier and then gasified with oxygen and steam in the dilute phase. Shift conversion to yield a 3 : 1 ratio of hydrogen to carbon monoxide is followed by methanation with a nickel catalyst.

stitute air for oxygen in order to avoid the expense of oxygen, the nitrogen in the air would dilute the product gas; therefore certain processes resort to a heat carrier as the means of providing heat. An inorganic material is heated in a separate vessel, with air as the oxidant. The material is then put into the gasifier, where it raises the temperature to the level required for the char or the coal to react with steam.

In making hydrogen, synthesis gas or high-B.t.u. gas the raw gas is next treated to remove tar and dust and is passed over a shift catalyst, which serves to speed up the reaction in which the four components of the gas (carbon dioxide, hydrogen, carbon monoxide and steam) reach equilibrium ($CO_2 + H_2 \rightleftharpoons CO + H_2O$). Any desired ratio of carbon monoxide and hydrogen can be achieved by adjusting the amounts of steam and carbon dioxide. When hydrogen is the desired final product, the carbon monoxide is all converted to carbon dioxide and scrubbed from the gas by any of several processes. In making synthesis gas, which figures in the manufacture of a wide range of chemical products, the ratio of carbon monoxide to hydrogen is adjusted to obtain the optimum composition for the chemical to be manufactured.

When high-B.t.u. gas is the objective, the appropriate ratio of hydrogen to carbon monoxide is produced. The gas is then purified to remove the sulfur compounds that may be present. The reason is that the catalysts that have been tested for the crucial step of methanation are all nickel-based and are highly sensitive to poisoning by sulfur compounds.

No full-scale commercial methanation plant has yet been built. A test is under way, however, at a Lurgi plant operated by the Scottish Gas Board. The test, which started last fall and is being conducted by a consortium of American firms, will use 10 million cubic feet per day of purified Lurgi gas to demonstrate the efficiency of various methanation catalysts and the amount of cleaning that must be done to keep the catalyst functioning for an acceptable period of time. A second major engineering problem is the rapid removal of heat released by the highly exothermic reaction; if the heat is not removed, it can cause deterioration of the catalyst through sintering or the deposition of carbon.

A major alternative in making high-B.t.u. gas is to gasify part of the coal to form hydrogen and then to produce methane by the reaction of hydrogen directly with coal or char ($C + 2H_2 \rightarrow CH_4$). Heat does not have to be supplied, since the reaction is exothermic. The products of the reaction are then methanated to eliminate any residual carbon monoxide and to bring the gas to a heating value acceptable for distribution through pipelines. The major advantages of direct hydrogenation are that it requires fewer materials and has a higher thermal efficiency than complete gasification followed by methanation over a catalyst.

Making a producer gas is a much simpler operation than making a high-B.t.u. gas. Because it requires fewer steps and employs air rather than oxygen, the cost of making it on a commercial scale should be lower than the cost of making high-B.t.u. gas. After the coal or char has been reacted with air the hot raw gas, containing from 110 to 160 B.t.u. per cubic foot, is treated to remove tar and dust and further treated to remove hydrogen sulfide. The product is a low-B.t.u., low-sulfur gas suitable for boiler fuel. Since a substantial amount of natural gas (34 percent in 1971) is consumed by industry, any substitution of producer gas made from coal would reduce or even eliminate the problems arising from the present short supply of natural gas.

The two new processes that have reached the demonstration-plant stage are the HYGAS process, which is being developed by the Institute of Gas Technology, and the CO₂ Acceptor process, which is a project of the Consolidation Coal Company. Other processes, which are at or approaching the pilot-plant stage, include the BI-GAS process of Bituminous Coal Research, Inc., and the Synthane process of the U.S. Bureau of Mines. All the processes under investigation can be classified in various ways: by the method of supplying heat for the gasification reaction (internal heating or external heating); by the method of achieving contact between the reactants (fixed bed, fluidized bed or entrainment in the gasifying medium); by the flow of reactants (cocurrent or countercurrent); by the gasifying medium (hydrogen or steam plus oxygen, air or enriched oxygen), and by the condition of the residue removed (slagging, which means that the residue is liquid ash, or nonslagging, which means that it is dry ash). Nearly all the combinations of ways to gasify coal represented by these classifications have been investigated.

In the absence of full-scale commercial plants the cost of coal gasification can be only roughly estimated, and the estimates must be viewed with caution.

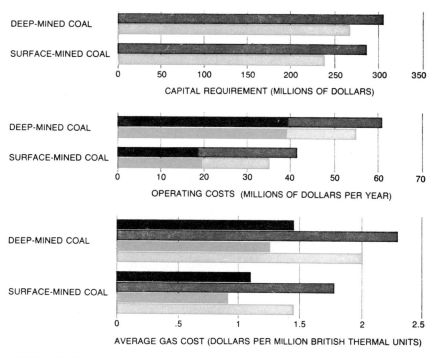

GASIFICATION COSTS are estimated for the Lurgi process (*gray*) and a typical new process (*color*). Darker parts of operating-cost bars represent coal cost, lighter parts other costs. Average gas cost is for 20 years from 1975 (*darker bars*) or from 1990 (*lighter bars*).

In a presentation to the Panel on Coal Gasification of the National Academy of Sciences representatives of the Lurgi process estimated that as of about the beginning of 1972 the capital cost of a gasifier producing 250 million cubic feet of gas per day would be from $180 million to $190 million. The estimate did not include working capital, interest during construction or start-up expenses; these items would increase the cost to about $250 million, based on 1970 dollars. In the fall of 1973 the El Paso Natural Gas Company estimated the cost of a similar plant at more than $400 million. All the newer processes are estimated to have somewhat lower capital costs than the Lurgi process [see illustration above].

An entirely different technology that is attracting interest is gasifying coal underground. The idea is not new, and a fair amount of research was done on it in various countries until about 1960. Concern about shortages of energy has focused attention on it again.

Any process would require the creation of enough permeability in the coal so that a stream of air could flow from one point in the seam to another point without undue loss of pressure. The coal could then be ignited at either end and gasification would begin. Part of the coal would burn with the injected air, producing a mixture of carbon monoxide, carbon dioxide and heat. If good contact between gas and solid could

be maintained, the hot carbon dioxide would then be reduced to carbon monoxide by a reaction with the hot coal. The product would be a producer gas.

Experiments in underground gasification of coal have created the required permeability by a number of methods that entail digging shafts or by one or another variation of the percolation method, in which two holes are drilled from the surface to the coal seam and then connected so that air can flow between them. The experiments have been able to produce a combustible gas, but they do not do so continuously and the gas does not have a constant heating value. Most of the tests have resulted in poor recovery of the available coal and have failed to achieve the level of control of the solid-gas contact that is required to produce consistently a gas of high quality. Many other problems, such as subsidence of land and contamination from ground water, have not been solved.

A number of new approaches have been proposed. They include breaking up the coal with explosives and linking boreholes by drilling with lasers. If a successful method could be developed, the energy from coal in the ground could be extracted with little or no requirement for underground manpower. Moreover, it might be possible to extract the energy from coal seams that are too thick, too thin or too poor in quality to be exploited by conventional methods.

# 7

# The Necessity of Fission Power

## COMMENTARY

The chief competitor for fossil fuels as our major energy sources is nuclear power. In this article, Hans Bethe contrasts our needs for energy with the various resources available. He concludes that the only reasonable solution for the energy deficit that will occur as we run out of oil and gas is to invest in nuclear fission power. His article was written as the United States was still involved in discussing President Ford's program, enunciated in January 1975, for energy independence. As we now know, that program got nowhere, and four years later conservation is still a desirable action that few have taken or are likely to undertake on the basis of exhortation alone.

Alternative sources of energy are treated briefly by Bethe. Fusion, ultimately the most attractive alternative, is not seen by Bethe as a likely candidate for the next 50 years, if indeed it will ever be possible. Solar power he likewise deems either impractical or too expensive, judging from plans to use solar energy as either auxiliary heating for small homes or as central power generation from a large array of mirrors. In January 1979, three years after this article was published, a committee of the National Academy of Sciences reported on another possible path of solar energy—photovoltaic processes, that is, the direct conversion of sunlight to electricity through the use of cells made of silicon and other materials. The committee saw that possibility as unlikely to provide us with much power by the year 2000, but worth much serious research for the long term.

Throughout this article, Bethe points out the need for research into new methods of power generation. However, he spends most of his effort on showing how nuclear fission is the best choice. In doing so, he concentrates on arguments for the safety of nuclear power. The dangers of small amounts of radioactivity from routine operations are compared with those of natural levels and are seen to be insignificant. Reactor accidents are likewise considered no real danger. In this argument, the author adopts the by-now-standard practice of comparing deaths from nuclear reactor use with those from all other sources, such as automobile accidents, and reasons that society is prepared to accept those kinds of death at a much higher rate than that expected for nuclear accidents. It is of course by no means clear that deaths due to self-generated decisions and actions, such as automobile accidents, falls, and drownings, are comparable with deaths imposed by actions generally impinging on a population with no alternative. The residents of the Harrisburg, Pennsylvania area near the Three-Mile Island reactor accident in 1979 may take a jaundiced view of Bethe's arguments.

Nuclear waste disposal is not seen as a difficult problem by Bethe. Yet, three years after he wrote this article, it is the subject of hot debate and is seen as a decisive issue for the future of nuclear power. The problem of nuclear proliferation does concern Bethe for the same reasons that President Carter imposed a moratorium on nuclear fuel reprocessing. He concludes that this danger should be minimized when the United States joins other nations in controlling by inspection. In spite of the possibility of proliferation and nuclear accidents, Bethe thinks our energy needs require that we take the risks to keep our economy going.

# The Necessity of Fission Power

by H. A. Bethe
*January 1976*

*If the U.S. must have sources of energy other than fossil fuels,
the only source that can make a major contribution between
now and the end of the century is nuclear fission*

The quadrupling of the price of oil in the fall of 1973 came as a rude but perhaps salutary shock to the Western world. It drew attention to the fact that oil is running out, and that mankind must turn to other fuels, to strict energy conservation or to both.

The price increase was not entirely unjustified. From 1950 to 1973 the price of oil, measured in constant dollars, had declined steadily. Moreover, it has been estimated that if world oil production were to continue to increase at the same rate that it has in the past two decades, the upward trend could persist only until about 1995; then the supply of oil would have to drop sharply [*see illustration on next page*]. Accordingly the oil-producing countries must see to their own economic development while their oil lasts so that they can rely on other sources of revenue thereafter. At the same time the rest of the world must take measures to become less dependent on oil—particularly imported oil—while there is still time.

What would it take for the U.S., which currently gets more than 15 percent of its energy in the form of imported oil, to become "energy independent?" In a report issued last June the Energy Research and Development Agency (ERDA) outlined its plans for the U.S. to achieve this goal. The ERDA projections are expressed in terms of quads, or quadrillions ($10^{15}$) of British thermal units (B.t.u.). According to ERDA, the drive to achieve energy independence calls for a two-pronged approach. First, the U.S. must be technologically geared not only to expand the production of its existing principal energy resources (oil, gas, coal and uranium) but also to develop several new energy sources. Second, a major energy-conservation effort must be initiated both to reduce total energy consumption and to shift consumption to sources other than oil. Only if both remedies are successfully applied can energy independence be achieved—and then it can be achieved only by 1995 [*see illustration on page 73*]. Without any new initiatives the need for imported oil will rise steadily from about 12 quads at present to more than 60 in the year 2000. At current prices the importation of that much oil would cost about $120 billion, compared with $25 billion in 1974, an increase of $95 billion.

Now, $95 billion may not sound like a gigantic sum when this fiscal year's Federal budget deficit is projected to be about $70 billion. The economics of international trade, however, is a different matter. Even a $10 billion trade deficit has a major effect on the stability of the currency. It is almost impossible to think of exports that could bring in an additional $95 billion. Besides, if current trends are allowed to continue, the U.S. would take about 30 percent of the world's oil production when that production is at its maximum. Clearly it is critical that the U.S. not follow this course.

What is critical for the U.S. is a matter of survival for Japan and the countries of western Europe. After all, the U.S. does have substantial amounts of oil and gas and plenty of coal. Japan and Italy have none of those fuels. England and Norway will have a limited domestic supply of oil in a few years, but other countries of western Europe have no natural oil resources of their own and have limited amounts of coal. If the U.S. competes for scarce oil in the world market, it can only drive the price still higher and starve the economies of western Europe and Japan. The bankruptcy of those countries in turn would make it impossible for the U.S. to export to them and thus to pay for its own imports.

For the next five years or so there is only one way for the U.S. to make measurable progress toward the goal of energy independence, and that is by conserving energy. There are two kinds of energy conservation. One approach is to have the country lower its standard of living in some respects, for example by exchanging larger cars for smaller ones. This measure has been widely accepted, probably at some cost in safety. To most Americans, however, it appears undesirable to continue very far in this direction.

The other approach to conservation is to improve the efficiency with which energy is consumed. A number of useful suggestions have been made, such as insulating houses better, increasing the efficiency of space-heating and water-heating systems, improving the way steam is generated for industry and upgrading other industrial processes. Conversions of this type require substantial investment, and their cost-effectiveness on a normal accounting scheme is not clear. Much leadership, public education and tax or other incentives will be needed to realize the potential for increased efficiency. If all these things are provided, the total energy consumption of the U.S. in the year 2000 could be reduced from 166 quads to 120.

ERDA predicts that if at the same time the generation of electricity from coal and nuclear fuel is allowed to expand as it is needed, the U.S. can achieve an intermediate trend in oil imports: a satisfactory decline in the first 10 years, followed by a rise until oil imports are higher in 2000 than they are now. Energy independence will not have been achieved by that course either.

In all three ERDA projections it is assumed that the U.S. will move gradually from liquid fuels (oil and gas) to solid fuels (coal and uranium). For example, in President Ford's State of the Union Message in January, 1975, the actual contribution of various fuels to our energy budget in 1973 was presented along with the President's aims for 1985 and the expected situation in 1985 if no action is taken [see illustration on page 74]. The latter situation would require the importation of 36 quads of oil, in fair agreement with ERDA's prediction of 28 quads for 1985.

The Ford projection envisions a total U.S. consumption of 103 quads in 1985, 28 quads more than in 1973. Since much of the added energy would go into the generation of electricity, with a thermal efficiency of 33 to 40 percent, however, consumable energy would increase by only 17 quads, or 26 percent. Taking into account an expected 22 percent increase in the working population during that period, the consumable energy per worker would stay roughly constant.

The Ford message projects that domestic oil production will increase by seven quads by 1985 and that natural-gas production will decrease by only two quads, in spite of the fact that in the U.S. oil production has declined in the past two years and natural-gas discoveries have run at less than half of consumption for the past eight years. The ERDA report agrees that by stimulating the domestic production of oil and gas the U.S. could attain just about the total production figure used by the President, 53 quads, with gas somewhat higher than his estimate and oil lower.

Of course, the country would be depleting its resources more rapidly and would have to pay for it by having less domestic oil and gas in the years after 1985. The proposed stimulation of domestic oil and gas production, however, would provide the breathing space needed to bring other forms of energy into play. The only energy resources the U.S. has in abundance are coal and uranium. Accordingly President Ford calls for a massive increase in coal production, from 600 million tons in 1973 to 1,000 million tons in 1985. Meanwhile the Administration's energy program calls for the building of 200 nuclear-fission reactors with an energy output equivalent to about 10 quads.

Coal should certainly be substituted for oil and gas in utilities and in other industrial uses wherever possible. The conversion of coal into synthetic gas or oil is essential; demonstration plants for these processes and price guarantees should be given the highest priority. The same applies to oil from shale.

Coal cannot do everything, however, particularly if it is used intensively for making synthetic fuel. The U.S. needs another, preferably nonfossil, energy source. The only source that is now sufficiently developed to play any major role is nuclear fission. Thoughtful people have raised a number of objections to nuclear-fission reactors, which I shall discuss below, but first let me review some of the alternative energy sources that have been suggested.

Nuclear fusion is the energy source that has most strongly captured the imagination of scientists. It is still completely unknown, however, whether useful energy can ever be obtained from the fusion process. It is true that both stars and hydrogen bombs derive their energy from the fusion of light atomic nuclei, but can such energy be released in a controlled manner on the earth? The requirements for accomplishing the task are tremendous: a mixture of heavy-hydrogen gases must be brought to a temperature of about 100 million degrees Celsius and kept there long enough for energy-releasing reactions between the hydrogen nuclei to take place at a rate sufficient to yield a net output of energy.

The most obvious way to try to satisfy this condition is by magnetic confinement. At 100 million degrees hydrogen is completely ionized, and the positively charged nuclei and negatively charged electrons can be guided by magnetic

FINITE SUPPLY OF OIL is responsible for the shape of this curve representing world oil production over a two-century span. The projection is based on the work of M. King Hubbert of the U.S. Geological Survey, who estimates that if world oil production were to continue to increase at the same rate that it has in the past two decades, output would peak in about 1995 and then drop sharply. Energy content of various fuels discussed in this article is expressed in quads, short for quadrillions ($10^{15}$) of British thermal units (B.t.u.).

fields. Since the early 1950's physicists in many countries have designed many intricate magnetic-field configurations, but they have not succeeded in attaining the break-even condition. Great hopes have alternated with complete frustration. At present the prospects seem better than ever before; a few years ago Russian experimenters developed the device named Tokamak, which has worked at least roughly according to theoretical expectations. This device has been reproduced in the U.S. with comparable success. More than $200 million has now been committed by ERDA for a much larger device of the Tokamak type, to be built at Princeton University; if that machine also fulfills theoretical expectations, we may know by the early 1980's whether or not power from fusion is feasible by the Tokamak approach.

There have been too many disappointments, however, to allow any firm predictions. Work on machines of the Tokamak type is also going forward in many other laboratories in the U.S., in the U.S.S.R. and in several countries of western Europe. If the problem can be solved, it probably will be. Money is not the limiting factor: the annual support in the U.S. is well over $100 million, and it is increasing steadily. Progress is limited rather by the availability of highly trained workers, by the time required to build large machines and then by the time required to do significant experiments. Meanwhile several alternative schemes for magnetic confinement are being pursued. In addition there are the completely different approaches of laser fusion and electron-beam fusion. In my own opinion the latter schemes are even further in the future than Tokamak.

Assume now that one of these schemes succeeds in the early 1980's. Where are we then? The problem is that the engineering of any large, complex industrial plant takes a long time, even after the principle of design is well known. Since preliminary fusion-power engineering is already under way, however, it is a reasonable hope that a prototype of a commercial fusion reactor could operate in about 2000, and that fusion might contribute a few percent of the country's power supply by 2020.

Solar power is very different. There is no doubt about its technical feasibility, but its economic feasibility is another matter. One should distinguish clearly between two uses of solar power: the heating of houses and the production of all-purpose power on a large scale.

Partial solar heating of houses may become widespread, and solar air-conditioning is also possible. ERDA is spon-

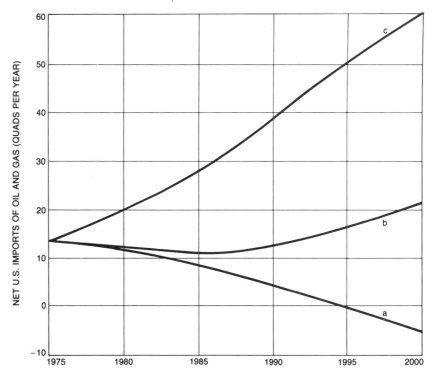

THREE PROJECTIONS of the extent to which the U.S. will continue to be dependent on imported oil and gas for the rest of this century were made in a 1975 report by the Energy Research and Development Administration (ERDA). Curve *a*, which shows the U.S. ending its dependence on imported fuel in about 1995, assumes that all the recommendations of ERDA's National Plan for achieving "energy independence" are put into effect. Curve *b* shows the effect of an intermediate approach emphasizing energy conservation. Curve *c* shows the expected trend in oil imports in the absence of any major new initiatives. All three curves assume that the energy efficiency of automobiles will improve by about 40 percent over the next five years or so as a result of the trend toward smaller cars and that the number of coal-burning and nuclear power plants will expand to meet rising demand for electricity. Any slowdown on nuclear plants would shift all three curves sharply upward.

soring the development of model solar-heated houses. Private estimates for solar-heating systems, for a "standard" house of 1,200 square feet, run between $5,000 and $10,000 in mass production, compared with about $1,000 for conventional heating systems. With such an installation one might expect to supply about 50 percent of the house's heating requirements (more in the South, less in the North, particularly in regions of frequent cloud cover). In any case an auxiliary heating system supplied with gas, oil or electricity must be provided; otherwise the cost of the solar-heating system becomes exorbitant.

ERDA estimates that 32 million new households will be established between 1972 and 2000, and that they will then comprise about a third of all dwelling units. If all the new units are equipped with solar heating, it would require a private investment of $150 to $300 billion. The heating requirement for all residential units in 1973 was close to 10 percent of the country's total energy consumption, and that fraction is likely to remain about the same. Some of the new

dwelling units will not use solar energy, but let us assume (optimistically) that an equal number of older houses will be converted to solar heat. In that case a third of all houses would derive on the average about half of their heat from the sun, which would then supply somewhat less than 2 percent of the country's total energy needs. This contribution would be helpful but clearly would not be decisive.

The use of solar heat on a large scale for power generation is something else again. (Here I shall assume electric power, but the situation would not be essentially different if the energy were to be stored in fuels such as hydrogen.) Of the many proposals that have been made, the most practical in my opinion is to have a large field (perhaps a mile on a side) covered by mirrors, all of which reflect sunlight to a central boiler. The mirrors would be driven by a computer-controlled mechanism; the boiler would generate electricity in the conventional manner. At least three separate groups, supported by ERDA, are working on this kind of project. The best estimates I have heard give about $2,500 per installed kilowatt (power averaged over the 24-hour day) exclusive of interest and the effects of inflation during construction. On the same basis nuclear-fission reactors cost about $500 per kilowatt, so that solar power is roughly five times as expensive as nuclear power.

That cost estimate may sound high, but a little thought will show that it is not. First of all, the sun shines for only part of the day. On a sunny winter day in the southern U.S. one square mile of focused mirrors is just about enough to generate an average of 100 megawatts of electric power at a cost of about $250 million. To achieve that output the full heat of the sun must be utilized whenever it shines. At noon such a system would generate about 400 megawatts; near sunrise and sunset it would generate correspondingly less; at night it would generate none. To get an average of 100 megawatts one must have equipment to generate 400 megawatts, so that the generating equipment (boilers, turbines and so on) would cost roughly four times as much as they would in a comparable nuclear or fossil-fuel power plant. To this total cost must be added

the cost of storing the energy that will be needed at night and on cloudy days. (The means of storage is so far a largely unsolved problem.)

Assume now that half of the cost is allotted to the mirrors and their electronic drive mechanisms; that would amount to $125 million for a plant of one square mile, or less than $5 per square foot. It is hardly conceivable that the mirrors and their drives could be built that cheaply, even in mass production, when a modest house costs $30 a square foot. I conclude therefore that all-purpose solar power is likely to remain extremely expensive.

Although it seems clear that solar power can never be practical for western Europe and Japan, the countries that need power most urgently, it might be just the right thing for certain developing countries, provided that the capital-cost problem can be solved. Many of those countries have large desert areas, rather modest total energy needs and abundant cheap manpower, which is probably required for the maintenance of any solar-power installation.

In addition to the alternative energy sources discussed above, a variety of

other schemes have been suggested, such as harnessing the wind or the tides, burning garbage or agricultural wastes, converting fast-growing plants into fuels such as methane or tapping the earth's internal heat. Each of these approaches presents its own special difficulties, and at best each can make only a minor contribution toward the solution of the energy problem.

I do not mean to imply that work on alternative-energy projects is worthless. On the contrary, I believe that research and development on many of them should be pursued, and in fact ERDA is stepping up this type of work. I want to emphasize, however, that it takes a very long time from having an idea to proving its value in the laboratory, a much longer time for engineering development so that the process can be used in a large industrial plant and a still longer time before a major industry can be established. Certainly for the next 10 years and probably for the next 25 years the U.S. cannot expect any of the proposed alternative energy schemes to have much impact.

For all these reasons I believe that nuclear fission is the only major nonfossil power source the U.S. can rely on for the rest of this century and probably for some time afterward. Let us now examine the objections that have been raised against this source of power.

Some concern has been expressed over the fact that nuclear reactors in routine operation release radioactivity through outflowing liquids. According to the standards originally set by the Atomic Energy Commission and now administered by the Nuclear Regulatory Commission, these releases must be kept "as low as practicable," and under no circumstances must the additional radiation exposure of a person living permanently near the fence of the power plant be greater than five millirem per year. Most modern fission power plants release far less than this limit. For the purposes of comparison an average person in the U.S. receives 100 millirem per year in natural radiation (from cosmic rays, radioactivity in the earth and in buildings and radioactive substances inside his body) and an average of about 70 millirem per year from diagnostic medical X rays. It has been estimated that in the year 2000 a person living in the U.S. would on the average receive an additional tenth of a millirem from nuclear reactors if 1,000 of them are deployed. Chemical plants for reprocessing the nuclear fuel may add a couple of tenths of a millirem, but the Nuclear Regulatory

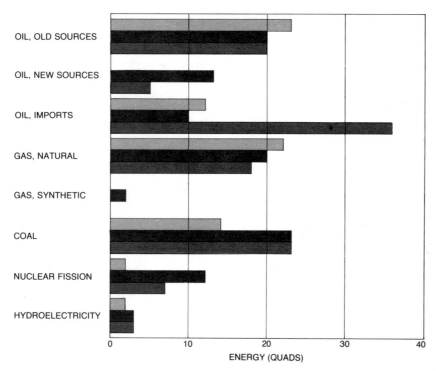

OIL, OLD SOURCES

OIL, NEW SOURCES

OIL, IMPORTS

GAS, NATURAL

GAS, SYNTHETIC

COAL

NUCLEAR FISSION

HYDROELECTRICITY

0          10          20          30          40
ENERGY (QUADS)

TWO ESTIMATES of the contribution of various fuels to the energy budget of the U.S. in 1985 are presented here along with the actual energy budget in 1973 (*light gray bars*). The chart is based on President Ford's State of the Union Message for 1975, in which he compared the expected impact of his administration's energy program (*dark gray bars*) with the expected situation if no action is taken (*colored bars*). The total U.S. energy consumption in 1973 was 75 quads; the total for 1985 in the absence of any major new programs is projected here to be about 112 quads, including some 36 quads of imported oil; Ford program, which includes a major energy-conservation effort aimed at saving about nine quads per year by 1985, envisions a total U.S. energy consumption of 103 quads for that year.

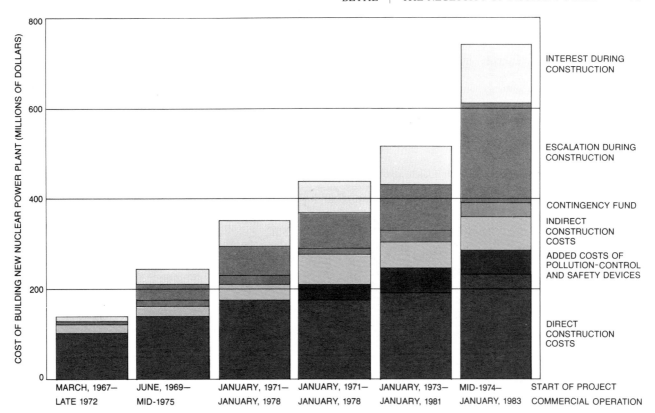

CONSTRUCTION COST of a 1,000-megawatt nuclear power plant of the light-water-reactor type has risen substantially for plants planned between 1967 and 1974 and expected to become operational between 1972 and 1983. As this ERDA bar chart indicates, however, a large fraction of the cost increase is due to inflation and interest during construction. Cost of building a coal-burning power plant has risen at a comparable rate during this period. (The bar for nuclear plants started in 1971 was revised upward in 1973.)

Commission is tightening the regulations further. In view of these very small numbers the controversy over the routine release of radioactivity, which was strong in the 1960's, has pretty much died down.

A more popular fear at present is that a reactor accident would release catastrophic amounts of radioactivity. Here it must be said first of all that a reactor is not a bomb. In particular, light-water reactors, which make up the bulk of U.S. reactors at present, use uranium fuel with a readily fissionable uranium-235 content of only 3 percent. Such material, no matter how large the amount, can never explode under any circumstances. (For breeder reactors, which can only come into operation about 20 years from now, the argument is slightly more complicated.)

It is, however, conceivable that a reactor could lose its cooling water, melt and release the radioactive fission products. Such an event is extremely unlikely, and one has never happened. There are at least three barriers to such a release. The radioactive fission products are enclosed in fuel pellets, and those pellets have to melt before any radioactivity is released. No such "meltdown"

has occurred in nearly 2,000 reactor-years of operation involving commercial and military light-water reactors in the U.S. Moreover, even if there were to be a meltdown, the release of radioactivity would be retarded by the very strong reactor vessel, which typically has walls six to 12 inches thick. Finally, once this reactor vessel melts through, the radioactive material would still be inside the containment building, which is equipped with many devices to precipitate the volatile radioactive elements (mainly iodine, cesium and strontium) and prevent them from escaping to the outside. Only if very high pressure were to build up inside the reactor building could the building vent and release major amounts of radioactivity. The chance of that happening is extremely small, even in the event of a meltdown.

One may nonetheless ask: Exactly how likely is such a reactor accident? Obviously it is very difficult to estimate the probability of an event that has never happened. Fortunately most of the conceivable failures in a reactor do not lead to an accident. Reactors are designed so that in case of any single failure, even of a major part of the reactor, the reactor can still be safely shut down. Only when

two or more essential elements in the reactor fail simultaneously can an accident occur. This makes a probabilistic study possible; an estimate is made of the probability of failure of one important reactor element, and it is then assumed that failures of two different elements are independent, so that the probability of simultaneous failure of the two is the product of the individual probabilities. This, however, is not always true. There can be "common mode" failures where one event triggers two or three failures of essential elements of the reactor; in that case the probability is the same as that of the triggering event, and one does not get any benefit from the multiplication of small probability numbers. The probability of such common-mode failures is of course the most difficult to estimate.

Working on the basis of these principles, a Reactor Safety Study commissioned three years ago by the AEC estimated the probability of various types of reactor accident. The results were published in draft form in August, 1974, in a document that has come to be known as the Rasmussen report, named for the chairman of the study group, Norman C. Rasmussen of the Massachusetts Institute of Technology. The final report was published last October.

The methods applied in the Rasmussen report have been used for several years in Britain to predict the probability of industrial accidents. Experience has shown that the predictions usually give a frequency of accidents somewhat higher than the actual frequency. Several groups, including the Environmental Protection Agency and a committee set up by the American Physical Society, have since studied various aspects of the problem and have come out with somewhat different results. Those differences have been taken into account in the final Rasmussen report; the most important of them will be discussed here.

The basic prediction of the Rasmussen report is that the probability of a major release of radioactivity is about once in 100,000 reactor-years. (Common-mode failures were found to contribute comparatively little to the total probability.) Such an accident would involve the release of about half of the volatile fission products contained in the reactor. A release of that scale would have to be preceded by a meltdown of the fuel in the reactor, an event for which the report gives a probability of once in 17,000 reactor-years. Finally, the report predicts that the water coolant from a reactor will be lost once in 2,000 reactor-years, but that in most cases a meltdown will be prevented by the emergency core-coolant system.

There is at least some check on those estimates from experience. For one thing, there has never been a loss of coolant in 300 reactor-years of commercial light-water-reactor operation. Furthermore, there has never been a fuel meltdown in nearly 2,000 reactor-years of commercial and naval light-water-reactor operation. If Rasmussen's estimate were wrong by a factor of 20 (in other words, if the probability of a meltdown were once in 850 reactor-years), at least one meltdown should have occurred by now.

What would be the consequences in the extremely improbable event of a major release of radioactivity? The immediate effects depend primarily on the population density near the reactor and on the wind direction and other features of the weather.

For a fairly serious accident (one that might take place in a million reactor-years) Rasmussen estimates less than one early fatality but 300 cases of early radiation sickness. He also predicts that there could be 170 fatalities per year from latent cancers, a death rate that might continue for 30 years, giving a total of some 5,000 cancer fatalities. In addition there might be 25 genetic changes per year; counting the propagation of such changes through later generations, the total number of genetic changes could be about 3,000.

The number of latent cancers in the final version of the Rasmussen report is about 10 times as high as it was in the original draft report; that change was largely suggested by the study of the American Physical Society, as modified by a very careful study made by the Rasmussen group. A major release of radioactivity under average weather and population conditions (probably one in 100,000 reactor-years) would cause about 1,000 latent cancers, but it would not result in any cases of early radiation sickness.

It is obvious that 5,000 cancer deaths would be a tragic toll. To put it in perspective, however, one should remember that in the U.S. there are more than 300,000 deaths every year from cancers due to other causes. A reactor accident clearly would not be the end of the world, as many opponents of nuclear power try to picture it. It is less serious than most minor wars, and these are unfortunately quite frequent. Some possible industrial accidents can be more serious, such as explosions and fires in large arrays of gasoline storage tanks or chemical explosions. The danger from dam breaks is probably even greater.

The probability of a serious reactor accident was predicted in the Rasmussen report to be once in 10,000 years when there are 100 reactors, which is about the number expected for the U.S. in the year 1980. What if the number of reac-

ROUTINE EMISSION OF RADIATION (2)    NUCLEAR REACTOR ACCIDENTS (2)

FALLS (18,000)

FIRES AND HOT SUBSTANCES (7,000)

DROWNING (6,000)

MOTOR-VEHICLE ACCIDENTS (50,000)

OTHER ACCIDENTS (30,000)

ACCIDENT RISKS estimated for the entire U.S. population as the result of the operation of 100 nuclear power plants are compared here with the risks from several leading causes of accidents in terms of the average number of deaths per year attributable to each cause. (The averages for the latter categories are rounded to the nearest 1,000 fatalities.) The figure for the risk of death from nuclear accidents is based on the conservative assumption that there is likely to be one major release of radioactivity in the U.S. every 1,000 years, resulting in about 1,000 eventual deaths from cancer, and that once in 10,000 years there could be a more serious accident resulting in approximately 5,000 eventual deaths. The average risk from nuclear reactors is obviously extremely small compared with other risks that society accepts. It must be noted, however, that the nuclear-power risk can only be predicted, whereas the other risks are actuarial, that is, derived from statistics of actual events.

COAL

OIL

URANIUM (LIGHT-WATER REACTOR)

EXPENSIVE URANIUM (LIGHT-WATER REACTOR)

EXPENSIVE URANIUM (BREEDER REACTOR)

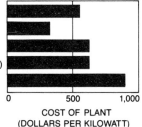

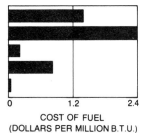

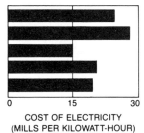

COST OF PLANT
(DOLLARS PER KILOWATT)

COST OF FUEL
(DOLLARS PER MILLION B.T.U.)

COST OF ELECTRICITY
(MILLS PER KILOWATT-HOUR)

COST ESTIMATES summarized in this bar chart were made in late 1973 by the Philadelphia Electric Company for prospective electric-power plants consuming three different types of fuel: coal, oil and uranium. The first three entries in each set of bars were made on the assumption that plant construction would start in 1974. (The bars representing fuel costs for coal and oil have been updated to 1975.) The bottom two entries refer to an indefinite date in the future when uranium is expected to become much more expensive. According to this study, electricity from nuclear fuel will continue to be substantially cheaper than that from fossil fuel.

tors increases to 1,000, as many people predict for the year 2000 or 2010? The answer is that reactor safety is not static but is a developing art. The U.S. is now spending about $70 million per year on improving reactor safety, and some of the best scientists in the national laboratories are engaged in the task. I feel confident that in 10 years these efforts will improve both the safety of reactors and the confidence we can have in that safety. I should think that by the year 2000 the probability of a major release of radioactivity will be at most once in 10 million reactor-years, so that even if there are 1,000 reactors by that time, the overall chance of such an accident will still be no more than once in 10,000 years.

Taking into account all types of reactor accidents, the average risk for the entire U.S. population is only two fatalities per year from latent cancer and one genetic change per year. Compared with other accident risks that our society accepts, the risk from nuclear reactors is very small [see illustration on opposite page].

A special feature of possible reactor accidents is that most of the cancers would appear years after the accident. The acute fatalities and illnesses would be rather few compared with the 5,000 estimated fatalities from latent cancers in the foregoing example. The problem is that many more than the 5,000 victims will think they got cancer from the radiation, and it will be essentially impossible to ascertain whether radiation was really the cause. The average probability that the exposed population will get fatal cancer from the released radioactivity is only about .1 percent, compared with the 15 percent probability that the average American will contract fatal cancer from other causes. Will the affected people in the case of a reactor accident be rational enough to appreciate this calculation? Or would an accident, if it occurs, have

a psychological effect much more devastating than the real one?

The problem of nuclear energy that is considered most serious by many critics is the disposal of nuclear wastes. Will such wastes poison the atmosphere and the ground forever, as has been charged? It is true that the level of radioactivity in a standard 1,000-megawatt reactor is very high: about 10 billion curies half an hour after the reactor is shut down. The radioactivity then decays quite quickly, however, and so does the resulting heat.

When the spent nuclear fuel is unloaded from a reactor, it goes through a number of stages. First the highly radioactive material, still in its original form, is dropped into a tank of water, where it is left for a period ranging from a few months to more than a year. The water absorbs the heat from the radioactive decay and at the same time shields the surroundings from the radiation.

After the cooling period the fuel will in the future be shipped in specially protected trucks or railcars to a chemical-reprocessing plant. (No such plant is currently in operation, but a large one is being built in South Carolina and could go into operation next year.) In the chemical plant the fuel rods will be cut open (still under water) and the fuel pellets will be dissolved. The uranium and the plutonium will be separated from each other and from the radioactive fission products. The uranium and plutonium can be reused as reactor fuel and hence will be refabricated into fuel elements. The remaining fission products are the wastes.

These substances are first stored in a water solution for an additional period to allow the radioactivity to decay further. Special tanks with double walls are now being used for that purpose in order to ensure against leakage of the solution.

After five years the wastes will be converted into solids, and after another five years they will be shipped to a national repository. Three different methods have been developed for solidifying wastes; one method now operates routinely at ERDA's reactor test station in Idaho to solidify the wastes from Government-owned reactors. The solid wastes can then be fused with borosilicate glass and fabricated into solid rods, perhaps 10 feet long and one foot in diameter. (Approximately 10 such rods will be produced by a standard 1,000-megawatt reactor in a year.) The rods are then placed in sturdy steel cylinders closed at both ends. It is difficult to see how any of the radioactive material could get out into the environment after such treatment, provided that the material is adequately cooled to prevent melting.

There are two possibilities for the national repository. One, for interim storage, would be in an aboveground desert area; the steel cylinders would be enclosed in a heavy concrete shield to protect the external world from the radiation. Cooling would be provided by air entering at the bottom of the concrete shield, rising through the space between the steel and the concrete and escaping at the top after having been heated by about 20 degrees C. Natural air circulation would be sufficient; no fans are required. The proposal for such a national repository has been studied and approved by a committee of the National Academy of Sciences.

The area required for such an interim-storage repository is not large. A standard reactor produces about two cubic meters of solid waste a year. The National Academy of Sciences committee estimated that all the wastes produced by U.S. reactors by 2010 could be stored on a tract of 100 acres. The cost is estimated at $1.5 billion, a small fraction of the probable cost of the reactors.

The second possibility for the national

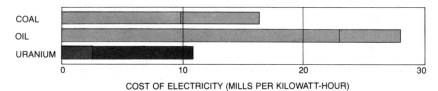

ACTUAL POWER COSTS for the first quarter of 1975 were obtained by averaging the total costs, including fuel (*color*), for 22 utilities that operate nuclear reactors as well as other plants. These figures, compiled by the Atomic Industrial Forum, are in accord with those in illustration on preceding page. (The capital investment in these currently operating plants was of course much lower than that estimated for the future plants in that example.)

repository is permanent storage deep underground. The preferred storage medium here is bedded salt, which presents several advantages. First, the existence of a salt bed indicates that no water has penetrated the region for a long time; otherwise the salt would have been dissolved. Water trickling through the storage site should be avoided, lest it leach the deposited wastes and bring them back up to the ground, an extremely slow process at best but still better avoided altogether. Second, salt beds represent geologically very quiet regions; they have generally been undisturbed for many millions of years, which is good assurance that they will also remain undisturbed for as long as is required. Third, salt flows plastically under pressure, so that any cracks that may be formed by mechanical or thermal stress will automatically close again.

The first attempt by the AEC to find a storage site in a salt mine in Kansas was unfortunately undertaken in a hurry without enough research. (Drill holes in the neighborhood might have allowed water to penetrate to the salt bed and the waste.) Now ERDA is carefully examining other sites. A promising location has been found in southeastern New Mexico. There are roughly 50,000 square miles of salt beds in the U.S.; only three square miles are needed for disposal of all the projected wastes up to the year 2010.

The method of disposal is this: In a horizontal tunnel of a newly dug mine in the salt bed, holes would be drilled in the wall just big enough to accommodate one of the steel cylinders containing waste. It has been calculated that the cylinders could be inserted into the salt 10 years after the waste comes out of the reactor. The residual heat in the waste, five kilowatts from one cylinder, is then low enough for the salt not to crack. (The high heat conductivity of salt helps here.) If the calculation is confirmed by experiment in the actual mines, the wastes could go directly from the chemical-processing plant into per-

manent disposal and interim storage would be unnecessary. Otherwise the wastes would be placed for some years in the interim repository and then be-shifted from there to permanent storage underground.

It seems to me virtually certain that a suitable permanent storage site will be found. It is regrettable that ERDA is so slow making a decision and announcing it, but after the difficulties with the Kansas site it is understandable that ERDA wants to make absolutely sure the next time.

Most of the fission products have short half-lives, from a few seconds to a few years. The longest-lived of the common products are cesium 137 and strontium 90, with half-lives of about 30 years. The problem is that the wastes also contain actinides: elements heavier than uranium. In the present chemical process .5 percent of plutonium and most of the other actinides go with the wastes. Plutonium 239 has a half-life of nearly 25,000 years, and 10 half-lives are required to cut the radioactivity by a factor of 1,000. Thus the buried wastes must be kept out of the biosphere for 250,000 years.

Scientists at the Oak Ridge National Laboratory have studied the possible natural events that might disturb radioactive-waste deposits and have found none that are likely. Similarly, it is almost impossible that man-made interference, either deliberate or inadvertent, could bring any sizable amount of radioactivity back to the surface.

The remaining worry is the possibility that the wastes could diffuse back to the surface. The rate of diffusion of solids in solids is notoriously slow, and experiments at Oak Ridge have shown that the rate holds also for the diffusion of most fission products in salt. Ultimately this observation will have to be confirmed in the permanent storage site by implanting small quantities of fission products and observing their migration.

In the meantime one can draw further confidence from a beautiful "experiment" conducted by the earth itself. It has been discovered that in the part of Africa now called the Gabon Republic there existed some 1.8 billion years ago a natural nuclear reactor. A metal ore in that area is extremely rich in uranium, ranging from 10 to 60 percent. Whereas the present concentration of uranium 235 in natural uranium is .72 percent, the concentration 1.8 billion years ago was about the same as it is in present-day light-water reactors (3 percent). The ore also contained about 15 percent water. Therefore conditions were similar to those in a light-water reactor (except for the cooling mechanism). In the natural nuclear reactor plutonium 239 was formed, which subsequently decayed by emitting alpha radiation to form uranium 235. The interesting point is that the plutonium did not move as much as a millimeter during its 25,000-year lifetime. Moreover, the fission products, except the volatile ones, have stayed close to the uranium, even after nearly two billion years.

Assuming that plutonium is made in appreciable amounts, it must be kept from anyone who might put it to destructive use. Contrary to a widespread fear, however, there is little danger that plutonium could be stolen from a working nuclear reactor. The reactor fuel is extremely radioactive, and even if an unauthorized person were to succeed in unloading some fuel elements (a difficult and lengthy operation), he could not carry them away without dying in the attempt. The same is true of the used fuel cooling in storage tanks. The places

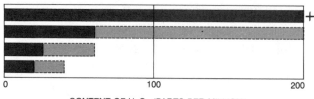

URANIUM RESOURCES OF THE U.S. are listed in this bar chart on the basis of ERDA estimates. The top row of bars refers to high-grade uranium ores. The prices throughout

from which plutonium might in principle be stolen are the chemical reprocessing plant (after the radioactive fission products have been removed), the fuel-fabrication plant or the transportation system between the plants and the reactor where the refabricated fuel elements are to be installed.

Transportation seems to be the most vulnerable link. Therefore it is probably desirable to establish the chemical plant and the fuel-fabrication plant close together, leaving only the problem of transportation from there to the reactor. Actually the problem of secure and safe transportation is essentially solved, at least in the U.S. The sophisticated safeguards now in force for nuclear weapons can be easily adapted for the transportation of nuclear materials. The protection of plants against theft is also being worked on and does not appear to present insuperable problems. For example, people leaving a plant (including employees) can be checked for possession of plutonium, even in small amounts, by means of automatic detectors, without requiring a body search. These direct measures for safeguarding plutonium are necessary and cannot be replaced by simple inventory-accounting procedures, which would be far too inaccurate. By ensuring that no plutonium (or fissionable uranium) has been diverted from U.S. plants one can be reasonably confident that no terrorists in this country can make an atomic bomb (which, by the way, is not as easy as some books and television programs have pictured it).

It has been asserted that the proposed measures for safeguarding plutonium and similar measures for protecting nuclear power plants from sabotage will interfere with everyone's civil liberties. I do not see why this should be so. The workers in the nuclear plants, the guards, the drivers of trucks transporting nuclear material and a few others will be subject to security clearance (just as people working on nuclear weapons are now). I estimate their number at less than 20,000, or less than 1 percent of our present armed forces. The remaining 200 million Americans need suffer no abridgement of their civil liberties.

Plutonium has been called the most toxic substance known. The term toxicity can be misleading in this context, because it implies that the danger lies in some chemical action of plutonium. Experiments with animals have shown that it is the level of radioactivity of the plutonium that counts, not the quantity inhaled, as is the case with a chemical poison. Nonetheless, the radioactive hazard is indeed great once plutonium is actually absorbed in the body: .6 microgram of plutonium 239 has been established by medical authorities as the maximum permissible dose over a lifetime, and an amount approximately 500 times greater is believed to lead to lethal cancer.

Plutonium can be effectively absorbed in the body if microscopic particles of it are inhaled. About 15 percent of the particles are likely to be retained in the lung, where they may cause cancer. Fortunately there is little danger if plutonium is ingested in food or drink; in that case it passes unchanged through the digestive tract, and only about one part in 30,000 enters the bloodstream. Therefore effective plutonium poisoning of the water supply or agricultural land is virtually impossible.

Some opponents of nuclear power have maintained that because of the very low maximum permissible dose even small amounts of plutonium in the hands of terrorists could cause great damage. This point has been put in perspective by Bernard Cohen, who has investigated in theory the effect of a deliberate air dispersal of plutonium oxide over a city. He finds that on the average there would be one cancer death for every 15 grams of plutonium dispersed, because only a small fraction of the oxide would find its way into people's lungs. Other, soluble compounds of plutonium would be even less effective than an insoluble oxide. A terrorist who manages to steal six kilograms or more of plutonium could probably do more damage by fashioning a crude bomb from it than by dispersing it in the air of a city.

Will the spread of nuclear reactors encourage the proliferation of nuclear weapons? That in my opinion is the only really serious objection to nuclear power. The availability of fissionable material is obviously a prerequisite for making nuclear weapons. Even after the material is available, however, the manufacture of a nuclear bomb is still a massive undertaking: in each of the six countries that have so far conducted nuclear explosions, thousands of scientists and technicians have worked on the development of the weapon. Nonetheless, a number of additional countries would be capable of this effort if they wanted to make it, and if they had the material.

Many countries in need of nuclear power will soon be in the market for the purchase of nuclear power plants from any country willing to sell them. Nuclear power plants sold in international trade are usually put under the inspection system of the International Atomic Energy Agency (IAEA) in order to ensure that no fissionable material is diverted for military purposes. The IAEA needs strengthening and more money for its force of inspectors. An important additional safeguard would be to prevent the proliferation of nuclear chemical-processing plants, since it is from those plants rather than from the reactors that fissionable material could be diverted. A good proposal is that the chemical processing be centralized in plants for an entire region rather than dispersed among plants for each nation. Another approach would be to have the country supplying the reactor lease the fuel to the customer country with the requirement that the used fuel be returned.

The original fuel for a light-water reactor is mostly uranium 238 enriched with about 3 percent of readily fissionable uranium 235. If an explosive were to be made from this fuel, the two isotopes would have to be separated, a procedure that requires a high level of technology. The used fuel contains in

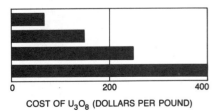

COST OF U$_3$O$_8$ (DOLLARS PER POUND)

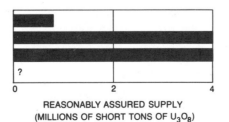

REASONABLY ASSURED SUPPLY
(MILLIONS OF SHORT TONS OF U$_3$O$_8$)

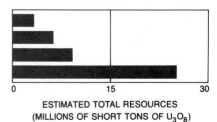

ESTIMATED TOTAL RESOURCES
(MILLIONS OF SHORT TONS OF U$_3$O$_8$)

are in 1975 dollars and include rehabilitation of the land in the case of low-grade materials (*bottom three rows of bars*). Other estimates of total resources, measured in millions of short tons of uranium oxide (U$_3$O$_8$), range up to three times those given here.

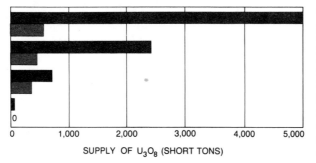

LIGHT-WATER REACTOR

HIGH-TEMPERATURE
GAS-COOLED REACTOR

CANDU REACTOR WITH
THORIUM BREEDING

BREEDER REACTOR

0

SUPPLY OF U₃O₈ (SHORT TONS)

URANIUM REQUIRED for the initial fueling (*colored bars*) and 40-year operation (*gray bars*) of a 1,000-megawatt nuclear power plant is indicated (again in millions of short tons of U₃O₈) for the four principal types of reactor system. For the breeder reactor the plutonium required for initial fueling is expected to be available as a by-product of previously operational light-water reactors. Candu is the Canadian name for their heavy-water natural-uranium reactor, which can be modified to convert thorium into the isotope uranium 233.

addition some plutonium, which can be separated from the uranium by chemical procedure, a less difficult task. The resulting plutonium has a high concentration of plutonium 240 (with respect to plutonium 239), which could be used to make rather crude bombs by a country just beginning in nuclear-weapons technology. Breeder reactors contain more plutonium per unit of power, with a smaller percentage of plutonium 240. I personally would therefore recommend that breeder reactors not be sold in international trade.

Proliferation would not be prevented if the U.S. were to stop building nuclear reactors for domestic use or if it were to stop selling them abroad. Western Europe and Japan not only need nuclear power even more than the U.S. does but also have the technology to acquire it. Moreover, they need foreign currency to pay for their oil imports and so they will want to sell their reactors abroad. The participation of the U.S. in the reactor trade may enable us to set standards on safeguards, such as frequent IAEA inspection, that would be more difficult if we left the trade entirely to others.

It has been alleged that nuclear power is unreliable. The best measure of reliability is the percentage of the time a plant is available for power production when the power is demanded. This "availability factor" is regularly reported for nuclear plants and runs on the average about 70 percent. There are fewer good data on the availability of large coal-fired plants, but where the numbers exist they are about the same as those for nuclear plants.

The "capacity factor" is the ratio of the amount of power actually produced to the amount that could have been produced if the plant had run constantly at full power. That percentage is usually lower than the availability factor for two

reasons: (1) some nuclear power plants are required for reasons of safety to operate below their full capacity, and (2) demand fluctuates during each 24-hour period. The second factor is mitigated by the operation of nuclear reactors as base-load plants, that is, plants that are called on to operate as much of the time as possible, because the investment cost is high and the fuel cost is low. A reasonable average capacity factor for nuclear power plants is 60 percent. One utility has estimated that at a capacity factor of 40 percent nuclear and coal-fired plants generating the same amount of electricity would cost about the same; operation at 60 percent therefore gives the nuclear plant a substantial edge.

But are not nuclear power plants expensive to build? An examination of the construction cost of such plants planned between 1967 and 1974, and expected to become operational between 1972 and 1983, shows that the cost of a 1,000-megawatt power plant of the light-water-reactor type has risen from $135 million to $730 million in this period [*see illustration on page 75*]. Closer inspection reveals, however, that a large fraction of the cost increase is due to inflation and to a rise in interest rates during construction; without those factors the 1974 cost is $385 per kilowatt of generating capacity. This figure represents a cost increase of about 300 percent, which is more than the general inflation from 1967 to 1974. The main cause must be looked for in the steep rise of certain construction costs, particularly labor costs, which rose about 15 percent per year, or 270 percent in seven years.

The cost of building coal-fired plants has risen at a comparable rate. A major factor here has been the requirement of "scrubbers" to remove most of the sulfur oxides that normally result from the burning of coal. Coal plants equipped

with scrubbers may still be about 15 percent cheaper to build than nuclear plants. Any massive increase in coal production would, however, call for substantial investment not only in the opening and equipping of new mines but also in the provision of additional railroad cars and possibly tracks, particularly in the case of Western mines. If this "hidden" investment is included, the capital cost of coal-burning power plants is not very different from that for nuclear plants. Even disregarding this factor the overall cost of generating electricity from nuclear fuel is already much less than it is for generating electricity from fossil fuel, and recent studies indicate that nuclear power will continue to be cheaper by a wide margin [*see illustration on page 77*].

There is some truth in the charge that "nuclear power does not pay its own way," since the Government has spent several billion dollars on research on nuclear power and several more billions will undoubtedly have to be spent in the future. On the other hand, the Government is also spending about $1 billion a year as compensation to coal miners who have contracted black-lung disease.

It has also been said that uranium will run out soon. It is true that the proved reserves of high-grade uranium ore are not very large, and the existing light-water reactors do require a lot of uranium. If all reactors were of this type, and if the U.S. were to set aside all the uranium needed for 40 years of reactor operation, then the total uranium-ore resources of the U.S. would only be enough to start up 600 reactors, a number that might be reached by the year 2000. Beyond that date it will be important to install reactors that consume uranium more efficiently. The most satisfactory alternative to emerge so far is the breeder reactor, which may be ready for industrial operation by 1990. The breeder in effect extracts the energy not only from the rare isotope uranium 235 but also from other isotopes of uranium, thereby increasing the supply of uranium about sixtyfold. Even more important, with the breeder the mining of low-grade uranium ore can be justified both economically and environmentally. With these added resources there is enough uranium in the U.S. to supply 1,000 reactors for 40,000 years [*see bottom illustration on preceding two pages*].

As interim alternatives two other types of reactor are attractive: the high-temperature, gas-cooled, graphite-moderated reactor and the Canadian natural-uranium reactor ("Candu"), which is moderated and cooled by heavy water.

The Candu reactor can be modified to convert thorium by neutron capture into the fissionable isotope uranium 233.

In weighing the overall health hazard presented by nuclear reactors it is appropriate to compare nuclear plants with coal-burning power plants. Recent findings indicate that even if scrubbers or some other technology could reduce the estimated health effects from coal burning by a factor of 10 (which hardly seems attainable at present), the hazard from coal would still exceed that from nuclear fuel by an order of magnitude [see illustration at right]. This comparison is not meant as an argument against coal. The U.S. clearly needs to burn more coal in its power plants, and even with coal the hazard is not great. The comparison does point up, however, the relative safety of nuclear reactors.

In sum, nuclear power does involve certain risks, notably the risk of a reactor accident and the risk of facilitating the proliferation of nuclear weapons. Over the latter problem the U.S. has only limited control. The remaining risks of nuclear power are statistically small compared with other risks that our society accepts. It is important not to consider nuclear power in isolation. Objections can be raised to any attainable source of power. This country needs power to keep its economy going. Too little power means unemployment and recession, if not worse.

MINING AND MILLING

TRANSPORTATION, MANUFACTURING AND OPERATION

POLLUTION

ACCIDENTS

**OVERALL HEALTH HAZARDS** presented by a nuclear power plant and a coal-burning power plant, both capable of generating 1,000 megawatts of electricity, are compared here in terms of the estimated number of deaths resulting from one year of operation. (Injuries and other health effects have been translated into equivalent deaths by a suitable formula.) The data were gathered primarily by C. L. Comar of the Electric Power Research Institute and L. A. Sagan of Stanford University. The coal-mining figure refers to underground mining; surface mining is much less dangerous. The figure for pollution from coal includes sulfur dioxide pollution only. As the second set of bars shows, even if sulfur dioxide "scrubbers" were to succeed in reducing the estimated hazard from coal-burning by a factor of 10, adverse health effects from coal power would still be greater than those from nuclear power.

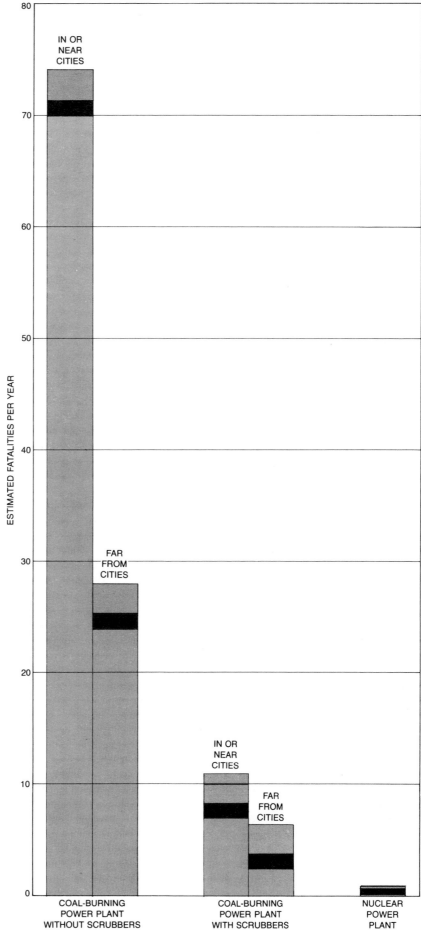

# 8

# Natural-Uranium Heavy-Water Reactors

## COMMENTARY

I f there is a nuclear future for all of us, what kinds of reactors will we use? There are a variety of models, the light-water reactors using boiling water or pressurized water being the most common in the United States and Europe. Other designs, however, may prove to be more advantageous for some purposes. In this article, Hugh McIntyre sets out the case for the Candu reactor, the heavy-water natural-nuclear fuel plant developed by the Canadian government over the past two decades. That reactor has been developed to the point where it is starting to assume a significant part in the planned energy resources of Canada. Some plants have been exported by Canada to India and Pakistan, and plans are underway for similar reactors in other countries.

It is interesting to follow McIntyre's history of the nuclear industry in Canada after World War II. It is surprising how little trouble the nuclear power industry in Canada has had in public acceptance of power-plant siting, fear of accidents, or general resistance based on fears of radiation. Perhaps it is a function of less public awareness, perhaps of a better public relations campaign. Perhaps the Canadians trust their government more than United States citizens do theirs. Whatever the reason, theirs is a success story.

Though there have been mishaps, and aspects of the design that had to be corrected after experience, the program in Canada has gone remarkably smoothly. A comparison is made by McIntyre between the United States and the Canadian experience. In the United States, General Electric and Westinghouse played a major role in the design and manufacture of plants after heavy subsidization of the basic research and development by the United States Atomic Energy Commission. In Canada, Atomic Energy of Canada Limited, a Crown Corporation, was the single entity responsible for the design and production of reactors. It may be that in this case the interrelation between the government research and development and regulatory agencies, as well as between government and industry, are more important than the inferred competition between the two major private corporations in the United States.

The advantages of the Candu system are by no means unqualified. Though it can use ordinary nuclear fuel without the necessity for the large uranium-enrichment plants needed for pressurized-and boiling-water reactors used in the United States, it needs large supplies of heavy water. Limitations on this supply have been important in restricting Canadian use of the Candu reactors to their full capacity. In addition, operation of the Candu reactors has disadvantages as well as assets. Plans are continuing for modification to improve their performance. However the Candu fares in competition with other types of reactors in the next generation, the history of how Canada planned and implemented its own nuclear power industry with self-sufficiency illustrates how complex the development of a new kind of energy technology can be.

# Natural-Uranium Heavy-Water Reactors

by Hugh C. McIntyre
October 1975

*In the U.S. power reactors are fueled with enriched uranium and are cooled by ordinary water. The Canadian "Candu" system, working with unenriched uranium and heavy water, offers interesting alternatives*

The U.S. nuclear-power industry, which has dominated the world market with its ordinary-water reactors fueled with enriched uranium, is in a period of deepening uncertainty. In spite of a clear need for nonpetroleum energy sources, a shortage of capital funds and the objections of environmentalists to the siting of nuclear power plants have created a situation in which

half of the nuclear power reactors planned for the U.S. over the next decade have been postponed or canceled. Indeed, there is much pessimism about whether nuclear power will be allowed to make its promised contribution to forestalling future energy shortages in the U.S.

Meanwhile, as opponents of nuclear power often point out, domestic uranium

supplies are being fed into uranium-235-enrichment plants at a rate that threatens to strip the U.S. of economic deposits of uranium by the year 2000. Acting with what seemed to be commendable foresight, the now superseded U.S. Atomic Energy Commission proposed to solve the long-range uranium-supply problem by developing the fast breeder reactor, which would produce more nuclear fuel

NUCLEAR POWER STATION at Pickering, Ont., has four Candu reactors. Each has a gross generating capacity of 540 megawatts of electricity (MWe); the net capacity after supplying station needs is 514 MWe. The "du" in Candu refers to deuterium oxide (heavy water) and uranium. In the Candu reactor concept deuterium oxide acts both as the moderator, for slowing down neutrons, and as the coolant, or heat-transport medium. The fuel is natural (unenriched) uranium in oxide form. The Pickering station, the first entirely commercial nuclear power facility in Canada, is owned by Ontario Hydro. First of Pickering's units began operating in 1971.

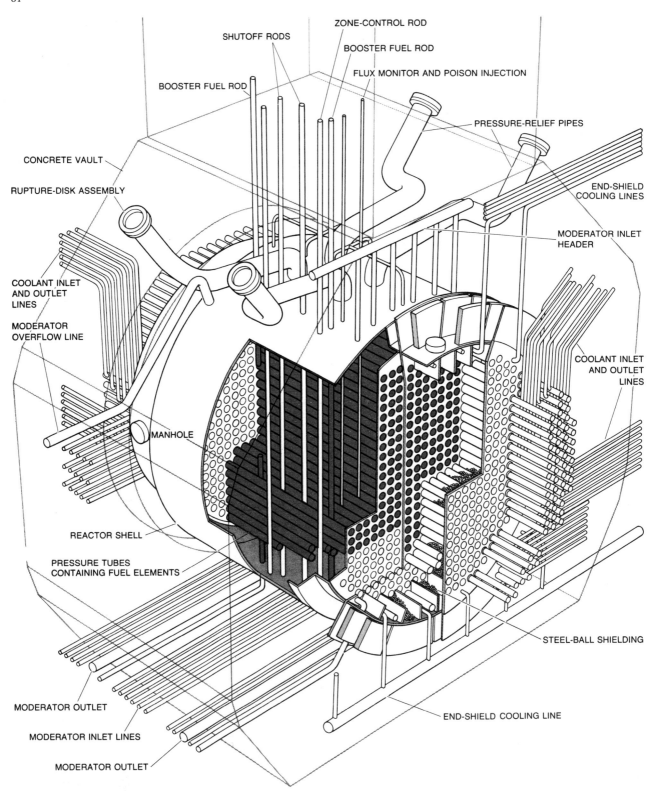

SHUTOFF RODS

ZONE-CONTROL ROD

BOOSTER FUEL ROD

FLUX MONITOR AND POISON INJECTION

BOOSTER FUEL ROD

PRESSURE-RELIEF PIPES

CONCRETE VAULT

RUPTURE-DISK ASSEMBLY

END-SHIELD COOLING LINES

MODERATOR INLET HEADER

COOLANT INLET AND OUTLET LINES

MODERATOR OVERFLOW LINE

COOLANT INLET AND OUTLET LINES

MANHOLE

REACTOR SHELL

PRESSURE TUBES CONTAINING FUEL ELEMENTS

STEEL-BALL SHIELDING

MODERATOR OUTLET

MODERATOR INLET LINES

END-SHIELD COOLING LINE

MODERATOR OUTLET

CANDU NUCLEAR REACTOR differs from U.S. nuclear power reactors not only in using natural uranium and heavy water but also in that the coolant for the Candu reactor flows through several hundred individual pressure tubes containing the fuel. In American systems the fuel elements are contained in a single massive pressure vessel through which the coolant flows (*see illustrations on pages 86 and 87*). As this diagram shows, the pressure tubes in the Candu reactor vessel are arranged horizontally. The outer shell for a reactor capable of generating 750 MWe is 28 feet in diameter, 19.5 feet long and 1.25 inches thick. The tubes are made of a zirconium alloy four millimeters (one-sixth inch) thick. The heavy,

water coolant, at a pressure of 1,450 pounds per square inch, leaves the reactor at a temperature of about 310 degrees Celsius (590 degrees Fahrenheit) and passes to a steam generator (not shown) where ordinary light water is converted into steam at a temperature of about 250 degrees C. (482 degrees F.) and a pressure of 570 pounds per square inch. The steam drives the turbogenerator that generates electricity. The many pipes that convey the coolant into and away from the reactor ultimately are gathered into two large headers that are connected to the steam generator. The Candu reactor is designed so that the fuel bundles in the individual pressure tubes can be replaced while reactor is running at full power.

| SYSTEM | CUMULATIVE LOAD FACTOR THROUGH JUNE, 1974 | ELECTRIC GENERATION (MEGAWATT HOURS) |
|---|---|---|
| CANDU REACTORS | 56.62 PERCENT | 37,065,523 |
| BOILING-WATER REACTORS | 49.89 | 189,229,239 |
| PRESSURIZED-WATER REACTORS | 49.35 | 248,553,124 |

CUMULATIVE LOAD FACTORS, expressed as a percent of design capacity over an extended period, have been consistently higher for nuclear power reactors of the Candu type than for either of two reactor types that currently supply all U.S. nuclear power. Figures in second column are cumulative load factors for all U.S. and Canadian (Candu) nuclear stations through June, 1974. Figures were assembled by *Nuclear Engineering International*.

than it consumed. The breeder program, since inherited by the Energy Research and Development Administration (ERDA), not only is running behind schedule but also has acquired its own critics. Even its supporters are beginning to ask not when the breeder will be ready but whether it will be ready before the uranium is exhausted. Moreover, not one spent-fuel recovery plant, designed to recycle U-235 and to extract plutonium for fast breeder reactors, has yet gone into operation.

Confronted with these problems, U.S. nuclear authorities are looking abroad for possible technological solutions. One promising concept that is gaining attention is the Canadian-designed line of power reactors named Candu. These reactors use deuterium oxide (heavy water) as a moderator and natural (unenriched) uranium as a fuel.

The 20-year development history of the Candu reactor is not well known outside Canada. The first prototype reactor in the Candu series went critical in June, 1962. The second reactor in the series and the first commercial installation began feeding 200 megawatts of electric power (MWe) into the Ontario power grid in 1967. The second commercial installation, a four-reactor complex at Pickering, Ont., went into operation in 1971. With a designed gross generating capacity of 2,160 MWe, it was for nearly two years the largest nuclear station in North America (until the completion of the Commonwealth Edison Zion 2 unit in Illinois surpassed it by 40 MWe). The Candu reactor concept is now available in standard "off the shelf" designs of 600- and 750-MWe capacity. Eighteen new reactors with a total capacity of some 12,500 MWe are scheduled for completion at five sites in three Canadian provinces by 1983. In addition Candu power stations are now operating in India and Pakistan; construction has been started on a station of 600 MWe in Argentina, and a similar station is planned for South Korea. It is noteworthy that Candu reactors have a record of cumulative availability that is better than that of either the boiling-water reactor or the pressurized-water reactor, which are the established power reactors in the U.S. and Europe.

Compared with the present troubled state of the U.S. nuclear industry, the history of the Candu reactors seems almost placid. There has yet to be a major public debate in Canada about the siting of a nuclear power plant. The Pickering station, for example, is within the city limits of Toronto, which has a population of 2.5 million. Although there have been several accidents and malfunctions in Candu nuclear plants, none has so far caused any injury, any radioactive contamination outside the reactor building or any stoppage in the delivery of electric power.

The use of natural uranium as fuel and heavy water as a moderator developed logically out of Canada's needs and background in reactor technology. A restrained effort to sell the Candu reactor abroad has been focused on the requirements of developing countries or medium-size developed countries outside the "nuclear club." So far Canada has made no serious effort to sell the Candu concept to U.S. utilities.

If the situation of the U.S. electric-utility industry should get worse, however, a proposal made last winter by Aaron L. Segal of Cornell University might be taken more seriously. He suggested (at hearings held in New York on Project Independence) that one way the U.S. could benefit from Canada's energy resources would be for it to finance a line of Candu stations along the border to pump electricity south, "like a giant power cow." The U.S. could also logically explore the feasibility of using light water or an organic liquid as the heat-transfer medium for a natural-uranium reactor moderated with heavy water. These are concepts that the Canadians, with limited resources, are just beginning to explore.

All the nuclear power plants built in the U.S. operate with uranium fuel that has been enriched in one of three giant gaseous-diffusion plants so that it contains between 1 and 4 percent U-235. In natural uranium the content of U-235 is only .72 percent. To sustain a nuclear reaction in a reactor fueled with either natural or enriched uranium it is necessary to use a moderator, a substance that is effective in slowing down the high-velocity neutrons released in the fission of U-235 so that they are maximally effective in splitting other nuclei of U-235. When a nucleus of U-235 splits, it releases on the average 2.5 neutrons. The objective in reactor design is to limit the loss of neutrons to competing processes so that exactly one neutron survives to split another nucleus of U-235 and thus maintain a chain reaction. The number of surviving neutrons is expressed by the multiplication factor $K$. When $K$ is less than 1, there is no chain reaction; when $K$ is greater than 1, the chain reaction proceeds exponentially. Most reactors are equipped with control rods made of a strong neutron absorber such as boron, which are automatically pushed in or out of the reactor core to maintain $K$ at exactly 1.

All nuclei absorb neutrons to a greater or lesser degree. Hence the reactor de-

| UNIT COST | PICKERING | LAMBTON (1) | LAMBTON (2) |
|---|---|---|---|
| CAPITAL | 4.60 | 1.70 | 1.70 |
| OPERATION AND MAINTENANCE | 1.10 | .96 | .96 |
| FUELING | .98 | 10.60 | 13.32 |
| HEAVY-WATER UPKEEP | .35 | | |
| TOTAL UNIT ENERGY COST (MILLS PER KILOWATT HOUR) | 7.03 | 13.26 | 16.18 |

COMPARISON OF ELECTRIC-POWER COSTS in the largest Candu nuclear power station at Pickering with costs in two equally new coal-fired units of comparable size at Lambton, Ont., shows that nuclear power is about half as expensive as fossil-fuel power. Although the capital investment at Pickering is more than two and a half times higher per kilowatt-hour than it is at Lambton, nuclear fuel and supplemental supplies of heavy water, needed for upgrading and replacement, cost only about a tenth as much as coal. It should be noted that the cost comparison is somewhat unfair to the coal units because their output changes with the demand. The nuclear station operates at maximum capacity to supply a base load.

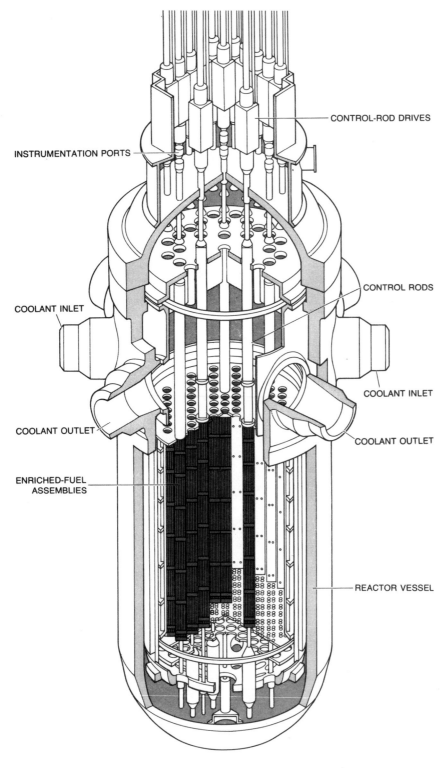

INSTRUMENTATION PORTS

CONTROL-ROD DRIVES

CONTROL RODS

COOLANT INLET

COOLANT INLET

COOLANT OUTLET

COOLANT OUTLET

ENRICHED-FUEL ASSEMBLIES

REACTOR VESSEL

**PRESSURIZED LIGHT-WATER REACTOR, developed to power U.S. nuclear submarines, is one of the two systems used in all U.S. nuclear power plants now operating (about 55). Because light water captures neutrons about 600 times more readily than heavy water does, a light-water reactor will not operate unless the fuel is enriched to contain 1 to 4 percent uranium 235 instead of the .72 percent naturally present. A pressurized light-water reactor capable of generating 1,100 MWe requires a pressure vessel about 15 feet in diameter, 45 feet tall and six to 11 inches thick. When the reactor is charged with 196,000 pounds of uranium oxide containing an average of 3.2 percent U-235, it will operate for 10 to 12 months before fresh fuel is needed. Initial charge for a 750-MWe Candu reactor is 292,000 pounds of unenriched uranium oxide. Light-water coolant is heated to 320 degrees C., and it circulates at 2,250 pounds per square inch. A separate steam generator produces steam for turbine at a temperature of 285 degrees C. and a pressure of 1,000 pounds per square inch.**

signer must carefully select all components—fuel containers, moderators, coolants and structural materials—to conserve neutrons. In addition certain fission products, such as xenon 135, have such an enormously large "capture cross section" for neutrons that they act as reactor poisons. The great virtue of heavy water as a moderator is that it has a neutron-capture cross section only about a 600th as large as the capture cross section of light water. (In Candu reactors the .2 percent of light-water impurity remaining in the heavy water captures about as many neutrons as the heavy water itself.)

If light water is used as a moderator in a power reactor, it is necessary to have a uranium fuel enriched in U-235 in order to raise the probability that at least one neutron per fission will encounter another nucleus of U-235 before being absorbed or lost from the reactor. When heavy water is used as a moderator, the concentration of U-235 in natural uranium is sufficient to sustain the chain reaction. The main drawback of heavy water, of course, is that it is fairly expensive (about $50 per pound). The compensating advantage is that the use of heavy water obviates the need for building expensive uranium-enrichment facilities or, what amounts to the same thing, buying enriched uranium from those who have the facilities.

The entire question of reactor economics, as one might suspect, is rich in controversy. In making comparisons between rival systems, utilities try to reduce everything to a single figure: the total unit energy cost (TUEC). Unfortunately it is hard to make comparisons between one country and another because of widely differing interest rates, fuel prices and operating policies. To speak only of the Canadian experience, the latest total energy cost figures from Ontario Hydro show that the Pickering nuclear station is generating power for less than half the cost of an equally new coal-fired station of similar size at Lambton, Ont. [see bottom illustration on preceding page].

The capital cost of the Pickering station came to about $365 per kilowatt of installed electric-generating capacity (KWe). It appears that the capital cost for a U.S. plant of the same size, at current prices, would be only about 80 percent as much, or roughly $300 per KWe. Thus if U.S. enriched-uranium reactors had been installed at Pickering instead of Candu reactors, Ontario Hydro might have saved .9 mill per kilowatt-hour (KWh) in capital cost plus another .35 mill per KWh in heavy-water upkeep charges. On the other hand, the indications are that enriched fuel in the U.S. is now about five times as expensive as Candu natural-uranium fuel, amounting to a credit of 3.9 mills per KWh in Pickering's favor. On that basis a station similar to Zion 2 would produce power at a cost of about 9.6 mills per KWh if it were sited in Ontario, whereas Pickering produces power for 7.03 mills. This conclusion might be disputed, but it is nevertheless clear that the Candu system is at least competitive with current U.S. nuclear generating systems.

The Candu system has other points in its favor. Unlike U.S. light-water reactors, in which the entire reactor core is enclosed in a single large pressure vessel with a wall as much as a foot thick, the Candu system has fuel rods encased in individual pressure tubes [*see illustration on page 84*]. Although the U.S. pressure vessels are acknowledged to be well designed and extremely safe, it is evident that the failure of one pressure tube or even several in a Candu reactor would have less serious consequences than a break in a large pressure vessel. In the event that one of the pipes supplying cooling water to a U.S. reactor should rupture, the reactor core would have to be cooled promptly by water from an emergency cooling system. How successfully such a system would operate in a real crisis is a matter of earnest dispute. The Candu reactors have a similar emergency cooling system, but in addition a large volume of heavy-water moderator, isolated from the heavy-water cooling cycle, is constantly available to absorb heat in a coolant-loss accident. A final safety advantage of the Candu scheme is the use of on-power fueling, which means that a smaller quantity of heat from decaying fission products is stored in the reactor at any one time than is stored in U.S. reactors, in which fission products accumulate for nine or 10 months between refuelings. On-power refueling also increases the overall availability of Candu reactors to the utility operator. No one of these features was chosen in isolation to enhance the characteristics of the system. Rather, each one stemmed logically from Canada's political, economic and technological position during the decade (1954–1964) in which Candu was developed.

Although assigning the paternity of any complex technical enterprise, involving the ideas of scores of contributors, is hazardous, it is generally acknowledged that the principal credit for the Candu concept goes to W. Bennett Lewis, who was appointed director of

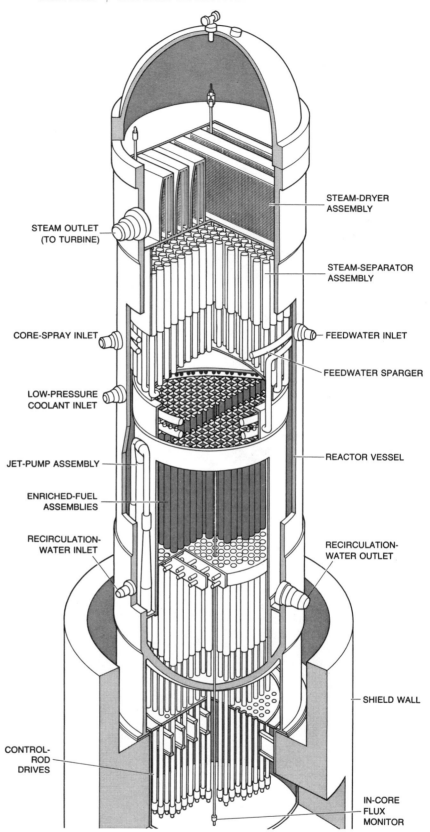

STEAM-DRYER ASSEMBLY

STEAM OUTLET (TO TURBINE)

STEAM-SEPARATOR ASSEMBLY

CORE-SPRAY INLET

FEEDWATER INLET

FEEDWATER SPARGER

LOW-PRESSURE COOLANT INLET

JET-PUMP ASSEMBLY

REACTOR VESSEL

ENRICHED-FUEL ASSEMBLIES

RECIRCULATION-WATER INLET

RECIRCULATION-WATER OUTLET

SHIELD WALL

CONTROL-ROD DRIVES

IN-CORE FLUX MONITOR

BOILING-WATER REACTOR requires a pressure vessel about three times larger in volume than the vessel needed for a pressurized-water reactor of the same power output. Therefore the vessel for a 1,065-MWe boiling-water reactor would be about 21 feet in diameter and 76 feet high. The vessel walls need to average only about six inches in thickness because the operating pressure of the vessel is only 965 pounds per square inch. The fuel charge is 362,000 pounds of uranium oxide containing an average of 1.1 percent U-235. Steam is generated in reactor and enters turbine at a temperature of about 280 degrees C. Like the pressurized-water reactor, boiling-water reactor must be shut down for refueling.

the Chalk River Nuclear Laboratories in 1946 after a distinguished wartime career in Britain in the development of radar. When Lewis came to Chalk River, a small community some 125 miles west of Ottawa, he found an isolated branch of the Manhattan project left over from World War II. The chief technical effort at Chalk River had been the design and construction of ZEEP-1 (Zero-Energy Experimental Pile No. 1), a reactor moderated by heavy water in which uranium 238 would be transmuted into plutonium. ZEEP did not, in fact, go critical until after the first atomic bomb had been dropped on Hiroshima. By 1947, however, a much larger heavy-water research reactor, NRX, was completed and a still larger one was planned, although it was not finished until 1957.

The design and operation of such reactors trained a corps of specialists in reactor physics, chemistry and engineering with special experience in heavy-water technology. Lewis recognized perhaps more clearly than anyone else that this resource of trained manpower could be used to develop a power reactor that employed heavy water as a moderator and natural uranium as a fuel. The concept would enable Canada to exploit her large resources of uranium without becoming involved in U-235 enrichment, which was then and for many years thereafter a secret technology. In this way Canada, and other nations if they wished, could enjoy the benefits of nuclear power without undertaking work that was closely associated with weapons technology.

In August, 1951, Lewis presented "An Atomic Power Proposal" to C. J. Mackenzie, president of Canada's National Research Council. Mackenzie passed the proposal on to C. D. Howe, Minister of Trade and Commerce, who responded favorably. The document, which was not declassified until 1955, listed three Chalk River findings that indicated the feasibility of a natural-uranium power reactor. First, the operation of NRX showed that energy could be extracted from uranium at a cost from a third to a fourth that of the equivalent thermal output from coal or oil, at prevailing prices. Second, one could expect that a charge of 15 tons of natural uranium, in the form of uranium oxide, would provide an output of 400,000 thermal kilowatts, equivalent after conversion to 120,000 KWe. Third, the system seemed capable of producing steam at 550 degrees Fahrenheit and a pressure of 1,500 pounds per square inch. Although these values were well below the temperatures and pressures achieved in modern fossil-

fuel power plants, they would compare favorably with temperatures and pressures achieved in enriched-fuel light-water reactors. The key to the concept was, in Lewis' words, "neutron economy." In order to conserve the much weaker neutron flux from unenriched uranium, every effort had to be made to prevent the thermal (slowed-down) neutrons from being absorbed before they could trigger new fissions in the fuel.

Following Lewis' proposal machinery was set in motion to initiate a Canadian nuclear-power effort. A Crown corporation, Atomic Energy of Canada Limited (AECL), was commissioned in 1952 to exploit the commercial possibilities of nuclear energy. The first board of directors included Richard L. Hearn, the general manager of Canada's largest utility, Ontario Hydro, which was already anticipating a shortage of new hydroelectric sites and was increasingly committed to thermal power generation.

In January, 1954, a group of engineers detached from Canadian utilities was assembled at Chalk River under the leadership of Harold A. Smith (now Ontario Hydro's vice-president for engineering and operations). They were to get an accelerated course in reactor physics from AECL personnel before designing a nuclear power plant. By 1955 a tripartite agreement was concluded: AECL would provide the scientific backing, Ontario Hydro would operate the demonstration power reactor and the Canadian General Electric Company would have the prime responsibility for the design and manu-

facture of the components. The three participants were to split the costs on a 70-25-5-percent basis. Eight of the senior Chalk River engineers moved to Peterborough, Ont., under J. S. Foster (now president of AECL) to undertake the actual engineering design of the Nuclear Power Demonstration plant (NPD).

The engineering group under Smith, which remained at Chalk River, was armed with a report, NPG-5, that summarized the reflections of Chalk River on the project. NPG-5 envisioned that the reactor would be enclosed in a pressure vessel, similar to those in U.S. designs, and that the fuel rods would consist of metallic uranium tightly jacketed in a light metal to resist attack by water.

Smith and his engineering group immediately began to modify NPG-5. In place of a pressure vessel they proposed that the fuel rods be enclosed in individual tubes through which the heavy-water coolant would flow at a pressure of 1,450 pounds per square inch. The heavy-water moderator would surround the tubes and would be roughly at atmospheric pressure. The pressure-tube configuration, which closely resembles the design of steam boilers in fossil-fuel power plants, was perhaps the most important single decision in the development of the Candu system.

The Chalk River scientific group had no objection to the pressure-tube scheme, but it pointed out that the tubes would interpose a substantial mass of potentially neutron-absorbing material among the fuel rods, which would not be the

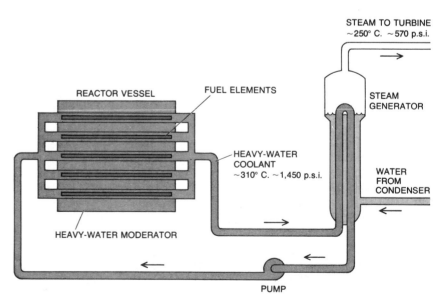

ORIGINAL CANDU CONCEPT (left) is compared with two variations in an advanced stage of development. In the first of the two variations (middle) light water replaces heavy water as the coolant and is allowed to boil inside the reactor, thereby producing steam directly to drive a turbine. In the second variation (right) the coolant is terphenyl, an

case in the pressure-vessel arrangement. In order to conserve the precious neutrons the pressure tubes would have to be made out of a material, such as zirconium, with a small neutron-capture cross section. At first this requirement baffled the design engineers; zirconium was so new as a commercial metal that neither reliable mechanical specifications nor accurate cost figures were available. Quoted prices ranged all the way from $60 to $500 a pound. Finally a new zirconium alloy called Zircalloy-2, developed for the U.S. submarine-reactor program, was found to be satisfactory.

The next change the engineering group made in the original NPG-5 design was to turn the reactor on its side so that the pressure tubes would be horizontal. In this way the structural members needed to support the reactor would not interfere with the hundreds of inlets in the reactor face for coolant, fuel and instruments. Loading a long, heavy fuel bundle into a narrow, hot horizontal tube presented problems of handling. The engineers asked: Why not cut the fuel elements into short lengths?

The physicists responded enthusiastically. Cutting the elements into chunks opened the way to shuffling the fuel, thereby solving the problem of getting the maximum burnup out of all the fuel in the reactor core. Burnup is expressed as the number of megawatt-days of thermal power generated per ton of fuel. In the typical case of a single long fuel element the region near the midpoint, which is exposed to the highest neutron

flux, may achieve a burnup of 10,000 megawatt-days per ton, whereas the ends of the element, which are exposed to a much lower flux, may reach only 40 percent of that value. A stubby element, on the other hand, could be inserted into the fuel channel at one end and gradually pushed into the central core by the insertion of more short pieces. By the time the element was finally ejected at the other end of the channel it would have achieved a burnup of nearly 10,000 megawatt-days, 30 times what had been thought possible only five years earlier.

The final significant change worked out in this interaction between engineers and scientists was the substitution of uranium oxide fuel for metallic fuel. The oxide fuel is better able to retain fission products, including gaseous ones, at high temperature without swelling. It also resists attack by water. Only its much lower thermal conductivity militated against it. That deficiency was solved by bundling together a number of thin oxide rods coated with Zircalloy, through which the heavy water would circulate. By December, 1956, a new report, NPG-10, was drafted by the Chalk River engineering-development group and was given to the Peterborough design-engineering group for assessment. The demonstration reactor envisioned in NPG-10 was essentially the Candu reactor of today.

The first prototype embodiment of the NPG-10 power reactor, the Nuclear Power Demonstration plant, was de-

signed to generate 22 MWe, a tenth of what was considered a commercial scale at the time. The NPD was sited 30 miles up the Ottawa River from the Chalk River Nuclear Laboratories. Even the modest scale of nuclear engineering required by the reactor was a challenge to existing Canadian manufacturing facilities.

For example, the vessel enclosing the reactor core was made of aluminum sheets with a total thickness of 1¼ inches, shaped into a cylinder 15 feet long and 17 feet in diameter. The fabrication of the vessel required 200 separate joints, which consumed two tons of weld metal. The welds were checked by taking 12,000 radiographs, which revealed 50 initial defects necessitating the removal of 20 feet of weld. Repeated inspections showed that there was only about a 50 percent chance of correcting the defect on the first try. The second round of inspection disclosed 26 remaining defects, the third round 13, the fourth round seven, the fifth round five and the sixth round none.

Further lessons were learned during the operation of the NPD. In the first attempt at refueling while the reactor was running, two leaks in the head of the fueling machine, operating at 1,200 pounds per square inch, allowed 75 tons of heavy water to escape over a period of two days until the leaks could be repaired. As fast as the heavy water leaked out it was collected in a sump and pumped directly back into the reactor, impure and oily as it was, to keep the fuel cool. The total volume of leakage

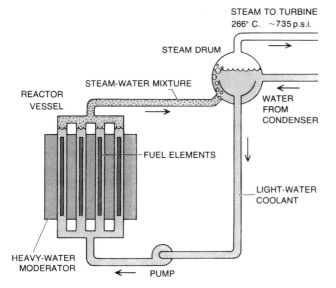

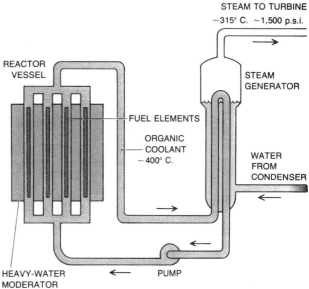

organic liquid with a boiling point much higher than that of water. With terphenyl as a heat-transport medium it should be possible to generate turbine steam with a temperature of at least 315 degrees C. (599 degrees F.), thereby raising the overall thermal effi-

ciency of a nuclear power plant from present value of 30 percent to 35 percent. (Modern fossil-fuel generating stations achieve 40 percent.) Atomic Energy of Canada Limited has been operating an experimental organic-cooled reactor at Whiteshell, Man., since 1966.

| CANDU POWER REACTORS | START-UP DATE | GENERATING CAPACITY (MEGAWATTS) |
|---|---|---|
| ROLPHTON, QUE.: NUCLEAR POWER DEMONSTRATION PLANT (NPD) | 1962 | 22 |
| DOUGLAS POINT, ONT.: OPERATING | 1967 | 200 |
| GENTILLY, QUE.: BOILING LIGHT WATER (BLW) (EXPERIMENTAL) | 1971 | 250 |
| UNDER CONSTRUCTION (CONVENTIONAL CANDU) | 1979 | 600 |
| PICKERING, ONT.: OPERATING | 1971 | 4 × 540 |
| UNDER CONSTRUCTION | 1980 | 4 × 540 |
| BRUCE, ONT.: UNDER CONSTRUCTION | 1976 | 4 × 745 |
| PLANNED | 1982 | 4 × 750 |
| POINT LEPREAU, N.B.: UNDER CONSTRUCTION | 1980 | 600 |
| DARLINGTON, ONT.: PLANNED | 1983 | 4 × 800 |
| PAKISTAN: OPERATING (KARACHI) | 1971 | 125 |
| INDIA: OPERATING (RANA PRATAP) | 1972 | 2 × 200 |
| PLANNED (KALPAKKAM) | 1980 ? | 2 × 200 |
| PLANNED (NARORA) | 1980 ? | 2 × 200 |
| ARGENTINA: UNDER CONSTRUCTION (RIO TERCERO) | 1979 | 600 |
| SOUTH KOREA: PLANNED (WOLSUNG) | 1980 | 600 |

**EIGHT CANDU POWER REACTORS, ranging in output from 200 to 540 MWe, are now operating in three countries. The count does not include the 22-MWe Nuclear Power Demonstration plant (NPD), which proved out the Candu concept, and the 250-MWe experimental unit at Gentilly, Que., which uses light water instead of heavy water as a coolant in a reactor that otherwise follows the Candu scheme. The two Candu units at Rana Pratap were a Canadian-Indian project in which Indian companies made many of the components. Candu-type units planned for Kalpakkam and Narora will be completed without further Canadian aid. Plutonium for India's nuclear explosion of 1974 was "cooked" in a small heavy-water natural-uranium reactor, a copy of Canada's NRX reactor at Chalk River, Ont.**

exceeded the total inventory of heavy water normally required in the NPD both as a moderator and as a coolant.

With the experience gained with the NPD, plans were drawn up for the first commercial station, to be located at Douglas Point, directly west of Toronto on the eastern shore of Lake Huron. This 200-megawatt station would be financed by the Canadian government and owned initially by the AECL but would be purchased by Ontario Hydro "as soon as it was operating efficiently." Two principal changes were made in designing the Douglas Point reactor: the vessel enclosing the reactor core was fabricated of stainless steel instead of aluminum, and a small number of "booster rods" containing slightly enriched uranium were introduced so that the reactor could be restarted faster after a shutdown. Otherwise the changes were few, since the original target date for the completion of the Douglas Point station

was 1964, only two years after the first operation of the 22-MWe prototype.

In spite of an intensive program of development, a variety of problems led to delays that prevented the start-up of the Douglas Point station until early in 1967. From the outset the seals on the transport pumps that circulated the heavy water leaked badly. Within a few months the station had to be shut down so that the pumps could be rebuilt and fitted with controlled-leakage throttle bushings. Ever since then the reactor operators have found it difficult to control the flow of heavy-water coolant because of the large gland flow required by the new bushings. To date Douglas Point's cumulative availability has been disappointing: only 45 percent compared with 60 percent for the NPD prototype.

To be fair it should be noted that much of Douglas Point's downtime can be attributed to a persistent shortage of

the most critical component of the Canadian nuclear-power program: heavy water. Many familiar with the problem blame the heavy-water drought upon an American company, the Deuterium Corporation. That company held patents to variants of the GS hydrogen sulfide ion-exchange process, which was used by the U.S. to produce heavy water at Savannah River, Ga., and was subsequently licensed to AECL.

The Deuterium Corporation persuaded political authorities in the coastal province of Nova Scotia to back its plan for producing heavy water at Glace Bay, near the depressed coal town of Sydney on Cape Breton Island. AECL refused to provide Deuterium Corporation's Canadian affiliate, Deuterium of Canada, with financial assistance but agreed to buy its product. Unfortunately the Sydney plant produced only a trickle of heavy water before it was forced to shut down, defeated by insoluble design problems and by corrosion caused by the use of salt water as a coolant. The Deuterium Corporation managed to sell its interest, leaving Nova Scotia with a useless $90-million plant. The plant has now been completely rebuilt by AECL at a cost of more than $100 million and is about to be restarted.

Following the collapse of the Deuterium of Canada venture AECL was left without a domestic supply of heavy water. Canadian General Electric was thereupon persuaded to build a plant at Port Hawkesbury in Nova Scotia. Beset by various problems of its own, the plant nevertheless proved capable by 1967 of achieving more than half of its design capacity of 400 tons of heavy water per year, using AECL's version of the GS process. Unfortunately for General Electric it had contracted to sell heavy water on an unrealistic declining price schedule, which turned out to be far below the prevailing world price of about $50 per pound. When the contract price fell to $17 per pound early this year, General Electric asked for relief. AECL has now agreed to buy back the plant for $90 million, a figure that at least allows General Electric to recover its investment.

Meanwhile the domestic success of the Candu concept had led to an acute shortage of heavy water in 1970. In order to provide heavy water for the four-reactor Pickering station, AECL had to buy the heavy-water inventory of the experimental Swedish Marviken heavy-water station for $11.9 million and pay an additional $55.8 million to the U.S. for almost two million pounds of heavy water extracted at Savannah River. A few million dollars' worth of heavy water was even imported from the U.S.S.R. in 1970 and 1971.

In spite of these purchases AECL had to juggle its limited heavy-water supplies. For example, Douglas Point had to be shut down in order to get enough heavy water to start up the larger and more efficient Pickering station. Douglas Point was subsequently restarted with heavy water borrowed from Quebec's first nuclear station at Gentilly. The plant at Gentilly is an experimental prototype to test the performance of a modified Candu system using heavy water as a moderator but light water as a coolant. The shortage of heavy water finally came to an end with the completion late in 1973 of a heavy-water plant with an annual design capacity of 800 tons, built by AECL at Bruce, near Douglas Point. The plant has since been bought by Ontario Hydro.

Roughly one ton of heavy water is needed for each additional megawatt of installed Candu capacity. At present the Bruce plant and a plant half as large at Port Hawkesbury are running at just over 70 percent of their design capacity. The start-up of the rebuilt Glace Bay plant will provide a total annual production of about 1,000 tons, or enough for a nuclear-power growth rate of 1,000 MWe per year. Beginning in 1980, however, Ontario Hydro alone expects to expand its nuclear capacity at the rate of 2,500 MWe per year. In addition AECL

has further commitments to Quebec and New Brunswick, and obligations to Argentina, South Korea and Britain as well. To provide the needed heavy water Ontario Hydro is building three more heavy-water plants, all at the Bruce site, bringing total capacity to 3,200 tons per year. (Some of the process heat for heavy-water production is being supplied by nuclear steam from the Douglas Point nuclear station.) AECL will supplement the heavy-water production of its two Nova Scotia plants with 800 tons per year from a plant at La Prade, near the Gentilly nuclear site. The total projected output of all the Canadian plants (assuming that they will operate at 70 to 75 percent of capacity) is 3,500 tons of heavy water per year, worth some $350 million at current prices.

As Canada's only utility with experience in nuclear engineering, Ontario Hydro has taken the lead in modifying the Candu concept. Its cautious approach is typical of a large utility, and it has stayed with the basic Candu concept for stations projected well into the 1980's. On the other hand, it has worked steadily to improve the details of the system: instrumentation, pumps and other subsystems needed to minimize leakage of the costly heat-transfer medium. Wherever possible, sophistication has been replaced by simplicity.

The performance of the 2,160-MWe Pickering station, in spite of a construc-

tion strike that delayed the completion of the first unit by nine months and an operators' strike that shut the plant down for a few months in 1973, has been exemplary. In February, 1973, the fourth unit was operating at full power only 12 days after first going critical—a record for any type of power reactor. Since the first two units went into service they have operated at a capacity factor of 80 percent (equivalent to producing 80 percent of theoretical capacity at continuous full power). Unit No. 4 has achieved a record capacity factor of 93 percent. Only unit No. 3, shut down for half of 1974 because of cracks in its pressure tubes, has scored no better than 65 percent.

The cracking incident, the only major technical malfunction at Pickering so far, led to vigorous corrective action. Within three months, at the end of 1974, a total of 17 leaking tubes were identified and were removed from the radioactively hot core. The tubes were sent to Chalk River, where it was determined that the tiny cracks (less than an inch in length) were in regions of high residual stress near rolled joints, and had resulted from faulty rolling technique. The cracks propagated only during cold shutdown; at operating temperature the zirconium hydride that had propagated the crack was reabsorbed into solution. Replacement tubes were installed within three months and the unit was restarted in April of this year. Similar tubes in unit No. 4 and in two of the Bruce units were

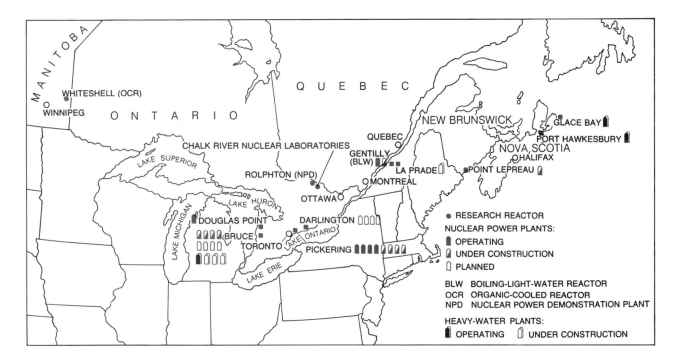

CANDU REACTORS AND HEAVY-WATER PLANTS are in four of Canada's 10 provinces. Candu reactors now supply 14 percent of the power in one province, Ontario. (For the U.S. as a whole nuclear energy supplies 8.5 percent.) The three heavy-water plants now operating have a capacity of 1,600 tons per year. When units now under construction are completed, capacity will be 4,800 tons.

removed and were relieved by repetitive stressing as a precaution against further cracking. A correct rolling technique was prescribed for all future tube installations.

It is perhaps obvious that the strength of the Candu system in contributing to the country's energy self-sufficiency is more than simply technical. It is also a matter of social organization. In contrast to the U.S. system of encouraging private industry to develop nuclear power under the supervision of public authorities at various levels, the Canadian approach has been one of government-guided development. Work on the Candu concept has from the first been a partnership involving a governmental regulatory authority (the Atomic Energy Control Board), a public development organization (AECL) and private manufacturers (mainly Canadian General Electric and Westinghouse of Canada), together with publicly owned utilities.

Unlike General Electric and Westinghouse in the U.S., which respectively promoted the boiling-water reactor and the pressurized-water reactor, no Canadian company was large enough to act as both a supplier and a designer of complete nuclear power stations. For a brief period in the 1960's the Civilian Atomic Power Department of Canadian General Electric attempted to fill this role. It sold one complete station to Pakistan, the Kanupp reactor, which went critical in 1971 and is still operating successfully (although not yet at its design capacity of 125 MWe because of limitations in the associated power grid).

Encouraged by this success, Canadian General Electric tried to market its own version of the Candu system, named HWR. This system was similar to the Candu one but had vertical pressure tubes. After a year or so without contracts the company liquidated the operation. Most of the designers and engineers were absorbed back into AECL's "power projects" group, and Canada was back to a single reactor-design group.

As things now stand (and they have changed very little since 1962) the Atomic Energy Control Board is the final authority in Canada's nuclear affairs. It regulates the siting, the design and the safety and security systems of all nuclear installations; the manufacture, transport and utilization of all nuclear equipment, nuclear fuel and other radioactive material, and all import and export of nuclear commodities and equipment. In its major actions the board works closely with its sister government organization AECL (from which it draws most of its personnel). This is not to say that there is always perfect harmony among the regulatory authorities. For example, AECL would like to sell more reactors abroad than the Atomic Energy Control Board has so far allowed it to.

There is no question that the Canadian government was acutely embarrassed by India's underground nuclear explosion in 1974. AECL had regarded India as an apt pupil in nuclear matters. The Canada-India Research reactor (CIR) in Trombay in which India "cooked" its plutonium (from its own natural uranium) was a copy of Chalk River's NRX, and Canada contributed technical assistance and a major share of the cost. AECL also took a prominent part in aiding and financing a two-unit power station of the Candu type at Rana Pratap. The Indian effort was a joint one in which AECL deliberately tried to encourage Indian self-sufficiency, including the development of a local component-manufacturing industry. The success of the policy is suggested by the fact that even when Canada had cut off all nuclear trade and aid after the 1974 explosion, India's Atomic Energy Commission announced that it was proceeding with two more two-unit stations of the Candu type at Kalpakkam and Narora. It conceded, however, that their completion might be delayed by as much as five years as a result of the withdrawal of Canadian help.

At present Canada's nuclear firms have full order books. For example, in Ontario the first unit of the 3,000-MWe Bruce station will start up early next year, with all four units scheduled to be operating by 1978. By that time the project of doubling the size of the Pickering station will be in full swing, with completion scheduled for 1985. By then another 3,000-MWe station will be well under way at the Bruce site and still another 3,000-MWe station at Darlington will have been started, with completion scheduled for 1984. By 1980 two more 600-MWe nuclear units will be in operation, one at Gentilly in Quebec and the other at Point Lepreau in New Brunswick; they will be the first commercial units in each province. Manitoba Hydro, still busy completing a huge hydroelectric system on the Nelson River, has intimated that it will make a nuclear commitment by 1980.

Beyond this, Candu stations will be running by 1979 at Rio Tercero in Argentina (which has built an expensive heavy-water prototype plant of its own at Atucha). A unit of similar size should be operating a year later in South Korea. Both countries have expressed interest in a second unit.

Meanwhile in Britain the nuclear authorities have recognized a technological gap between its gas-cooled, graphite-moderated reactor program and the fast breeder reactor, which is expected to prevail in the future. The gap, expected to last for at least a decade, is being filled by the "steamer," a heavy-water moderated, vertical-pressure-tube reactor using slightly enriched uranium, which owes much to the Candu experience and for which Canada has agreed to supply 1,000 tons of heavy water by 1980.

AECL scientists and engineers, however, are far from complacent about today's Candu system. They point out several major weaknesses: the pressurized-heavy-water coolant cannot be raised to a temperature high enough to generate steam of a pressure and temperature comparable to that in conventional fossil-fuel stations. The Candu units therefore require large turbines with a special blade design to prevent erosion from wet steam. If a way could be found to generate hotter and higher-pressure steam from a Candu reactor, the overall thermal efficiency of the station could be raised from the present 30 percent to about 40 percent, which is now achieved in the best fossil-fuel power plants.

Another deficiency is that the Candu reactor cannot be controlled as finely as the utilities would like. Among the fission products of uranium 235 is iodine 137, which decays in a few minutes to gaseous xenon 135. The last has such an enormously large capture cross section for thermal neutrons that even in low concentrations it can devour enough thermal neutrons to lower $K$ below the critical value of 1. When a Candu reactor is running at close to full power, the steady-state equilibrium between the neutron flux and the concentration of xenon 135 is such that criticality is maintained. If one wanted to cut back the reactor abruptly to half power because of lower power demand, however, the delicate equilibrium would be upset and the reactor would "poison out," that is, shut itself down. The reactor cannot be restarted until the xenon 135 decays into daughter products with lower capture cross sections, which takes about 40 hours. This deficiency is overcome in the latest Candu designs by the insertion of rods of slightly enriched uranium.

Finally, Candu reactors, like the present generation of U.S. reactors, are admittedly wasteful of uranium because of their once-through fueling. Even Canada, richly endowed with uranium though it is by world standards, sees an increasing shortage, even for its own purposes, by the end of the century. AECL believes some relief can be gained by turning to a thorium cycle in a reactor that is something less than a true breeder. AECL experts state that with little, if any, change in the Candu reactor it should be possible to burn thorium in combination with either U-235 or plutonium. Calculations show that a self-sufficient thorium cycle with a capacity of 1,000 MWe could be launched with an initial inventory of no more than 1,200 metric tons of natural uranium to provide the initial supply of U-235. In the thorium cycle the common isotope of thorium, thorium 232, is converted to fissionable uranium 233 by the absorption of a neutron.

Meanwhile, until the development work on the thorium cycle has progressed further, AECL is pursuing a more direct route toward upgrading the

low efficiency of the all-natural-uranium cycle. It has nearly completed a modest fuel-fabrication pilot plant at the Chalk River Nuclear Laboratories to produce plutonium-enriched uranium fuel elements for testing in research reactors. The idea is to add about half a gram of plutonium 239 to each kilogram of uranium. Since a kilogram of natural uranium contains 7.2 grams of U-235, the "spiked" fuel would contain a total of 7.7 grams of fissionable material. Even with this minor enrichment it should be possible to approximately double the total power output of each fuel pellet before it must be replaced. The anticipated improvement is from 8,000 megawatt-days per ton to 15,000 megawatt-days.

In addition to considering new fuel cycles for Candu, AECL is restudying heat-transport mediums. A prototype reactor using light water as a coolant instead of heavy water has been operating at Gentilly since 1971. A research reactor at Whiteshell in Manitoba has been operating since 1966, cooled by ter-

phenyl, an organic liquid that boils at something above 700 degrees F.

Ontario Hydro is directing its efforts toward operating the present Candu reactors more efficiently. One proposal is to run the reactors at close to full power and to store excess steam at high pressure in large underground caverns to handle peak loads. Another use for off-peak steam would be to supply a large-scale district heating system. Since the Pickering station is less than 20 miles from downtown Toronto, engineers of Ontario Hydro have been studying district-heating systems in Sweden to see how they might be adapted to Canadian circumstances. Another attractive possibility, based on the use of waste heat rather than on primary steam production, is for year-round fish farming. A feasibility study is now under way to see how the waste heat from a nuclear power station can be used most effectively for aquaculture. In Canada's frigid climate heat must be considered a valuable resource rather than a pollutant.

HEAVY-WATER PLANT on the shore of Lake Huron at Bruce, Ont., is the towers beyond the smokestack at right center in this photograph. On the point beyond the towers is the Bruce Nuclear Power Station, which is still under construction. The domed building in the left foreground is the Douglas Point Nuclear Power Station, the prototype of the Candu system. When the Bruce heavy-water plant is completed in 1980, it will consist of four units with a total capacity of 3,200 tons per year. Only one unit is now in opera- tion. A typical sample of water from Lake Huron, which supplies the Bruce plant, contains from 145 to 148 molecules of deuterium oxide in every million molecules of water. The separation of deuterium oxide from light water is carried out by a modified distillation process that exploits the fact that deuterium oxide has a slightly higher boiling point than light water: 101.52 degrees C. as against 100 degrees at normal atmospheric pressure. The distillation process yields deuterium oxide with a minimum purity of 99.75 percent.

# 9

## Superphénix:
## A Full-Scale Breeder Reactor

### COMMENTARY

A recurring question about nuclear reactors is the future supply of uranium ore. There is no doubt that the fission reactors of various kinds all use up our high-grade uranium fuel at a rapid rate, so rapid that some economic geologists have estimated the exhaustion of high-grade ore in the United States if there is an extensive program of building conventional nuclear power plants by the year 2000. In the breeder reactor, whose operation is discussed in this article by Georges Vendryes, fuel is actually produced as well as used. The breeder reactor, then, is the clear choice for nuclear power if we have to conserve uranium reserves. The picture today includes some disparity between government and private estimates of uranium reserves, partially because some have estimated ultimate resources and others, only proven reserves. Whatever the precise numbers, it is likely that 20 years from now uranium reserves will be much less plentiful and much more expensive. Thus the quest for the breeder reactor.

The breeder has excited much controversy in the United States for several reasons. The safety issue has troubled many, particularly with the liquid-sodium moderated breeder now seen as the model likely to be developed in this country. The fact that the breeder will produce plutonium on a large scale is also disturbing in view of the prospects for nuclear proliferation among the many nations using such reactors. Some fear that terrorists will sooner or later gain access to such plutonium and be able to make a crude bomb. Consequently, we are going much more slowly in developing a breeder than we might have anticipated a few years ago. The costs of just a prototype to test reactor materials is now in the vicinity of a billion dollars.

French nuclear engineers, however, have been systematically exploring the breeder over the past 10 years, first with Rapsodie (from *rapide* and sodium) and then Phénix, and now with the planned Superphénix. This reactor is designed to use liquid-sodium coolant for the intense heat generated, a choice that is being followed by most of the working groups in all countries with active research breeders. Sponsored by a consortium of leading European electric companies, Superphénix will be the working prototype of the commercial breeder of the future. If successful, it will lead to a major power source with minimum fuel depletion, all that was hoped for in nuclear power.

Phénix and Rapsodie had good running and relatively accident-free records. If Superphénix can be built with the same kind of relative speed as its fore-runners and is able to operate without difficulty, it will go a long way to overcoming resistance to this step in advancing nuclear power. Though nuclear power has had a relatively quiet history in Europe, in the last few years there has been an increasing public controversy akin to that in the United States. There were large demonstrations in France and Germany in 1977 and 1978, and in 1978, Austria, in a referendum, rejected operation of a nuclear reactor that had already been built. Sweden had a change of government partly because of the nuclear power issue. Yet Superphénix is being built, and France is already counting on its contribution to its nuclear future, for France's oil and gas supplies are small and much of its coal reserves are depleted. All of the countries developing breeders will be hoping for the best from the French scientists and engineers.

# Superphénix: A Full-Scale Breeder Reactor

by Georges A. Vendryes
*March 1977*

*The decision has been made to begin the construction in France of a 1,200-megawatt breeder-reactor power station. The joint European project will be the prototype of future nuclear plants*

The need to resort to nuclear fission to help meet the anticipated world demand for energy over the next few decades is widely, if not universally, recognized. What is often not appreciated sufficiently, however, is the fact that if the construction of new nuclear power plants is limited to the same basic types of reactor generally in service today, the respite gained will be only a brief one. Most experts agree that at current prices the world's economically recoverable uranium reserves are inadequate to ensure a lifetime supply of fuel for light-water nuclear reactors built after the year 2000. This means that unless uranium is used in a more efficient way than it is in such reactors, it will turn out to be an energy resource not very different in scale from oil.

Only breeder reactors—nuclear power plants that produce more fuel than they consume—are capable in principle of extracting the maximum amount of fission energy contained in uranium ore, thus offering a practical long-term solution to the uranium-supply problem. Breeder reactors would make it possible to obtain some 50 times more energy from a given amount of natural uranium than can be obtained with present-day light-water reactors. Hence the minimum uranium content of economically recoverable ore could be significantly lowered. For these two reasons (of which the second is by far the more important) the useful supply of natural uranium could be greatly enlarged. Uranium would then constitute a virtually inexhaustible fuel reserve for the world's future energy needs.

Recognizing the importance of these considerations, a number of nations have undertaken intensive research programs aimed at developing an economically competitive breeder reactor before the uranium-supply situation becomes critical. Last fall a consortium of major European electric-utility companies, acting through a joint subsidiary, decided to start the construction of a 1,200-megawatt breeder-reactor power plant at Creys-Malville in France. The new full-scale breeder reactor, named Superphénix, will be described here. First, however, it is necessary to explain just what is meant by the term breeding, which serves to characterize the operation of such plants.

Two types of heavy isotope are present in the active core of every nuclear reactor. One type, called the fissile (or fissionable) isotope, undergoes most of the fission reactions and is the source both of the heat energy released by the reactor and of the neutrons that sustain the chain reaction in the core. The only fissile isotope that exists in nature is uranium 235, which constitutes .7 percent of natural uranium; the nonfissionable isotope uranium 238 accounts for the remaining 99.3 percent. Two other fissile isotopes, plutonium 239 and uranium 233, are expected to play an increasingly important role in the future as substitutes for uranium 235.

The second type of heavy isotope in the core of every reactor is said to be fertile; it undergoes practically no fission reactions, but by capturing a stray neutron a fertile nucleus can be transmuted into a fissile nucleus at the end of a series of radioactive disintegrations. A typical example of a fertile nucleus is uranium 238, which is transmuted by neutron capture into fissile plutonium 239. Similarly, fertile thorium 232, the only form of thorium extracted from the ground, can be transmuted into fissile uranium 233.

In every nuclear reactor, as the fissile nuclei are being consumed new fissile nuclei are being created by the transmutation of fertile nuclei. Most reactors in operation today, however, use either ordinary (light) water or deuterated (heavy) water to moderate, or slow, the neutron flux in the active core. In such a slow-neutron reactor it is impossible to produce as many fissile nuclei by neutron capture as are consumed. As a result the proportion of fissile nuclei in the fuel quickly falls below a certain minimum level, and the depleted fuel must be removed from service with most of the fertile nuclei still not transformed. A set of special conditions must be satisfied to raise the breeding ratio (the ratio of the amount of fissile material produced from fertile material to the amount of fissile material consumed during the same period) to a value greater than 1. The most favorable conditions for breeding are obtained when fissile plutonium 239 and fertile uranium 238 are used together in a fast-neutron reactor, in which the neutrons from the fission reactions are not slowed down by a moderating substance such as water between the time they are emitted by one fission reaction and the time they cause the next reaction. Only under these conditions can the breeding ratio be raised to a value significantly higher than 1.

In a fast-neutron reactor the initial fuel load of plutonium is needed to start the fission chain reactions and the production of power. During this period plutonium is bred from natural uranium (or from uranium depleted in uranium 235) in the reactor core and in the surrounding "breeding blanket." When the fuel subassemblies that make up the core and the blanket have undergone prolonged neutron irradiation, they must be reprocessed chemically in order to separate and remove the fission products. In each reprocessing operation more plutonium is recovered than existed at the start of the irradiation. The excess plutonium is set aside and is replaced in the reactor by natural or depleted uranium. Everything proceeds as though the reactor were consuming only natural or depleted uranium and simul-taneously furnishing new plutonium as a by-product of the plant's operation.

The time required for a breeder reactor to produce enough plutonium to fuel a second identical reactor is called the reactor's doubling time. This time factor is inversely proportional to the reactor's breeding ratio. In the future it is expected that breeding ratios on the order of

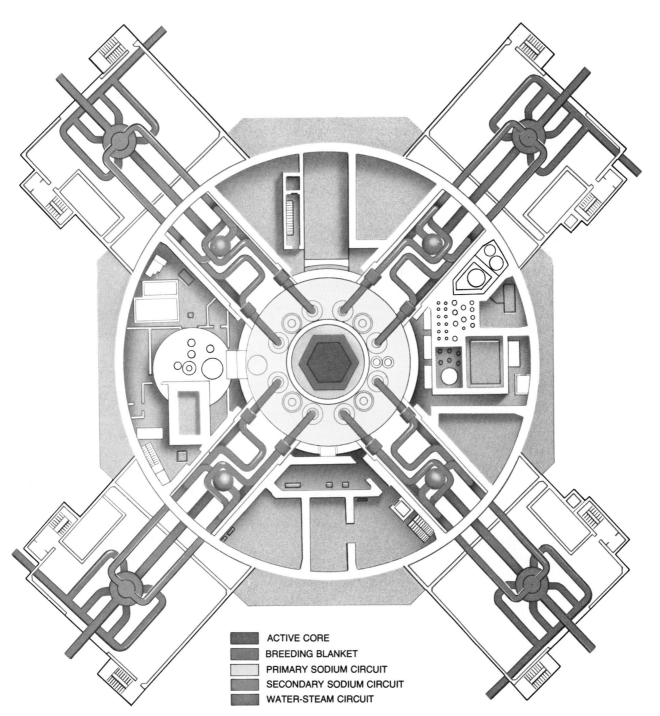

ACTIVE CORE
BREEDING BLANKET
PRIMARY SODIUM CIRCUIT
SECONDARY SODIUM CIRCUIT
WATER-STEAM CIRCUIT

**HORIZONTAL SECTION of the proposed Superphénix breeder-reactor power station shows the overall layout of the plant, which will consist essentially of a large circular reactor building with four steam-generator buildings laid out radially around it. The central reactor building, which is designed to house all the plant's nuclear components, will be built of reinforced concrete one meter thick; the building will have an inside diameter of 64 meters and a height of about 80 meters. Each steam-generator building will serve one segment of the** secondary sodium circuit. (The associated turbogenerator building is not shown in this view.) The site selected for Superphénix is at Creys-Malville in France. Construction of the plant has received the backing of a consortium of European utilities, representing France (51 percent), Italy (33 percent), West Germany (11.04 percent), the Netherlands (2.36 percent), Belgium (2.36 percent) and the United Kingdom (.24 percent). The color coding adopted for this drawing and the ones on the next three pages is given in the key at the bottom.

98

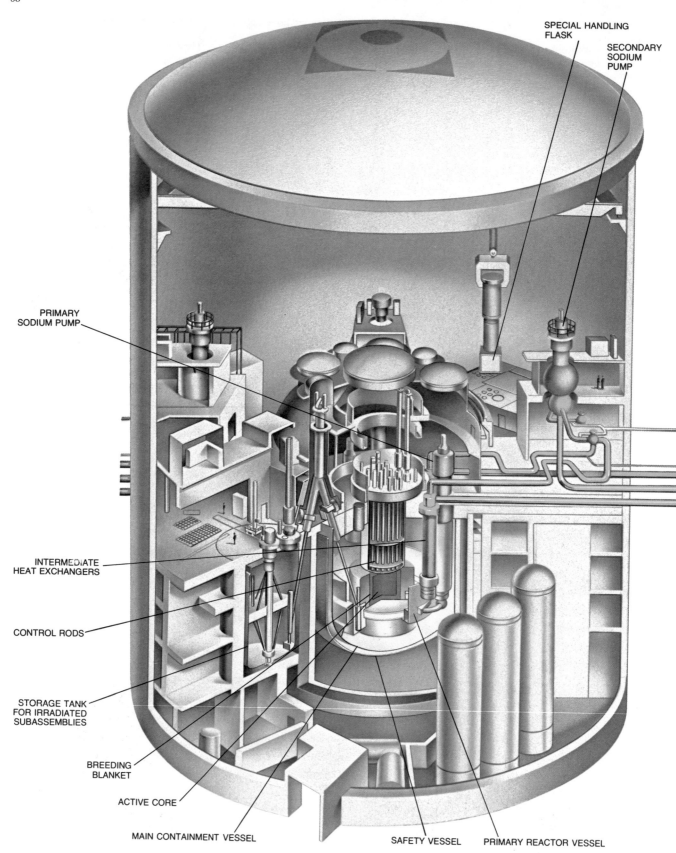

PRIMARY
SODIUM PUMP

SPECIAL HANDLING
FLASK

SECONDARY
SODIUM
PUMP

INTERMEDIATE
HEAT EXCHANGERS

CONTROL RODS

STORAGE TANK
FOR IRRADIATED
SUBASSEMBLIES

BREEDING
BLANKET

ACTIVE CORE

MAIN CONTAINMENT VESSEL

SAFETY VESSEL    PRIMARY REACTOR VESSEL

**VERTICAL SECTION** of the Superphénix reactor building and one of the four identical steam-generating buildings shows the main operating components of the plant in somewhat greater detail. Superphénix is classified as a pool-type breeder reactor, which means that the active core, the primary sodium pumps and the intermediate heat exchangers are all located within a single large vessel; in this particular design the main steel containment vessel, which is hung from a steel-and-concrete upper slab, is 21 meters across and is filled with

3,300 tons of molten sodium. A cylindrical structure welded to the main vessel supports the control-rod mechanism and the fuel subassemblies, which constitute the active core of the reactor. The four primary pumps convey the sodium upward through the core. The primary reactor vessel separates the "cold" sodium, which enters at the bottom of the subassemblies at a temperature of 395 degrees Celsius, from the "hot" sodium, which leaves at the top at 545 degrees C. The hot sodium then flows downward through the eight intermediate heat

1.4 or so will be achieved, in part by exploiting the concept of the heterogeneous core [see illustration on next page]. The corresponding doubling times will then be between 10 and 20 years. Since it is unlikely that the consumption of electricity will double at shorter intervals toward the end of the century, a doubling time in this range will enable fast-neutron reactors to cope with the rising demand for energy unaided, by virtue of their self-fueling feature.

The breeding ratios of the fast-neutron reactors built today are not significant, since for several years the plutonium produced by light-water reactors will constitute the major, if not the exclusive, source of the initial fuel for fast-neutron reactors. Thus a remarkable complementarity exists between these two types of nuclear reactor. Over a fairly long period a two-pronged strategy of nuclear-power generation can be established, with the light-water plants leading the way for the gradual penetration of the market by the fast breeder plants.

Although fast-neutron plants are capable of producing more plutonium than they consume, that potential can be exploited or not. At the discretion of the user plutonium production can be higher or lower than consumption. The amount of plutonium available can be matched exactly to the demand, whether the latter rises, remains stable or even declines; hence a stock of unused plutonium need never be created. In the absence of fast-neutron reactors, on the other hand, it would be impossible to completely burn the plutonium and its transplutonium derivatives produced by the slow-neutron plants. These highly radioactive elements would constitute wastes that would have to be set aside and stored for thousands of years.

The fact that fission reactions are caused by fast neutrons in a breeder reactor makes the dimensions of the core very compact; the core volume of a 1,000-megawatt fast-neutron plant does not have to exceed 10 cubic meters. Fast-neutron reactors by their very nature generate a great deal of heat per unit of volume. To remove this intense heat output from the fuel subassemblies that make up the reactor core it is necessary to use a coolant endowed with outstanding thermal properties. Water is unsuitable because hydrogen is a powerful neutron moderator, and any material of that kind must be avoided.

Of all conceivable fluids molten sodium is the one that combines the most attractive array of properties. A liquid at 98 degrees Celsius, it boils at 882 degrees C. at atmospheric pressure. Since the maximum sodium temperature in the reactor core never exceeds 550 degrees C. in normal operation, it is not necessary to pressurize the vessels and the circuits that contain the sodium. More-

over, the excellent thermal properties of sodium mean that the steam produced in the steam generators has characteristics equivalent to those required to drive the turbines of the most modern fossil-fuel power plants. The overall efficiency of a fast-neutron reactor is equal to or greater than 40 percent, whereas the efficiency of a typical light-water power plant does not exceed 33 percent; the comparatively high efficiency of fast-neutron reactors is a positive feature with respect to thermal discharges into the environment.

Every fast-neutron reactor that has been or is being built in the world today calls for molten sodium as the coolant. The fact that all the countries with active breeder programs (including the U.S., the U.S.S.R., France, Britain, West Germany, the Benelux nations, Italy, Japan and India) have made the same basic technological choice is a very favorable factor. It avoids the spreading of effort mounted along divergent lines and enhances overall efficiency. The approach followed has been much the same in all the countries involved. Reactors built and planned during the still prevailing development phase belong to three categories that follow in a logical succession: experimental reactors, demonstration plants and prototype power stations.

In line with this logical sequence the forerunners of Superphénix were Rapsodie and Phénix. The experimental reactor Rapsodie (the name associates the words *rapide* and sodium) was commissioned in 1967. Its power level is low (40 megawatts of thermal output) and it does not produce any electricity. Nevertheless, its main features are representative of the breeder regime from a technical standpoint with respect to temperature and other factors. Rapsodie has operated in a satisfactory manner for almost 10 years, with an average availability of nearly 90 percent during the operating runs. It is in continuous use as a test facility for investigating the effects of prolonged irradiation on various fuel assemblies.

One year after Rapsodie went into operation the decision was made to build the Phénix demonstration plant, named for the mythological bird that was reborn from its own ashes. The achievement of a high breeding ratio was not of particular concern in the design stage. The principal purpose of Phénix was to confirm the validity and reliability of the entire system by demonstrating the possibility of building a fast-neutron power plant within a reasonable period of time and of running it satisfactorily. Phénix was put into regular operation in July, 1974. The record of the first two years is particularly gratifying. These excellent results do not mean that the demonstration is over. The day-to-day operation of the reactor is being closely watched, and unforeseeable incidents

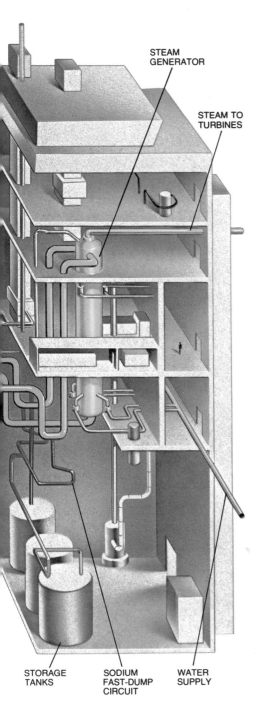

STEAM GENERATOR

STEAM TO TURBINES

STORAGE TANKS

SODIUM FAST-DUMP CIRCUIT

WATER SUPPLY

exchangers, which form part of a secondary circuit of nonradioactive sodium, inserted for reasons of safety between the primary sodium circuit and the water-steam circuit. Each of four secondary loops consists of two intermediate heat exchangers, a secondary pump installed inside spherical expansion tank and a steam generator in the adjacent building.

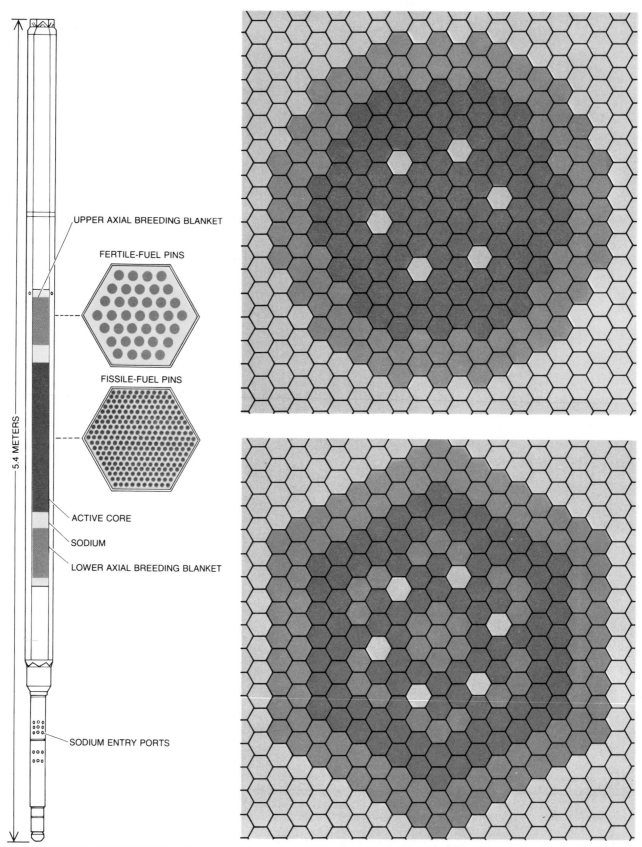

UPPER AXIAL BREEDING BLANKET

FERTILE-FUEL PINS

FISSILE-FUEL PINS

ACTIVE CORE

SODIUM

LOWER AXIAL BREEDING BLANKET

5.4 METERS

SODIUM ENTRY PORTS

**NUCLEAR-FUEL SUBASSEMBLY** of the Superphénix reactor is shown in the cutaway vertical diagram at left. In each active-core subassembly the fuel is subdivided into 271 long, thin pins along which the sodium of the primary circuit (*yellow*) flows; the fissile material (*red*) occupies the central portion of the pin, fertile material (*orange*) being placed at both ends. (The fertile subassemblies contain fewer, larger pins.) Two alternative core designs under consideration for the breeder reactors of the future are represented by the sche-matic horizontal sections at the right. The two designs differ in the arrangement of the stainless-steel subassemblies: in the conventional core design (*top*) the central zone of fissile subassemblies is surround-ed by an outer "breeding blanket" of fertile subassemblies; in the new heterogeneous core design (*bottom*) fertile material is inserted into core in the form of clusters of fertile subassemblies. Gray hexagons are control rods. Designs are idealized here; in reality active core and breeding blanket will account for a total of about 600 subassemblies.

could still occur. Small sodium leaks detected during the summer of 1976 in two intermediate heat exchangers have led to the temporary shutdown of the plant for repairs to the observed defects, which are minor and do not call the design into question. The initial results are considered encouraging enough to proceed with confidence.

Superphénix, the next step in the development sequence, will be the prototype for the commercial breeder power plants of the future. In design it is very similar to Phénix. It was thought essential for overall efficiency and success to maintain the continuity of technological choices as far as possible. In spite of this constraint continuous progress in acquired know-how led in some cases to significant changes with respect to Phénix, if only to meet increasingly stringent safety criteria. Creys-Malville, where Superphénix will be built, is in the upper Rhône valley, not far from the electric-power grids of Italy and Germany. The site selected for the plant, on the banks of the Rhône 40 miles east of Lyons, is in a sparsely populated farming region where no other major industrial projects are planned.

From the geological standpoint the Creys-Malville site is in a low-seismicity zone of Degree VI on the international macroseismic scale (which has a range of 12 degrees, with an interval of one degree corresponding to a factor of two in ground acceleration). The Superphénix plant is designed to continue operating after being subjected to a Degree VI earthquake, which corresponds to the maximum intensity already observed in the region. Furthermore, the design guarantees that all essential safety functions of the plant, such as the neutron shutdown of the reactor, the removal of residual power from the core and the integrity of the containment, will be maintained in the event of an earthquake of Degree VII in intensity.

The Superphénix power station will be designed to adapt its operation to variations in demand on the electric-power grid. It will be operated as a baseload plant. The gross power output of the plant has been set at 1,200 megawatts of electricity, which is similar to the power level of light-water nuclear plants scheduled for construction at the same time. In 1985, 1,200 megawatts will represent between 1.5 and 2 percent of the total installed power of the French grid. The choice of this figure for Superphénix results from a compromise. On the one hand there is a trend toward large nuclear power plants on the grounds of economics; on the other hand extrapolation from Phénix to Superphénix must remain within reasonable limits.

A fast breeder plant does not differ greatly in its general layout and operating scheme from any other nuclear pow-

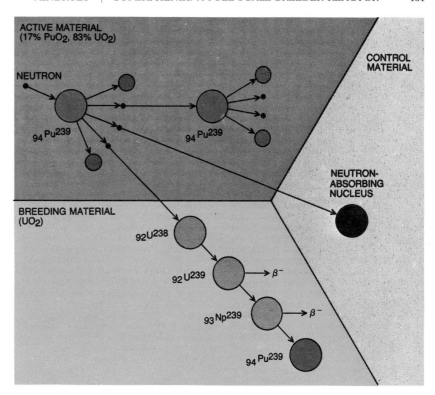

NUCLEAR REACTIONS that take place in the core of a breeder reactor are diagrammed. As in any nuclear reactor, the fissile active-core material (in this case plutonium 239) undergoes a self-perpetuating chain of fission reactions, yielding both the heat energy produced by the reactor and the neutrons that sustain the chain reaction. In the breeder fertile nuclei in the core and in the blanket material (in this case uranium 238) can also be transmuted into fissile nuclei by capturing a stray neutron each, thereby creating new fissile material. The absorption of neutrons by nuclei in the control rods can be adjusted to regulate the rate of the reactions (right). In a "fast" breeder the neutrons are not slowed down by a moderating substance such as water.

er station. Heat produced in the reactor core is conveyed by a fluid (molten sodium in this case) to water, producing steam, which feeds an electric-generating turbine unit. In order to avoid any accidental reaction between the radioactive sodium and the water an intermediate, or secondary, loop of nonradioactive sodium is inserted between the primary circuit conveying the sodium through the core and the water-steam circuit. Instead of one 1,200-megawatt turbogenerator of advanced design, two 600-megawatt units will be used in parallel, incorporating only conventional equipment that has proved its reliability in many oil-fired plants.

The design of the core and the fuel assemblies is a key factor in the realization of Superphénix. The core, as the seat of heat generation, is the most highly stressed of all the parts of a nuclear plant. This is all the more true in a fast-neutron core, where the heat production per unit of volume is exceptionally high (up to 500 kilowatts per liter) and all the structures are subjected to an intense flux of fast neutrons ($6 \times 10^{15}$ neutrons per square centimeter per second). To ensure that the heat is evacuated without giving rise to excessive temperatures the nuclear fuel is subdivided into long, thin pins (less than a centimeter in diameter) along which the sodium flows at a

speed of six meters per second. The fissile material is located in the central portion of the pin, fertile material being placed at both ends. A cluster of 271 pins are fastened together within the hexagonal stainless-steel structure known as a fuel subassembly. All together 364 subassemblies, packed in a regular array, constitute the reactor's active core, which is in turn surrounded by 232 similar subassemblies containing larger pins of fertile material, representing the breeding blanket. The sodium flows upward, entering at the bottom of the subassemblies at 395 degrees C. and leaving at the top at 545 degrees. At the center of the active core 450 watts of heat energy is generated per centimeter of fuel pin.

A fuel mixture with a mean composition of 17 percent plutonium oxide ($PuO_2$) and 83 percent uranium oxide ($UO_2$) has been selected as the fissile material; the fertile material consists of uranium oxide alone. Long and satisfactory experience with these materials has been gained in the operation of Rapsodie and Phénix. Of the 25,000 $PuO_2$-$UO_2$ fuel pins that have been irradiated so far in Rapsodie, 3,000 survived a burnup of 80,000 megawatt-days per ton and some have reached 150,000 megawatt-days per ton. Less than one pin per 1,000 irradiated failed. So far

PHÉNIX, a 250-megawatt demonstration breeder-reactor power station, is located on the Rhône River near Avignon. The plant began generating electricity at full power in July, 1974.

15,000 fuel pins have been irradiated in the Phénix core. At present subassemblies are taken out of the reactor as soon as they reach a burnup of 50,000 to 65,000 megawatt-days per ton. Not a single pin has failed while in service in Phénix.

Development work is also being devoted to new carbide and nitride fuels, which are likely to exhibit breeding characteristics superior to those of the oxides of plutonium and uranium currently called for. It remains to be seen whether this potential advantage will be offset by increased difficulties in fabrication, irradiation behavior and chemical reprocessing. The use of carbide and nitride fuels in Superphénix is not contemplated at this time.

Another important technical problem concerns the choice of the material for the hexagonal structure of the subassemblies and for the pin tubes, which must meet very stringent requirements. They must maintain good mechanical strength at temperatures approaching 650 degrees C. Furthermore, the internal pressure in the pin tubes may be as high as 30 kilograms per square centimeter, owing to the buildup of gaseous fission products. The pins are also subjected to considerable thermal stresses. Last but not least, they are exposed to a peculiar phenomenon: under prolonged irradiation by fast neutrons, vacancies form in the crystal lattice of the metal and grow into tiny cavities, causing the metal to swell. Some idea of the intensity of neutron bombardment in a high-power fast-neutron reactor can be gained from the fact that every atom of the material "cladding" the fuel pins is struck or at least caused to vibrate once

every 100 hours on the average by the passage of a neutron or another atom recoiling from a neutron collision. Another impressive figure is the cumulative number of fast neutrons crossing any given square centimeter of the cladding material after irradiation in the reactor core: this figure approaches one full gram of neutrons! The swelling of metallic alloys under neutron irradiation must be kept low enough to avoid deformation of the subassembly, which is liable to raise problems in the operation of the reactor, particularly in the fuel-handling maneuvers. A great deal of research-and-development work has already been accomplished but more is required in order to find a complete solution to the problem.

The different types of fast-neutron reactor are distinguished essentially by the organization of the primary sodium circuit. In the pool design the reactor core, the intermediate heat exchangers and the primary sodium pumps are all within a single large vessel. In the loop design only the reactor core is housed within the vessel and the intermediate heat exchangers and pumps are connected to it by loops. It must be stressed that the two systems rely on the same technology, that most development work on components is common to both and that the differences between the two concepts are much less than those between, say, pressurized-water and boiling-water reactors. In most countries loop-type reactors were built first, since the separation of components facilitated construction, operation and maintenance, justifying such a choice at an early stage of development. The first pool-type

breeder reactor in the world was built in the U.S. more than 10 years ago. Following the loop-type construction of Rapsodie, the pool concept was adopted for Phénix and, owing to the excellent record of that plant, it was maintained fundamentally unchanged for Superphénix.

It is clear that both the pool system and the loop system can be built and run, and that both have advantages and drawbacks only long operating experience can distinguish. Among the main reasons for the selection of the pool system for Phénix and Superphénix, following a meticulous comparison with the loop system, was a safety consideration. For a large plant, say 1,000 megawatts or more, it was thought the integrity of the primary sodium circuit could be maintained in all reasonably foreseeable circumstances more readily by enclosing it within a single vessel of simple design than by dispersing it in a highly intricate system of pipes and vessels involving many hundreds of meters of piping up to one meter in diameter. Although the main pool-type vessel is larger than the loop-type reactor vessel (roughly 20 meters in diameter as against 10), the pool-type vessel is much more straightforward in design. As a result construction, inspection and maintenance are far easier. The main problem encountered in the pool design concerned the cover of the main vessel. The solution implemented in Phénix could not be extrapolated to the dimensions of Superphénix. It was decided to hang the steel main vessel directly from the steel-and-concrete upper slab, and to put under the slab a layer of metallic thermal insulation that is in contact with the argon atmosphere above the sodium. The tests performed to date indicate that this arrangement is entirely satisfactory.

Experience with nuclear power plants of every type has shown that the steam generator is a crucial component. In fast-neutron reactors particular care must be taken in design and construction to prevent any violent chemical reaction between the sodium and the water, which would result from a leak in the exchanger tubes. The steam-generator model selected for Phénix, the only one with which extensive experience had been gained at the time, was subdivided into 36 low-power modules (17 megawatts each). The subdivision made it possible to subject three complete full-scale modules to thorough tests in simulated operational conditions. Although this approach was justifiable for an initial project, it could not be maintained for a large power plant because of its prohibitive cost. Research for Superphénix was therefore oriented toward units of different design, with a higher power per unit (several hundred megawatts). The problems presented by the fabrication and the operation of these units did not appear to grow with size, but the large modules do have certain drawbacks, the main ones being the near impossibility of conducting full-scale tests prior to installation in the power plant and the increased electric-power loss in case of the unavailability of a unit.

The tests performed under normal and accidental conditions on two "once through" mock-ups, one with straight ferritic steel tubes and the other with helical Incoloy tubes, provided complete satisfaction and showed good agreement with the design forecasts. The helical-tube model was finally selected for Superphénix, with each secondary loop including a steam generator with a thermal power of 750 megawatts. A steam-reheat stage can be added with either sodium or steam. The sodium system was employed for Phénix, raising the net efficiency of the plant to 42 percent. The steam system was adopted for Superphénix, simplifying the steam generator and the associated circuits, because a cost study showed that the lowered investment cost offset the loss in efficiency.

It is obviously important to prevent the development of even the smallest leak in the tubes separating the water from the sodium and to minimize the effects of any contact of the two fluids that may nevertheless occur. Ultrasensitive hydrogen detectors (capable of detecting a leak of as little as two milligrams of hydrogen per second) will be housed in several locations in each steam generator. Automatic systems designed to limit the consequences of an incipient reaction are also available. Two such systems consist of automatic valves that immediately shut off the sodium circuits and discharge systems designed to remove the products of the reaction and to limit the ensuing pressure surge.

The maneuvers required to convey the fuel subassemblies to their core positions and to withdraw them from the reactor after irradiation will be conducted exclusively during plant shutdown. They will be carried out by a series of devices that manipulate the assemblies in sodium at all times, in order to allow the removal of the residual heat released by the fission products. Two eccentric rotating plugs housed in the upper slab of the reactor will make it possible to position the device that grips the subassembly heads above any point of the core and blanket. This system, which allows direct service above each subassembly, also copes with potential deformations of the subassemblies due to swelling under irradiation. One of the main drawbacks of sodium is its opacity, which makes it impossible to follow

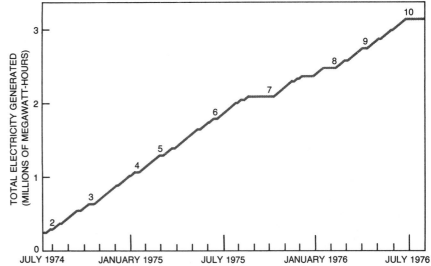

OPERATING RECORD OF PHÉNIX during its first two years was considered encouraging enough to proceed with Superphénix, the next stage in the French breeder-development program. The level parts of this cumulative electric-generating curve correspond to plant shutdowns; the numbers refer to refueling shutdowns. An extended work period scheduled after one year of operation took place during seventh refueling shutdown. In its first two years of operation Phénix generated electricity at full power for the equivalent of 530 days, a better performance than is typical of present-day light-water reactors in their first two years of operation.

the progress of the handling operations visually. Ultrasonic transmitter-receiver units, employing the principle of sonar, have been developed to surmount this obstacle. These devices, operating within the sodium itself, provide a guarantee that the subassemblies manipulated will occupy their correct positions at all times, without the risk of colliding with the handling devices.

The principles underlying the control of a fast-neutron reactor are identical with those of any other nuclear reactor. The existence of delayed neutrons gives the mechanisms acting on core reactivity the time to act smoothly, whether to raise or lower the power of the plant or to keep it stable. These operations are performed by means of control rods containing a suitable neutron-absorbing material, which move in channels parallel to the fuel subassemblies. Superphé-

|  | PHÉNIX | SUPERPHÉNIX |
|---|---|---|
| GROSS ELECTRICAL RATING (MEGAWATTS) | 264 | 1,240 |
| THERMAL RATING (MEGAWATTS) | 590 | 3,000 |
| GROSS EFFICIENCY (PERCENT) | 44.75 | 41.5 |
| VOLUME OF CORE (LITERS) | 1,227 | 10,820 |
| LENGTH OF FUEL ASSEMBLIES (METERS) | 4.3 | 5.5 |
| NUMBER OF FUEL PINS PER ASSEMBLY | 217 | 271 |
| OUTSIDE DIAMETER OF FUEL PINS (MILLIMETERS) | 6.6 | 8.65 |
| MAXIMUM LINEAR POWER (WATTS PER CENTIMETER) | 430 | 450 |
| RATE OF FUEL BURNUP (MEGAWATT-DAYS PER TON) | 50,000 | 70,000 |
| MAXIMUM TOTAL NEUTRON FLUX (NEUTRONS PER SQUARE CENTIMETER PER SECOND) | $7.2 \times 10^{15}$ | $6.2 \times 10^{15}$ |
| BREEDING RATIO | 1.12 | 1.24 |
| NOMINAL CLADDING TEMPERATURE (DEGREES CELSIUS) | 650 | 620 |
| INTERVAL BETWEEN REFUELING OPERATIONS (MONTHS) | 2 | 12 |

PHÉNIX AND SUPERPHÉNIX are compared in this table. The continuity of technological choices was maintained as far as possible in going to the larger plant, although a number of significant changes were incorporated in Superphénix design, partly to meet new safety criteria.

| PRIMARY CIRCUIT | NUMBER OF PUMPS | 4 |
|---|---|---|
| | TEMPERATURE AT CORE INLET | 395 DEGREES CELSIUS |
| | TEMPERATURE AT CORE OUTLET | 545 DEGREES CELSIUS |
| | OVERALL SODIUM FLOW RATE | 16.4 METRIC TONS PER SECOND |
| | WEIGHT OF SODIUM | 3,300 METRIC TONS |
| SECONDARY CIRCUIT | NUMBER OF PUMPS | 4 |
| | NUMBER OF INTERMEDIATE HEAT EXCHANGERS | 8 |
| | TEMPERATURE AT INLET OF INTERMEDIATE HEAT EXCHANGER | 345 DEGREES CELSIUS |
| | TEMPERATURE AT OUTLET OF INTERMEDIATE HEAT EXCHANGER | 525 DEGREES CELSIUS |
| | OVERALL SODIUM FLOW RATE | 13.2 METRIC TONS PER SECOND |
| | TOTAL WEIGHT OF SODIUM IN THE FOUR LOOPS | 1,700 METRIC TONS |
| TERTIARY CIRCUIT | NUMBER OF STEAM GENERATORS | 4 |
| | TEMPERATURE OF SUPERHEATED STEAM | 490 DEGREES CELSIUS |
| | PRESSURE OF SUPERHEATED STEAM | 180 BARS |
| | OVERALL STEAM FLOW RATE | 1.36 METRIC TONS PER SECOND |

**SPECIFICATIONS for the steam-generating system of Superphénix are summarized in this table. The use of sodium in the reactor's primary and secondary circuits is expected to give the new electric station a comparatively high overall thermal efficiency of at least 40 percent.**

nix will be provided with a highly redundant system of control rods, divided into three independent groups. One of these is specially designed to penetrate the core even in the extreme and improbable case of its undergoing a large deformation. Uninterrupted monitoring of the Superphénix core is provided by a diversified set of detectors, whose output is processed and correlated by computer. The temperature of the sodium leaving each subassembly is measured by three thermocouples; two of them are of the chromel-alumel type and the third uses a sodium-steel couple and responds almost instantaneously. The boiling-sodium detectors, flowmeters and devices for the detection and localization of any cladding failures are improved versions of those employed in Phénix. The neutron detectors and electronic instruments for measuring variations in reactivity have proved their reliability through long experience with them.

The many precautions implemented in the design of Superphénix were subjected to detailed scrutiny by the licensing authorities before their approval was secured. These safety measures reduce the probability of an accident to an extremely low level. The procedure followed went to the extent of considering the case in which a total shutdown of forced sodium circulation through the core at full power is not accompanied by any action of the many control systems designed to shut down the fission chain reaction and energy production imme-

diately. Even in this case the considerable thermal inertia represented by the large mass of sodium present in the primary vessel (3,300 tons) and the interval of several hundred degrees C. between the sodium temperature in normal operation and its boiling point furnish a substantial time interval for manual emergency action. Nevertheless, it is necessary to ensure that even in the highly improbable case of a serious accident involving a core meltdown the consequences will be contained in such a way that no significant quantity of plutonium or fission products can escape into the environment.

The containment system for Superphénix therefore consists of a series of successive enclosures, which can withstand both internal reactor accidents and external aggression such as an airplane crashing into the power plant. Finally, special arrangements have been made to prevent potential sodium fires and to limit their spread should they occur. Sodium fires would not actually jeopardize the safety of the installation, but it is nonetheless necessary to take full precautions to maximize the reliability and the availability of the power station.

In all areas, not just in the priority area of safety, a considerable research-and-development effort has preceded the design and construction of Superphénix. This program, which calls for full-scale tests in sodium of all components where innovations have been made, will continue to back up con-

struction of the reactor in the coming years.

Phénix was built in slightly more than four years. Preliminary site preparation began in the fall of 1968, and the filling of the primary and secondary circuits with 1,400 tons of sodium was started before the end of 1972. For Superphénix a building schedule spread over 68 months has been adopted. Construction deadlines are comparable to those set for other types of nuclear power plant. The fact that breeder reactors are not pressurized and that their components, even the large ones, are made of comparatively thin stainless-steel sheet and pipe makes it possible to perform most of the final assembly on the site. The Phénix experience clearly showed the advantages of this approach and the flexibility that it engendered in adherence to the construction schedule.

The investment cost of the Superphénix power plant will significantly exceed that of a light-water plant of comparable output. This cost differential is unavoidable since Superphénix is the first plant of its kind, whereas light-water plants (of which more than 100 have been built to date in the world) have amply profited from the fruits of technical progress and above all of series production. In spite of the fact that Superphénix is a prototype, it should be emphasized that the cost of a kilowatt-hour of electricity produced by Superphénix will be in the same range as that produced by an oil-fired power station. It is probable that the investment cost of fast breeder plants, which will progressively decline as larger numbers are constructed, will remain for some time higher than that of light-water plants, if only because of the larger amounts of stainless steel employed and the presence of an intermediate sodium circuit added for safety reasons. Economic competitiveness with light-water plants will derive from a cheaper fuel cycle, made possible by fuel breeding, and this factor will become increasingly important with the foreseeable increase in the price of natural uranium.

The expansion program of the French national utility company Électricité de France (EDF) already calls for a series of breeder plants, employing plutonium provided by a large number of pressurized-water reactors built simultaneously. It is reasonable to expect that two pairs of fast-neutron plants will be initiated in France between 1980 and 1985, representing, together with Superphénix, about 8,000 megawatts of electric-generating capacity in service in the early 1990's. Commitments may grow to 2,000 megawatts per year after 1985, so that by the year 2000 fast-neutron plants may account for about a fourth of the installed capacity and a third of the total energy output of all the nuclear plants in France. Simultaneous with the successive launching of these plants will be the construction of plants for the fabrication and reprocessing of fast-breeder fuels, thus closing the fuel cycle. The latter will be high-capacity plants (with an output of about 200 tons of oxides per year) aimed at achieving a low overall fuel-cycle cost.

The importance of Superphénix must be gauged in relation to the coming generation of power plants derived from it. It is in a way the culmination of the technological development phase and the final stage before the commercial series, the technical definition of which will rely directly on the Superphénix experience. If everything proceeds as planned, by the mid-1980's, thanks to Superphénix, one may expect to have at least a preliminary operating record with a large fast-neutron power plant. This experience, which will be shared by several large electric utilities, symbolizes the joining of efforts by the European countries involved in aiming at the earliest possible commercial launching of a type of reactor that is indispensable to their economies.

| REACTOR | LOCATION | POWER (MEGAWATTS) | FORM OF OUTPUT | BASIC DESIGN | SCHEDULE |
|---|---|---|---|---|---|
| EXPERIMENTAL BREEDER REACTOR 1 | U.S. | .2 | ELECTRICAL | LOOP | |
| DOUNREAY FAST REACTOR | U.K. | 15 | ELECTRICAL | LOOP | |
| EXPERIMENTAL BREEDER REACTOR 2 | U.S. | 20 | ELECTRICAL | POOL | |
| B.R. 5 | U.S.S.R. | 10 | THERMAL | LOOP | |
| ENRICO FERMI FAST BREEDER REACTOR | U.S. | 66 | ELECTRICAL | LOOP | |
| RAPSODIE | FRANCE | 40 | THERMAL | LOOP | |
| B.N. 350 | U.S.S.R. | 150 | ELECTRICAL | LOOP | |
| SOUTHWEST EXPERIMENTAL FAST OXIDE REACTOR | U.S. | 20 | ELECTRICAL | LOOP | |
| B.O.R. 60 | U.S.S.R. | 12 | THERMAL | LOOP | |
| PROTOTYPE FAST REACTOR | U.K. | 250 | ELECTRICAL | POOL | |
| FAST-FLUX TEST FACILITY | U.S. | 400 | THERMAL | LOOP | |
| K.N.K. 2 | GERMANY | 20 | ELECTRICAL | LOOP | |
| PHÉNIX | FRANCE | 250 | ELECTRICAL | POOL | |
| P.E.C. | ITALY | 116 | THERMAL | LOOP | |
| S.N.R. 300 | GERMANY | 300 | ELECTRICAL | LOOP | |
| JOYO | JAPAN | 100 | THERMAL | LOOP | |
| B.N. 600 | U.S.S.R. | 600 | ELECTRICAL | POOL | |
| FAST BREEDER TEST REACTOR | INDIA | 15 | ELECTRICAL | LOOP | |
| CLINCH RIVER BREEDER REACTOR | U.S. | 380 | ELECTRICAL | LOOP | |
| COMMERCIAL FAST REACTOR | U.K. | 1,300 | ELECTRICAL | POOL | |
| SUPERPHÉNIX | FRANCE | 1,200 | ELECTRICAL | POOL | |
| MONJU | JAPAN | 300 | ELECTRICAL | LOOP | |
| S.N.R. 2 | GERMANY | 1,300 | ELECTRICAL | | |
| B.N. 1500 | U.S.S.R. | 1,500 | ELECTRICAL | | |
| PROTOTYPE LARGE BREEDER REACTOR | U.S. | 1,200 | ELECTRICAL | | |

1945  1950  1955  1960  1965  1970  1975  1980

| TYPE OF FACILITY | DESIGN PHASE | CONSTRUCTION PHASE | OPERATION PHASE |
|---|---|---|---|
| EXPERIMENTAL REACTOR | | | |
| DEMONSTRATION PLANT | | | |
| COMMERCIAL PROTOTYPE | | | |

**WORLD SURVEY** of progress in the development of liquid-metal-cooled fast breeder reactors includes all facilities with a thermal-power output greater than one megawatt. The plants are listed in chronological order according to the beginning of their design stage. Different colors are used to distinguish the three main categories of reactors built or planned so far: experimental reactors, demonstration plants and prototype commercial power stations. Different intensities of color denote design, construction and operation phases. Projections are made only to 1980; bars that stop short of the present represent decommissioned facilities. S.N.R. 300, Superphénix and S.N.R. 2 are multinational European projects. The German K.N.K. reactor has been in operation since 1968 with a slow-neutron core; beginning in 1977 it will be run with a fast-neutron core as K.N.K. 2. The British Prototype Fast Reactor at Dounreay in Scotland and the Russian B.N. 350 at Shevchenko, two demonstration plants comparable in size to the French Phénix, are both completed but have not yet been run at full power, owing to difficulties with their steam-generating equipment. Preliminary site work is about to begin on the closest comparable U.S. plant, the 380-megawatt Clinch River project near Oak Ridge, Tenn., which is expected to be completed in the early 1980's.

# III

# ENVIRONMENTAL COSTS
# OF FOSSIL FUELS

One of the great advantages of oil and gas, as seen from the viewpoint of the last half of the twentieth century, is their clean-burning nature. They leave no solid wastes; unlike coal, most are relatively low in sulfur. They are also convenient and cheap to transport and easy to burn. But burning oil and gas, like coal, inevitably produces carbon dioxide, which is vented to the atmosphere. For the past 40 years, we have known that the burning of fossil fuels over the past century has increased the amount of carbon dioxide in the atmosphere. How much more we will add if we continue to burn fossil fuels, and how serious a threat to our environment that will be, is not yet determined. As a result, more attention is now given to this problem than to a great many others.

Other aspects of the Earth's environment are changing—for the worse, many people assume—in response to all of the production, refining, transport, and burning of fossil fuels. These changes are both global in nature, like the carbon dioxide problem, and local, ranging from oil tanker spills to the coal dust that affects miners' lungs. The most serious global pollutant other than carbon dioxide is sulfur, and a most serious source of that sulfur is the burning of high-sulfur coal. The global distribution of sulfur oxide gases in the atmosphere is governed not only by coal burning but also by the natural weathering of sulfur-containing rocks and the sulfur oxide gases arising from swamp and marsh areas.

The amount of sulfur added by coal burning is still less than that coming from natural causes, but this does not mean it is no problem. Most of the sulfur in the atmosphere remains in the lower part of the atmosphere, the troposphere, and is washed out by rain relatively quickly so that its abundance in the atmosphere does not build up. Its major effects are felt locally, where the sulfur gases wash out in rain, mainly in the form of sulfuric acid, and adversely affect soils and vegetation, lakes, and rivers. Over major urban areas, the sulfur gases may accumulate, particularly during temperature inversions, and they may be associated with a pronounced increase in the death rate among the most vulnerable groups of the population, the very young and the very old. The suggestion that we could build tall stacks to inject the sulfur higher into the atmosphere gained some acceptance until it was demonstrated that the pollution was simply displaced downwind rather than being diluted. Sweden pays the price for the wind-carried sulfur pollution from the Ruhr Valley and adjointing areas of France, Belgium, and the Netherlands. In the United States, the people of central Illinois and Indiana have a higher sulfur content in their air and fallout because they are downwind from St. Louis. These are only a few examples of the consequences of sulfur oxide gases produced by coal-burning power plants in metropolitan and industrial areas.

For these reasons, it is imperative that we find a reasonably efficient and inexpensive way of removing the sulfur from coal by some combination of cleaning the coal during preparation, suitable burning, and recovery from the stacks. If we take the path of substituting coal for dwindling oil and gas reserves and do not adequately face this problem, we might kill a good many more people than we would by investing in nuclear power.

Another aspect of environmental damage that we must consider is the occupational safety of those who work to produce or burn the fuel for our energy. The loss of life from accidents and the shortening of lives from miners' diseases are no less the consequence of extracting coal or uranium from the ground than other effects. Here again we have been spoiled by the experience with oil and gas. Though there certainly are accidents in drilling for oil and gas, they are fewer than those in underground mines and vanishingly small in relation to the total energy content of the product produced per worker. Refinery workers have health hazards too, but they are less serious than those in other energy industries.

In this section, we are introduced to some of the impacts of energy production on the environment. In the first article, the carbon dioxide question is explored from the perspective of a biologist (see also "The Carbon Cycle," by Bert Bolin; SCIENTIFIC AMERICAN Offprint 1193). Following this is an article about a hitherto unknown effect of our energy use—or rather, energy waste— the light of our planet at night that comes from giant flares of gas being burned off from oil fields. The safety of importation of natural gas in liquified form, which would avoid flaring, is evaluated in the third article, which shows that the hazards of transportation are no less grave than those of production or burning. The widespread distribution of pelagic tar from the prevalent oil spills by the huge tankers that cross the oceans is covered in the fourth article. Finally, the last article discusses the effects on the land of coal strip-mining in the western United States.

# 10

# The Carbon Dioxide Question

## COMMENTARY

The outlines of the carbon dioxide story have been clear for some time. The carbon dioxide that is naturally present in our atmosphere is the consequence of a balance of contributions and losses from photosynthesis and respiration of all of the plants and animals of the world's lands and seas, volcanoes, weathering of rocks, and precipitation of calcium carbonates in the sediments of the oceans. For the last century, we have been disturbing that balance with the carbon dioxide added from fossil-fuel burning. In this article, George Woodwell presents one current view of the problem, emphasizing a point that has not been made too strongly in many past discussions: Major forested areas of the world may be as important as the oceans in removing excess carbon dioxide from the atmosphere. Woodwell sees the cutting of the forests of the Amazon leading to an environmental cost that is potentially more serious than the effects of soil erosion, landslides, and other local geologic effects.

The heart of the carbon dioxide story today entails the evaluation of two different areas. The first is getting the right numbers on the credit side of the budget, how much carbon dioxide is steadily being gained by the atmosphere. We thought we knew that figure pretty well, but it now seems that there may be a bigger contribution than we thought from the organisms of the world. On the debit side of the ledger, some carbon dioxide steadily leaves the atmosphere, even though the total amount present is increasing. Getting the right figures for that loss is the other difficulty. Oceanographers are convinced that the answer lies in determining how much the carbon dioxide of the atmosphere exchanges with the shallow and deep oceans. Those who work with land flora think the problem is in the biomass on land, and there is where it ought to be controlled. The best we can say at the moment, in spite of the many multidisciplinary conferences and workshops, is that the answer is not clear to everyone's satisfaction.

The ultimate question is how the projected increase in carbon dioxide will affect the world climate. How much the carbon dioxide "greenhouse effect" will raise the average world temperature is not yet settled. It depends on knowledge of the degree to which a slight rise in air temperature will affect the amount of water vapor in the atmosphere and thus the density of cloud cover over the planet, a cloud cover which reflects much of the incident sunlight away from the Earth. Furthermore, the quantitative effects of volcanic and human-made dust on climate are not yet worked out. In some models, that dust may serve to reflect back more of the sun's light and thus exert a cooling effect.

We are engaged in a giant experiment with the atmosphere; oceans; and the flora, fauna, and climate of the Earth. Yet we are not sure of the outcome. If ever there was a need to understand more fully a scientific problem for the good of our future, it is in this area.

# The Carbon Dioxide Question

by George M. Woodwell
*January 1978*

*Human activities are clearly increasing the carbon
dioxide content of the earth's atmosphere. The question
is: Will enough carbon be stored in forests and the
ocean to avert a major change in climate?*

In the century and a quarter since
1850 human activities have increased the amount of carbon dioxide in the atmosphere of the earth from
290 parts per million or less to slightly
more than 330 parts per million. Perhaps a fourth of the total increase has
come within the past decade. By the
year 2020, if present trends continue,
the amount of carbon dioxide in the atmosphere could approach twice the current value. Until recently the increase
was commonly attributed to the burning
of fossil fuels. Now there is evidence
that it may be due in equal degree to
another source: the worldwide destruction of forests.

Although carbon dioxide is only a
trace gas in the atmosphere of the earth,
present at a concentration of about .03
percent by volume, it plays a possibly
critical role in controlling the climate
of the earth because it absorbs radiant
energy at infrared wavelengths. Heat
trapped in this way has a large potential for altering the world climate substantially. And quite apart from possible effects on the climate, the carbon
dioxide in the atmosphere also plays a
critical role as the source of the carbon
that is fixed in photosynthesis by green
plants and therefore provides the basis
for all plant and animal life.

Mankind therefore faces a historic dilemma. The human activities that are
increasing the carbon dioxide content of
the atmosphere promise to bring a general warming of the climate over the
next several decades. Although one cannot be certain of how much the climate
will change, or of the precise mechanisms that will be involved, the results
of a steadily rising amount of carbon
dioxide in the atmosphere will almost
certainly be destabilizing. An increase
in the average world temperatures will
probably enlarge the area of the arid

zones and significantly affect agricultural production.

The other horn of the dilemma is that
the kinds of corrective action that might
be contemplated would surely have effects that would be equally destabilizing. The most obvious corrective action
would be a major reduction in the consumption of fossil fuels. Equally important would be measures to lower the rate
at which the forests of the world are
being reduced or cleared by logging, by
the expansion of agricultural and grazing lands, by toxification and by other
consequences of industrial development. A major effort to change the balance of land use between agriculture
and forest, in addition to an effort to
restrict the burning of fossil fuels, would
so upset established patterns of social
and economic development as to be
equivalent to the drastic changes in the
human condition that a warming of the
climate might lead to.

Although the carbon dioxide problem
has been with us for more than a
century, unambiguous data on changes
in the carbon dioxide content of the atmosphere have been available only
since 1958. In that year Charles D. Keeling of the Scripps Institution of Oceanography established a continuous carbon dioxide monitoring station on the
volcano Mauna Loa on the island of Hawaii. Mauna Loa was chosen because it
offered an opportunity to study the carbon dioxide content of the mixed air of
the troposphere, or lower atmosphere,
in the middle latitudes. The records now
available from Mauna Loa and other
stations show two clear patterns. First,
there has been throughout the period
since 1958 a regular upward trend in the
carbon dioxide content of the atmosphere. The amount of the increase at
Mauna Loa has been about .8 part per

million per year, although there have
been obvious variations in the rate of
increase. Second, there is a systematic
oscillation in the carbon dioxide content
of the atmosphere correlated with the
seasons. The carbon dioxide content rises to a peak in late winter, usually April
in the Northern Hemisphere, and falls
to a minimum at the end of the northern
summer, in late September or October.
The data from Mauna Loa are the long-
est and most accurate continuous record
of carbon dioxide concentration ever
made anywhere in the world.

Records of carbon dioxide concentration have been kept for various periods
at the South Pole, in Australia, at Point
Barrow in Alaska, on Long Island in
New York and at other locations. Investigators in the U.S., Sweden, Australia
and elsewhere have also sampled the atmosphere extensively from airplanes.
The data all show a winter-summer oscillation with a minimum in late summer and a maximum in late winter. The
oscillation follows the seasons of each
hemisphere. The data also show a more
or less continuous increase in the carbon
dioxide content of the atmosphere, with
the amount varying with time and place
between about .5 part and 1.5 parts per
million annually.

The seasonal change in atmospheric
carbon dioxide reflects one of the most
important factors affecting the atmosphere: the metabolism of the biota, or
the totality of living matter. The seasonal change in carbon dioxide concentration in the atmosphere is correlated with
the "pulse" of photosynthesis that occurs
during the summer in middle latitudes
of both hemispheres. Recently it has
been recognized that the primary cause
of the seasonal change is most probably
the pulse of photosynthesis in forests
of the middle latitudes. The emphasis is
on the forests because they are extensive

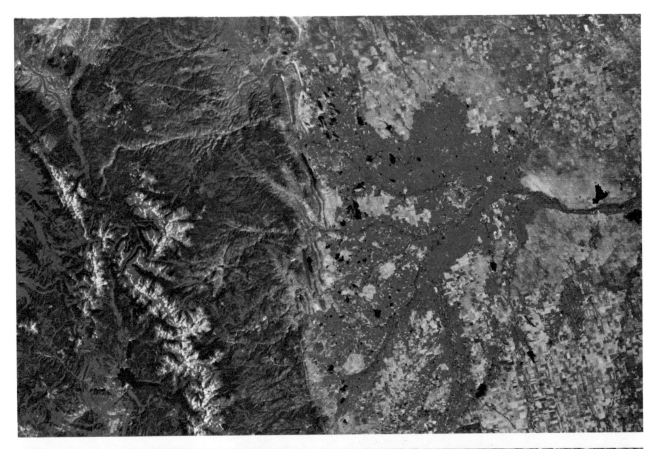

**SUMMER AND FALL** Landsat satellite images of an area along the eastern edge of the Rockies near Boulder, Colo., show the annual "pulse" of carbon dioxide fixation characteristic of the temperate zones. In this type of imagery the green of vegetation comes out red. In the top image, made in August, the intense red of the area to the right of the mountains at left reflects a peak of photosynthetic activity, in which plants take up carbon dioxide from the atmosphere to build themselves. In the bottom image, made in October, red has substantially faded, reflecting a diminution of the photosynthetic activity. In this area the activity is that of both forest and crop plants.

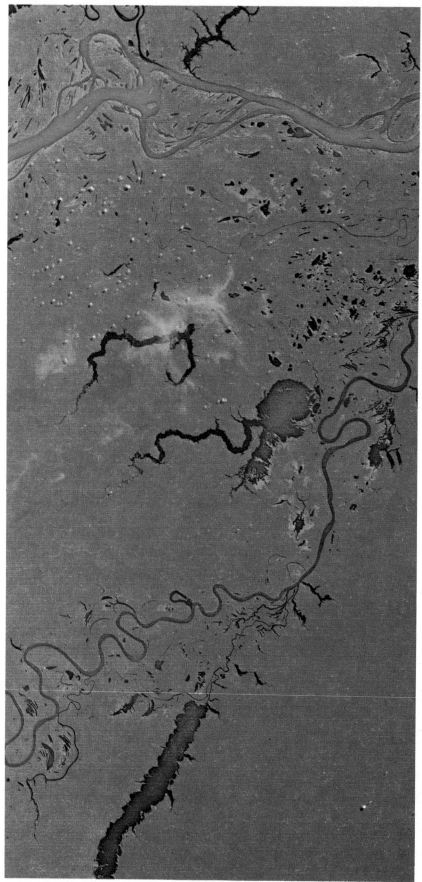

**RAIN-FOREST AREA of the Amazon Basin of northwestern Brazil that appears in this Landsat image is almost uniformly red, reflecting the intense year-round photosynthetic activity that is characteristic of tropical rain forests. Natural forest communities fix more carbon per unit area than most agricultural cropland. The area of such forests, however, is being reduced.**

in area, conduct more photosynthesis worldwide than any other type of vegetation and have the potential for storing carbon in quantities that are sufficiently large to affect the carbon dioxide content of the atmosphere.

The variation in the amplitude of the difference between the winter concentration of carbon dioxide and the late-summer concentration is consistent with this hypothesis. The difference ranges from about five parts per million at Mauna Loa to more than 15 parts per million in central Long Island. The difference drops toward the Tropics, where the seasonal pulse of metabolism is either less pronounced or absent; the difference is also less at higher elevations at all latitudes. The amplitude is substantially less in the Southern Hemisphere, apparently because the smaller continental land mass limits the area of forests. The clear conclusion is that the forests of the earth have a pronounced influence on the short-term carbon dioxide content of the atmosphere.

The cause of the long-term increase in the carbon dioxide content of the air, an increase of 10 to 15 percent since 1850, has usually been ascribed to the accelerating release of carbon dioxide through the combustion of fossil fuels. Recent analyses have thrown this assumption into doubt. My colleagues and I at the Ecosystems Center of the Marine Biological Laboratory in Woods Hole, Mass., in collaboration with R. H. Whittaker and Gene E. Likens of Cornell University, W. A. Reiners of Dartmouth College and C. C. Delwiche of the University of California at Davis, have shown that there is probably a substantial additional release from the biota. Similar findings have been published by other workers, notably Bert Bolin of the University of Stockholm and J. R. Adams and his colleagues at Rice University. The release from the biota has been chiefly through the destruction of forests and the oxidation of humus. The assumption that the increase in the carbon dioxide content of the atmosphere has been a consequence of burning fossil fuels, without regard to possible changes in the biota, has led to what now appears to be a serious miscalculation of the world carbon budget.

The difficulty has arisen from the assumption that the biota has been a sink for atmospheric carbon dioxide when in reality it has probably been a source of carbon dioxide released to the atmosphere. This probable error means that at the moment it is not possible to resolve major questions about the world carbon budget. If the biota has not been a sink for atmospheric carbon dioxide, and if the absorption of carbon dioxide by the oceans of the world is no greater than we have thought, then the amount of carbon dioxide in the atmosphere should be increasing even faster than the observations show. Obviously the estimates are wrong. But where does the error lie?

The issue can be seen more clearly by comparing the magnitudes of the pools that are more or less continuously exchanging carbon with one another. The atmosphere holds at present about $700 \times 10^{15}$ grams of carbon in the form of carbon dioxide, which is continuously being exchanged with the biota and with the surface waters of the ocean. The amount of carbon held in the total worldwide biota is about $800 \times 10^{15}$ grams, or somewhat more than is held in the atmosphere. A still larger pool of carbon, variously estimated at between $1,000 \times 10^{15}$ and $3,000 \times 10^{15}$ grams, is held in the organic matter of the soil, mainly humus and peat. The harvest of the forests, the extension of agriculture onto soils that contain large amounts of organic matter and the destruction of wetlands all speed the decay of humus, which is transformed into carbon dioxide, water and heat. The carbon dioxide released enters the atmospheric pool.

Although these three pools of carbon in continuous interaction are all roughly the same size, the total amount of carbon held in the oceans is much larger. The largest part of the carbon is in the form of dissolved carbon dioxide, which is a part of the carbonate-bicarbon-

ate system. The total in this pool approaches $40,000 \times 10^{15}$ grams when the waters of the great oceanic basins are included. On a time scale measured in thousands of years the carbon dioxide content of the atmosphere may well be determined by the equilibrium established with the inorganic carbon of the deep ocean. The rate of exchange between the atmosphere and the ocean as a whole, however, is low. The most rapid exchanges are between the atmosphere and the mixed surface layer, roughly the top 100 meters above the colder abyssal waters. The surface layer contains about $600 \times 10^{15}$ grams of inorganic carbon. The second-largest reservoir in the ocean is in the form of dissolved organic matter (the "humus" of the ocean), which seems to be everywhere about one part per million and may total as much as $3,000 \times 10^{15}$ grams in the oceans as a whole.

The deep waters of the ocean vastly exceed in volume the waters of the mixed layer and hold by far the largest pool of carbon that is in exchange with the atmosphere: from $35,000 \times 10^{15}$ to $38,000 \times 10^{15}$ grams. (Excluded from this pool is the carbon in the carbonaceous sediments, which contain a far larger amount.) The capacity of the abyssal regions for absorbing carbon is virtually unlimited. The problem is that the carbon appears to move from the

atmosphere through the mixed layer of the ocean into the oceanic depths very slowly.

When one tries to construct a flow chart showing the net transport of carbon from one pool to another, one finds that the available estimates vary widely in quality. The most accurately known figures are for the carbon dioxide released by the worldwide combustion of fossil fuels, currently about $5 \times 10^{15}$ grams of carbon per year, and the increase in the carbon dioxide content of the air, equivalent to about $2.3 \times 10^{15}$ grams of carbon per year. That leaves $2.7 \times 10^{15}$ grams of fossil-fuel carbon to be removed by some combination of terrestrial and oceanic processes. Let us assume for the moment that the terrestrial biota represents a stable pool of carbon, neither augmenting nor reducing the amount of carbon dioxide in the atmosphere. In that case (which I shall argue is unlikely) the ocean must provide the sink for $2.7 \times 10^{15}$ grams of carbon per year. Is that rate of removal supported by the evidence?

According to the best estimates of chemical oceanographers, it is difficult to explain how the ocean could absorb that much annually. Their analyses are based on a detailed knowledge of the amount of carbon held in the carbonate-bicarbonate system of the surface layer

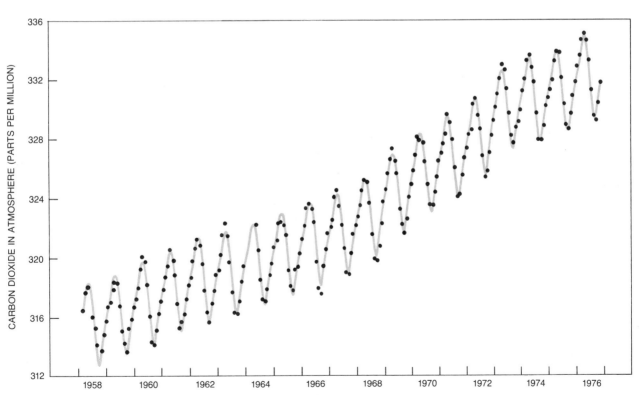

TREND IN ATMOSPHERIC CARBON DIOXIDE has been measured since 1958 at the Mauna Loa Observatory on the island of Hawaii by Charles D. Keeling of the Scripps Institution of Oceanography. The dots indicate the monthly average concentration of carbon dioxide. The seasonal oscillations are caused by the removal of carbon dioxide by photosynthesis during the growing season in the Northern Hemisphere and the subsequent release during the fall and winter months. The Mauna Loa measurements and those made elsewhere show that the average carbon dioxide content of the atmosphere has risen more than 5 percent since 1958. Rate of increase has varied from year to year from causes not yet known. Current rate is one part per million per year, equivalent to $2.3 \times 10^{15}$ grams of carbon.

combined with carefully constructed models of the mechanisms of mixing in the oceans. The radioactive isotopes carbon 14 and tritium (hydrogen 3), both produced in large quantities by the atomic bomb tests of the 1950's and early 1960's, have been exploited as tracers to examine the rates at which water of the mixed layer is exchanged with the water of the oceanic depths. The studies seem to show that the mixing rate is very low indeed. The transfer of carbon from the atmosphere through the surface layer and into abyssal waters, according to

some calculations, is unlikely to exceed $2.5 \times 10^{15}$ grams per year. In sum, according to these studies, the oceans seem to be barely adequate as a sink for the difference between the $5 \times 10^{15}$ grams per year of carbon currently being released into the atmosphere by the burning of fossil fuels and the $2.3 \times 10^{15}$ grams that the atmosphere actually retains.

This balance of flows has to be completely reexamined if the biotic pool of carbon, instead of either expanding or being in net balance with the carbon in

the atmosphere, is actually a net source of atmospheric carbon dioxide. Whittaker and Likens have recently provided a tabulation of current information about the size of various segments of the biota. Their work shows that the largest pools of carbon in the biota are in forests. It also shows that the largest amount of net photosynthesis is on land, not in the ocean as had been assumed previously on the basis of earlier guesses about the rates of net primary production in the oceans. (Net primary production is the net amount of fixed carbon, or

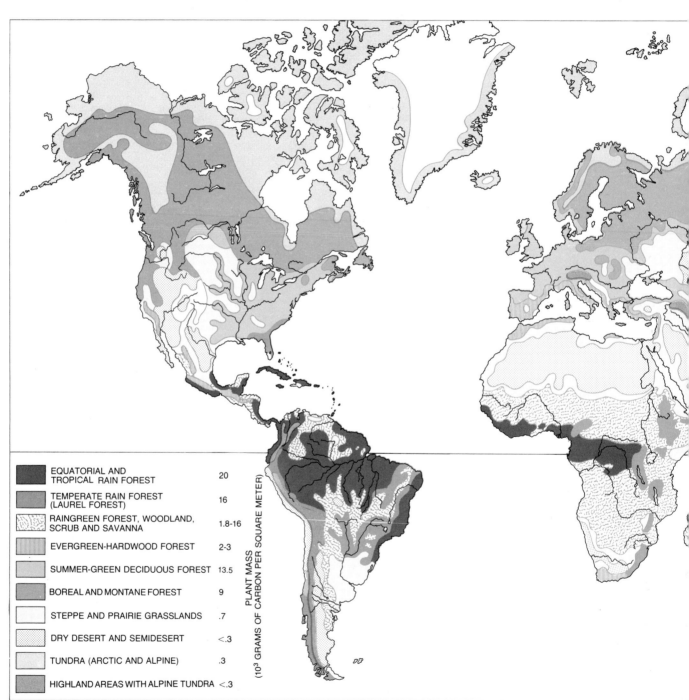

| | | PLANT MASS ($10^3$ GRAMS OF CARBON PER SQUARE METER) |
|---|---|---|
| ■ | EQUATORIAL AND TROPICAL RAIN FOREST | 20 |
| ■ | TEMPERATE RAIN FOREST (LAUREL FOREST) | 16 |
| | RAINGREEN FOREST, WOODLAND, SCRUB AND SAVANNA | 1.8-16 |
| | EVERGREEN-HARDWOOD FOREST | 2-3 |
| | SUMMER-GREEN DECIDUOUS FOREST | 13.5 |
| | BOREAL AND MONTANE FOREST | 9 |
| | STEPPE AND PRAIRIE GRASSLANDS | .7 |
| | DRY DESERT AND SEMIDESERT | <.3 |
| | TUNDRA (ARCTIC AND ALPINE) | .3 |
| | HIGHLAND AREAS WITH ALPINE TUNDRA | <.3 |

**CARBON STORED IN PLANTS is distributed as is shown in this world map based on the work of H. Brockmann Jerosch. The total amount of carbon stored in terrestrial biomass is about $830 \times 10^{15}$** grams. In comparison the carbon in the total oceanic biomass is negligible: less than $2 \times 10^{15}$ grams. About 40 percent of all plant carbon is stored in the tropical rain forests. Another 14 percent is held

organic matter, left from photosynthesis after the needs of the plant for respiration have been met. It is the organic matter available for the growth of the plant and is ultimately available for storage or for consumer organisms such as animals or organisms of decay.)

Perhaps the most significant finding of the Whittaker-Likens study is that the tropical rain forests, with their big trees, represent the largest single pool of carbon in the biota and also have the highest total net primary production. This observation emphasizes the importance

of the tropical forests in the earth's carbon budget. If these and other forests are harvested rapidly and the stored carbon is released, they have the potential for contributing significantly to the amount of carbon dioxide in the atmosphere. Conversely, if deforested lands are allowed to become forested again, the forests will absorb some of the carbon dioxide from the atmosphere, retarding the rate of increase.

Curiously, the question of whether the biotic pool is getting larger or smaller has only recently become contro-

ver-sial. For example, at a 1970 conference titled "Study of Critical Environmental Problems," organized by the Massachusetts Institute of Technology and held in Williamstown, Mass., the conferees assumed that the biotic pool must be getting larger and encouraged oceanographers to believe their models of oceanic circulation and carbon dioxide absorption were adequate. A subsequent series of conferences appeared to reinforce this assumption, although in 1972 doubts were raised at a Brookhaven National Laboratory conference titled "Carbon and the Biosphere."

The first serious challenge to the oceanographers' model was contained in two papers presented at the Dahlem Conference on Biogeochemistry, held in West Berlin in November, 1976. In one paper R. A. Houghton and I estimated that the biota may be releasing about as much carbon dioxide to the atmosphere annually as is released by the combustion of fossil fuels. In the other paper Bolin arrived at a somewhat lower value for the biotic release by drawing on data on forest harvests collected by the United Nations Food and Agriculture Organization (FAO). Bolin's estimate was about $10^{15}$ grams of carbon. The subject dominated the Dahlem conference, stimulating much discussion.

The possibility of a significant release of carbon dioxide from the biota also dominated two subsequent conferences, one arranged by the Department of Energy (formerly the Energy Research and Development Administration) last March in Miami Beach and the other held in April at Ratzeburg in West Germany under the auspices of the Scientific Committee on Problems of the Environment of the International Council of Scientific Unions. Recent papers in *Science* and other journals support the conclusion that the biota is a net source of atmospheric carbon dioxide and not a sink. The oceanographers' models are clearly in question. What does this mean for the world carbon budget?

The answer is far from clear. Substantially larger quantities of carbon are entering the atmosphere than are stored in it. In addition to the $5 \times 10^{15}$ grams of carbon released annually from the combustion of fossil fuels, another $4 \times 10^{15}$ to $8 \times 10^{15}$ grams, possibly more, may be being released currently through the destruction of forests and the accelerated oxidation of humus. Of this combined amount, $9 \times 10^{15}$ to $13 \times 10^{15}$ grams of carbon per year, only $2.3 \times 10^{15}$ grams accumulate in the atmosphere. The remainder, $7 \times 10^{15}$ to $11 \times 10^{15}$ grams, perhaps more, is stored somewhere on the earth. But where? As we have seen, the present models of oceanic uptake provide for the removal of less than $3 \times 10^{15}$ grams of carbon per year. Oceanographers are now reviewing their assumptions to see if they have overlooked mechanisms

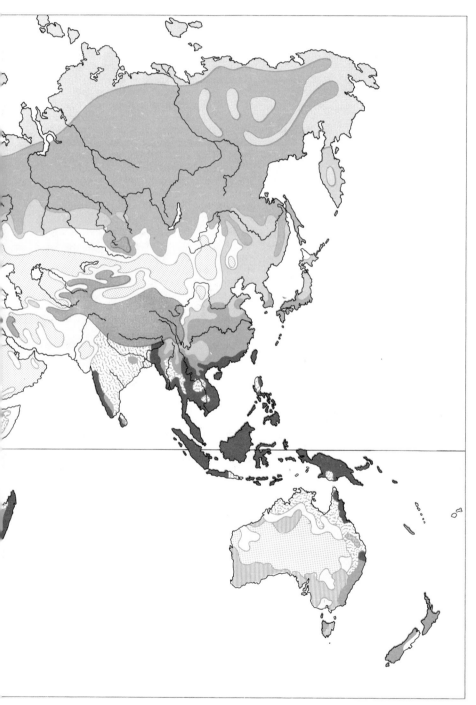

in tropical seasonal forests. Forests at all latitudes hold nearly 90 percent of all the carbon stored in the world's ecosystems, both terrestrial and marine. Author believes reduction in the area of forests has contributed significantly to increase of carbon dioxide in the atmosphere.

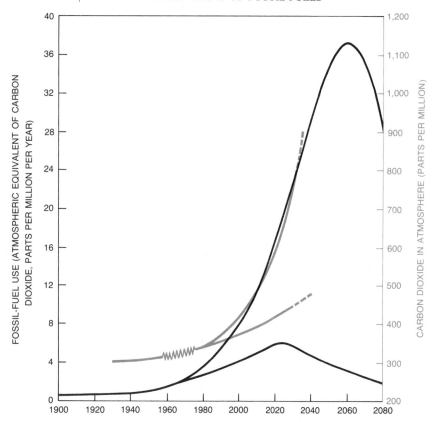

**PROJECTIONS OF FOSSIL-FUEL CONSUMPTION** (*black curves*) and carbon dioxide content of the atmosphere (*color*) are shown for minimum and maximum plausible rates of increase. The fuel-consumption rates are taken from a recent study done at the Oak Ridge National Laboratory. The minimum projection assumes an annual increase of 2 percent per year until 2025, followed by a symmetrical decrease. The maximum projection assumes a growth rate of 4.3 percent per year until the rate is limited by the depletion of resources in the middle of the next century. The uncertainty of such predictions makes estimates of the future carbon dioxide content of the atmosphere extremely risky. The uncertainty is greatly aggravated by the newly recognized possibility that the destruction of forests may also be releasing large amounts of carbon dioxide to the atmosphere. The sawtooth part of the curve represents the Mauna Loa measurements that were begun in 1958. At present the fossil fuel burned each year releases to the atmosphere an amount of carbon dioxide equivalent to about two parts per million. About half of that amount of carbon dioxide is actually retained in the atmosphere.

appraisal of the changes in the forest vegetation of Europe spanning the millennium from A.D. 900 to 1900. In that period the forest cover of western Europe was reduced from about 90 percent to about 20 percent. A similar change took place earlier in the lands of the Mediterranean, particularly the Levant. This great reduction in forest area released a quantity of carbon that was a significant fraction of the total previously held in the atmosphere. It is reasonable to assume that since 1900 continued industrialization and population growth have resulted in similar changes in the forests elsewhere.

Timothy Wood and Daniel B. Botkin of the Ecosystems Center at Woods Hole recently conducted a study of the changes in the forest area of New England over the period since the arrival of European settlers. They found that up to 1900 there was a continuous reduction in the total standing crop of forests but that since then there has been a period of recovery owing to the abandonment of agriculture and the expansion of forests into the former agricultural land. The recovery, however, has not resulted in a pool of carbon equivalent to that of the original forests. The forests have been harvested regularly and have never reached the stature or extent of the original ones; the standing crop of carbon today is no more than half the original one. The newest data indicate that the increase in the forested area has now ended, probably because of a renewed expansion of agriculture and an intensified harvest of trees.

The Wood-Botkin study shows that in a Temperate Zone forest that was allowed to recover from intensive harvest the storage of carbon amounted to 3 or 4 percent per year of the net primary production over the entire period of recovery, about 70 years. If a similar fraction of the net primary production of other Temperate Zone forests were stored and an equal additional quantity were stored in humus, the amount of carbon accumulated in all the Temperate Zone forests of the earth would come to about $.5 \times 10^{15}$ grams per year. The experience with New England forests suggests the regrowth of forests in the temperate zones probably does not at present provide a large sink for atmospheric carbon dioxide.

Meanwhile there has been a continuous expansion of agriculture into other forested lands, a continuous harvesting of primary forests elsewhere and a general toxification of the earth as a result of human activities. The most conspicuous inroads into the forests have been in the Tropics. The largest remaining forested area on the earth is the Amazon Basin, and we have sought data on the rate of harvest of Amazonian forests. There is no thoroughly satisfactory survey that can be applied to the entire Am-

that would be able to sequester additional amounts of carbon.

Because the issue is so important those who are familiar with terrestrial ecosystems are closely examining their own data, particularly the data covering changes in forest mass. How certain can we be that terrestrial communities are indeed a net source and not a sink? The problem has been addressed in several ways in recent months. The data are not as good as one might hope, but they seem compelling to those who are familiar with them.

The analysis is based first on knowledge of the relative magnitudes of the pools of carbon held within the biota and on the net primary production for each of the major plant communities on the earth. For example, the Whittaker-Likens study shows that tropical rain forests hold about 42 percent of all the carbon locked up in terrestrial vegetation and account for about 32 percent of the total net primary production. Forested areas of all kinds—tropical, tem-

perate and boreal—hold 90 percent of all the carbon held in vegetation and contribute more than 60 percent of the net primary production. The only other large single contributor to the net primary production is the savannas, or grasslands, which account for about 12 percent of it and for only about 3 percent of the standing mass of carbon. All the cultivated land on the earth accounts for about 8 percent of the total net primary production and for less than 1 percent of the standing mass of carbon. The Whittaker-Likens estimates lie about midway between the extremes of other analyses that were carried out under the direction of P. Duvigneaud of the University of Brussels at the Ratzeburg conference. Since the various studies all confirm the importance of forests, particularly the tropical forests, it is essential to establish whether or not these ecosystems are changing in size and, if they are, at what rate.

The data are scarce. We have the experience of Henry C. Darby, a British geographer, who in 1954 published an

azon Basin without all the hazards associated with any extrapolation. Nevertheless, Lawrence S. Hamilton of Cornell University and his colleagues have recently published a series of reports on changes in Venezuelan forests.

One of the reports, by J. P. Veillon,

shows a 33 percent reduction in forest area in the western llanos of Venezuela between 1950 and 1975. Hamilton, in an introduction to the series, cites FAO data that "suggests an estimate of moist forest cleared per year at...0.6 to 1.5 percent of the still existing area." Stud-

ies from other sections of the Amazon Basin attest to the high rate of development of highways, the expansion of agriculture at the expense of forests and the failure of revegetation after the forest has been cleared. Virtually no knowledgeable investigator with experi-

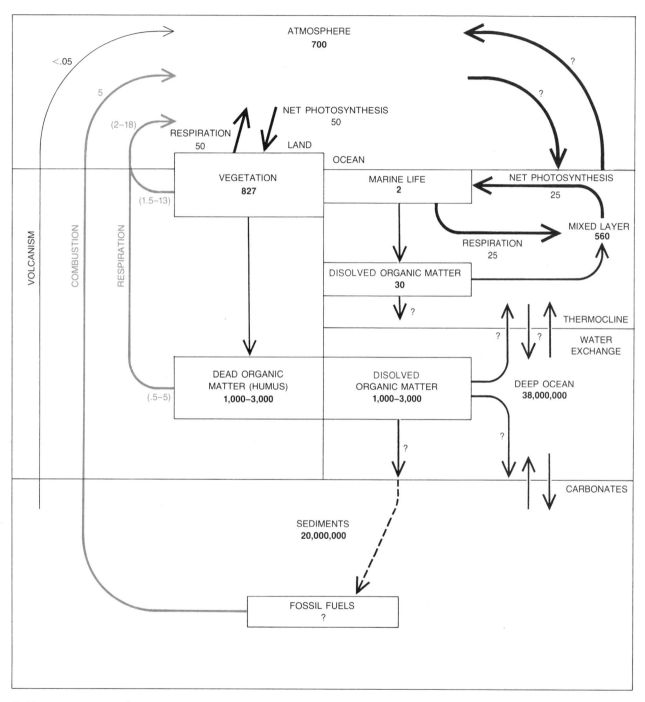

**GLOBAL BALANCE SHEET** shows major carbon repositories and annual exchange rates among depots that are in contact. Quantities are expressed in units of $10^{15}$ grams, or billions of metric tons. Annual releases to the atmosphere governed by human activities are shown in color. Land plants fix a net of about $50 \times 10^{15}$ grams of carbon per year. This carbon is either consumed and promptly respired by various terrestrial organisms or stored in the plant mass. The balance between fixation (net photosynthesis) and storage plus the total respiration of all terrestrial organisms determines whether there is a net flux of carbon dioxide to or from the biota. Many biologists now believe that there has been a long-term net flow of car-

bon dioxide from the biota into the atmosphere and that the flow is continuing. The carbon fixed by marine organisms is either respired or stored. It has been commonly assumed that most of it is respired immediately and recycled. It now seems possible that sinking fecal pellets may carry more carbon into the oceanic depths than had been thought. This transfer would supplement the normally slow diffusion of carbon dioxide into the surface layers of the ocean, where it comes into equilibrium with the carbonate-bicarbonate system. Although the deep ocean provides a virtually unlimited sink for carbon dioxide, gas must enter mixed layer and then penetrate thermocline, a thermally stratified layer that impedes mixing with deeper layers.

ence in the Tropics believes the Amazonian forest will escape substantial inroads from harvest and clearing over the next 30 years.

The best assumptions available to me suggest that the rate of clearing of tropical forests for all purposes is probably in the range of .5 to 1.5 percent of the existing area annually. If the rate is 1 percent, and if most of the clearing is through the expansion of agriculture and grazing lands into areas that were formerly forested, the release of carbon from forests alone would be about $4.5 \times 10^{15}$ grams per year. By applying such estimates to the entire terrestrial biota, allowing for additional storage through regrowth, my colleagues and I have recently estimated that the net release of carbon dioxide to the atmosphere from the biota is $6 \times 10^{15}$ grams of carbon annually. The magnitude of an additional release through the decay of soil humus is hard to calculate but we have estimated the loss at $2 \times 10^{15}$ grams per year. The total estimated release is therefore about $8 \times 10^{15}$ grams. The uncertainties are so great, however, that we have guessed that the actual loss from the biota might lie between $2 \times 10^{15}$ and $18 \times 10^{15}$ grams per year. Although one must always bear in mind the limitations of the data on which such assumptions are based, it is difficult to avoid the conclusion that the destruction of the forests of the earth is adding carbon dioxide to the atmosphere at a rate comparable to the rate of release from the combustion of fossil fuels, and if the oxidation of humus is included, at an appreciably higher rate.

These observations have come as a surprise to many agriculturists and foresters. The assumption in their experience has been that modern agricultural and forestry practices have improved the net primary productivity of terrestrial systems under human management and that the improvement of net primary production must have resulted in a faster storage of carbon in the humus of soils under management than in natural soils. But the average productivity of agriculture, measured in the ecologist's units of total organic matter available to man or other animals, is substantially less than the average primary productivity of the natural communities the agriculture replaced. Agricultural plant communities are managed not for the storage of large quantities of carbon but for the rapid turnover of carbon pools through their utilization by man. This means that lands under agriculture do not store as much carbon as the forests that were replaced by agriculture did. Similarly, grasslands turned to agriculture tend both to lose the organic matter in the soil through decay and not to accumulate additional organic matter.

Forests that are managed intensively, although they may produce increased amounts of wood, tend to have at the time of harvest a standing crop much smaller than the stands of the primary forests they replaced. This again means that the turnover time has been reduced and that the standing pool of carbon never achieves the same size as the pool of the original forests. Thus the replacement of primary forests with secondary forests that are managed for lumber or pulp results in a net release of carbon dioxide. There is a further release of carbon through the decay of humus. The decay is stimulated by the harvest of the forests and may continue for several years after the harvest during the early stages of the plant succession that follows the cutting. All these factors lead to a net release of carbon when unmanaged primary forests are replaced by managed ones.

One further line of evidence seems to support the conclusion that the terrestrial biota has for many decades been a net source of carbon dioxide rather than a sink. By comparing the ratios of carbon isotopes in trees Minze Stuiver of the University of Washington has calculated that in the century between 1850 and 1950 the biota appears to have released

| | AREA ($10^6$ SQUARE KILOMETERS) | NET PRIMARY PRODUCTION ($10^{15}$ GRAMS OF CARBON PER YEAR) | PLANT MASS ($10^{15}$ GRAMS OF CARBON) |
|---|---|---|---|
| TROPICAL RAIN FOREST | 17.0 | 16.8 | 344.0 |
| TROPICAL SEASONAL FOREST | 7.5 | 5.4 | 117.0 |
| TEMPERATE EVERGREEN FOREST | 5.0 | 2.9 | 79.0 |
| TEMPERATE DECIDUOUS FOREST | 7.0 | 3.8 | 95.0 |
| BOREAL FOREST | 12.0 | 4.3 | 108.0 |
| WOODLAND AND SHRUBLAND | 8.5 | 2.7 | 22.0 |
| SAVANNA | 15.0 | 6.1 | 27.0 |
| TEMPERATE GRASSLAND | 9.0 | 2.4 | 6.3 |
| TUNDRA AND ALPINE MEADOW | 8.0 | 0.5 | 2.3 |
| DESERT SCRUB | 18.0 | 0.7 | 5.9 |
| ROCK, ICE AND SAND | 24.0 | 0.03 | 0.2 |
| CULTIVATED LAND | 14.0 | 4.1 | 6.3 |
| SWAMP AND MARSH | 2.0 | 2.7 | 13.5 |
| LAKE AND STREAM | 2.0 | 0.4 | 0.02 |
| TOTAL CONTINENTAL | 149.0 | 52.8 | 826.5 |
| OPEN OCEAN | 332.0 | 18.7 | 0.45 |
| UPWELLING ZONES | 0.4 | 0.1 | 0.004 |
| CONTINENTAL SHELF | 26.6 | 4.3 | 0.12 |
| ALGAL BED AND REEF | 0.6 | 0.7 | 0.54 |
| ESTUARIES | 1.4 | 1.0 | 0.63 |
| TOTAL MARINE | 361.0 | 24.8 | 1.74 |
| WORLD TOTAL | 510.0 | 77.6 | 828.0 |

**MAJOR PLANT COMMUNITIES of the earth are listed along with their area, their net primary production and the amount of carbon they hold in storage. Net primary production is the amount of carbon a plant community provides annually for harvesting or for the support of various consumer organisms, either wild or domesticated. Although only about 30 percent of the earth's surface is covered by land, the net primary production of terrestrial vegetation is slightly more than twice the primary production of the oceans. The quantity of carbon stored in land plants is some 500 times greater than the quantity stored in marine ecosystems. The carbon stored in trees is roughly equal to the carbon in the atmosphere. The figures in the table were recently compiled by R. H. Whittaker and Gene E. Likens of Cornell University.**

to the atmosphere $1.2 \times 10^{15}$ grams of carbon per year. Over the same period the release from fossil fuels averaged $.6 \times 10^{15}$ grams of carbon per year.

Stuiver exploited the fact that the ratio of carbon 12 to carbon 13 varies among the atmosphere, the biota and fossil fuels. The biota and fossil fuels are enriched slightly in the lighter isotope, carbon 12. In addition a third isotope of carbon, carbon 14, is present only in the atmosphere and in the biota. Carbon 14 is produced in the upper atmosphere through the cosmic-ray bombardment of the common isotope of nitrogen, nitrogen 14. It has also been produced in large quantities by atomic bomb tests in the atmosphere. Because carbon 14 has a half-life of some 6,000 years it has long since disappeared from fossil fuels, which were formed millions of years ago. The combustion of fossil fuels therefore releases a pool of carbon that is deficient in carbon 14 and tends to dilute the carbon 14 of the atmosphere. By measuring the concentration of various carbon isotopes in the rings of trees of known age and comparing the ratios with those of the atmosphere and of fossil fuels Stuiver was able to estimate the amount of carbon released from the biota. The measurements are technically difficult; moreover, the ratios of carbon isotopes in trees are affected by various environmental factors that make the results less clear-cut than one might like. Nevertheless, the technique offers an important additional means for testing the magnitude of the release of carbon dioxide from the biota.

In view of the available evidence there seems to be little question that the increase in carbon dioxide content of the atmosphere is due not only to the combustion of fossil fuels but also to the destruction of forests. G. Evelyn Hutchinson of Yale University made this point in a chapter in *The Earth as a Planet,* a book edited by Gerard P. Kuiper in 1954. Hutchinson guessed that the release of carbon from the biota was about equal to the release from fossil fuel. The best evidence we have at present indicates that this relation persists.

There is enough carbon held within the biota for the relation to continue for another decade or two through the expected peak in the worldwide consumption of oil. By that time, if not sooner, the earth will have been committed to climatic change as a result of the accumulation of carbon dioxide in the atmosphere—if indeed such a change is to take place. The question of whether or not it will take place depends on the scale of the carbon dioxide effect, an appraisal that is extremely difficult to make with any certainty. It is now recognized that changes in the output of the sun, changes in the reflectivity of the earth (as it is influenced by the extent of cloud, snow and ice cover) and other

| FORESTS: | PLANT MASS ($10^3$ GRAMS OF CARBON PER SQUARE METER) | NET PRIMARY PRODUCTION (GRAMS OF CARBON PER SQUARE METER PER YEAR) | |
|---|---|---|---|
| | | RANGE | MEAN |
| TROPICAL (WET) | 3.0–36.0 | 450–1,600 | 990 |
| TEMPERATE | 3.0–90.0 | 270–1,125 | 560 |
| BOREAL | 3.0–18.0 | 180–900 | 360 |
| SAVANNAS | 0.1–7.0 | 90–900 | 400 |
| GRASSLANDS | 0.1–2.3 | 90–675 | 270 |
| CULTIVATED LAND | 0.2–5.4 | 45–2,800 | 290 |

**TRANSFER OF LAND INTO AGRICULTURE** usually results in a sharp reduction in the carbon stored in the biomass and a somewhat smaller reduction in the carbon dioxide removed annually from the atmosphere and fixed by photosynthesis. The table, also based on the work of Whittaker and Likens, indicates the range of published estimates for the standing biomass and the net primary production of major natural ecosystems compared with cultivated land.

factors all influence the climate. Whether or not the carbon dioxide content of the atmosphere is great enough to be the dominant factor remains to be seen. If the carbon dioxide effect is indeed dominant, the probability is that the earth will be warmed differentially, with temperatures increasing toward the poles. Such a change can be expected to move the desert zones poleward, enlarging the areas of aridity and reducing the areas suitable for agriculture. The prospect is not encouraging for a world whose human population may double within the next 30 to 35 years.

If the evidence were overwhelming that the risk of a deleterious change in climate over the next few decades was unacceptably great, the course of action would be clear enough. The burning of fossil fuels would be restricted to reduce that source of carbon dioxide. Strong moves would also be made to prevent the harvest of primary forests around the world, to expand the areas devoted to forests and to allow such areas to develop massive standing crops of trees. Whether such drastic measures could be effected is much in doubt; the social problems that would result would clearly be profound.

Other suggestions have been made, including the suggestion that because the availability of phosphorus is considered by some to limit net primary production in the oceans the advanced nations should apply some of their industrial energy to the mining of phosphorus with the objective of transferring it as rapidly as possible to the relatively infertile oceans, thereby stimulating photosynthesis and the storage of carbon. The scheme is superficially attractive because it seems to offer a way of speeding the storage of carbon in the oceans. The possibility exists, however, that any additional photosynthesis stimulated in the ocean would be offset by an equivalent stimulation of respiration, so that there would be no net increase in

carbon storage. There are many questions about the feasibility of such a step, including the basic one of whether phosphorus is indeed critically limiting in oceanic waters. There is a reasonable possibility that nitrogen is also limiting, in which case the stimulation of marine photosynthesis could prove to be substantially more difficult than has been assumed.

Nevertheless, recent experience has emphasized to all of us who work in these fields that important details of the world carbon budget are substantially unknown at present. Some improvement in our knowledge of such details seems feasible through measurement of the changes in the areas and structures of forests worldwide from satellite photographs. Investigations are also under way to see if biotic mechanisms might facilitate the transfer of considerably more carbon into the oceanic depths than we assume is being transferred today. The immediate prospect of establishing with high precision all the details of the world's carbon budget, however, is not bright.

The potential hazards associated with a steady increase in the carbon dioxide content of the atmosphere will loom large in the coming decades and will doubtless bear heavily on such decisions as whether to accelerate the development of power plants based on nuclear fuel instead of those based on coal and whether to preserve forest areas instead of encroaching on them (and, if the forests are to be preserved, how to provide the new lands that are almost certain to be needed for agriculture). There is almost no aspect of national and international policy that can remain unaffected by the prospect of global climatic change. Carbon dioxide, until now an apparently innocuous trace gas in the atmosphere, may be moving rapidly toward a central role as a major threat to the present world order.

# 11

# Nighttime Images
# of the Earth from Space

## COMMENTARY

A nyone who has ever lived near or passed an oil field may have seen a large flare of natural gas burning night and day. Such flares are characteristic of those oil fields in which the amounts of gas are too small to be economically piped to users or which are too far away from major markets. It is hard for people who face a shortage of such a priceless commodity to accept the fact that the costs of building the equipment and pipelines for providing such gas to the customer costs more—not only in dollars, but in energy itself—than the amount recovered. That net loss could be justified only as paying a premium for the cleanliness and convenience of gas use.

In the United States, flaring of natural gas has been restricted because of environmental reasons as well as the growing demand for gas in the markets. But in other parts of the world, much natural gas is flared because there is no other cheap way to dispose of it. Pending arrangements for pipelines, other methods of transport, or industrial use, the Mexican government oil company is flaring gas from its newly discovered large fields. This gas can easily be marketed in the long run now that the United States and Mexico have reached a purchase agreement and the gas will be transported by pipeline to the United States. The large amounts of gas being flared in gas fields in North Africa and the Persian Gulf may pose more of a problem, for there the gas is far from markets and by present technology must be liquified and shipped in very cold (cryogenic) tankers.

In this article, Thomas Croft has shown by an unusual application of satellite photography how abundant and obvious these flares are from space. The amounts of flared gas have never been very well known, and this ingenious method may prove a good way to estimate their size and distribution. Certainly the photographs dramatize their possible importance. How the images are produced and analyzed makes a fascinating story in itself, a combination of advanced methods of photography and satellite control and placement. Computers play an important role in enhancement of the images to reveal more detail and resolve the imagery.

Flared natural gas is not the only source of the bright lights our planet displays to space, as Croft shows. The lights of agricultural burning in the less-developed countries of the world show up on these photographs, too, as do large forest flares. The question of agricultural burning is problematic. It undoubtedly contributes to soil erosion and may be a poor way to deal with farmland. However, we still have not discovered a better way to rid fields of harvested stalks, weeds, and overgrowth in many poorly developed regions where soils are thin and impoverished, where jungles compete with agriculture, and climates are disadvantageous.

# Nighttime Images
# of the Earth from Space

by Thomas A. Croft
*July 1978*

*An unusual aspect of the earth is revealed in pictures recorded at
midnight by U.S. Air Force weather satellites. The brightest lights
on the dark side of the planet are giant waste-gas flares*

When the earth is viewed from space during the day, cloud patterns and geographic features dominate the scene. The evidence of man's presence, when it is visible at all, constitutes a minor modification of the picture. At night, however, particularly at midnight on a moonless night, the darkened image of the earth sparkles with the bright lights of man's creations. In addition to the transient brilliance of such natural phenomena as lightning, forest fires and the aurora, the nocturnal side of the earth is girdled with complex arrays of city lights and more diffuse bands of agricultural fires. By far the brightest of man's works, however, are the gas flares found in association with some of the world's major oil fields.

This unusual aspect of the earth has become apparent only recently as an outgrowth of the U.S. Air Force's Defense Meteorological Satellite Program. The primary mission of the spacecraft put into orbit in the course of this program is to provide imagery on which to base short-range cloud-cover forecasts. At first the pictures that were relayed electronically back to the earth for this purpose were routinely discarded after a day's use, but the waste of potential scientific data was soon recognized and steps were taken to save the better auroral images. These pictures were finally made public in 1973. Provisions were then made for the establishment of an archive of the original films at the University of Wisconsin and for the distribution of the auroral images on microfilm to interested investigators through the facilities of the Department of Commerce. Most of the pictures that accompany this article were obtained in this way from the Wisconsin archive.

## Characteristics of the System

The Air Force meteorological satellite is not the only system capable of supplying nighttime images of the earth from space. The three Landsat spacecraft launched by the National Aeronautics and Space Administration in 1972, 1975 and 1978 could also operate at night, although they were not designed for that purpose and have seldom been called on to make nighttime exposures. The Landsat system offers the advantage of four-color imagery and a finer ground resolution than the Air Force meteorological satellite can achieve, but the latter system is much more sensitive to faint light sources. For a study of the brighter light sources the two systems are complementary: the Air Force satellite is well suited for conducting a wide-ranging survey of the entire earth, whereas the Landsat system can provide high-resolution color pictures of specific areas selected from the survey.

The spacecraft of both of these U.S. programs are in near-circular orbits at altitudes of about 800 or 900 kilometers. The orbits are designed to miss the earth's poles by about nine degrees, making the plane of the orbit precess around the earth at the same rate as that with which the earth moves around the sun. For photographic missions such sun-synchronous orbits offer an important advantage: the time of day (or night) below the camera does not change with the passing of the seasons, and hence shifts in lighting are minimized. The practical effect of such a scheme is that the images are recorded in the form of successive strips that run approximately north-south, with each strip representing one orbit along the track of the satellite. The time of day in each area photographed is unchanged from strip to strip. The overlap between adjacent strips increases at high latitudes: at 90 degrees north and south latitude the poles appear in each strip; they are photographed alternately every 102 minutes.

One of the most striking things about many of the images obtained with this system is the light source: moonlight at midnight. A similar but more detailed picture of the earth is recorded by the satellite in daylight on the other half of its orbit. The satellite program thereby provides cloud-cover pictures anywhere on the earth every 12 hours or so, during periods when moonlight falls on the night side of the earth (about half the time). There are several other types of sensor on each of these satellites. One device makes simultaneous infrared images, relying on thermal radiation from the earth and from the clouds. The resulting films show the relative temperatures of different clouds, and they provide a means for mapping cloud cover even on moonless nights.

In images made in full moonlight, when the satellite's cameras are operated at reduced sensitivity, many man-made lights and fires are visible, but only the gas flares are bright enough to stand out clearly [*see illustration on pages 124 and 125*]. As the moonlight decreases however, the pictures undergo a transformation much like the change that takes place in the evening sky when the sun sets and the stars come out, except that here the cities and the fires come out! For example, consider the satellite image on the opposite page. To the north the boot of Italy stands out clearly in the lingering moonlight, and it is easy to locate many of the major cities of Europe. The brightest spots in this strip are gas flares coincident with known oil fields in Algeria, Libya and Nigeria. The fairly uniform band of small lights sprinkled across Africa south of the Sahara appears to originate with fires set deliberately to clear agricultural or pastoral land. Many similar fire patterns are seen elsewhere in the world.

Several shortcomings of the Air Force meteorological-satellite system are apparent in this picture. The details near the edges are quite fuzzy, owing to the low altitude of the spacecraft, which is only about a third as high as this image is wide. A redesigned scanning device now flying on the Air Force meteorological satellite contains features that improve the resolution of such images near the edges.

The imaging system that produced these pictures works as follows. The image originates in an optical telescope that scans the earth's surface in an "across track" direction with a constant angular resolution. (In nonpolar regions the scan is roughly east-west.) At the focal plane of the telescope is a light sensor, which resembles a photographer's light meter except that the field of view is only two-tenths of a degree. The edges of the scene are far from the satellite and are viewed obliquely, so that the telescope's angular field of view covers a surface area some six or seven times larger there than the area covered at the nadir (that is, with the camera pointing straight down). Data from this system are sent to the ground in the form of a stream of binary numbers representing the variations in brightness recorded by the scanning sensor. Later, on the earth, the numbers are converted back into light spots and the images are reassembled on film in a conventional maplike form. In the process some approximate corrections are made for distortions, which can result from a variety of sources. (The orbit is not exactly circular, the earth is not exactly spherical, the spacecraft is not always at the same altitude, and so forth.)

Some of the larger gas flares are so bright that the internal reflections within the body of the telescope become visible; this effect accounts for the rings around the gas flares in some of the images. Similar artifacts appear in astronomical telescopes, which are also designed to detect objects that are very small and yet very bright in relation to their surroundings. Except in conditions of extreme contrast, such as the contrast that exists between the bright flares and their dark surroundings, this artifact causes no problem for the imaging system of the satellite.

From a comparison of such images with their infrared counterparts, which are exactly the same size and easy to match by overlaying the two films on a light table, one can see that the city

**THREE MAJOR LIGHT SOURCES** associated with human activities are visible in this nighttime satellite image, made recently in the course of the Air Force's Defense Meteorological Satellite Program. The numerous bright spots arrayed across the upper third of this picture are the city lights of Europe. The larger isolated lights near the middle and bottom arise from gas flares at oil fields in Algeria, Libya and Nigeria. (The rings around the brighter flares are caused by internal reflections within the body of the telescope.) The uniform band of smaller lights scattered across Africa south of the Sahara appears to originate with agricultural and pastoral fires.

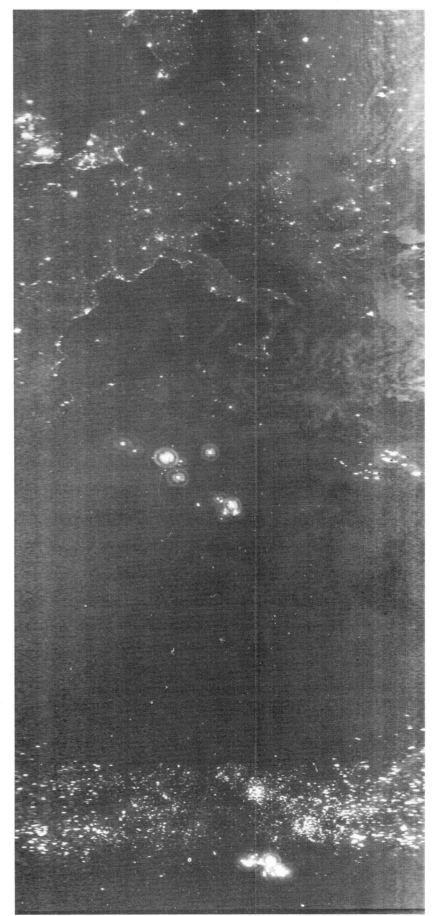

lights penetrate thin clouds with little degradation. Moderately heavy clouds diffuse the image, whereas very heavy clouds can completely block the light.

### Gas Flares

The nighttime satellite images show bright gas flares in many parts of the world, but by far the greatest concentration of them is in the vicinity of the Persian Gulf. Even in full moonlight this area is aglow with numerous large flares [*see bottom illustration on page 126*]. The burning of waste gas in the Persian Gulf oil fields has been a spectacular sight in that part of the world for decades and was reported by aviators flying over the region as early as 1933. The practice of venting unwanted gas from oil wells to the air without burning goes back even further; more than 100 years ago an article in *Scientific American* reported such waste from early oil wells in Pennsylva-

nia; the writer estimated that one well released a million cubic feet of gas per hour and had been doing so "for years."

Since gas flares are the most conspicuous features of these nighttime images, they warrant closer attention. The imaging system of the Air Force meteorological satellite is designed to measure only the average brightness over each of its picture elements, called pixels, which are roughly three kilometers on a side. (The exact size varies from place to place on the image, and from sensor to sensor.) The contribution of a single flame to this average brightness must therefore depend not only on its intrinsic brightness but also on the percentage of the area of the pixel that is occupied by the flare's image. In other words, the flares must be either very bright or very big to show up so clearly on the images. It turns out that they are both. The large areas covered by the flares result from the practice of spreading the fire lateral-

ly to ensure complete combustion. Usually this is done by dispensing the gas from a series of standpipes placed in a row 50 or more meters long [*see top illustration on page 127*].

In an effort to analyze more closely two of the larger gas flares in Algeria seen in the illustration on the preceding page, I obtained Landsat photographs of the same region made during the day [*see bottom illustration on page 127*]. Two flames are clearly visible in several of these photographs, with a north-south separation of about 11 kilometers. In terms of the Air Force satellite's imaging system the two flares are three pixels apart.

By scrutinizing enlarged transparencies of the Landsat photographs under a magnifying glass I was able to determine that the red flames are some 500 meters across, much larger than the flares usually seen in ground-level photographs. In daytime satellite imagery such gas

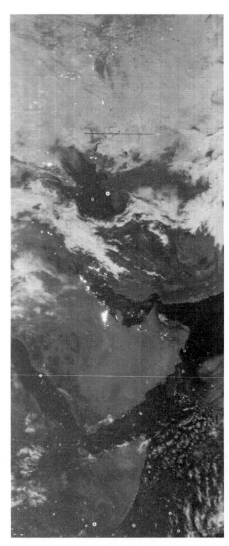

**MOONLIT PANORAMA of an expanse of earth stretching from northwestern Africa to southeastern Asia is composed of parts of six images obtained on six successive north-south orbits by the Air Force** **meteorological satellite. All of the pictures were made at local midnight on February 6, 1974. The primary illumination was provided by reflected light from the moon. The overlap between adjacent strips**

flares are easy to spot, since their smoke trails extend many tens of kilometers downwind. In an attempt to avoid giving such graphic evidence of pollution, the more modern gas flares are equipped with "smokeless" burners. This practice is no doubt justified from the standpoint of appearances, but in view of the concern about the rising level of carbon dioxide in the atmosphere, mankind might be better off in the long run if some of the carbon particles in the smoke were left unburned.

A more precise estimate of the lateral extent of these flares can be obtained from nighttime Landsat images. For this purpose one of the Landsat spacecraft was activated over Algeria on the night of January 31, 1976, at the request of the U.S. Geological Survey. An extreme enlargement of one of the flares photographed on this occasion is shown in the top illustration on page 128. The flare corresponds to the larger, more souther-

ly one shown in the daytime Landsat picture at the bottom of page 127.

To understand what this particular nighttime image shows, it is necessary to know something about how it was made. As the Landsat satellite passes overhead, its multispectral scanning telescope looks downward by means of a 45-degree mirror that rocks back and forth to scan the scene from left to right (that is, in the across-track direction). Patterns of light falling on the focal plane of the telescope are conveyed to electronic sensors by way of tiny glass light pipes, each of which has a square cross section corresponding to a square 79 meters on a side on the earth's surface at the nadir. (At the edge of the image, 93 kilometers from the projection of the satellite's track on the earth, each light pipe covers a slightly larger area, so that the stated resolving power of the system is usually rounded off to 80 meters.) The electronic sensors are

"read" once for every 57 meters of the scan; hence the Landsat pixels are rectangles measuring 57 meters by 79 meters at the nadir. A large bright object can affect two or three consecutive sensor readings, partly because the light pipes are larger than the 57-meter pixel and partly because of a lag in the electronics. (A few months ago the Russian delegates to the United Nations suggested that 50-meter pixels should be the smallest allowed; anything finer would be considered a violation of a nation's right to privacy.)

Within each pixel the Landsat imaging system obtains four separate sensor readings, one for each of four spectral ranges, or colors. (The term "color" is used loosely here; two of the ranges are actually in the infrared and near-infrared regions of the spectrum and are therefore invisible to the human eye.) For each color and for each pixel the Landsat sends to the ground a separate

increases at high latitudes. In this case the strips were cropped at top and bottom; the originals include both poles in each strip. Although some city lights and agricultural fires are visible in such brightly moon-lit scenes, only the gas flares are bright enough to stand out clearly. An enlargement of the bright cluster of waste-gas flares in the Persian Gulf area is shown in the bottom illustration on the next page.

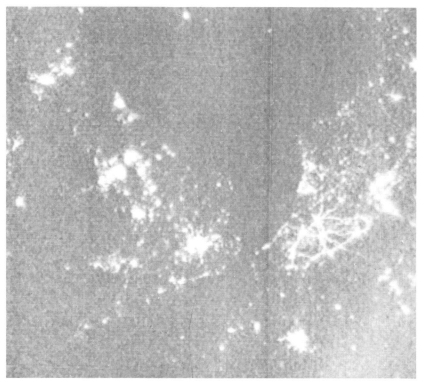

**CITY LIGHTS** of the countries bordering the English Channel and the North Sea show up with unusual clarity in this enlarged Air Force satellite image, in spite of the comparatively poor contrast. The picture was made on a moonless night in May, 1977, when the satellite's sensors were operating at peak sensitivity. The British Isles are at left. Network of lights at center right is in Belgium. Well-lighted night spot near the edge of the image at lower right is Paris.

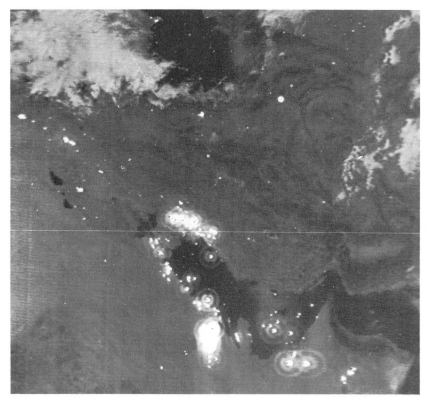

**GAS FLARES** are concentrated conspicuously in the Persian Gulf area, as evidenced by this enlarged moonlit image recorded by the Air Force satellite's optical system. Dark area at top is Caspian Sea; bright spot on promontory is Baku in the U.S.S.R.; larger spot due south of the Caspian is Tehran, Iran; similar spot near large lakes at center left is Baghdad, Iraq.

binary number coded to represent the power level of the light. Since there are only 35 illuminated pixels in the particular enlargement under consideration here, it was feasible to produce each small colored rectangle individually by ordinary photographic means. To make the infrared and near-infrared data visible I adopted a "false color" method of reproduction, shifting each digital power level toward the shorter-wavelength end of the spectrum by about a fifth of a micrometer. Thus the original infrared reading is reproduced as red, the near-infrared as green and the red as blue. (There was practically no green in the original image.)

A standard Landsat picture is made up of 7,581,600 pixels, each with four separate spectral readings. It follows that a single daytime image represents more than 30 million numbers sent down from space. No simple photographic method could be practical for reassembling such a color image on film. In fact the system now in operation for making Landsat films does not even use light. Instead the film is held in a vacuum and exposed to direct bombardment by an electron beam. This approach enables one to expose very fine lines on the film, with each line corresponding to an across-track string of contiguous pixels. Color composites are then made by mechanically superposing the black-and-white films, each of which represents one of the original spectral bands. The reconstruction of the Air Force satellite program's images is done in much the same way, except that a light beam is used instead of an electron beam.

With this understanding of the basis of the Landsat imagery in mind, let us reexamine the top picture on page 8 and try to visualize the flame that produced this light. Many of the pixels along the border of the image reveal only a weak light, which is what one would expect if only a wisp of flame intruded into that rectangle. Although the overall image is about 500 meters long, it appears that it might be caused by two flares 200 meters apart. On the other hand, the dark center might be smoke obscuring part of the flame. (The flames of this same fire in the daytime Landsat image did not appear to be separated.) The matter could probably be resolved by examining several more Landsat images of the same site.

From a comparison of the larger-scale Air Force images with published charts of the world's principal oil and gas fields it is clear that many such flares coincide with oil fields but few coincide with gas fields. This is not surprising; a gas well can simply be capped if the gas cannot be sold, whereas an oil well unavoidably releases gas as the oil is extracted from the ground. Oil often reaches the surface in the form of a

GAS FLARES ARE SPREAD over a large area in remote regions in order to ensure complete combustion. This photograph, made from the vantage point of a nearby drilling rig, shows such a flame at an oil field in Kuwait. The standpipes used to dispense the gas are roughly eight feet tall. The photograph was made by David F. Cupp and appeared originally in the May 1969 issue of *National Geographic*.

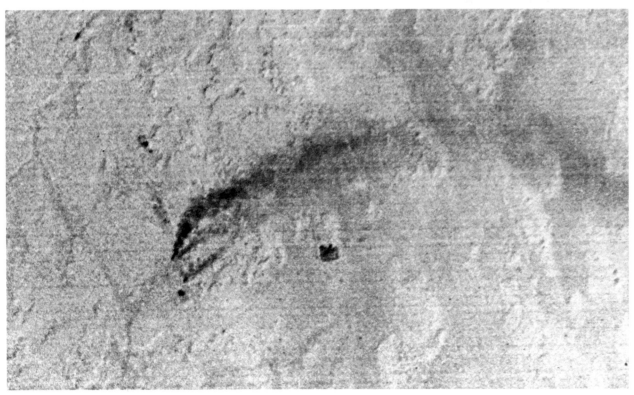

FOUR-COLOR SATELLITE IMAGE of two large gas flares in Algeria was obtained in daylight by the *Landsat 1* spacecraft, operated by the National Aeronautics and Space Administration. The flames of the burning gas are seen here as red splotches at the head of long smoke plumes. A greatly magnified nighttime Landsat image of the more southerly flame of the two appears at the top of the next page.

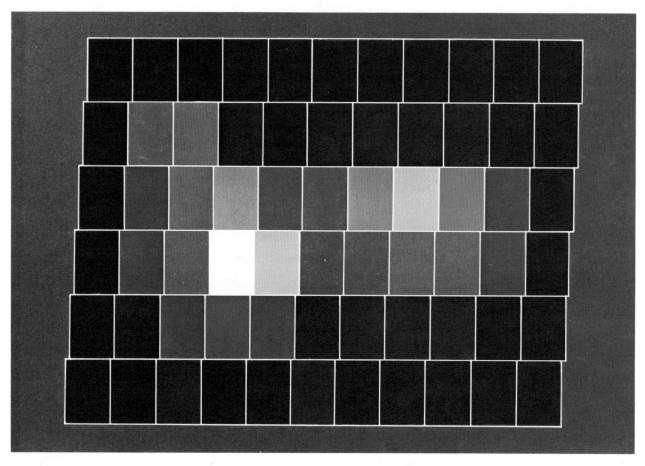

BLOWUP of an extremely small portion of a nighttime Landsat image containing one of the Algerian gas flares shown in the bottom illustration on the preceding page was made by the author in an effort to estimate the lateral extent of the flare. Every Landsat image is composed of millions of tiny picture elements, called pixels, that correspond to rectangular areas on the earth's surface 79 meters long and 57 meters wide. Within each pixel the Landsat imaging system obtains four separate sensor readings, one for each of four spectral ranges. In this case there were only 35 illuminated pixels in the enlarged image, so that it was feasible to produce each small colored rectangle individually by ordinary photographic means. A "false color" method of reproduction was adopted in order to shift the normally invisible infrared and near-infrared ranges of the Landsat data into the visible part of the spectrum. The resulting image suggests that the overall length of the gas flare was about 500 meters, although the possibility remains that it was composed of two flares 200 meters apart.

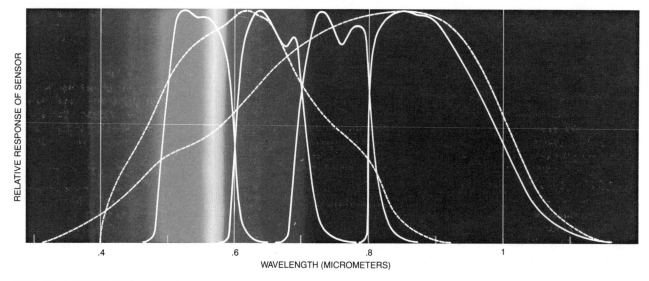

SPECTRAL RANGES of the Landsat multispectral scanning system and two versions of the sensor carried on board the Air Force meteorological satellites are compared here. The six curves are all shown with the same peak value, although in actuality both the old Air Force sensor (represented by the broken white curve on the right) and the new Air Force sensor (represented by the broken white curve on the left) are more sensitive than any of the Landsat sensors (represented by the four solid white curves). The band of colors running across the graph from top to bottom in the wavelength range from approximately .4 to .7 micrometer corresponds to the visible portion of the electromagnetic spectrum. A comparison of the curves of the satellite sensors with this visible range shows why both spacecraft are particularly effective at detecting fires: much of the energy from fires is transmitted at wavelengths to which the human eye is insensitive.

frothy mixture with various gases, and the oil must settle before it can be piped away. The associated gas must be disposed of in some way, and in remote areas it may be more economical to burn the gas than to transport it to a buyer. Government policymakers might well ponder the significance of these pictures in setting domestic price controls on natural gas. The artificial depression of gas prices in the U.S. and other developed countries can be viewed as an encouragement to such waste in the remote oil fields of the less-developed countries. Presumably the economic dilemma of the policymakers in the controlled economies of the world is similar, since large gas flares can be seen in association with oil fields in the U.S.S.R. and other Communist countries.

Since mankind has been venting or burning such gas for more than 100 years, it is only natural to ask how much has been wasted in this way. The answer is difficult to determine, since the parties most directly involved have little motivation to be frank about the details. In spite of these difficulties Ralph M. Rotty of the Oak Ridge Institute for Energy Analysis has compiled annual estimates of the total world volume of flared gas from 1935 through 1976 [*see illustration at right*]. His figures show that the amount of gas flared has grown at a steady pace that exceeds the growth rate of a simple exponential model, at least prior to the recent rise in oil prices. By adding these yearly estimates, and extending the numbers forward to 1978 at a fixed rate and backward to the discovery of oil in 1859 at an exponential rate, I have arrived at a total volume of wasted gas (at atmospheric pressure) of 4,200 cubic kilometers, or roughly 1,000 cubic miles. Rotty estimates that in recent years flare gas accounts for about 3 percent of all the hydrocarbons burned by man. The nighttime satellite observations I have described here might offer an independent means for reappraising this estimate of the rate at which gas is currently being flared in the world.

## Japanese Lanterns

One of the strangest sights on the dark side of the earth is seen in the satellite image at the bottom of the next page. On the right is Japan, one of the world's brightest nations at night, owing to its dense population and advanced state of development. On the left, in the middle of the Sea of Japan, an area that is normally black on such a moonless night, there is a great swirling mass of bright lights. The lights seem to be arrayed in an orderly fashion, and their pattern changes from night to night. It has long been known that this region is subject to severe thunderstorms accompanied by extraordinary displays of light-

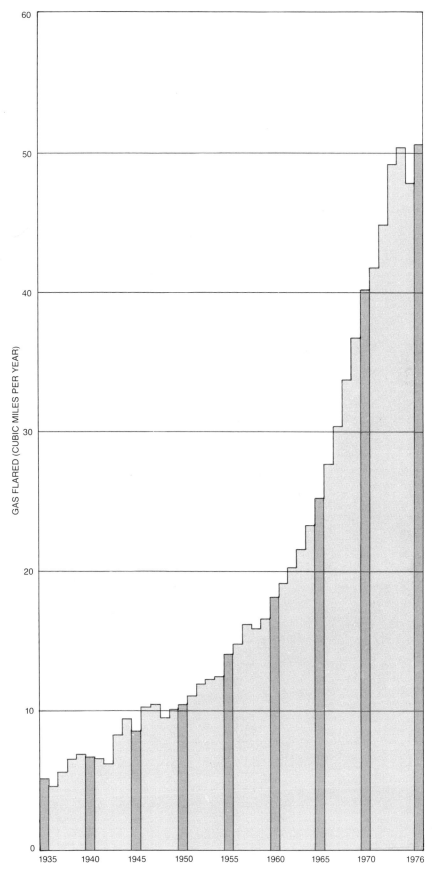

**ANNUAL ESTIMATES** of the total volume of gas (at atmospheric pressure) flared in the world's oil fields between 1935 and 1976 were compiled by Ralph M. Rotty of the Oak Ridge Institute for Energy Analysis. Using rough approximations to carry these figures backward to the discovery of oil in 1859 and forward to the present, the author has arrived at a grand total of 1,000 cubic miles for the volume of gas wasted in this way in a little more than a century.

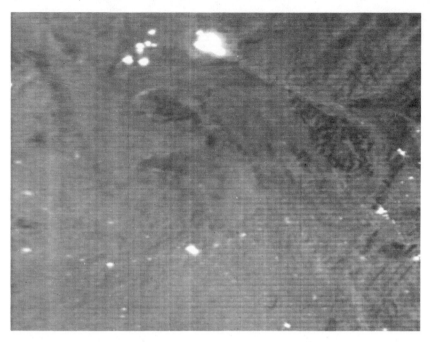

**GIANT GAS FLARE IN SIBERIA** is seen in this nighttime satellite image, made in January, 1975. The flare, one of the biggest yet detected by the author in his examination of the Air Force pictures, is located near Surgut in northern Siberia. The large oil field known to exist in this remote region apparently lacks a gas pipeline to places where more productive use could be made of the waste gas. The route of the Trans-Siberian railroad is marked by the regularly spaced large and small cities strung out like a necklace across the bottom of the picture.

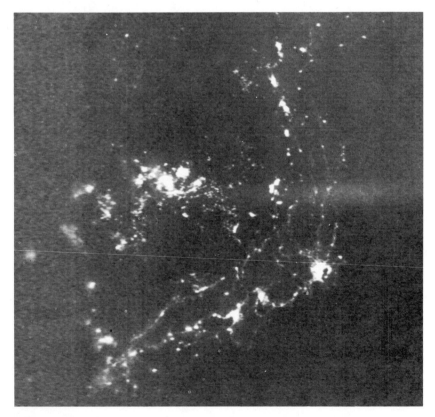

**BRIGHT LIGHTS IN THE SEA OF JAPAN** appear at left in this Air Force satellite image, made on a moonless night in June, 1975. The lights coincide with the known position of the Japanese squid-fishing fleet at this time. The several thousand boats of this fleet are strung with incandescent bulbs totaling hundreds of millions of watts, which serve to attract the squid to the surface. Japan itself is sharply delineated by city lights of its densely populated coastal regions.

ning. In response to my inquiry, however, the Japanese Meteorological Agency reported that there were no major thunderstorms in the Sea of Japan on the night this image was recorded. A second inquiry brought a more satisfactory answer. Scientists at the Japanese government's fisheries bureau sent me charts showing the location of the squid-fishing fleet on the date in question. The match between the charts and the satellite images was unmistakable.

I was informed that during the squid-fishing season vast fleets of both Korean and Japanese boats operate in the Sea of Japan. The Japanese fleet alone is composed of some 2,600 boats, each weighing between 60 and 100 tons and each carrying as many as 50 incandescent lamps with an average power of 3,500 watts per lamp. That adds up to a total of more than 400 million watts of electric light! The lamps are used to attract the squid to the surface, where they are netted. Each boat strings its bulbs in a double row about two or three meters above the deck. Half the bulbs have no shades, and the other half have only small shades. On the average only about half of the Japanese fleet fishes at any one time, so the total emitted light might be only on the order of 200 million watts. Even so, it must seem like daylight out there. Moreover, in addition to these boats there is the smaller Korean squid-fishing fleet and a lighted Japanese fleet in shallower waters seeking another fish: the saury. (A separate Japanese squid-fishing fleet reportedly works the waters near New Zealand, but so far I have not found evidence of their activities in the Air Force weather-satellite imagery.)

One can get a better feel for the magnitude of this wattage by comparing it to the total power sent skyward by the U.S. population in the form of visible light. A decade ago this output was measured from space and was found to be about 40 million watts—roughly a fifth of a watt per person. Making allowance for the low efficiency of the fishermen's incandescent lamps compared with the combination of lights used in the U.S. at night, I estimate that the sum of all the light detected by the Air Force satellite from the U.S. is only two or three times greater than that detected from the squid-fishing fleet in the Sea of Japan.

To be sure, the city lights of any country, including the U.S., are much more dispersed. In fact, their pattern rather accurately reflects the distribution of population. That correspondence can be readily appreciated by comparing the montage of three nighttime satellite images of the U.S. shown at the top of the opposite page with the computer-assisted census map of the U.S. reproduced at the bottom of the same page. There are only a few discrepancies; for example, two lights appear east of Salt Lake City

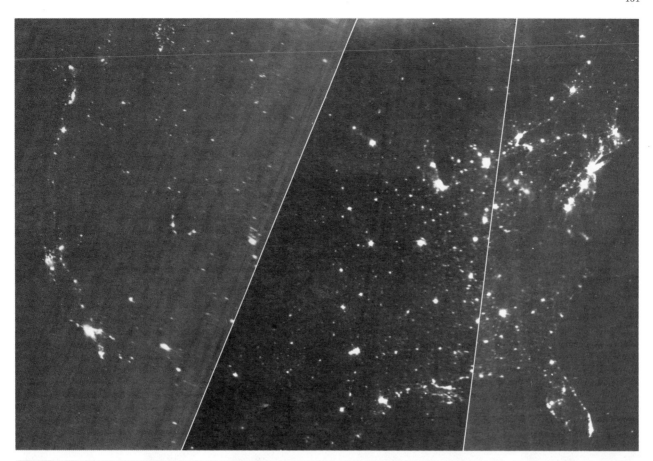

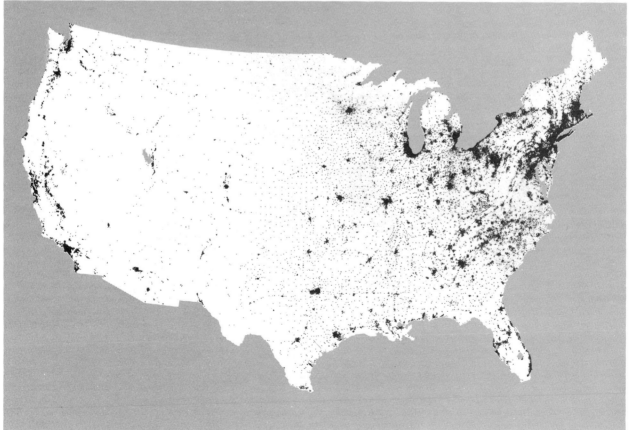

**POPULATION DISTRIBUTION** of the U.S. is accurately reflected by the pattern of city lights revealed in the montage of three night-time satellite images at top. A computer-plotted population map, obtained from the Bureau of the Census, is reproduced at bottom.

**BRILLIANT AURORA** extending across Canada as far south as the Great Lakes is the most conspicuous feature of this picture, recorded by the Air Force meteorological satellite on the night of April 18, 1974. City lights of U.S. occupy middle portion of this strip. Smaller lights scattered along the western side of Mexico at lower left are agricultural fires. The large bright gas flare at lower right is associated with the Reforma oil field on the eastern coast of Mexico.

that have no counterparts on the census map.

## Agricultural and Natural Fires

In many cultivated parts of the earth vegetable matter is regularly burned as part of the seasonal cycle of growth. I have already pointed out the band of agricultural fires that runs across central Africa south of the Sahara. Another good example closer to home is seen in the satellite image at the left. Since the lights scattered all along the western side of Mexico are absent at other times of the year, I surmise that they must be also caused by agricultural burning. The gas flares in this image, on the other hand, show little variation in the course of the year. The bright gas flares visible in this strip are associated with the Reforma oil field on the eastern coast of Mexico. (This particular strip also illustrates beautifully how far south the aurora can appear at times.)

Similar agricultural fires can be seen in many other parts of the world. The agricultural or pastoral origin of these fires can usually be determined by the fact that they disappear in certain seasons. Daytime Landsat images are useful for studying the broad band of agricultural burning across central Africa, since the burned areas appear blackened on subsequent passes. The total area of land cleared in this way has been measured by means of the Landsat images.

It appears that the less-developed countries are the only regions where there is much agricultural burning. Presumably the practice is related to the lack of powered machines to prepare the land for planting; as a result fire is used instead to help clear the residue of the previous season's crop. Some crops of course require fire even in circumstances where other alternatives exist. Nevertheless, it is somewhat surprising to see the extent to which fire is still used in countries that lack modern agricultural machinery. A century ago similar fires were set to help clear the vast forests that once covered the central U.S.

Natural fires are also seen in the Air Force satellite imagery, for example in northwestern Australia [*see illustration on page 133*]. Unlike the fires in cultivated lands, these fires are very large. Two aspects of the fires make them appear to be accidental: they are in remote regions not generally cultivated, and they are so large that men could probably control them only with difficulty, if at all. (On the other hand, it has been reported that the aborigines once burned the scrub in this area to maintain grazing lands for kangaroos; perhaps the practice is still followed on a large scale.) Apparently these large fires are destructive to wildlife; I have received an inquiry from the Australian Wildlife Service expressing interest in the use of such satellite images to monitor the recurrent fires in the region. It is clear that such a project is both feasible and, given the concurrence of the observed country, desirable as a means for assessing the damage caused by large natural fires. Except for times of heavy clouds, the fires could be charted daily.

Another civilization watching the earth from space would see no evidence of an energy shortage here; indeed, nighttime viewing would reveal great waste, indicating a glut of energy. The waste arises in part from the unwillingness of the developed countries (particularly those that are well lighted at night) to depend on energy imports because of a perceived threat to their national security and economic well-being resulting from any such dependence.

The city lights of the developed world and the gas flares of the less-developed world are a comparatively recent event in history. Only a century ago nocturnal images of the earth from space would have revealed neither cities nor flares and far less agricultural burning. What will the dark side of the earth look like in another 100 years? I would venture to suggest that the inhabitable regions will look much like the U.S. does today, covered with city lights but with no gas flares. Gas and oil will probably be highly prized as chemical stocks, and they will be used as fuels only in certain systems at premium prices.

Why do the operators of oil fields not stop the waste of flare gas now by installing liquefaction machinery? The answer to this obvious question apparently has three parts. First, billions of dollars are in fact being invested in gas-liquefaction equipment and in the ships to carry the liquefied gas. The speed and scale of this effort have been hampered by statements from the leaders of the developed countries indicating their aversion to the purchase of such liquefied gas for fear of becoming too dependent on it. Here again balance of payments problem and the concern for national security indirectly result in the burning of more waste gas.

A second factor also plays an important role: present-day gas-liquefaction machinery is inherently economical only when the plant is large. Small flaring centers must be connected to large centers or their gas probably cannot be saved economically. A small but economical gas-liquefaction plant needs to be designed. Perhaps these satellite images will reveal that the small flares are numerous enough to warrant a substantial investment in the development of such plants.

The third factor standing in the way of the productive use of flare gas is simply that many flares currently dispose of highly corrosive waste gas for which no economic use has yet been found.

Concerning the agricultural fires, it seems likely that this kind of burning on such a large scale removes valuable soil nutrients, casting them to the winds. Although fire is known to be necessary for the survival of some ecological systems, it seems too great a coincidence that the regions of poorest agricultural productivity are also the regions of greatest agricultural burning. Perhaps the use of fire to prepare the land for planting made more sense when people were not so numerous. Alternatives to burning that conserve soil nutrients could clearly have worldwide significance in view of the scope of the practice, as revealed in these satellite images.

NATURAL FIRES appear to be responsible for the large bright spots seen in this nighttime satellite image of western Australia. These fires are much larger than the controlled fires seen in cultivated regions. Short bright horizontal streaks visible above clouds nearby are caused by lightning. Southwestern corner of Australia is clearly illuminated by moonlight at lower left.

# 12

# The Importation of Liquefied Natural Gas

## COMMENTARY

I f a great amount of natural gas is being flared or capped for lack of transport facilities, it would seem imperative to invent efficient and safe means of carrying that gas to its markets. The cryogenic liquified natural gas tanker is one answer. The nagging question is whether it will be sufficiently safe, for there is little doubt that it works well enough. In this article, Elisabeth Drake and Robert Reid describe the plans and proposals for a carefully designed system of tanker transport and shore facilities. Some such systems are now being built; others are still on the drawing boards. Many experiments have been performed to model the various events that could occur in the course of loading, sailing, and unloading, and so far the outcome seems favorable, although since the Three-Mile Island reactor accident, the inadequacies of modeling may give us some pause. The technology, it seems, is ready.

In this kind of transport, there are uncomfortable possibilities for something going wrong that could lead to serious accidents with loss of life and property. The authors explore how some of these risks can be minimized to the point of acceptability, as we accept the risk for any activity of society, from construction accidents to air travel. The risks described are local; that is, they affect those who work on the tankers, loading docks, or tank farms, or those who live around the tanks on shore. To the extent that the general population can be fenced off from the facilities, the risk are solely occupational. This is not to say that the hazards are therefore inconsequential.

More global dangers may be posed by the spills of liquified natural gas at sea. We know from bitter experience with the Torrey Canyon, the Argo Merchant, and the Amoco Cadiz the enormous amounts of oil that can be spilled through an error in navigational judgement or a violent storm. What would be the consequences of a spill of liquified natural gas of that magnitude? We know that it could ignite, just as oil or gasoline does, but we have little information on what damage to the oceanic flora and fauna might result from a great flood of unburned, slowly boiling liquid gas covering the sea surface. Most of the liquid is methane, and there is ample evidence of the presence of methane, in very low concentrations, as a normal component of marine sediments. In fact, formation of methane is normally associated with the processes that form natural gas and petroleum in buried marine sediments. It may be that an analysis of the situation, followed by large-scale tests, will show that the consequences of a large spill at sea would be completely local and short-lived, a far smaller hazard than an oil spill. Valuable oyster and other fisheries may be unaffected. But so far any prediction is not backed by experience.

The authors concentrate primarily on accidents at or near shore facilities. In this, as in other issues related to the environmental dangers of any new enterprise, particularly one related to energy, we face two separate issues. One is the fear that people have of accidents with materials that are unfamiliar to them; the other is the understandable desire to put possibly unsafe material in someone else's backyard. A final issue is worth considering: If the world will run out of natural gas in the next 50 years, how much capital is worth investing in a time-limited operation? There are many reasons for thinking that such an industry will be economic even though we know it will last for only a limited time. After all, most modern technologies become obsolete before long because something new is invented that replaces them. Lastly, a caution. We have too often seen the adoption of a new technology that was promised as economical, efficient, and safe, only to learn about the serious defects after large-scale operation.

# The Importation
# of Liquefied Natural Gas

by Elisabeth Drake and Robert C. Reid
*April 1977*

*The shortages of the past winter have dramatized the increasing uncertainty of U.S. gas supplies. The importation of liquefied natural gas by ship may ameliorate the situation, but is it safe?*

The consumption of energy in the U.S., which reached a peak of 75 quads (quadrillion British thermal units) in 1973 and then declined slightly, is now on the rise again and is expected by the Federal Energy Administration to be at a level of 85 quads in 1980 and 95 quads in 1985. About 30 percent of the energy comes from gas, and the incentives for maintaining that proportion as the demand for energy rises are strong. Yet domestic production of natural gas has fallen off sharply since it reached a peak in 1973 and appears likely to decline even more rapidly in the future unless new sources are found and developed. One way to supplement the dwindling supplies of natural gas is to import liquefied natural gas on a large scale from areas overseas that have an abundance of natural gas and little or no market for it. It is relevant to ask how promising this option is, that is, whether the arguments for the importation of liquefied natural gas outweigh those against it.

The obvious problem in transporting large amounts of natural gas by any means other than a pipeline is that at ordinary temperatures a gas occupies a large volume. If natural gas is cooled to a temperature of $-162$ degrees Celsius ($-259$ degrees Fahrenheit), however, it becomes a liquid with a six-hundredth the volume of the gas. The problems of transporting the fuel to places that cannot be reached by pipeline and of storing it in large quantities thereby become manageable. With liquefied natural gas the main problems are to find materials that will hold such a cold substance reliably and to determine what safety measures must be adopted against the possibility that the liquid might escape.

The arguments in favor of the large-scale importation of liquefied natural gas can be summarized quickly, since they are not complex. The U.S. needs additional sources of energy. Gas is particularly desirable as a fuel because it burns cleanly and is easy to distribute to consumers. Gas heating is now installed in many homes, factories and public buildings. Natural gas, much of which is produced as a by-product of the petroleum with which it is associated, is still wasted in many areas by being vented into the air or burned, since there is no local market for it. The technology for liquefying natural gas, for transporting it on the high seas and for storing it on land is in hand. Moreover, that technology is less complex and less expensive than the technology for making synthetic gas out of oil or coal. A considerable international trade in liquefied natural gas already exists: Japan imports about 80 percent of its gas in liquid form, Western Europe 5 percent and the U.S. somewhat less than .1 percent. Indeed, the U.S. is at present a net exporter of liquefied natural gas: exports from Alaska to Japan are about three times greater than imports from Algeria to a terminal in Massachusetts. (In last winter's gas-supply emergency the shipment of liquefied natural gas from Alaska to Massachusetts by way of the Panama Canal was authorized for the first time.) In 1976 the figures were exports of 32 trillion B.t.u.'s to Japan and imports of 10.8 trillion B.t.u.'s to Massachusetts. Put in more familiar terms, the annual imports were 450,000 cubic meters (three million barrels or 10 billion standard cubic feet); in terms of the size of the ships currently fitted out to transport liquefied natural gas the imports amounted to about 12 shiploads.

The arguments against the large-scale importation of liquefied natural gas focus on the question of the safety of the undertaking. Liquefied natural gas, like gasoline and natural gas, can be dangerous if it is handled carelessly or if large amounts are released in an accident against which insufficient safeguards have been provided. Allowance must also be made for the fact that the liquefied gas is at a very low temperature.

A facility for liquefying natural gas and storing the liquid was built in Cleveland in 1941. In 1944 one of the storage tanks failed and a disastrous accident resulted. No dike had been built around the tank to contain all the liquid in the event of a leak, so that the liquefied gas flowed unimpeded into the surrounding area. The cold liquid boiled rapidly, and the vapors soon reached a source of ignition that touched off a huge fire in which 128 people died.

This accident set the fledgling liquefied natural gas industry back many years. Nearly two decades passed before the advantages of this form of the fuel were explored again. The possibility of doing so arose in part from work in the National Aeronautics and Space Administration and the Department of Defense on rocket fuels; that work yielded improved materials for storing cryogenic liquids and new safety precautions for handling them.

In the 1960's several municipal gas

**TANKER FOR LIQUEFIED NATURAL GAS is under construction at the Quincy Shipbuilding Division of the General Dynamics Corporation. Here a crane lowers one of the five metal spheres that will hold the liquefied natural gas into a space in the hull that has** been prepared for it. The sphere has a capacity of 25,000 cubic meters of liquefied natural gas, and the ship will carry five such spheres. The spheres are protected by the white hemispherical structures. The spheres are built separately and shipped to the tanker by barge.

companies designed and built facilities that employed liquefied natural gas for "peak shaving," that is, for supplying fuel at times of unusually high demand. A company would buy, liquefy and store pipeline gas during periods when the demand was low and the price was below normal. Later, during cold spells when the capacity of the pipeline was strained and the price of gas was higher, the liquefied natural gas could be revaporized and fed into the mains serving the company's customers. More than 60 such plants are now operating in the U.S. and Canada.

The peak-shaving plants have proved to be economically successful and have had an excellent safety record. They played an important role in maintaining gas service to residential customers during the unusually cold periods last winter. On this scale, then, the use of liquefied natural gas as a fuel appears to be a sound concept. With the depletion of gas reserves in the region of the 48 contiguous states of the U.S., however, the incentive to import liquefied natural gas for base-load operations is increasing. A base-load terminal would receive liquefied natural gas on a regular basis from a fleet of tankers, store it in large tanks and revaporize it continuously to send it to the mains as fuel.

The tankers projected for operations on this scale would each have a capacity of up to 165,000 cubic meters, which is enough liquefied natural gas to cover a regulation American football field to a depth of about 40 meters (125 feet). The storage tanks at the receiving terminal would be from two to four times the size of the 50,000-cubic-meter structure typical of present peak-shaving facilities. Contemplating these prospects, many people have voiced concern about what would happen if a tanker carrying liquefied natural gas were involved in a collision or an airplane hit a storage tank or an earthquake occurred in an area occupied by a tank or a facility were sabotaged. The question to be faced is whether the safety provisions that can be devised would be sufficient to allow the large-scale importation of liquefied natural gas to proceed with acceptable risks to the public.

One cause for the concern about liquefied natural gas is an accident that took place in 1973 at a storage facility on Staten Island, which is part of New York City. The accident involved a tank that had been used to store liquefied natural gas. From outside to inside the tank consisted of a concrete wall, an insulating layer of polyurethane foam and a container for the liquid. The container was a membrane made of aluminized Mylar plastic film.

After the tank had been in operation for about two years a leak developed in the Mylar film. The tank was shut down

and the liquefied natural gas in it was pumped out and vaporized for local consumption. Nitrogen gas was then blown into the tank to warm it and to eliminate any residue of flammable vapor. Eventually air was admitted to the tank and workmen entered to begin repairs.

While the workmen were in the tank the insulation somehow caught fire. Hot gases from the combustion raised the internal pressure. The roof rose, as it had been designed to do if excessive pressure developed in the tank; in settling it collapsed into the tank, killing 40 workers. Even though the accident did not involve any liquefied natural gas or endanger the public safety, it aroused local opposition to a terminal that was under construction nearby for the importation of liquefied natural gas. Another source of concern was the fact that the terminal would bring ships carrying liquefied natural gas into waters where marine accidents had occurred. The issue of whether or not the terminal is to be operated remains unresolved.

Most of the questions concerning the safety of liquefied natural gas relate to tankers and storage tanks. We shall discuss some typical designs before returning to the safety question.

The 35 liquefied natural gas tankers now in operation have an average capacity of 46,000 cubic meters of liquid; 41 other tankers that are under construction or in the design stage have a mean capacity of 124,000 cubic meters. As we have mentioned, plans are being laid for vessels that will carry 165,000 cubic meters.

The tanks on a ship carrying liquefied natural gas must have double walls and insulation more than a meter thick to reduce the vaporization rate. Accordingly a collision that might lead to a loss of cargo would have to be considerably severer than it would if the ship were built like a petroleum tanker, where the tank is the hull of the ship itself. Accidents such as ramming and grounding are highly unlikely to cause the release of cargo from a ship carrying liquefied natural gas.

The tanks on a given liquefied natural gas ship have one of three basic designs. The first is freestanding tanks, which are separate from the hull except for support members. The outside of each tank is insulated, and a clearance may be left between the insulation and the hull. The second design is membrane tanks, which receive support from the

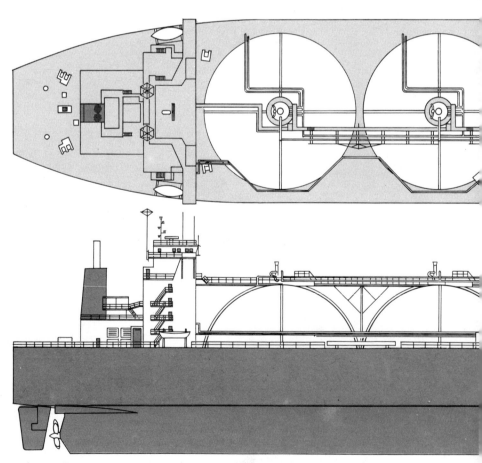

SPECIALIZED SHIP of the type that is under construction by the General Dynamics Corporation is designed to carry 125,000 cubic meters of liquefied natural gas in five spherical tanks.

hull through load-bearing insulation. The third design is spherical tanks that are built outside the ship and then lowered into prepared spaces during the final stages of its construction. With all three types of tank the primary container for the liquid is made of welded metal. In addition the freestanding tanks and the membrane tanks are required by the U.S. Coast Guard to have a secondary cryogenic barrier. (The requirement does not apply to spherical tanks because they are built under conditions where the welds can be pretested for integrity.)

At sea a tanker carrying liquefied natural gas presents an unusual profile. The density of the cargo is less than half the density of seawater, so that the ship rides high in the water. A typical ship has a draft of only 10 meters and a main deck that is from 20 to 25 meters above the waterline. Ballast tanks, which are filled with water, are required to provide stability on return voyages. At such times the tanker nonetheless carries a residual "heel" of liquefied natural gas; part of it is allowed to vaporize slowly to provide fuel for the ship, and the remainder serves to keep the temperature in the tanks low so that they do not have to be cooled before being loaded again.

Since it is expensive to build and operate such a large and highly specialized vessel, its operators seek to minimize the amount of time the ship is idle. This approach has led to the development of elaborate and efficient schemes for loading and unloading. Pipes carry liquefied natural gas between a ship and a tank on shore at a rate as high as some four cubic meters per second (50,000 gallons per minute).

The storage tanks must be built of materials that retain their strength at −162 degrees C. Carbon steel, which is the basic material for most steel construction, is not satisfactory because it gets brittle at low temperatures. Certain materials, however, have been extensively tested with liquefied natural gas and found to be suitable for the construction of the inner tank, the one that actually holds the cold liquid. The materials include high-nickel steels, some aluminum alloys and prestressed concrete. The insulation that is a requisite for every tank holding liquefied natural gas is put outside the structure that contains the liquid and is held in place by an outer tank. The outer tank is what an observer sees. The insulation is usually the noncombustible material known as perlite.

Storage tanks for liquefied natural gas at an import terminal are never small. A typical tank has an inner diameter of 55 meters, an outer diameter of 58 meters and a height of 55 meters. It holds some 90,000 cubic meters (550,000 barrels) of liquefied natural gas.

Each tank is surrounded by an impoundment dike that must be capable of containing at least the entire contents of a full tank. In many cases the dike is built at some distance from the tank and is therefore fairly low (from two to 10 meters high). Some recent designs have put the dike close to the tank, partly because in the event of a fire the flames would be confined to a smaller area. Such a dike is likely to be almost as high as the tank itself. In addition to the diking requirement, Federal regulations stipulate that a buffer zone wide enough to prevent another disaster of the Cleveland type must be provided between the dike and the boundary of the facility.

In the early stages of the development of facilities for liquefied natural gas there were plans to store the material in roofed holes in the ground. The liquefied natural gas was expected to create a sealed cavity by freezing the adjacent soil. Experience with such tanks in the U.S. showed, however, that stresses

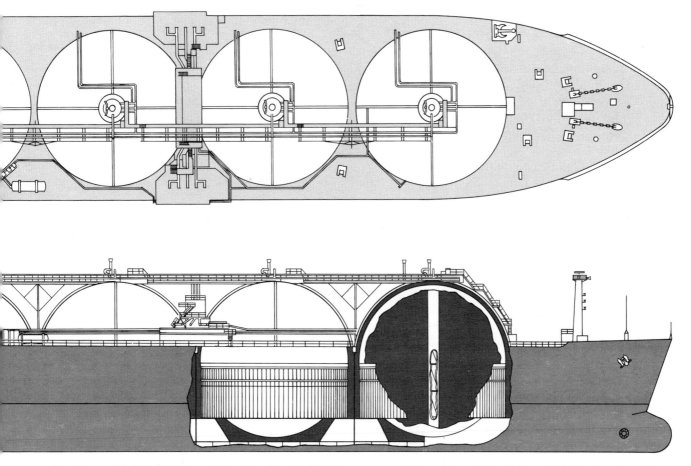

Here the vessel is depicted in plan and elevation views. Each tank has an inside diameter of 120 feet and is heavily insulated to minimize vaporization of the cold liquid. Vapor that does form is put to use as supplemental fuel for the ship's engines, which usually burn oil.

build up in the frozen soil and cracks develop. The increase in the amount of contact between the liquefied natural gas and the soil leads to an increased rate of heat transfer into the cavity, and the economics of the facility become marginal. Four such tanks in the U.S. have been abandoned; a few remain in operation in other countries, but they too are being phased out of service.

In Japan, where land is scarce and earthquakes are a severe hazard, a number of buried concrete tanks for liquefied natural gas have recently been built. A tank of this kind typically has a foamed polymer inside the concrete as insulation. The insulation supports a membrane that functions as the seal for the liquefied natural gas.

Liquefied natural gas has a number of interesting characteristics arising from the fact that methane, which is its main constituent, is mixed with small amounts of other compounds such as ethane, propane and nitrogen. One characteristic is the possibility of a "flameless vapor explosion" when liquefied natural gas comes in contact with water. The phenomenon was first reported in 1970 by David S. Burgess and his colleagues at the U.S. Bureau of Mines, who were measuring the boiling rate of liquefied natural gas spilled on water. In the 56th test of an otherwise uneventful series a sharp explosion destroyed the experimental tank containing the water. Later a similar but larger explosion took place after about a quarter of a cubic

meter of liquefied natural gas had been spilled on an open pond. In neither case did the material catch fire.

To determine the cause of these explosions Torr Enger and David E. Hartman of the Shell Pipe Line Corporation carried out an extensive program of testing. They concluded that the explosions resulted from the fact that a thin layer of the liquefied natural gas on the water had become so superheated that homogeneous nucleation of vapor occurred very rapidly. A flameless vapor explosion can happen only when the liquefied natural gas incorporates significant fractions of ethane and propane. The range of composition is quite different from that of typical liquefied nat-

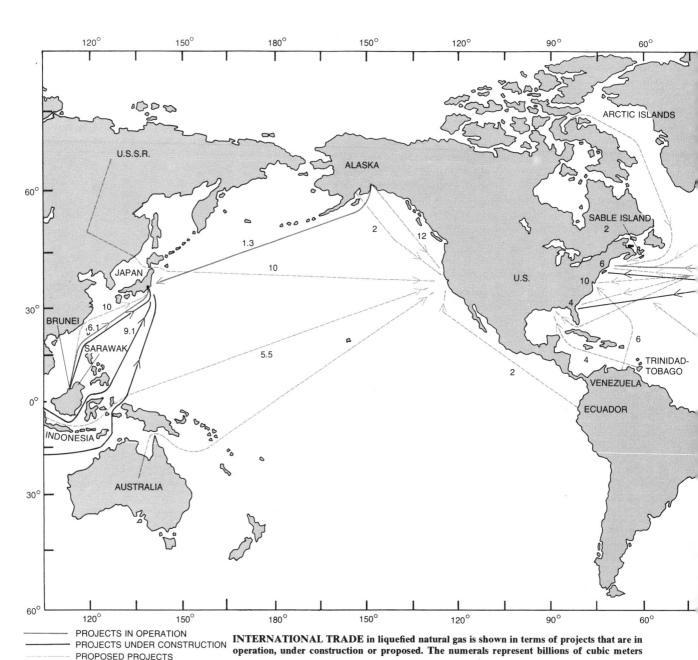

PROJECTS IN OPERATION
PROJECTS UNDER CONSTRUCTION
PROPOSED PROJECTS

**INTERNATIONAL TRADE** in liquefied natural gas is shown in terms of projects that are in operation, under construction or proposed. The numerals represent billions of cubic meters

ural gas, which incorporates only small percentages of ethane and propane.

Even when a flameless vapor explosion takes place, the damage is slight. At the Liquid Natural Gas Research Center of the Massachusetts Institute of Technology we measured pressures in the liquid close to the surface where the explosion occurs and found they were well below 690 kilonewtons per square meter (100 pounds per square inch). Since the pressure wave would attenuate rapidly with distance, if such an explosion took place on water adjacent to a tanker, it would have little effect on the hull of the ship. Pressures in the air above the explosion are of course even lower.

A second interesting effect is that mix-

tures of liquefied natural gas with differing composition and density can stratify. This phenomenon was first recognized in 1971 after an incident at an import terminal in Italy. About 18 hours after a cargo of liquefied natural gas had been put into a storage tank the pressure in the tank began to rise. Soon the safety valves were actuated, and in the course of an hour some 150,000 kilograms of natural gas were vented. Fortunately the vented gas did not ignite and the pressure in the tank did not go high enough to cause any serious damage.

An analysis of the incident revealed that the new load of liquefied natural gas had a higher density than the material that was already in the tank. It was also warmer. Because of the difference

in density the new material, which had been loaded into the bottom of the tank, remained there, creating a two-layer system. Over the following 18 hours heat flowed into the tank through the bottom and the side walls, since even though the liquefied natural gas in the bottom layer was warmer than that in the top layer, it was still much colder than the surroundings. Such a flow of heat is normal, and in an unstratified storage tank it drives a convective circulation of liquefied natural gas that maintains the entire contents of the tank well mixed and at essentially the same temperature.

In a two-layer system the liquid in each layer still flows convectively, but the denser fluid is not sufficiently buoyant to enable it to penetrate the less dense upper layer. Thus energy can be stored in the denser layer. In time the transfer of heat and mass between the layers tends to equalize the difference in density. Then the layers may mix rapidly. As the material attempts to achieve thermal equilibrium, the intrusion of the warm bottom layer leads to a rapid generation of vapor to release the excess energy that was accumulated while there were two layers. The contents of the tank have suddenly mixed. The phenomenon is commonly called rollover.

Modern facilities have standard procedures for preventing rollover. The less dense liquid may be loaded into the bottom of the tank and the denser into the top. This procedure tends to prevent stratification. Another option is to always load the tank from the top; then, even if stratification occurs, the time required for rollover is much longer than the residence time of liquefied natural gas in a storage tank at a typical import terminal.

Problems other than flameless vapor explosions and rollover have received considerable attention. If liquefied natural gas is spilled, it boils rapidly. Although the vapor is not toxic, it may in high concentration cause asphyxiation by excluding oxygen. Moreover, the low temperature of the material may result in frostbite for anyone in the immediate vicinity of a spill. Both of these potential hazards are too localized to be of concern outside the boundaries of the facility.

The major hazard of liquefied natural gas is fire. If a spill is ignited, it burns much like a pool of gasoline. If it is not ignited quickly, the flammable vapor may be carried by the wind until a source of ignition is encountered. Experiments in the U.S., France and Japan have shown that once the vapor has been ignited a flame front burns back through the vapor toward the source from which the vapor came.

Another serious question is whether a

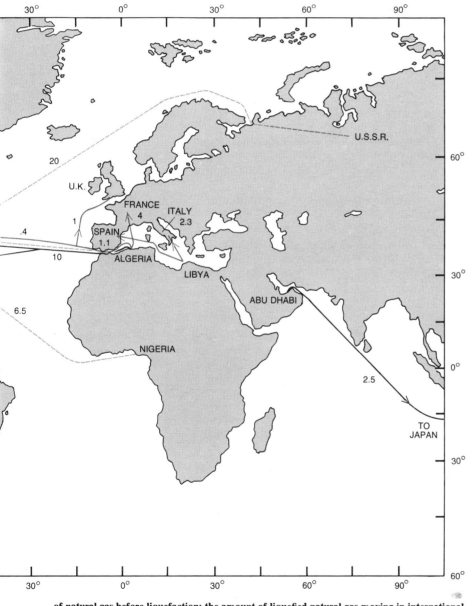

of natural gas before liquefaction; the amount of liquefied natural gas moving in international trade or planned to be moved is about a six-hundredth the volume of the gaseous material.

fire in a cloud of vaporized liquefied natural gas might develop into a detonation capable of producing a damaging blast wave. The consensus among workers who have studied the problem is that the probability of such an explosion in an unconfined space is small. The detonation of a vapor in open air has not been confirmed even when a high-explosive charge served as the initiator. Charles D. Lind of the Naval Weapons Center at China Lake, Calif., has been unable to obtain detonations even with charges of up to two kilograms.

Lind carried out his tests with mixtures of methane and air enclosed in thin polyethylene hemispheres up to 20 meters in diameter. Ignition sources or explosive charges were placed in the center at ground level, and the results were followed with high-speed photography. The polyethylene enclosure was destroyed by either the detonation of the high explosive or the resulting blast wave, but in no case did the combustion wave of the methane accelerate to become a detonation. Explosions of methane-air mixtures have been demonstrated in rigid enclosures, but normally the combustion wave must travel 30 meters

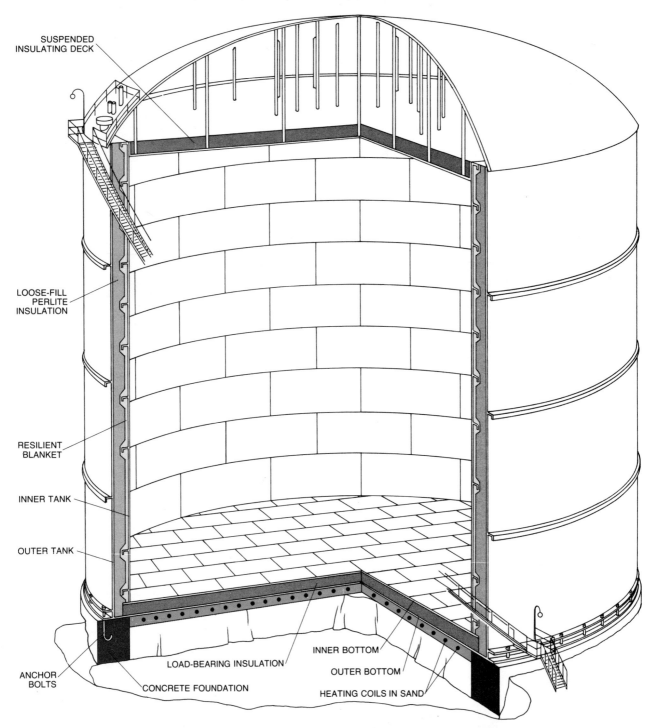

SUSPENDED
INSULATING DECK

LOOSE-FILL
PERLITE
INSULATION

RESILIENT
BLANKET

INNER TANK

OUTER TANK

ANCHOR
BOLTS

LOAD-BEARING INSULATION

CONCRETE FOUNDATION

INNER BOTTOM

OUTER BOTTOM

HEATING COILS IN SAND

**STORAGE TANK designed to hold liquefied natural gas after it has been delivered by tanker to an import terminal has a capacity of 90,000 cubic meters. The tank is well insulated so that the liquefied natural gas, which is stored at slightly more than atmospheric pressure, does not vaporize too rapidly. Heating coils under tank serve to prevent frost heaves caused by temperature variations in the ground.**

or more before it can become a self-supporting detonation wave.

Liquefied natural gas inside a storage tank is innocuous; it cannot burn unless it is vaporized and mixed with air. Only if it is released can there be a hazard. Accordingly tankers and storage facilities for liquefied natural gas are designed and operated to prevent accidental release.

Typically tanks for liquefied natural gas are designed to meet standards that specify the severity of wind, earthquakes and so on that the tank must withstand. The standard usually is the severest condition experienced within the past 50 or 100 years. Safety factors, which are also laid down in building codes, ensure that a tank will be able to withstand an even severer event. Moreover, in a storage facility it must be demonstrated that the public would not be endangered if the largest pipe connection to the tank should fail at the maximum rate of flow of liquefied natural gas.

Similar analyses of hazard are made for a liquefied natural gas tanker entering a port. Data are collected on the traffic density and the type, speed and length of other vessels in nearby waters. Since the probability of collision should approach zero if the rules of the road are followed, analysts frequently make the conservative assumption that all ships move in a random manner. In any event, not all collisions would be severe enough to penetrate the double hull of a ship carrying liquefied natural gas deep enough to release any of the cargo. Therefore the analysis is carried further to estimate the minimum momentum and angle of impact for a striking ship to cause a major release of liquefied natural gas.

Only after careful analyses can one estimate the potential hazards to the public of an operation involving liquefied natural gas. As an example, the risk associated with the proposed importation of liquefied natural gas to Staten Island is estimated to be about one fatality every 10 million years for people living or working along the approach route to the harbor. That level of risk is about 10 times less than the risk of dying from a fire at home and about the same as the risk of being struck by lightning.

Nevertheless, even though a facility can be designed to provide a high degree of safety in the event of the kind of accident envisioned in the design standards, one may still postulate severer accidents resulting, say, from a massive earthquake or from a sophisticated act of sabotage. The sudden destruction of a tank containing liquefied natural gas would be expected to lead to a major fire with potentially disastrous consequences. Can society tolerate such a risk?

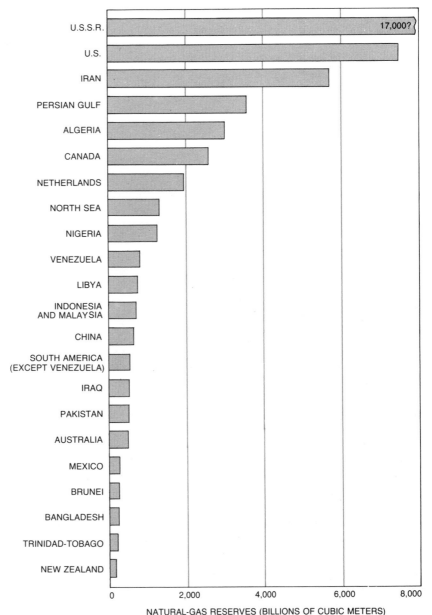

GAS RESOURCES OF THE WORLD are listed. The figures are for gaseous natural gas. Much of it is unlikely to be liquefied and exported, but many of the countries have little or no domestic market for natural gas and are therefore likely to consider exports of liquefied gas.

The general problem is not unlike the problems faced daily by industrial engineers and governmental regulatory agencies. For example, should a big jet airplane be allowed to fly over a crowded public facility such as an athletic stadium? There is a low but always finite possibility of a crash with catastrophic results.

Similar examples reveal that society tolerates certain highly improbable risks—risks that cannot feasibly be eliminated by design—in order to reap the benefits of energy, consumer products, transportation, central water-supply systems and so on. On the basis of the studies that have been made of the hazards of liquefied natural gas and the experience that has been gained in several countries in handling the fuel on a large scale, it seems reasonable to say that the hazards are similar to those involved in handling other fuels such as gasoline, propane (liquefied petroleum gas) and gaseous natural gas. Liquefied natural gas therefore appears to be a promising alternative source of energy. Moreover, it can be expected that further experience in handling liquefied natural gas and further research by the industry and by regulatory agencies will raise the level of safety in its use even higher.

# 13

## Pelagic Tar

## COMMENTARY

Ever since sailors first ventured out on the seas, they have dumped their waste there. Once we thought the oceans were so immense that any waste would be diluted enough to be essentially gone. That thought dominated until the middle of the twentieth century. The relics of former voyagers are rare. The remains of an ancient Greek amphora (storage jar for wine or oil) might be worthy of a museum, and a nineteenth-century sherry bottle might be prized by a collector. Now, however, the garbage is commonplace, at least in the major shipping lanes and certainly on the beaches of the world: the pieces of plastic bottles and other manufactured products that so obviously come from overboard dumping. Not so obvious are the microscopic or poorly identifiable particles, the chemicals, and the bacteria and viruses.

This article by James Butler tells the story of one such contaminant of the oceans—tar lumps: how we discovered them, where they must have come from, and how they might interact with ocean currents and the flora and fauna whose life cycles and behavior they may affect. Because there are natural oil seeps under the oceans and a variety of pollution sources from shoreline installations and sewage disposal points, it was not immediately obvious where the oil lumps came from. Butler shows how, by a combination of modern chemical detection and an understanding of biological and physical oceanography, the origin of the pelagic tar lumps was traced to the dumping overboard of tanker sludge and wax. These materials accumulate on the inside walls of the oil tankers and have to be cleaned out frequently. This source was identified as chemically distinct from natural seeps and accidental oil spills of large tankers.

Of what importance are the tar lumps? Granted that they violate our sense of the cleanliness of the oceans, just as a discarded beer can on a beautiful hillside grates against our sensibilities. Do they, however, cause any harm? Although it is not certain that they do over the wide expanse of the oceans, there are some grounds for believing that the more volatile hydrocarbons may interfere with the chemical sensing and behavior of micro- and macroorganisms. It is this possibility that worries some marine biologists, and it should worry us, for to the extent that the oceans provide food for the populations of many countries, they are another valuable resource that ought not to be sacrificed to negligence in our hunger for energy.

One thing is certain. As our oil and gas economy has gone global, particularly since the 1950s, the tanker fleets of the world have continually
expanded in number and size. The newer ships are load-on-top supertankers,
which eliminate much of the clean-out problem though they magnify the
dimensions of the spill problem, as the fishermen of Brittany found out from the
wreck of the Amoco Cadiz in the winter of 1978. Eventually, however, as our
supplies of oil and gas start to decrease and the world turns to nuclear energy,
coal, or solar energy, the tankers will slowly vanish. If the integrity of the seas
outlasts them, the seas will be safe after the second half of the twenty-first
century. Future generations of marine geologists will see the relics of our time
in the tar lumps incorporated in the marine sediments of the oceans.

# Pelagic Tar

by James N. Butler
*June 1975*

*Fine nets towed in the open ocean pick up ubiquitous black lumps, apparently the residue of sludge washed out of the hold of tankers. The stuff could probably be eliminated by good tanker procedures*

Until a few years ago the term pelagic tar and the material to which it is applied were virtually unknown. The term describes tarry residues of petroleum that are found on the surface of the ocean. (They are also found on ocean beaches, but a precise definition of "pelagic," which comes from the Greek for sea, limits its application to the open sea.) The tar appears to originate mainly from the discharge of waste by oil tankers. Tar residues of this type probably could have been found long ago, but the recent rapid increase in the transportation of oil by tanker and the shift of tanker routes as a result of the closing of the Suez Canal have made the tar considerably more conspicuous.

One naturally asks what becomes of the pelagic tar and what effects it has on marine organisms. My colleagues and I at Harvard University and the Bermuda Biological Station for Research have been investigating pelagic tar in an attempt to answer these questions and others. We do not have complete answers to any of our questions, but a good deal of information about pelagic tar is now in hand.

A factor contributing to the recognition that pelagic tar had become widespread in the world's oceans was the development of the neuston net [*see illustration on page 149*]. It was designed in 1962 by Peter M. David of the National Institute of Oceanography in Britain. The net is towed beside a vessel to sample the population of neuston, which are tiny organisms that float in the film of water at the surface of the ocean. It has been widely employed by oceanographers, many of whom have found that their nets are scooping up significant amounts of tar as well as neuston.

David seems to be the first person to have reported tar lumps at sea. In a communication to me he wrote: "The first tar lumps I caught were taken in hand nets at about 40°N, 20°W [between Portugal and the Azores] in 1954. Many of them were colonized by hydroids and barnacles....

"I began to make neuston nets in 1962 and used them in the International Indian Ocean Expedition in 1963 and 1964. Tar lumps were caught in many, possibly most, of the Indian Ocean samples, although often very tiny fragments in small quantities. The Mediterranean samples taken on the way out to the Indian Ocean were heavily contaminated. I remember thinking that the area off Southeast Arabia where we were going to do our first survey would probably be thick with oil, being right on the main tanker route, but it turned out to be very free of contamination."

In December, 1968, the research ship *Chain* encountered such a heavy concentration of oil and tar residues on the North American side of the Atlantic that investigators aboard reported the matter to the Smithsonian Institution's Center for Short-Lived Phenomena. (As it has turned out, pelagic tar is a short-lived phenomenon only on a geologic time scale.) The ship was on a cruise from the Woods Hole Oceanographic Institution south through the western Sargasso Sea. Victor E. Noshkin, Jr., and James Craddock, who made many tows with neuston nets, reported on one episode as follows. "In a 30-minute tow the nets skimmed about 1,800 meters of sea surface and contained a cupful of oil-tar lumps.... After from two to four hours of towing the mesh became so encrusted with oil that it was necessary to clean the nets with a strong solvent. On the evening of December 5, at 25°40′N, 67°30′W, the nets were so fouled with oil and tar material that towing had to be discontinued."

In the Mediterranean Sea three other workers from Woods Hole (Michael H. Horn, John M. Teal and Richard H. Backus) found large amounts of tar during a cruise of *Atlantis II* in 1969. Reporting in *Science* that they had collected tarry lumps in 75 percent of more than 700 tows with neuston nets, they wrote that the lumps were irregular in shape, with the greatest dimension varying from one or two millimeters to about 10 centimeters. "Hardness varied," they wrote, "although all lumps were easily deformed by a touch of the finger.... Some of the lumps were very sticky, had a rough, uneven surface and were relatively soft and black. Other lumps were firmer, with a smoother, more even surface, and were usually lighter (brownish black); this type frequently had barnacles attached and appeared to be older than the first."

Several organisms were associated with the tar lumps collected by the Woods Hole group. An isopod, *Idotea metallica*, was collected in large numbers. When these organisms were left with a tar lump in a tank on the ship, they tended to remain attached to the lump. The goose barnacle (*Lepas pectinata*) was frequently found attached to the lumps, particularly to the firmer, older-looking ones. At one station 150 barnacles ranging from two to eight millimeters in length were attached to four lumps. The growth rate of the barnacles was measured and found to be approximately one millimeter per week, thus establishing that the tar lumps to which they were attached were at least two months old. Tar was also found in the stomach of the saury (*Scomberesox saurus*), a fish that feeds on surface-dwelling crustaceans, in three of 10

LARGE TAR LUMP, somewhat magnified here, appears in a clump of the alga *Sargassum,* for which the Sargasso Sea of the western North Atlantic Ocean is named. Many organisms are associated with the alga. They are being studied to see if they are affected by tar.

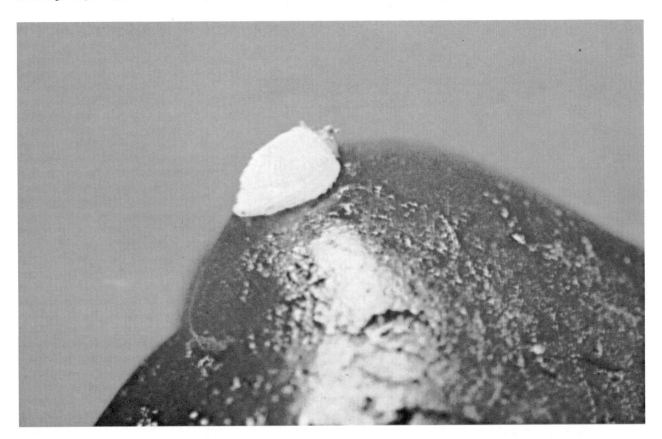

LUMP OF TAR found in the ocean near Bermuda carried a goose barnacle, *Lepas pectinata.* Barnacles of this species are frequently found attached to pelagic tar, particularly the older and firmer lumps. By ascertaining the growth rate of the barnacles one can estimate the minimum time the tar has been in the water. It is not known whether or not the barnacles are affected by pelagic tar.

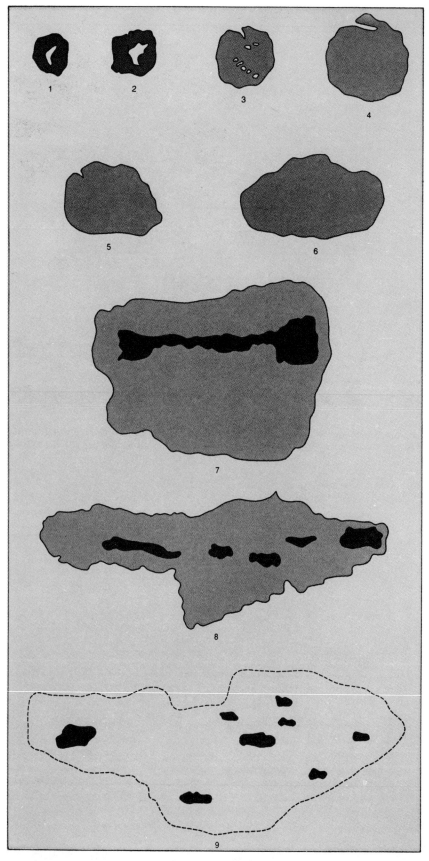

**EVOLUTION OF OIL SLICK** was traced in an experiment. The oil was dumped in the water by a ship that moved in a circle. Initially (*1*) the slick is about .2 kilometer in diameter, with an open area in the center. Succeeding panels (*2–6*) show it at four minutes, 22 minutes, 42 minutes, two hours and seven hours. After two days (*7*) it consists of a dark patch of thick oil surrounded by a much larger area of thin oil. Half a day later (*8*) the thick patch is breaking up. After four days (*9*) slick is 2.4 kilometers wide but indistinct.

specimens collected by the expedition. Several lumps covered with a grayish film were found to take up oxygen because of the microorganisms on their surface; when the lumps were treated with formalin to kill the microorganisms, the uptake of oxygen dropped to essentially zero.

Observations of tar by Thor Heyerdahl and his associates on their expeditions across the Atlantic on the papyrus rafts *Ra I* and *Ra II* in 1969 and 1970 attracted much more notice than the other reports because the raft voyages were widely publicized. Since the rafts traveled slowly (at a speed of about two knots) and the crew members rode only a foot above the surface of the water, the tar was much more noticeable than it could be to observers on larger ships, who would be from 15 to 40 feet above the water and moving at speeds of from eight to 12 knots. The log of *Ra II* records tar sightings on 40 of the first 43 days of sailing; the rest of the voyage (56 days) was in relatively clear water. The route of both voyages was from North Africa to Barbados, following the natural surface current that forms the southern boundary of the Sargasso Sea.

At approximately the same time Byron Morris, then a graduate student in biological oceanography at Dalhousie University and now my co-worker at the Bermuda Biological Station, was investigating surface-dwelling plankton with a fine-mesh net similar to the one designed by David. "I discovered on my very first tow with the net that plankton was not all I would catch," he told me. "In the bag with the animals were numerous pebble-sized lumps of black tar. I should have expected this, since I had recently heard that workers from Woods Hole had found tar . . . in the North Atlantic. . . . Nevertheless, my first encounter with floating tar came as a sad surprise." Since then Morris has made hundreds of tows in the western North Atlantic and the Sargasso Sea. He has reported that "on only one occasion did I fail to catch any tar."

One of the tar lumps collected by David was analyzed in the gas chromatograph by J. V. Brunnock, D. F. Duckworth and G. G. Stephens of the British Petroleum Company Research Centre in 1968. Their chromatogram showed a large component of paraffinic waxes that have a high boiling point. This finding indicated to the investigators that the lumps were not simply evaporated crude oil but were the sludge of crude oil, which clings to the inner walls of tankers and must be removed with the ballast before the next cargo is loaded. Some of

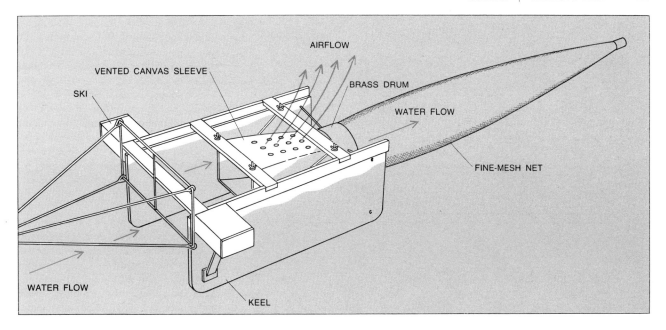

NEUSTON NET was designed to sample the population of neuston, which are small organisms living at the surface of the ocean. The nets also have collected significant amounts of tar, which had gone largely unnoticed until the nets came into wide use about a decade ago. The net and its supporting framework are designed to be towed alongside a boat from a boom or a crane near the bow.

the tar found in the Mediterranean by the Woods Hole group was analyzed at Woods Hole by Max Blumer, whose gas chromatogram showed it to be a residue of crude oil. His finding was in agreement with the one obtained by the British workers.

Tanker waste, consisting of the heavier and waxier fractions of crude oil, probably forms into tar lumps quickly on entering the water. It is also reasonable to suppose some lumps form more slowly as a result of accretion from oil slicks such as the ones resulting from tanker accidents. A slick would be likely to contain the lighter fractions of petroleum in addition to the heavier ones, but the lighter fractions would evaporate fairly rapidly, leaving the heavier fractions in the water as tar.

Since 1971 Morris and I have been studying the pelagic tar of the Sargasso Sea and the many organisms living within clumps of the alga Sargassum, for which the sea is named. We have had the benefit of data accumulated over a long period of time from the hydrographic station that was established 20 miles southeast of Bermuda by Henry M. Stommel of the Massachusetts Institute of Technology in 1954. The station, which is now called Station S, has been monitored continuously by a succession of people from the staff of the Bermuda Biological Station, using the research vessels Panulirus and Panulirus II.

The first samples of pelagic tar to turn up at Station S were collected in 1970 by Roger Pocklington. Morris has carried out a regular series of neuston-net tows in the region since 1971. We have measured the wet weights of tar, Sargassum and surface zooplankton. Many of the tar lumps have been analyzed chemically by gas chromatography. Most of the communities found in the alga are being analyzed ecologically, that is, the animals (ranging in size from hydroids to crabs and fishes) are separated, identified and counted. This task can be quite tedious, particularly with the smaller hydroids, worms, copepods, isopods and amphipods.

On two occasions (once in February, 1972, and again six months later) we made several tows through a given area during a period of 24 hours. Surprisingly, the amount of tar collected per tow between 4:00 P.M. on February 15 and 7:00 A.M. the next day varied by a factor of almost 10, and the amount of Sargassum varied by a factor of almost 30. There was no correlation between the two. Six months later we found the average amount of tar was 10 times higher than it had been in February, but again the factor of 10 separating the highest and lowest amounts appeared and so did the lack of correlation with the amount of Sargassum collected. The ratio of Sargassum to tar ranged from a high of nearly 5,000 : 1 to a low of .2 : 1. The lack of correlation between the tar pattern and the Sargassum pattern offers us the possibility of studying relatively independent colonies of Sargassum with widely different amounts of tar and thus

of ascertaining whether or not the presence of tar affects the ecology of the Sargassum communities.

One fact established by these brief repeated tows is that a single measurement in one place at one time tells almost nothing about the amount of either tar or Sargassum that would be found in an adjacent area at the same time or in the same place at another time. Even on a time scale as short as one hour the amount of tar or Sargassum collected can vary by a factor of 10. One explanation for these variations is provided by visual observations of Sargassum, which show that if the wind is steady, the clumps of weed line up in rows parallel to the wind direction. The spacing of these windrows increases with the velocity of the wind from about 20 meters at five knots to about 50 meters at 25 knots.

Nearly 50 years ago the physicist Irving Langmuir demonstrated that the wind is only indirectly the cause of these windrows. He showed that the action of wind over open water produces counter-rotating eddies and that between such eddies are bands of sinking water where floating weeds would collect. The Langmuir currents, as they are called, evidently affect accumulations of tar in the same way.

The windrows provide a possible explanation for the large amounts of tar observed by Heyerdahl. Since his rafts moved essentially downwind they could have spent long periods of time in windrows of tar lumps. In sampling at Station S the Panulirus II towed the net in a cir-

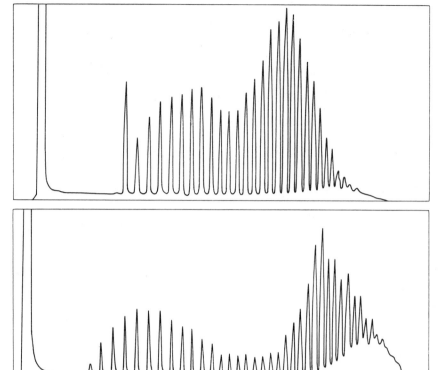

GAS CHROMATOGRAMS of crude-oil sludge (*top*) and pelagic tar (*bottom*) are compared. A chromatograph separates the molecular components of a sample. Here each peak represents a different paraffin molecule of hydrocarbon. The profiles are similar, indicating that the tar originated in crude-oil sludge, which is a waste discharged by oil tankers.

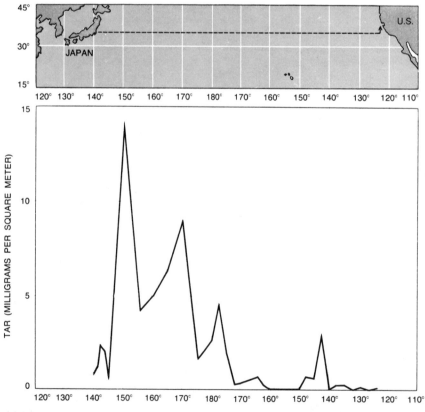

PATTERN OF TAR found on a crossing of the Pacific Ocean is displayed. The route of the ship is marked by the broken line. The largest amount of tar, comparable to the amount found in the Sargasso Sea, was collected in the Japan Current system, which is east of Japan.

cle so that a single haul would contain material collected not only while the ship was going across the windrows but also while it was going parallel to them; thus this particular source of variation tended to be averaged out. Here one is dealing, however, with a variation that appears from hour to hour. The evidence obtained from two years of sampling at Station S indicates that the concentration of tar also varies over longer periods, possibly as a result of seasonal weather patterns.

The initial reports on pelagic tar were concerned mainly with the physical appearance of the lumps. We wanted also to characterize the lumps chemically. The analysis would not be complete, since crude oil contains hundreds of thousands of different chemical compounds. Instead we chose a simple method of gas chromatography that had been developed by Blumer. It gives a characteristic "fingerprint" of a sample, displaying in the chromatogram primarily the sharp peaks for the normal paraffins. Those peaks are superposed on a background of unresolved materials of greater complexity.

The chromatograph's column of silicone separates the components of a sample approximately in the order of their boiling points. Two important branched-chain compounds, pristane (19-carbon isoprenoid) and phytane (20-carbon isoprenoid), are also resolved. They are found in virtually all crude oils. Pristane is also found in some marine organisms, whereas phytane almost never appears except in organisms that have been contaminated by petroleum. The presence of phytane at about half the concentration of pristane therefore helps in distinguishing hydrocarbons originating in petroleum from hydrocarbons of biological origin. Olefins provide another means of making this distinction, although our analysis did not separate olefins from hydrocarbons. Crude oil contains essentially no olefins, whereas they are a common constituent of marine organisms.

Another distinctive feature of petroleum residues from tankers is the large group of chromatographic peaks that represent compounds with molecules that have from 30 to 40 carbon atoms. They are the paraffin waxes that precipitate from crude oil during shipping. About a third of our samples show this pattern clearly.

The absence of the components of low boiling point, such as are found in gasoline and kerosene, indicates that a sam-

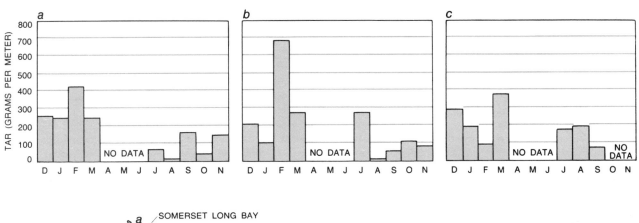

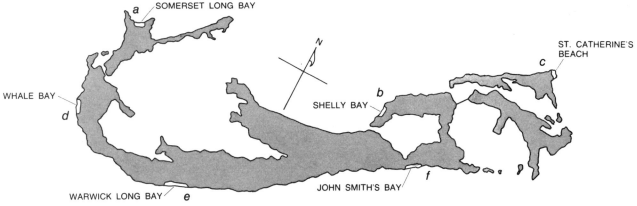

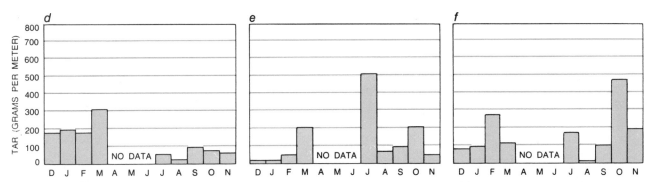

TAR ON BEACHES was sampled by workers in Bermuda. Here the beaches where samples were taken are identified by letters, and the amount of tar collected on each beach is shown in the correspondingly lettered chart. The method of sampling involved collecting all the tar from a path one meter wide, extending from the surf zone of the beach to the high-tide mark. The charts show the weekly average of tar collected in each transect. The workers were volunteers assisting the Bermuda Biological Station for Research.

ple is weathered and therefore has been at sea for at least several days. Unfortunately the loss of volatile components provides a good time scale only in the early stages of weathering. The difference between a residue of tar a month old and one a year old is small, judging from chromatographic analyses of tar stranded on a rock in Bermuda.

We have now analyzed a large number of tar lumps chromatographically. Our experience has been that any two lumps caught in the same net may have distinctly different chemical properties or may be essentially the same. On a number of occasions lumps of almost identical composition were found at in-

tervals of up to two months or at places separated by 100 kilometers. This evidence suggests that the tar comes from many different sources and that the sea tends to mix the lumps from a number of them.

The island of Bermuda itself tends to act as a giant net, collecting whatever is swept onto its beaches of pink sand by the intricate currents of the Sargasso Sea. Since November, 1971, several volunteers assisting our group have sampled six public beaches that face in different directions. The method has involved collecting all the tar lumps from a path one meter wide, extending from the surf zone to the high-tide mark

on the beach. The size of the lumps turned out to be relatively large; most of them were between five millimeters and five centimeters in diameter.

On several occasions we marked lumps of tar with orange wax and replaced them on the beach. They subsequently were redistributed on the beach or washed out to sea within one cycle of the tide. In one experiment the lumps were strewn as far as 80 meters along the beach after one tide cycle. On another occasion they had all disappeared by the next day, washed out to sea.

Almost all the Bermuda residents I talked with were quite certain that the lumps of tar were brought in by the prevailing winds. Therefore we measured the wind speed and direction at the beach and also obtained more precise records from the weather station at the airport. Surprisingly, we found little or no correlation between the prevailing wind and the amount of tar discovered on the beach. Apparently the delivery of tar to the beach, like its distribution in the open ocean, is controlled by the small-scale currents of the Sargasso Sea rather than by the wind.

The beach tar is chemically indistinguishable from the lumps found on the open ocean. The occasional large lump obtained from the beach did, however, provide an opportunity for studying the internal structure of the lumps. Blumer and Jeremy Sass made the study at Woods Hole on samples collected in Bermuda by Pocklington.

One analysis involved a 155-gram lump that the investigators froze in dry ice. At the low resulting temperature the tar is quite brittle and can be cracked with a hammer and a spatula, giving clean fracture faces. The appearance of different parts of the lump varied from brown to black, from dull to shiny and from liquid to waxy to crusty in texture. This particular lump contained an in-

clusion of hard yellow wax in the form of a crystal about seven millimeters long and two millimeters wide.

On chromatographic analysis the crystal was shown to consist solely of paraffins of high carbon number. Analysis of three lumps of tar showed that the dull black crust contained relatively low amounts of paraffins and consisted mostly of unresolved components. The relative amount of paraffins was probably reduced because of bacterial degradation at the surface. The light brown waxy parts contained relatively more paraffins.

The waxy inclusions are strong evidence that the lumps originate in the material clinging to the inner walls of tankers after their cargo has been unloaded. This sludge and wax is dumped overboard into the sea by about 20 percent of the tanker fleet. The other tankers employ the "load on top" method, in which the residue of the cargo is separated from the ballast water in one compartment and combined with the new cargo instead of being dumped at sea. This procedure is reported to reduce the amount of oil lost with the ballast water to less than 10 percent of what it would be otherwise.

The amount of tar found at sea tells us that the lumps do not accumulate indefinitely. Rough estimates that have been made of the total source of petroleum residues that might form tar, and even rougher estimates of the total amount of tar in the oceans of the world, lead to a guess that the amount of tar now on the surface of the sea is about 700,000 tons. The amount is approximately equal to the estimated annual waste from tankers that do not use the load-on-top method and is about a fourth of all the petroleum wastes deposited in the open ocean.

Since many of the nontanker sources deposit oil containing large fractions of volatile or soluble compounds, their contribution to pelagic tar would not be as large as the contribution from waxy wastes deposited by tankers. A correlation between the estimated standing crop of tar and the estimated influx of petroleum for several oceans gives an average residence time of 2.4 months for petroleum of all kinds reaching the sea. When the figure is corrected for the approximate proportion (80 percent) of volatile and soluble compounds, which disperse in a few weeks, the residence time for tarry residue is estimated to be about a year.

Since the tar lumps do not grow indefinitely and do not seem to weather significantly, where do they go? One hypothesis is that the tar breaks up into fine particles (too fine to be caught by a neuston net) and that the particles are distributed by currents in the top few hundred meters of the ocean. When large amounts of seawater are filtered, black particles are sometimes found on the filter. Preliminary analysis indicates that they are similar to tar lumps in composition. When large amounts of seawater are extracted with an organic solvent, which removes both dissolved and particulate hydrocarbons, one finds concentrations of hydrocarbons near the surface that are small by analytical standards (and hence difficult to verify) but large enough to account for the residue of most of the petroleum ever put into the ocean. As yet no distinction can be made in these analyses between hydrocarbons produced by marine organisms and hydrocarbons resulting from pollution.

Ultimately the fate of petroleum residues at sea is not to remain as oil slicks or tar lumps; they are relatively transient states. The residues either remain in the water as dissolved or particulate hydrocarbons, or they sink to the sediment, or

INPUT OF PETROLEUM to the oceans is charted on an annual basis. For each source the black line represents the best estimate and the colored area indicates the probable range.

they are degraded to carbon dioxide by various organisms. In the laboratory, cultures of bacteria, yeasts and fungi can be developed that will metabolize hydrocarbons rapidly in the presence of enough nutrient. Indeed, the growth of this type of culture in the ballast water of a tanker has been tried experimentally to emulsify and disperse the waxy waste that apparently is the source of tar lumps. In the open sea, however, the population of microorganisms and the concentration of nutrients and hydrocarbons are much lower than they are in typical laboratory experiments, so that the rate of degradation is probably also much lower.

An unresolved matter of major concern is the effect of petroleum wastes on marine organisms. A few large spills of oil near coastlines and a few areas where petroleum wastes are chronically discharged have been studied, but even in these studies there is controversy about how much one may generalize to other situations. The interplay between natural processes of degradation, recolonization by organisms from nearby areas and changes in the kinds of organisms that make up a marine community are all under investigation.

In the open sea, as I have indicated, some organisms find tar lumps suitable as a solid substrate to grow on. Other organisms can take hydrocarbons into their system without changing them or appearing to be affected by them. The average concentration of hydrocarbons in open water is too low for any immediate toxic effects to be observed, although near oil slicks and in association with tar lumps the concentration may be much higher. What is not known is the long-term, low-level effect of compounds from petroleum.

Many marine organisms, ranging in size from bacteria to lobsters, appear to communicate by means of chemical signals. The compounds involved in such communications are in many cases similar to the compounds in petroleum. The communication is effected at concentrations so low that even the relatively small average concentration of hydrocarbons in seawater may be high enough to cause "static" that confuses the chemical senses of some organisms. The possibility of subtle effects of this kind calls for detailed and sophisticated research.

Other investigators are studying the nature of chemical signals between marine organisms in an effort to ascertain what compounds are critical for these communications. We hope to learn from

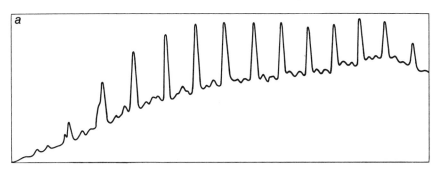
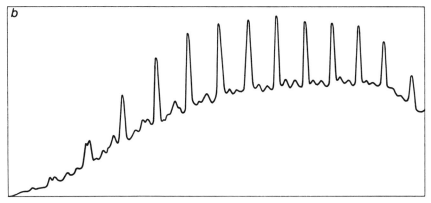
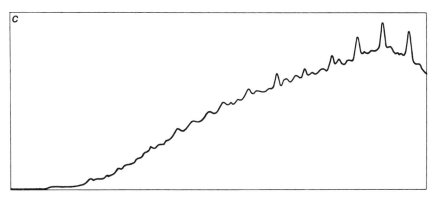

WEATHERING OF TAR is portrayed in chromatograms of a sample stranded on a rocky shore in Bermuda. The tar came ashore in December, 1970. The chromatograms were made in April, 1971 (a), October, 1971 (b), and February, 1972 (c). The tar was not significantly degraded in that time except for the outermost layer (c). Inside the softer material was almost as fresh as when it was deposited. Since tar lumps on the open ocean do not endure indefinitely, they must be disappearing by some mechanism other than simple weathering.

our studies of Sargassum communities exposed to varying amounts of tar just how much effect such a pollutant has on the ecological structure of the community. Still other workers are trying to make a clearer distinction between hydrocarbons produced by marine organisms and hydrocarbons introduced by oil pollution. Eventually all these factors may be brought together to form a realistic and quantitative picture of the effect of oil pollution on life in the oceans.

Concern about irreversible damage to the life in the oceans as a result of pollution is widespread among marine scientists, but the question of how much effect petroleum discharges at present levels are having is still unanswered. It may be possible for the oceans to accommodate much higher levels of petroleum waste without significant changes. On the other hand, the critical damage to subtle chemical communication signals between organisms may have already begun; if it has, the measurements that can be made now are simply too crude to detect it. In a situation of such importance for the future, where so little is known, it seems wise to err on the side of caution and attempt to control the dumping of petroleum wastes in the ocean with whatever international sanctions are available.

# 14

# The Strip-Mining
# of Western Coal

## COMMENTARY

Where the environmental costs of exploiting and transporting oil and gas seem to be mainly in the sea and the air, the environmental damage caused by coal is on the land. Strip-mining in particular has almost always resulted in eyesores at the least, serious and long-term despoliation of the surface at the worst. In this article, Genevieve Atwood writes about the possibilities for strip-mining western coals without causing such harm to the land. It is evident that if we are to rely increasingly on coal to cushion the depletion of our oil and gas supplies, we must make a crucial decision. How well can our need for large supplies of cheap coal from the West be made compatible with the preservation of another valuable resource—land for agriculture, grazing, and recreation?

The advantages of strip-mining are many: It is usually cheaper, much more highly productive per worker, and certainly less dangerous to the miner in terms of both serious and fatal accidents and lung diseases. In addition, most western coals are low in sulfur, thereby requiring less drastic cleanup operations before or during burning and contributing little to air pollution. The recovery of the resource is also much greater than for underground mining, which has low recovery because of the necessity for leaving enough coal to support the roof of the mine.

As Atwood points out, the only drawback of strip-mining—and it is a big one that has been known for a long time—is the damage it can do to the land surface and the quality of surface and ground water. In the past, much of the damage to the land came as a result of sheer neglect. The present generation of mining companies is paying for the behavior of those who simply took the coal and left the spoils dumps behind, unaltered. The drastic consequences of acid drainage of both mines and spoils dumps was left to local communities to take care of as best they might. These were the national sacrifice areas of the past; the decision to abandon them was made by unregulated mining companies. Because much of the mining in the eastern United States and the countries of northern and central Europe was in temperate, relatively humid climates, where vegetation and growth of primitive soils could progress rapidly, many of the spoils dumps of 50 years ago now are wooded and green. At the same time, some intelligent reclamation efforts, particularly in the United Kingdom and western Europe, were remarkably successful at returning the land to normal agricultural use only a few short years after mining.

The problem in the western United States is water. Even without mining, water-resources inventories for large parts of the West are in a precarious state. Continuous pumping of underground wells in some regions has gone on so long that groundwater levels have dropped significantly in many areas. The surface water supply in these semiarid or truly arid regions remains sparse. The large needs of the mining companies for reclamation water may not be met without diminishing the available supplies for agricultural or other needs.

Reclamation in many areas is possible, Atwood thinks, if enough water can be found; in other areas, it seems impossible from what we know today about the Earth's surface processes. The slow rates of weathering and soil formation, coupled with the surface water cycle and patterns of stream flow, erosion, and sedimentation downstream, are a complexly interwoven system. Interference by strip-mining may cause important changes in that system, some of them irreversible for many years. Are those changes we can tolerate?

# The Strip-Mining of Western Coal

by Genevieve Atwood
*December 1975*

*If the U.S. is to become self-sufficient in energy terms,
it will have to take huge amounts of coal from the
thick shallow deposits of the Western states. Can it be
done without despoiling the land?*

The availability of low-cost natural resources within the U.S. has been a major contributing factor to the country's economic and social growth. With oil and gas no longer plentiful, coal has become the mainstay of Project Independence: the effort to make the U.S. self-sufficient in energy terms. The coal industry is hoping to increase production from the 1974 level of 603 million tons to 1.3 billion tons by 1980 and to 2.1 billion tons by 1985. Since a ton of coal has the approximate heating value of four and a half barrels of oil, such an achievement would substitute coal for billions of barrels of oil.

Although people in the coal industry are delighted by the prospect, they are concerned that it may prove to be just another "boom and bust" cycle of the kind that has characterized the industry's history. Prosperity in the coalfields has never been predictable, since it fluctuates according to the availability of other fuels and the development of new energy technologies. There are currently no real alternatives to oil, gas and coal as energy sources; a large-scale role for such sources as oil shale, nuclear energy, geothermal and solar energy is a long way off, and many such sources are subject to attack by environmentalists. Just as steel has had its ups and downs in the market but has never been replaced, so coal may become essential to the U.S. economy.

Thus it seems almost certain that the country will turn increasingly to the vast coal deposits of the Western states, where 150,000 square miles of land are underlain by an estimated 2.9 trillion tons of coal. These deposits constitute 72 percent of the country's identified and hypothetical coal resources. Two distinctive things about minable Western coal reserves (198 billion tons) are that most of the coal has a low sulfur content and that a good deal of it (43 percent, or 86 billion tons, underlying 24,000 square miles) is close enough to the surface for strip-mining, in which the overburden is removed and coal is excavated from an open trench. Strip-mining in the West and in other parts of the country, however, has proved to have catastrophic effects on the land. The questions that arise are: Can the land be restored to its original capacity? If it can be, at what cost? Should the cost be borne by the public that needs the fuel or be covered by the mine operator and incorporated in the cost of the coal? Interested citizens and mine operators in the Western states with large deposits of coal accessible to strip-mining are actively debating these questions.

The amount of coal mined in the Western states (Montana, North Dakota, Wyoming, Utah, Colorado, Arizona and New Mexico) has increased substantially in recent years. The increase, from 75,000 tons per mine in 1961 to an average of a million tons in 1972, was brought about by the escalating market for low-sulfur coal and made possible by advances in mining technology.

Although the production of Western coal has risen sharply, the number of mines operating at any one time has remained fairly constant. Whereas in the past 40 years the number of operating strip mines in the Appalachian region of the East increased from 29 to 2,089, the number of strip mines in the West has remained at about 50 at any given time. Fewer than 35 of those mines account for more than 90 percent of Western coal production. Most Western strip mines are new: three-fourths of the area's tonnage comes from mines that are less than 10 years old.

Each mine has its special characteristics, but most of the mines follow the same six-step mining process. First, scrapers remove the topsoil and other unconsolidated material and put it on spoil piles. Second, the consolidated strata overlying the coal are drilled and blasted. Third, this overburden is removed by a huge dragline or power shovel. Fourth, the coal is drilled and blasted. Fifth, it is loaded into trucks. In the final step the spoil piles are graded by bulldozers.

In the East and the Middle West, where strip mines occupy areas smaller than those of the Western mines, the mining machinery tends to be smaller and more versatile. In the large Western mines the machines are of heroic size. The major workhorse is the dragline, which is employed to remove the overburden and put it in the pit opened by previous mining. The largest dragline now in operation stands more than 300 feet high and weighs 13,000 tons.

Nonetheless, the dragline is the limiting factor in coal production. In most Western mines these machines work full time, whereas the machines used for loading, hauling and reclamation work part time. Production can be increased only by increasing the rate of removing overburden. Bigger machines are not the answer; some draglines are already so large and heavy that the ground can barely support them as they move on to the next cut.

The trend from underground mining to surface mining has resulted in an enormous increase in productivity. The output per man-hour at a strip mine is approximately eight times the output at a fairly modern underground mine. The same trend has affected the geographic distribution of coal production in the Western states. From 1950 to 1967 Utah was the leading producer of coal west of the Mississippi, with an output of from four to five million tons per year from underground mines. In 1961 Utah International, Inc., opened the first big strip mine, the Navajo Mine in New Mexico. The production capacity of that mine alone is more than seven million tons per year. As a result of the trend toward strip-mining, Utah, where production is from underground mines only, has slipped almost to the bottom of the list of Western coal-producing states. First place has been taken over by Wyoming, where several huge strip mines are in operation.

In Wyoming, Montana and much of the northern Great Plains the conditions for surface mining approach the ideal. Coal seams from 50 to 75 feet thick, with an overburden of a mere 30 to 40 feet, are common. In Eastern and Middle Western mines a 10-foot seam is regarded as being exceptionally thick. There is also more overburden at those mines; at one mine in Oklahoma 95 feet of material must be removed to reach an 18-inch seam of coal.

The level of coal production from Western mines is expected to rise steeply in the near future. In Montana alone it is foreseen that 50 million tons of coal per year will be taken from five large mines by the early 1980's. Burlington Northern, Inc., expects to be hauling 90 million tons of coal per year out of the area by the same time. Plans are under consideration for thousands of miles of slurry pipelines to move millions of tons of coal per year across the country: from Wyoming to Arkansas, Montana to Washington, Wyoming to the Great Lakes and Utah to Nevada.

Although the projections for coal production in the West have virtually no ceiling, the current fraction of the nation's energy supplied by coal has risen only slightly (from 17.6 percent in 1973 to 17.8 percent in 1974). Total coal production rose only 1.4 percent (to about 603 million tons) from 1973 to 1974. Even the present low rate of coal production has subjected Western strip-mining to environmental constraints; sharp increases in production can only result in the multiplication of such constraints. Among the principal environmental concerns, of course, is whether or not Western land disturbed by strip-mining can be restored to something approximating its original condition.

Even though each mine site is different from all the others, a few generalizations can be made about the physical characteristics of Western mines and their potential for reclamation. Part of what can be said about reclamation is based on academic research and part on what the surface-mining industry has done (intermittently for 30 years and quite vigorously for the past five years) toward reclaiming mined land.

Geology and climate have the most significant bearing on a site's potential for reclamation. On the basis of their complex geological history the Western coal lands can be divided into two provinces: the Rocky Mountain province and the northern Great Plains province. The Rocky Mountain province includes the coal lands of the cordillera from Idaho to New Mexico, which lie between forested, granite-cored mountain ranges in broad basins that are comparatively flat but have been dissected by streambeds. The basins are covered by grasses and other dry-environment plants, shrubs and trees. The southwestern section is generally drier than the rest of the province, and the slopes of its mountains are less rugged and less forested than those in Utah, Idaho and Colorado.

The coal laid down in the Rocky Mountain province originated some 100 million years ago in the Cretaceous period. During later epochs of mountain building, forces that compressed the deposits and drove out volatile components upgraded some of the deposits from lignite to bituminous coal. After several million years coal swamps once again formed in the area on the flatlands between emerging highlands. Eventually material eroded from the highlands covered those coal deposits with thick layers of sediment.

The northern Great Plains province adjoins the Rocky Mountain province. During Paleocene time, some 65 million years ago, extensive beds of lignite were laid down over vast swampy areas. The mountains were low, and moisture-bearing winds from the west reached far into the interior of the continent. As the Rockies continued to be uplifted the winds were gradually cut off and the

STRIP COAL MINE is operated by the Western Energy Co. at Colstrip in southeastern Montana. The prominent ribbed ridge at lower right is a spoil pile made up of ma-

swamps gave way to grasslands. Today coal underlies thousands of square miles of basins covered at lower elevations by mixed-grass prairies and at higher ones by ponderosa pine.

Since Western coals formed under such a variety of geological conditions, they include all grades of coal (the main grades are lignite, subbituminous coal,

bituminous coal and anthracite). They are buried under a variety of overburden materials and call for different techniques of both mining and reclamation. Much of the coal underlying several large structural basins is accessible only to underground mining and will not be discussed here. In the current state of the technology the coal has to be within

about 225 feet of the surface to be accessible to strip-mining methods.

The present climate of the Western coal lands is arid or semiarid. The annual mean precipitation is low, ranging from four inches or less in the Four Corners area (where the boundaries of Utah, Colorado, Arizona and New Mexico meet) to 20 inches or more in some of

terial that lay over the seam of coal. The conspicuous rills are caused by erosion. Where the trench running toward the top of the photograph bends to the right, a dragline is removing overburden from the coal seam. In the trench a large shovel loads coal into

hauling trucks. Running diagonally at left center is a railroad where coal cars are being loaded through a conveyor and a hopper. In the area below the hopper are several old piles of spoil that have been graded as a preliminary step in the reclamation process.

the Colorado coalfields. Droughts are common, and when precipitation does occur, it may come as a cloudburst. The temperature in summer reaches levels that desiccate seedling plants, so that only the hardiest organisms, tolerant to both summer heat and winter cold, survive.

The soils at arid and semiarid Western sites are poorly developed. Rocks weather slowly, and what sparse vegetation

there is adds little organic matter to the soil. Only terrain where glaciers have deposited material has a supply of soil that is more than barely adequate for reclamation. Wind, unimpeded by vegetation, dries the soil and drives sand and soil before it, killing tender plants. The rates of erosion are among the highest in North America.

Under such conditions natural processes are slow. It might take decades or

centuries for a disturbed site in a desert to be restored without assistance. Indeed, no successful reclamation after stripping has yet been achieved at any of the more arid sites, although considerable success has been achieved in parts of Colorado and in the more favorable conditions of the semiarid northern Great Plains. Fortunately glaciated and semiarid conditions are more typical of areas where the largest increases in the sur-

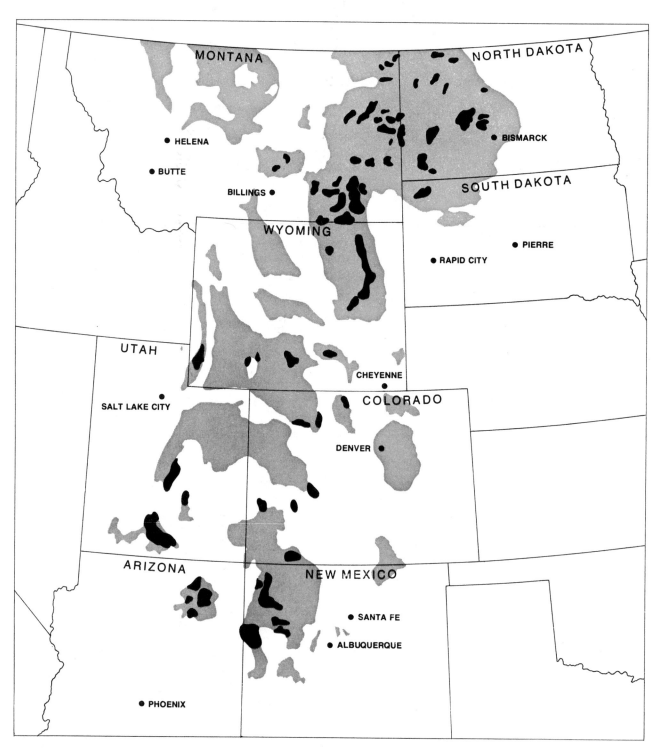

**LOCATION OF RESERVES** of Western coal is indicated. The parts of the map in color indicate the areas in the region that have major reserves of coal. The areas where the coal is close enough to the surface to be accessible by strip-mining are indicated in black.

face production of coal can be expected.

On the northern Great Plains rainfall ranges between 12 and 16 inches per year; the terrain is gently rolling; the overburden consists of alkaline shales and sandstones, and most of the land is grazed. Reclamation can be successful at most of these sites if enough planning, management, money and time are put into it. The prerequisites to successful reclamation include stability of the site, a nontoxic soil medium capable of holding moisture, proper plant-seeding techniques (which generally require slopes that can be traversed by farm machinery), occasional supplementary water and adequate management of grazing animals.

In the Appalachian region much of the damage has been done by water; the land has been scarred by acid drainage, instability of slopes, erosion and sedimentation. Water is scarce in most of the West, where the most difficult reclamation problems are revegetation and the maintenance of the hydrologic conditions in and around the mine site. Let us examine more closely how strip-mining can give rise to such problems.

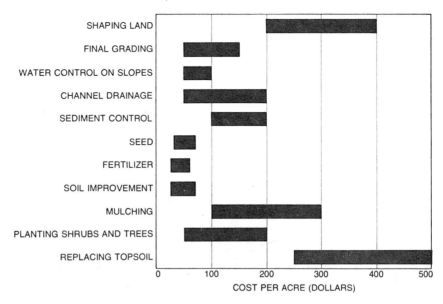

COST OF RECLAMATION of Western land where coal has been removed by strip-mining is given as a range of estimates. The figures cover the direct cost of reclamation and are based on data in a report prepared by the National Academy of Sciences for the Ford Foundation. Cost estimates made by mining companies range from $500 to $5,000 per acre.

Nearly all the Western lands underlain by coal can be classified according to some productive purpose and are capable of serving a range of uses: grazing, farming, recreation, watershed management or wildlife management. Surface mining without reclamation removes the land forever from productive use; such land can best be classified as a national sacrifice area. With successful reclamation, however, surface mining can become just one of a series of land uses that merely interrupt a current use and then return the land to an equivalent potential productivity or an even higher one.

Before 1950 most surface mines in the West (for all minerals, not just coal) operated according to the unwritten principle that the mined land would be treated as a sacrifice area. Today some states have strict regulations requiring reclamation. The regulations are not uniform, and they are not uniformly enforced. Moreover, none of them has been in effect for more than five years. Accordingly it cannot yet be determined whether the reclamation efforts made so far have either succeeded or failed.

Mining an area for coal must always disturb the land to some extent, but detrimental changes in topography brought about by mining can be remedied in most areas by employing earth-moving machines to grade and reshape the spoil. The Four Corners region may prove to

be an unfortunate exception. The mesa topography of the area has largely been created by flash floods that have cut gullies through layers that are otherwise resistant to erosion. Mining operations involving blasting and the overturning of strata leave a fairly homogeneous non-resistant material. This material is subject to rapid erosion, and if the erosion is widespread, badlands will be formed. In any event the material cannot give rise to the mesa topography that was displaced.

Strip-mining usually buries topsoil under subsurface unconsolidated material. Natural processes will not soon regenerate such soils. Although certain soil characteristics can be artificially created, some mine operators have found it cheaper simply to segregate the topsoil during strip-mining operations. Then when the coal has been removed and the other overburden has been put back, the original topsoil can be spread over it. In a semiarid area reclamation is virtually impossible unless the ground is covered with a nontoxic material capable of holding water.

The changes in surface material brought about by strip-mining may result in changes in vegetation that are in themselves detrimental to the productive capacity of the land. Even in relatively nonproductive regions the impact can be heavy. For example, halogeton, a toxic weed, is among the first and most tenacious plants to revegetate disturbed desert land, to the dismay of ranchers. In more productive areas much can be done to restore or even to enhance the

productivity of mined areas by irrigating them. That, however, calls for a long-term commitment to land management that many mining companies are unwilling or unable to make.

Water, in fact, is the key to reclamation in the West. Mined areas, unlike those in the Appalachians, cannot be regarded as having been reclaimed when they have simply been reshaped and revegetated. Their hydrologic function must also be restored. In areas where productive activities, such as ranching, depend on a barely adequate supply of water, any disturbance of that supply can be critical.

The hydrologic measures normally taken after mining can usually reduce such surface-water problems as erosion, sedimentation, silting, ponding and changes in the quality of the water. A variety of techniques for handling material, impounding water and treating water (developed at Appalachian and Middle Western mines and at a strip mine in Washington) can be applied in Western mines. After mining, surface water usually infiltrates the spoil material rapidly, which tends to promote revegetation and the recharge of aquifers. If a soil material has not been successfully established over the spoil, however, a layer of hardpan can form. Then the surface runoff increases, quite likely giving rise to undercutting and the erosion of gullies downstream. Such effects are almost always irreversible. They are similar to the widespread damage to streambeds caused at the turn

**STRIP-MINING OPERATION** is shown at the Peabody Coal Company's Black Mesa Mine in Arizona. At top a dragline removes overburden from the coal seam. The seam is visible in the trench below the dragline, as are two large trucks that haul the coal out of the trench. At bottom center is a drilling machine employed to prepare the overburden for blasting.

**REMOVAL OF COAL** proceeds at the Black Mesa Mine. At left a large power shovel digs coal from the seam and stands by to load it into a haulage truck. The rock wall with the drilling machine at its lip (*far right*) is the overburden that must be removed from coal.

of the century by the excessive runoff brought on by overgrazing.

Changes in the quality of the surface water caused by the mining operation can be controlled by treatment at the site. Subtler and more serious are the consequences of leaching and the mechanical erosion of the highly alkaline overburden. An excess of dissolved salts, a high content of trace metals and an increased load of sediment are the commonest symptoms. Although such effects may not be detected at first, they can eventually cause the groundwater to become contaminated.

Groundwater can also be contaminated by the percolation of water through the spoil, the residue of chemicals used in the mining process, the mixing of groundwater layers during the mining cycle and the seepage of low-quality groundwater from one stratum to another. Effects of this kind, which are difficult to prevent and almost impossible to reverse, may not be detected for decades. The groundwater at Colstrip, Mont., is only now being found to have been contaminated by mining operations of 50 years ago.

Pumping water out of a mine so that the mining itself can proceed often gives rise to another set of problems. The water table in the vicinity of the mine is drawn down and thereby lowers the water level in nearby wells. In Gilette, Wyo., for example, it is estimated that intensive mining could result in the lowering or dewatering of some 200 wells used for livestock.

Mining may also change the characteristics of aquifers. It is almost axiomatic that mining alters the porosity and permeability of the overburden. On the northern Great Plains the most valuable aquifer may be the coal seam itself, and the overburden may also be an aquifer. In addition water of poor quality may be contained in pockets in the overburden and in the strata just below the coal. By disturbing these components of the aquifer and by introducing their contents into the rest of the aquifer, mining can lower the quality of the water in it.

The problem of maintaining the aquifer is even more difficult when mining is done on an alluvial valley floor, which is by definition an area of unconsolidated overburden and a high water table. In the West such areas act as buffers to the seasonal fluctuations of surface water and provide the naturally irrigated land where winter hay is grown for cattle. Where surface mining interrupts the alluvial aquifer and reduces the amount of water in it, the surface-water table downstream is lowered and vegetation with short roots is desiccated. Without its protective cover of vegetation the unconsolidated material of the valley rapidly erodes, downstream areas are undercut and gouged and the productivity of the area can be lost for decades.

If the essential hydrologic functions of alluvial areas could be maintained during mining and restored after mining, there would be no reason not to mine them, particularly since the handling of overburden tends to be cheaper in such areas than it is in the hillier country around them. It is by no means certain, however, that the hydrologic functions can be maintained during mining. Until reliable methods of doing so are devised, surface mining will inevitably endanger the long-term productivity of an area for a cash crop of coal that can be harvested only once.

The environmental damage caused by strip-mining can be viewed in at least four ways. One is to accept the damage, on the basis that the cost to society of controlling it is excessive. The second is to insist that enough remedial work be done to reclaim the area after mining. The third is to forestall the problems by requiring preventive measures during the mining cycle. The last is to avoid the problems by not mining the area at all.

Some threats to the environment, such as the slowing of photosynthesis in leaves coated by the dust stirred up at the mine site, seem hardly worth the trouble involved in eliminating the cause, but others are clearly quite serious and must be balanced against the importance of coal to the national economy. Society can, either consciously or by default, treat strip mines as national sacrifice areas.

Most citizens and most coal-mining companies find the concept of sacrifice areas unacceptable, particularly in view of the fact that most mined areas can be reclaimed. For the past 20 years or so the general rule has been remedial action; when an environmental problem arose after the mining cycle had been completed, it was patched up. Usually this meant covering the mined area with a suitable soil material.

This "add on" method of reclamation proved to be inefficient, expensive and frequently unsuccessful. Accordingly the trend has been toward preventive measures such as segregating spoil, burying toxic material and incorporating grading operations into the mining cycle. As a result revegetation has been more successful and certain of the hydrologic problems have been avoided.

The policy of not mining areas that cannot be reclaimed is regarded as a

RECLAMATION OF STRIP MINE is in progress at the Big Sky Mine of the Peabody Coal Company in Montana. Here the spoil banks have been shaped and partly seeded with oats and alfalfa, which serve as cover crops for a mixture of native grasses. The view is southeast toward hills and coniferous trees that were not affected by the strip-mining operation.

harsh one by coal companies. It would be devastating to a couple of existing mines and would create hardships for companies that have invested heavily in such operations. Yet so much Western coal is easily available for mining that the nation can afford in the future to avoid mining areas that are in one way or another irreplaceable.

Based on estimates made by the Western mining companies themselves it can be concluded that the cost of reclamation (from $500 to $5,000 per acre) has not jeopardized the competitive position of coal in the market. The higher estimate would add, to strike a rough average, less than 10 cents per ton to the price of Western coal. Moreover, most operators of Western coal mines hold the view that reclamation does not interfere with production, although they do believe that it reduces productivity. (Production, which is output in tons per day, should not be confused with productivity, which is output in tons per man-day. Production will not necessarily decrease when productivity decreases.)

Certain issues other than reclamation must be considered in any discussion of Western coal mining. One is the concern being voiced in the mining states over the fact that much of the money for and the direction of the mining activity will

come from outside the region. Another has to do with the shortage of water in the West. Numerous objections to what may be in effect an allocation of scarce water resources for the production of energy for other states have been made, and more can be expected as coal production increases. Although there appears to be ample water for reclamation, the conversion of coal into electricity requires large quantities of water and will force the reallocation to energy production of water now dedicated to agriculture and recreation. At the same time voices are heard in the East warning that the shift to Western mines will be a severe blow to Eastern mines.

Such issues are more political than economic. So too is the question of how much reclamation should be undertaken and what timetable should be followed in the work. The choices that will shape the development of coal mining in the West and the reclamation of the mined lands will be made less in the marketplace than in the political arena. It seems clear, however, that large amounts of coal can be removed from a relatively few large mines in the Western states, that such operations can be limited to sites that can be reclaimed within an acceptable period of time after mining and that the cost of reclamation can be absorbed in the price of the coal.

# IV

# ENVIRONMENTAL COSTS OF NUCLEAR ENERGY

Little as we are accustomed to thinking about all the ways we have to pay for the energy we use, in the past ten years we have started to realize some of the sacrifices we make for the use of oil, coal, nuclear, and other sources of energy. Most obvious, next to the direct costs of production and distribution, have become the public-health consequences. These may be global or local and may affect the population at large or only those occupationally involved. Just as important as public health for some people is the preservation of the surface environment in terms of natural beauty. Then, too, there are the costs of using the resource or the land for this purpose as opposed to other purposes. If we set aside so much land for energy production—for strip-mining or solar energy collectors, for example—it is no longer possible to use it for agriculture or recreation.

The costs of nuclear power are even more disconcerting. Release of radiation to the environment from a reactor accident such as the major one at Three Mile Island, Pennsylvania, in the spring of 1979 is the most worrisome, but there have also been releases during ordinary operations. The occupational health costs associated with mining uranium ore and preparing it are not negligible. In addition, nuclear-process capability may play a role in the means to wage nuclear war. The short-term dangers of nuclear proliferation contrast with the long-term threat that may be posed by the improper storage of radioactive waste from both weapons manufacture and power stations. Whereas estimates of the danger of weapons proliferation are wholly dependent on an analysis of the world's political future, the possible threat of radioactive waste disposal is based on scientific extrapolations of the geological future of underground or undersea repositories.

For this section, I have selected four articles that discuss aspects of the general problem of nuclear energy. The first is on a prospective solution to the radioactive waste problem through underground storage. Though the groundrules for this particular argument—using reprocessed fuel and planning only for salt bed disposal—have changed as a result of intense discussion both in and out of government, the attractiveness of underground storage remains. The second article ties to the first in that it discusses the vital question of recovering valuable uranium and plutonium isotopes from spent nuclear fuel by reprocessing. Some people see this as the first along a dangerous path to the plutonium economy and nuclear proliferation. The third article explores the political factors behind the nuclear test ban treaty, the agreements to limit nuclear and other weapons systems, and the reasons the nuclear "club" has grown and is likely to continue growing unless we revise our thinking. The last article puts into perspective the relation of nuclear weapons to nuclear energy choices and seeks to analyze the two as aspects of a single problem. Reading these articles, one is impressed by how constant the nature of the general discussion of nuclear power and war has remained over the past 10–15 years, even though the specific details vary from year to year and seem at first to be topical in nature. I suspect that these choices will remain a central issue in politics, economics, and public policy for a long time to come.

# 15

# The Disposal
# of Radioactive Wastes
# from Fission Reactors

## COMMENTARY

The environmental hazard of nuclear power development that has received greater and greater public recognition over the past few years is the chance that radioactive waste buried underground will leak radioactivity to the surface environment. Both advocates and opponents of nuclear power have seen this issue as crucial and possibly decisive in the continuing political battle over the future of nuclear power. Some states now require adequate provisions for storage of such waste before they will allow reactors to be built. The issue cannot go away, for there is now a large amount of such waste, both that generated from nuclear weapons development since 1944 and that from the nuclear power generators built so far. Something will have to be done about containing the existing waste adequately, even if another reactor is never built.

In this article, Bernard Cohen lays out one design for an underground storage scheme. It is predicated on nuclear reprocessing, an option that was, at least temporarily, set aside by the Carter administration. Plans of the Department of Energy now favor disposal of raw spent fuel rods that will not involve the risk of producing large quantities of plutonium that might be diverted in some way to production of nuclear weapons. Burial of raw spent fuel rods may entail different arrangements than envisioned for reprocess and fuel, both, however, requiring encapsulating the waste in as nearly inert an armour as possible. Whether the material chosen for burial is salt—the focus of Cohen's article—shale, granite, or some other rock type, the general nature of the argument is the same.

The first part of the argument is based on the fact that the most highly radioactive, and therefore potentially most dangerous, products of a fission reactor decay sufficiently rapidly that we need only worry seriously about the first 1000 years, after which the remaining lower-level products decay more slowly for the next few million years. This time scale may seem long, but it presents far fewer problems to the geologist than guaranteeing periods up to a million years. The second part of the argument is that leakage from properly chosen underground sites can be minimized over long time spans. Even if some leakage were to take place, it would be so diluted by the time it reached the surface and entered the food chain and water supplies that it would be as harmless as the background radioactivity from natural sources that we live with every day.

These arguments are not universally accepted by any means. There are those who think that the radiation levels of waste materials remaining after 1000 years are still too high to neglect and so would like to see more assurance that they will stay safe for the million years it takes for them to decay to near-background levels. A number of people have calculated that the storage vessels themselves are not likely to last as long as they should. And finally, there are those who argue that we simply do not know enough yet about this kind of burial to be at all sure of the results. In the fall of 1978, a Draft Report of a Federal Interagency Review Group on this subject was made public; the conclusion was that safe burial appeared feasible but that it called for some intensive research and planning, particularly the detailed evaluation of specific sites to be chosen for repositories.

Whatever the approach taken toward the problem of radioactive waste, we will inevitably have to rely on long-term computer predictions of complex systems involving geology, geochemistry, and geophysics, as we have relatively little experience to go on. Such computer models are no better than the modeler's understanding of earth sciences and the quality of the data used to make the calculations. Thus far the models are limited in their sophistication and rely on poor and fragmentary data. We will have to do much better to approach the kind of assurance of reasonable safety that most earth scientists would accept.

# The Disposal
# of Radioactive Wastes
# from Fission Reactors

by Bernard L. Cohen
June 1977

*A substantial body of evidence indicates that the high-level radioactive wastes generated by U.S. nuclear power plants can be stored satisfactorily in deep geological formations*

The task of disposing of the radioactive wastes produced by nuclear power plants is often cited as one of the principal drawbacks to the continued expansion of this country's capacity to generate electricity by means of the nuclear-fission process. Actually the task is not nearly as difficult or as uncertain as many people seem to think it is. Since 1957, when a committee of the National Academy of Sciences first proposed the burial of such wastes in deep, geologically stable rock formations, a substantial body of evidence has accumulated pointing to the technical feasibility, economic practicality and comparative safety of this approach. In recent years a number of alternative schemes—some of them involving undersea burial—have also been put forward, but deep underground burial remains the best understood and most widely favored solution to the problem of nuclear-waste disposal.

In what follows I shall describe the nature of the wastes produced by nuclear reactors, evaluate their potential impact on public health and the environment and outline current plans to dispose of them in secure underground repositories.

What are the special characteristics of nuclear-plant wastes, and how do they differ from the wastes produced by the combustion of other fuels to generate electricity? For the sake of comparison it might be helpful to consider first the wastes resulting from the operation of a large (1,000-megawatt) coal-burning power plant. Here the principal waste is carbon dioxide, which is emitted from the plant's exhaust stacks at a

rate of about 600 pounds per second. Carbon dioxide is not in itself a dangerous gas, but there is growing concern that the vast amounts of it being released into the atmosphere by the combustion of fossil fuels may have deleterious long-term effects on the world's climate. The most harmful pollutant released by a coal-burning power plant is sulfur dioxide, which is typically emitted at a rate of about 10 pounds per second. According to a recent study conducted under the auspices of the National Academy of Sciences, sulfur dioxide in the stack effluents of a single coal-fired plant causes annually about 25 fatalities, 60,000 cases of respiratory disease and $12 million in property damage. Among the other poisonous gases discharged by coal-burning power plants are nitrogen oxides, the principal pollutants in automobile exhausts (a large coal-fired plant releases as much of these as 200,000 automobiles do), and benzpyrene, the main cancer-causing agent in cigarettes. Solid wastes are also produced, partly in the form of tiny particles. In the U.S. today such "fine particulate" material is considered second in importance only to sulfur dioxide as an air-pollution hazard; approximately a sixth of all man-made fine-particulate pollution comes from coal-burning power plants. Finally there is the residue of ashes, which for a 1,000-megawatt coal-fired plant accumulate at a rate of about 30 pounds per second.

The wastes from a nuclear power plant of equivalent size differ from the by-products of coal combustion in two important ways. First, their total quantity is millions of times smaller: when the wastes are prepared for disposal,

the total volume produced annually by a 1,000-megawatt nuclear reactor is about two cubic meters, an amount that would fit comfortably under a dining-room table. The comparatively small quantities of radioactive materials involved here make it practical to use highly sophisticated waste-management procedures, whose cost must be viewed in relation to the price of the electricity generated. For a 1,000-megawatt plant that price is roughly $200 million per year.

The second distinguishing characteristic of nuclear wastes is that their potential as a health hazard arises not from their chemical properties but from the radiation they emit. There appears to be a widespread misapprehension that this factor introduces a considerable degree of uncertainty into the evaluation of the potential health hazards associated with nuclear wastes, but the truth is quite the opposite. The effects of radiation on the human body are far better understood than the effects of chemicals such as air pollutants, food additives and pesticides. Radiation is easy to measure accurately with inexpensive but highly sensitive instruments; indeed, that is why radioactive isotopes are used so widely in biomedical research. Moreover, a large body of information has been compiled over the years from human exposure to intense radiation, including the atomic-bomb attacks on Japan, medical treatment with different forms of radiation and the inhalation of radon gas by miners. The available data have been analyzed intensively by national and international groups, including the National Academy of Sciences Committee on the Biological Effects of

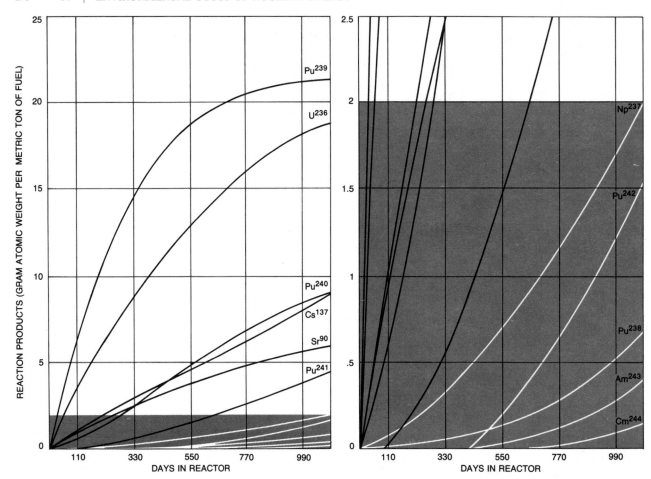

**BUILDUP OF REACTION PRODUCTS** per metric ton (1,000 kilograms) of uranium fuel in the active core of a typical U.S. power reactor of the light-water type is plotted here on two different vertical scales as a function of time over the three-year period the fuel customarily resides in the core. The hundreds of products resulting from the fission of uranium-235 nuclei in the fuel are represented by two characteristic fission fragments, strontium 90 and cesium 137, which together constitute about 5 percent of the total. All the other isotopes shown result from nuclear reactions in which uranium nuclei in the initial fuel are transmuted by neutron-capture reactions, followed in some cases by radioactive decay. Leveling off of the curve for fissionable plutonium 239 means that near the end of the effective life of the fuel this isotope is being consumed by fission reactions and neutron-capture reactions almost as fast as it is being created.

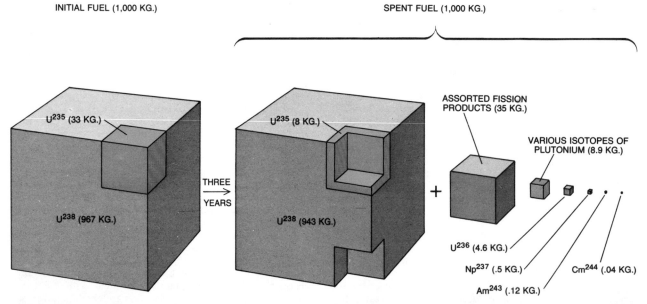

**BLOCK DIAGRAM** provides another graphic view of the transformation that takes place in the composition of the nuclear fuel in a light-water reactor over a three-year period. For every 1,000 kilograms of uranium in the initial fuel load (*left*) 24 kilograms of uranium 238 and 25 kilograms of uranium 235 are consumed (*center*), reducing the "enrichment" of uranium 235 from 3.3 percent to .8 percent. Uranium that is consumed is converted into 35 kilograms of assorted fission products, 8.9 kilograms of various isotopes of plutonium, 4.6 kilograms of uranium 236, .5 kilogram of neptunium 237, .12 kilogram of americium 243 and .04 kilogram of curium 244 (*right*).

Ionizing Radiation and the United Nations Scientific Committee on the Effects of Atomic Radiation. The result is a fairly reliable set of estimates of the maximum effects of various levels of radiation on the human body.

What are the radioactive substances in the waste products of a nuclear reactor, and how are they formed? In a light-water reactor (the type of nuclear plant now in general service for generating electricity in this country) the fuel consists initially of a mixture of two isotopes of uranium: the rare, readily fissionable isotope uranium 235 ("enriched" to 3.3 percent) and the abundant, ordinarily nonfissionable isotope uranium 238 (96.7 percent). The fuel mixture is fabricated in the form of ceramic pellets of uranium dioxide ($UO_2$), which are sealed inside tubes of stainless steel or a zirconium alloy. In the course of the reactor's operation neutrons produced initially by the fission of some of the uranium-235 nuclei strike other uranium nuclei, either splitting them in two (and thereby continuing the chain reaction) or being absorbed (and thereby increasing the atomic weight of the struck nucleus by one unit). These two types of reaction result in a variety of nuclear products, which can be plotted as a function of the time the fuel is in the reactor, usually about three years [see top illustration on opposite page].

The most important reaction in a light-water reactor is the fission of uranium 235, which creates hundreds of different products, of which strontium 90 and cesium 137, two characteristic fission fragments, constitute about 5 percent of the total. Another important reaction is the capture of neutrons by uranium-238 nuclei, which gives rise to plutonium 239. (Actually the neutron-capture reaction first yields uranium 239, which then decays radioactively in two steps to plutonium 239.) The plutonium 239 does not continue to build up linearly with time, because it may also participate in nuclear reactions. For example, a nucleus of plutonium 239 may fission when it is struck by a neutron, or it may absorb the neutron to become a nucleus of plutonium 240. The leveling off of the plutonium-239 curve means that near the end of the effective life of the fuel load this isotope is being destroyed by such processes at nearly the same rate as the rate at which it is being created.

Plutonium 240 can also capture a neutron and become plutonium 241, which can in turn either fission or capture another neutron and become plutonium 242. Plutonium 242 can be converted by the capture of still another neutron into americium 243 (after an intermediate radioactive decay from plutonium 243), and there is even an appreciable amount of curium 244 created by an additional neutron capture followed by a radioactive decay. By the same token successive neutron captures beginning with uranium 235 can respectively give rise to uranium 236, neptunium 237 and plutonium 238.

For every metric ton (1,000 kilograms) of uranium in the initial fuel load 24 kilograms of uranium 238 and 25 kilograms of uranium 235 are consumed in the three-year period, reducing the enrichment of the uranium 235 from 3.3 percent to .8 percent. In the process 800 million kilowatt-hours of electrical energy can be generated, and the uranium that is consumed is converted into 35 kilograms of assorted fission products, 8.9 kilograms of various isotopes of plutonium, 4.6 kilograms of uranium 236, .5 kilogram of neptunium 237, .12 kilogram of americium 243 and .04 kilogram of curium 244. Since only 25 kilograms of uranium 235 are consumed and a fifth of that amount is converted into uranium 236 and neptunium 237, one can easily calculate that only 60 percent of the energy-releasing fission reactions actually take place in uranium 235. Thirty-one percent occur in plutonium 239, 4 percent occur in plutonium 241 and 5 percent are induced by high-energy neutrons in uranium 238. (These figures are averages over the three years the fuel customarily is in the reactor. Near the end of that period only 30 percent of the fission reactions take place in uranium 235, with 54 percent occurring in plutonium 239, 10 percent in plutonium 241 and 5 percent in uranium 238. In view of the current public controversy over the projected future recycling of plutonium in nuclear reactors, it is inter-

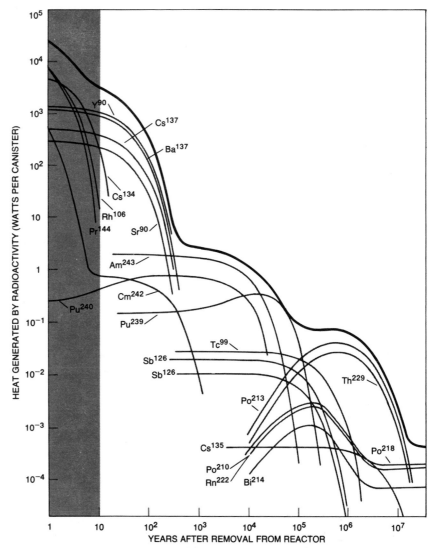

HEAT GENERATED by the various radioactive isotopes in the spent fuel from a nuclear power plant must be allowed to dissipate safely, which means that in any long-term storage plan the canisters containing the high-level wastes must be spread out over a fairly large area. The problem can be substantially alleviated by resorting to an interim-storage period of about 10 years (colored panel at left), after which the heat generated by each canister will have fallen off to about 3.4 kilowatts. The gray curves trace the contributions of the more important radioactive isotopes to the overall heating effect, which in turn is indicated by the black curve.

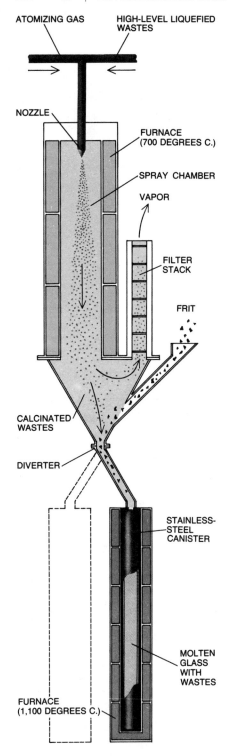

ATOMIZING GAS

HIGH-LEVEL LIQUEFIED WASTES

NOZZLE

FURNACE (700 DEGREES C.)

SPRAY CHAMBER

VAPOR

FILTER STACK

FRIT

CALCINATED WASTES

DIVERTER

STAINLESS-STEEL CANISTER

MOLTEN GLASS WITH WASTES

FURNACE (1,100 DEGREES C.)

**CURRENT PLAN for handling high-level radioactive wastes calls for their incorporation into glass cylinders about 300 centimeters long and 30 centimeters in diameter. In the single-step solidification process depicted here the liquid high-level waste is first converted into a fine powder inside a calcining chamber (top), then mixed with glassmaking frit (middle) and finally melted into a block of glass within the thick stainless-steel canister in which it will eventually be stored (bottom). When canister is full, flow is switched by a diverter valve into a new canister (broken outline); hence the process is continuous.**

esting to note that plutonium is already in intensive use as a nuclear fuel.)

After the spent fuel is removed from the reactor it is stored for several months in order to allow the isotopes with a short radioactive half-life to decay. (This temporary storage is particularly important with respect to an isotope such as iodine 131, one of the most dangerous fission products, which has a half-life of only eight days.) Thereafter one of the options would be to send the spent fuel to a chemical-reprocessing plant, where the fuel pins would be cut into short lengths, dissolved in acid and put through a series of chemical-separation processes to remove the uranium and plutonium, which would then be available to make new fuel. Everything else (except for certain gases, which would be discharged separately, and the pieces of the metal fuel pins that do not dissolve in the acid) is referred to as "high level" waste. In addition to all the fission products, which are responsible for the bulk of the radioactivity, the high-level wastes would in this case include the isotopes of neptunium, americium and curium, along with the small amounts of uranium and plutonium that would not be removed in reprocessing, owing to inefficiencies in the chemical separations.

The simplest and most obvious way to dispose of the remaining high-level wastes (once an economically sufficient quantity of them began to accumulate) would be to bury them permanently deep underground. On the face of it such an approach appears to be reasonably safe, since all rocks contain traces of naturally radioactive substances such as uranium, thorium, potassium and rubidium, and the total amount of this natural radioactivity in the ground under the U.S. down to the proposed nuclear-waste burial depth of 600 meters is enormously greater than the radioactivity in the wastes that would be produced if the country were to generate all its electric power by means of nuclear fission. Of course, the radioactivity of the nuclear wastes is more concentrated, but in principle that does not make any difference; the biological effects of radiation are generally assumed to have a linear relation to dosage, so that distributing a given total dosage among more people would not change the number of adverse health effects. (If this "linearity hypothesis" were to be abandoned, current estimates of the potential health hazards from nuclear wastes and all other aspects of the nuclear power industry would have to be drastically reduced.)

The detailed procedures for handling the high-level wastes are not yet definite, but present indications are that the wastes will be incorporated into a borosilicate glass (similar to Pyrex), which will be fabricated in the form of cylinders about 300 centimeters long and 30

centimeters in diameter. Each glass cylinder will in turn be sealed inside a thick stainless-steel casing. These waste canisters will then be shipped to a Federally operated repository for burial. One year's wastes from a single 1,000-megawatt nuclear power plant will go into 10 such canisters, and the canisters will be buried about 10 meters apart; hence each canister will occupy an area of 100 square meters, and all 10 canisters will take up 1,000 square meters. It has been estimated that an all-nuclear U.S. electric-power system would require roughly 400 1,000-megawatt plants, capable of generating 400,000 megawatts at full capacity, compared with the present average electric-power usage of about 230,000 megawatts. Accordingly the total high-level wastes generated annually by an all-nuclear U.S. electric-power system would occupy an area of less than half a square kilometer.

The main reason for spreading the canisters over such a large area is to dissipate the heat generated by their radioactivity. The problem of dealing with this heat can be substantially alleviated by waiting for 10 years after the reprocessing operation, at which time the heat generated by each canister will have fallen off to about 3.4 kilowatts. The advantage of delayed burial is seen more clearly when the heating effect is translated into the estimated rise in temperature that would result at the surface of a canister buried alone in rock of average thermal conductivity [see top illustration on page 174]. It is evident that burial after a wait of a year would lead to a temperature rise of 1,900 degrees Celsius, whereas waiting for 10 years would reduce the rise to 250 degrees C. The difference is critical, since glass devitrifies (crystallizes and becomes brittle) at temperatures higher than 700 degrees. In rock of average thermal conductivity the maximum average temperature of the rock just above and below the burial depth would be reached 40 years after burial, when the average temperature at the burial depth would be increased by 140 degrees [see bottom illustration on page 174]. If the canister were to be buried in salt, which has a much greater thermal conductivity, the rise in temperature at the burial depth after 40 years would be less: 85 degrees.

In salt an additional effect must be taken into account, since the heat will cause the migration of water toward the waste canister. Typical salt formations contain about .5 percent water trapped in tiny pockets. The solubility of salt in water increases with temperature, so that if the temperature on one side of the pocket is raised, more salt will go into solution on that side. This raises the salt content of the water above the saturation point for the temperature on the opposite side of the pocket, however, causing the salt to precipitate out of solution on that side. The net effect is a migration of the water pocket in the direction of the higher temperature, which is of course the direction of the buried waste canister. The rate of the migration depends on how rapidly the temperature increases with distance, and on how rapidly the temperature gradient, as I have explained, falls off with time.

This process is expected to lead to the collection of water around each canister at an initial rate of two or three liters per year; within 25 years a total of 25 liters will have collected, with very little further collection expected thereafter. Since the temperature at the surface of the canister would be higher than the boiling point of water, the water arriving at the canister would be converted into steam and would be drawn off by the ventilation system (assuming that the repository is not sealed). Small amounts of water would continue to migrate toward the canisters after 25 years, carrying corrosive substances such as hydrochloric acid arising from chemical reactions induced in the salt by the radiation from the canister. It is therefore usually assumed that the stainless-steel casings will corrode away, leaving the waste-containing glass cylinders in contact with the salt.

How can one evaluate the health hazards presented by such radioactive waste materials? The most direct hazard is from the gamma radiation emitted by the decaying nuclei. Gamma rays behave much like X rays except that they are even more penetrating. The effect of gamma rays (or any other form of ionizing radiation) on the human body is measured in the units called rem, each of which is equal to the amount of radiation that is required to produce the same biological effect as one roentgen of X radiation. ("Rem" stands for "roentgen equivalent man.") In analyzing the impact of radioactive wastes on public health the only significant radiation effects that need to be considered are those that cause cancer and those that induce genetic defects in progeny. According to the best available estimates, for whole-body radiation such as would be delivered by a source of gamma rays outside the body the risk of incurring a radiation-induced fatal cancer is approximately 1.8 chances in 10,000 per rem of radiation exposure. The estimated risk for total eventual genetic defects in progeny is about 1.5 chances in 10,000 per rem of radiation delivered to the gonads (with the effects spread out over about five generations). In the discussion that follows I shall be referring only to cancers, but it should be kept in mind that there are in addition a comparable (but generally smaller) number of genetic defects caused by exposure to gamma radiation.

The biological damage done by a gamma ray is in most situations roughly proportional to the ray's energy, so that

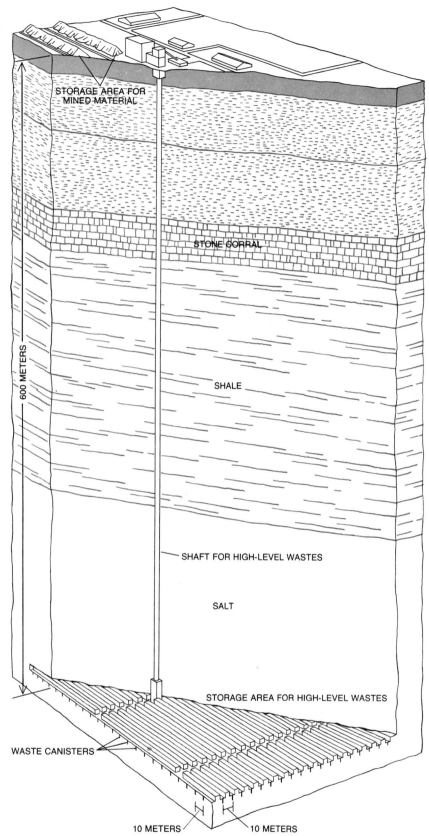

DEEP UNDERGROUND BURIAL is at present the method favored by most nuclear power experts in the U.S. for the long-term storage of high-level radioactive wastes. In this idealized diagram of a proposed Federally operated repository in southeastern New Mexico the waste canisters are shown emplaced at a depth of 600 meters in a geologically stable salt formation. In order to dissipate the heat from the canisters they would be buried about 10 meters apart; thus each canister would occupy an area of about 100 square meters. On this basis the total high-level wastes generated annually by an all-nuclear U.S. electric-power system (assuming roughly 400 1,000-megawatt plants) would occupy an area of less than half a square kilometer.

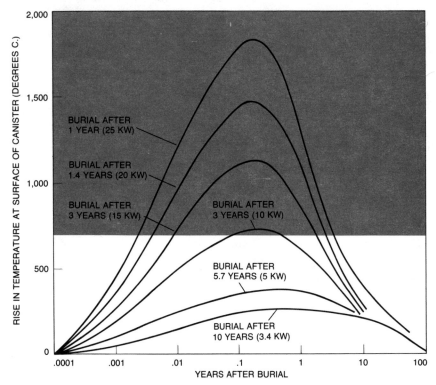

**ADVANTAGE OF DELAYED BURIAL** is evident in this graph, in which the heating effect of a single waste canister is translated into the estimated rise in temperature that would result at the surface of the canister if it were buried alone in rock of average thermal conductivity. The numbers labeling each curve indicate the heat generated by the canister (in kilowatts) after a given interim-storage period (in years). Thus burial after one year (*top curve*) would cause a temperature rise of 1,900 degrees Celsius, whereas waiting for 10 years (*bottom curve*) would reduce the increment to 250 degrees C. Colored area at top symbolizes critical fact that glass devitrifies (crystallizes and becomes brittle) at temperatures higher than 700 degrees C.

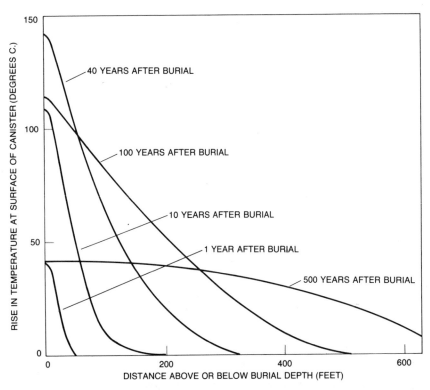

**MAXIMUM AVERAGE TEMPERATURE** of the rock just above and below the burial depth of the waste canister would be reached 40 years after burial, when the average temperature at the burial depth would be increased by about 140 degrees C. If the waste canister were to be buried in salt, the corresponding temperature increments would be considerably reduced.

one first plots the gamma-ray energy emitted per second (in watts) by the wastes resulting from one full year of a U.S. energy budget based on all-nuclear generation of electric power [*see bottom illustration on opposite page*]. From such a graph one can see that for the period between eight and 400 years after reprocessing the dominant contribution to the total gamma-ray emission is made by cesium 137 and its immediate decay product barium 137. During this four-century period the total gamma-ray hazard falls by more than four orders of magnitude.

One way to grasp the potential hazard presented by this amount of gamma radiation is to consider what would happen if the source of radiation were to be distributed over the entire land surface of the U.S. The number of fatal cancers per year induced in that case could be as high as many millions. Clearly the material that gives rise to the radiation must be confined and handled with great care. On the other hand, gamma rays are attenuated by about a factor of 10 per foot in passing through rock or soil, so that there would be no danger of this type from wastes that remain buried deep underground.

A measure of the care that must be taken in handling the waste canisters is indicated by the fact that a dose of 500 rem (which has a 50 percent chance of being fatal) would be received in 10 minutes by a human being standing 10 meters away from an unshielded new waste canister. There is no great technical difficulty, however, in providing shielding adequate for safe and effective remote handling of the waste canisters.

If any of the radioactive wastes were to enter the human body, their biological effects would be enhanced, since the radiation they would emit would strike human tissue in all directions and since the exposure would continue for some time. Accordingly one must consider the two major possible entry routes: ingestion and inhalation. The ingestion hazard can be evaluated in terms of the number of cancer-causing doses in the wastes produced by one year of all-nuclear electric power in the U.S. [*see illustration on page 176*]. In this graph the value of $10^6$ at $10^4$ years, for example, means that if all the wastes, after aging for 10,000 years, were to be converted into digestible form and fed to people, one could expect a million fatal cancers to ensue. This "worst case" scenario assumes, of course, that many millions of people are involved, but in view of the linear relation between dose and effect generally assumed for calculating such radiation risks it does not matter how many millions there are. The derivation of such a graph is rather complex, involving for each radioactive species the probability of transfer across the intestinal wall into the bloodstream; the probability of transfer from the blood into each body organ; the time the radioactive substance spends in each organ; the energy of the radiation emitted by the substance and the fraction of the energy absorbed by the organ; the mass of the organ; the relative biological effects of the different kinds of radiation emitted, and finally the cancer risk per unit of radiation absorbed (in rem).

Feeding all this radioactive material to people is hardly a realistic scenario, however, so that one might consider instead the consequences if the wastes were to be dumped in soluble form at random into rivers throughout the U.S. For this scenario, which comes close to assuming the most careless credible handling of the disposal problem, the graph shows that a million fatalities could result. It is unlikely anyone would suggest such dumping, but in any event it is clearly not an acceptable method of disposal.

In evaluating the inhalation hazard by far the most important effect that must be taken into account is the induction of lung cancers [see illustration on page 177]. Here again the graph shows the consequences of a situation approximating the most careless credible handling of the wastes: spreading them as a fine powder randomly over the ground throughout the U.S. and allowing them to be blown about by the wind.

Much attention is given in public statements to the potential hazards represented by the scales in such graphs that show the number of cancers expected if all the radioactive materials involved were to be ingested or inhaled by people. One often hears, for example, that there is enough radioactivity in nuclear wastes to kill billions of people. To put such statements in perspective it is helpful to compare the known hazards of nuclear wastes with those of other poisonous substances used in large quantities in the U.S. [see illustration on page 178]. Such a comparison shows that there is nothing uniquely dangerous about nuclear wastes. Nevertheless, it is often emphasized that radioactive wastes remain hazardous for a long time. Nonradioactive barium and arsenic, on the other hand, remain poisonous forever. It might also be argued that the other hazardous substances are already in existence, whereas nuclear wastes are a newly created hazard. Roughly half of the U.S. supply of barium and arsenic, however, is currently imported, and hence these hazards are also being introduced "artificially" into our national environment. One other important difference often goes unnoted, and that is that the chemical poisons are not carefully buried deep underground as is the plan for the nuclear wastes; indeed, much of the arsenic is used as a herbicide and hence is routinely scattered around on the ground in regions where food is grown.

IN SALT the heat from the waste canister would cause the migration of tiny pockets of water in the direction of the higher temperature, since the salt would tend to go into solution on the hotter side of the pocket (*right*) and to precipitate out of solution on the cooler side (*left*).

Actually such quantitative representations of potential hazards are virtually meaningless unless one also takes into account the possible pathways the hazardous agents can take to reach man. Therefore I shall now turn to that subject. It is generally agreed the most important health hazard presented by nuclear wastes arises from the possibility that ground water will come in contact with the buried wastes, leach them into solution, carry them through the overlying rock and soil and ultimately into food and water supplies. Human exposure would then be through ingestion. From the analysis of the ingestion route outlined above one can deduce that the hazard from ingested radioactive mate-

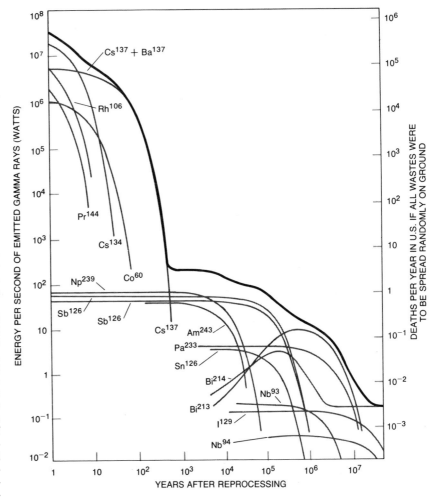

MOST DIRECT HEALTH HAZARD presented by radioactive wastes arises from the gamma radiation emitted by the decaying nuclei. The biological damage done by a gamma ray is in most situations roughly proportional to its energy; hence in this graph the gamma-ray energies emitted per second by various radioactive isotopes in the wastes resulting from one full year of an all-nuclear U.S. electric-power system (again assuming 400 1,000-megawatt plants) are plotted according to the scale at left. The black curve shows that between eight and 400 years after reprocessing the total gamma-ray hazard falls by more than four orders of magnitude. Scale at right indicates the total number of fatal cancers expected per year if the source of this amount of gamma radiation were to be spread at random over entire land surface of the U.S.

rial is high at first but much less after a few hundred years. In fact, one can calculate that after 600 years a person would have to ingest approximately half a pound of the buried waste to incur a 50 percent chance of suffering a lethal cancer. It is reasonable to conclude that it is very important the wastes be isolated from human contact for the initial few hundred years. I shall first take up that problem but shall return to the longer-term one.

When people first learn that nuclear wastes must be isolated for hundreds of years, their immediate response is often to say this is virtually impossible: man's social institutions and political systems and the structures he builds rarely last that long. This response, however, is based on experience in the environment encountered on the surface of the earth. What one is actually dealing with are rock formations 600 meters below the surface. In this quite different environment the characteristic time intervals required for any substantial change are on the order of millions of years.

In addition to the general security of the deep underground environment a great deal of extra protection is provided for the critical first few hundred years by the various time delays intrinsic to any conceivable release process. The most important of these additional safeguards has to do with the selection of a storage site, which is determined by geological study to be not only free of circulating ground water now but also likely to remain free of it for a very long time to come. In geological terms a few hundred years is a short time, so that predictions of this kind can be highly reliable. Since the patterns in which ground-water flows can be changed by earthquakes, only tectonically stable areas would be chosen. Salt formations offer additional security in this regard, because when salt is subjected to pressure, it flows plastically. Thus it is capable of sealing cracks that develop from tectonic activity. This property of salt also removes the scars of the burial operations, leaving the canisters sealed deep inside a gigantic crystalline mass.

Suppose, however, water does somehow manage to get into cracks in the rock formation in which the waste is buried. What happens then? The rock would of course be chosen to be impervious to water, so that there would be a second delay while the rock was being leached away before the waste glass was exposed to water. It would seem that there would not be much delay in salt because it is so soluble in water, but in fact the quantities of water deep underground are not large and the mass of salt is huge. For example, if all the ground water now flowing in the region of the proposed Federal waste-repository site in New Mexico were somehow diverted to flow through the salt, it would take 50,000 years for the salt enclosing one year's deposit of nuclear wastes to be dissolved away.

A third delay arises from the time it would take to leach away the waste glass itself. There is some uncertainty on this point, and the matter is complicated by the fact that leaching rates increase rapidly with temperature, but it seems fairly certain that the low rate at which the glass can be leached away will offer considerable protection for at least a few hundred years. If new leaching-rate studies indicate otherwise, it would not be too difficult or expensive to switch to ceramics or other more resistant materials for incorporating the wastes.

A fourth delay arises from the length of time it ordinarily takes water to reach the surface. Typical flow rates are less than 30 centimeters per day, and typical distances that must be covered are tens or hundreds of kilometers. For anything to travel 100 kilometers at 30 centimeters per day takes about 1,000 years.

The radioactive wastes would not, however, move with the velocity of the ground water even if they went into solution. They would tend to be filtered out by ion-exchange processes. For example, an ion of radioactive strontium in the wastes would often exchange with an ion of calcium in the rock, with the result that the strontium ion would remain fixed while the calcium ion would move on with the water. The strontium ion would eventually get back into solution, but because of continual holdups of this type the radioactive strontium would move 100 times slower than the water, thus taking perhaps 100,000 years to reach the surface. For the other important waste components the holdup is even longer.

IF ALL WASTES WERE TO BE INGESTED, the biological effects on the human population of the U.S. would be considerable. As this graph shows, the number of cancer-causing doses in the wastes produced by one year of all-nuclear electric power in the U.S. is such that if all the wastes, after aging for 10,000 years, were to be converted into digestible form and fed to people, one would expect a million fatal cancers to ensue (scale at left). If instead the wastes were to be converted into soluble form and immediately after reprocessing dumped at random into rivers throughout the U.S., the result could again be a million fatalities (scale at right).

As a result of all these delays there is an extremely high assurance that very little of the wastes will escape through the ground-water route during the first few hundred years when they are most dangerous. Indeed, the time delays offer substantial protection for hundreds of thousands of years. I shall give no credit for this factor, however, in the following discussion of the potential longer-term hazard.

As we have seen, the "50 percent lethal" dose of nuclear wastes ingested after 600 years would be half a pound. This is hardly a potent poison, and its dangers seem particularly remote when one considers that the material is carefully buried in low-leachability form isolated from ground water a third of a mile below the earth's surface. Many more potent poisons are routinely kept in the home. It is true, however, that nuclear wastes remain poisonous for a very long time, so that they could conceivably present a hazard.

To evaluate this long-term risk one must develop an estimate of the probability that the wastes will escape into the environment. How can this be done? One way is to make a comparison between an atom of nuclear waste buried at a depth of 600 meters and a typical atom of radium somewhere in the rock or soil above the waste canister, assuming that the waste atom is no more likely than the radium atom to escape and find its way into a human being. This would seem to be a conservative assumption, since "the rock or soil above the waste canister" includes the material near the surface, where the erosive forces of wind, surface runoff, freeze-thaw cycles, vegetation and so on are active.

It is difficult to calculate the escape probability for an atom of radium in a particular area, but the average escape probability over the entire continental U.S. can be estimated. To make such a comparison meaningful one can assume that the wastes are buried in a uniform distribution over the entire country, but for calculating averages it is equivalent to assume that they are buried at random locations across the country and always at the same depth. When the assumption is stated this way, it is clearly conservative; one would think that by making use of all the information available from geology, hydrology and lithology one could choose a burial site that would be much securer than a randomly chosen one.

Having made these two basic assumptions—random burial and an equal escape probability for atoms of waste and radium—one need only estimate the average probability that an atom of radium in the top 600 meters of the U.S. will escape. One approach has two steps: calculating the probability that a radium atom will escape from the soil into rivers and multiplying this number by the probability that a given sample of water will be ingested by a human being. The average concentration of radium in rivers (two grams per 10 trillion liters) and the total annual water flow in U.S. rivers (1.5 quadrillion liters) are known quantities; the annual transfer of radium

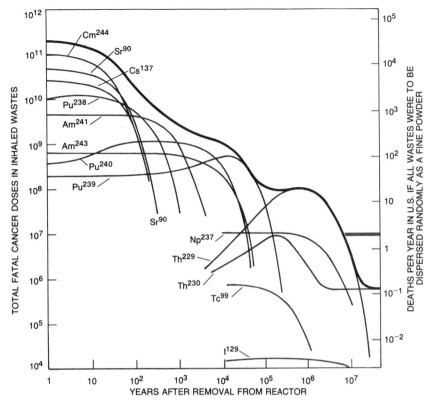

IF ALL WASTES WERE TO BE INHALED, the most important health hazard would be the induction of lung cancers. In this graph again the scale at left shows the total number of cancer-causing doses in the wastes produced by one year of all-nuclear electric power in the U.S. The scale at right shows the number of deaths expected by the inhalation route if all these wastes were to be spread as a fine powder randomly over the ground throughout the U.S. In both this graph and the one on the opposite page the short colored line at the lower right indicates the corresponding long-term health hazard represented by the natural radioactivity in the uranium ore that would be consumed by such an all-nuclear electric-power system in the U.S.

from the soil into rivers is the product of these two numbers, or 300 grams. Since radium is a product of the radioactive decay of uranium, from the average concentration of uranium in rock (2.7 parts per million) one can readily estimate the amount of radium in the top 600 meters of the U.S. as being 12 billion grams. The annual transfer probability is the ratio of the annual transfer to the total quantity, or .000000025 per year. The inverse of this number, 40 million years, is then the average lifetime of rock in the top 600 meters of the U.S. Therefore the assumption is that each atom of buried nuclear waste has less than one chance in 40 million of escaping each year. About one part in 10,000 of river flow in the U.S. is ingested by human beings, but owing to various purification processes the fraction of the radium in river flow that is ingested is closer to 1.5 part in 100,000. Multiplying this number by the annual probability for escape into rivers (.000000025), one finally obtains the total annual transfer probability of a radium atom from the rock into a human being. It is roughly four chances in 10 trillion.

There are at least two flaws in this calculation. It ignores transfer through food, a factor that reduces the transfer

probability, and it assumes that all the radium ingested is taken up by the body, a factor that increases the transfer probability. These problems can be avoided and the calculation can be simplified by estimating the number of human cancers induced annually by ingested radium (12) and dividing that number by the number of cancer-causing doses of radium in the top 600 meters of the U.S. (30 trillion). The first quantity is obtained from actual measurements of the amount of radium in cadavers combined with generally accepted estimates of the risk of a person's getting cancer from the radium. The result for the annual transfer probability obtained by this method is in close agreement with the figure derived by the preceding method. It therefore is reasonable to multiply the dosage scale in the ingestion graph on the opposite page by .0000000000004 (four chances in 10 trillion) to obtain the number of fatalities expected annually from the nuclear wastes produced annually by an all-nuclear U.S. electric-power system.

What all of this means is that after the first few hundred years of storage, during which we would be protected by the time delays discussed above, one could expect about .000001 fatality per year or less attributable to the buried waste. When this toll is added up, it comes to .4 fatality for the first million years plus an additional four fatalities over the next 100 million years.

If one is to consider the public-health effects of radioactivity over such long periods, one should also take into account the fact that nuclear power burns up uranium, the principal source of radiation exposure for human beings today. For example, the uranium in the ground under the U.S. is the source of the radium that causes 12 fatal cancers in the U.S. per year. If it is assumed that the original uranium was buried as securely as the waste would presumably be, its eventual health effects would be greater than those of the buried wastes. In other words, after a million years or so more lives would be saved by uranium consumption per year than would be lost to radioactive waste per year.

The fact is, however, that the uranium now being mined comes not from an average depth of 600 meters but from quite near the surface. There it is a source of radon, a highly radioactive gaseous product of the decay of radium that can escape into the atmosphere. Radon gas is the most serious source of radiation in the environment, claiming thousands of lives in the U.S. per year according to the methods of calculation used here. When this additional factor is taken into account, burning up uranium in reactors turns out to save about 50 lives per million years for each year of all-nuclear electric power in the U.S., more than 100 times more than the .4

life that might be lost to buried radioactive wastes.

Thus on any long time scale nuclear power must be viewed as a means of cleansing the earth of radioactivity. This fact becomes intuitively clear when one considers that every atom of uranium is destined eventually to decay with the emission of eight alpha particles (helium nuclei), four of them rapidly following the formation of radon gas. Through the breathing process nature has provided an easy pathway for radon to gain entry into the human body. In nuclear reactors the uranium atom is converted into two fission-product atoms, which decay only by the emission of a beta ray (an electron) and in some cases a gamma ray. Roughly 87 percent of these emission processes take place before the material even leaves the reactor; moreover, beta rays and gamma rays are typically 100 times less damaging than alpha-particle emissions, because their energies are lower (typically by a factor of 10) and they deposit their energy in tissue in less concentrated form, making their biological effectiveness 10 times lower. The long-term effect of burning uranium in reactors is hence a reduction in the health hazards attributable to radioactivity.

In this connection it is interesting to note that coal contains an average of about 1.5 parts per million of uranium, which is released into the environment when the coal is burned. The radon gas from the uranium released by one year of an all-coal-powered U.S. electric-generating system would cause about 1,000 fatalities per million years, a rate

three orders of magnitude greater than the result obtained above for the wastes from an all-nuclear-powered system.

If the risk of ingesting radioactive waste materials with food or water is so low, what about the risk of inhaling them as airborne particulate matter? The potential hazards from inhaling such materials are much greater and longer-lasting than the hazards from ingesting them. It is difficult, however, to imagine how buried nuclear wastes could be released as airborne particulates. The largest nuclear bombs yet considered would not disturb material at a depth of 600 meters. Meteorites of sufficient size to do so are extremely rare, so that their average expected effect would be a million times lower than that from ingestion. Volcanic eruptions in tectonically quiet regions are also extremely rare; moreover, they disturb comparatively small areas, so that their effects would be still smaller.

Release through ground water could lead to a small fraction of the radioactivity being dispersed at the surface in suspendable form, but calculation indicates that for this pathway to be as hazardous as ingestion all the wastes would have to be dispersed through it. Wastes dispersed at the surface would also constitute an external-radiation hazard through their emission of gamma rays, but another calculation demonstrates that this hazard too is less than that of ingestion.

None of the estimates I have given so far takes into account the possible release of nuclear wastes through human intrusion. Let us therefore consider that

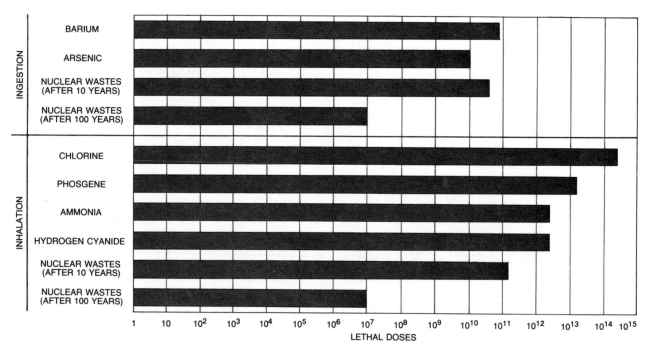

**COMPARISON OF HEALTH HAZARDS** presented by high-level radioactive wastes from nuclear reactors with those of other poisonous substances routinely used in large quantities in the U.S. demonstrates that there is nothing uniquely dangerous about the nuclear wastes. Moreover, the author notes, "chemical poisons are not carefully buried deep underground as is the plan for the nuclear wastes; indeed, much of the arsenic is used as a herbicide and hence is routinely scattered around on the ground in regions where food is grown."

possibility. Buried waste would not be an attractive target for saboteurs because of the great amount of time, effort, equipment and personal danger that would be needed to remove it. Only release through inadvertent human intrusion, such as drilling or mining, needs to be considered. The current plan is to retain Government ownership of repository sites and to maintain surveillance and long-lasting warning signs, so that this problem would exist only if there were a total collapse of civilization. One of the criteria for the choice of a repository site is that there be a lack of valuable minerals and the prospect of discovering them. (Indeed, the principal factor delaying the development of the proposed New Mexico site is the possibility that it may hold potash deposits.) Nevertheless, if there were random exploratory drilling in the area at the rate of the current average "wildcat" drilling for oil in the U.S., the effects would still be much less than those of release in ground water. If there were mining in the area (presumably for minerals not now regarded as valuable), the operations would have to be on a scale approaching that of the entire current U.S. coal-mining enterprise before their effects would equal those of ground-water release.

Wastes buried in salt might seem to be a poor risk against the possibility of intrusion by mining, since salt is widely mined. The quantity of salt underground, however, is so huge that on a random basis any given area would not be mined for tens of millions of years. Again the probability of release through this pathway is comparable to that through ground water, except that here the wastes are in insoluble form and, if ingested, much less likely to be taken up by the body. A pathway would seem to exist through the use of salt in food, but only 1 percent of the salt mined in the U.S. is so used, and it is purified by allowing insoluble components to settle out. Thus exposure through this pathway would be reduced roughly to that through the use of salt in industrial processes. All in all, then, the probability of the release of stored nuclear wastes through human intrusion is less than that of their release through ground water.

It is often said that by producing radioactive wastes our generation places an unjustifiable burden on future generations in requiring them to guard against their release. Here it should first be recognized that the estimate of the health effects of nuclear wastes I have given—an eventual .4 fatality for each year of all-nuclear power—was based on no guarding at all. The estimate was derived from a comparison with radium, and no one is watching this country's radium deposits to prevent them from getting into rivers through various earth-

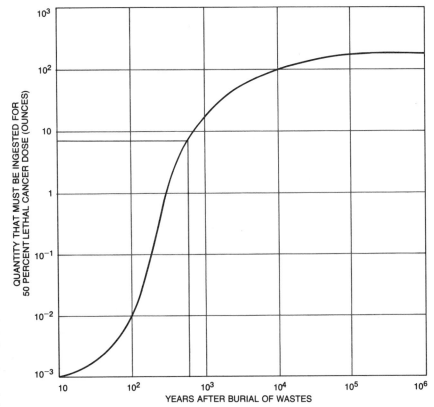

DANGER FROM INGESTED WASTES can be shown to be very great at first but much less after a few hundred years. As this graph shows, after 600 years a person would have to ingest approximately half a pound of the buried wastes to incur a 50 percent chance of contracting a fatal cancer. Such a calculation suggests that although it is obviously very important to isolate such wastes from human contact for a few hundred years, it is less imperative thereafter.

moving operations. Therefore guarding buried nuclear wastes would only serve to reduce that already small toll.

Even if guarding should be considered advisable, it would not be very expensive or difficult. Once the repository is sealed the guarding would consist only in making periodic inspections of the surface area—about 10 miles square for the wastes from 1,000 years of all-nuclear power—to make sure that the warning signs are in good order and to see that no one has unexpectedly undertaken mining or deep drilling. In addition occasional water samples might be drawn from nearby rivers and wells to check for increased radioactivity. Hence keeping watch on the wastes accumulated over 1,000 years of all-nuclear electric power in the U.S. would provide a job for only one person at a time.

Perhaps the best way to put into perspective the burden we are placing on our descendants by storing nuclear wastes is to compare that burden with others we are placing on them. Probably the worst will be the burden resulting from our consumption of the earth's high-grade mineral resources. Within a few generations we shall have used up all the world's economically recoverable copper, tin, zinc, mercury, lead and dozens of other elements, leaving fewer

options for our descendants to exploit for materials. Moreover, we are burning hydrocarbons—coal, oil and gas—at the rate of millions of tons each per day, depriving our descendants not only of fuels but also of feedstocks for making plastics, organic chemicals, pharmaceuticals and other useful products. These burdens are surely far heavier than any conceivable burden resulting from the appropriate burial of nuclear wastes.

What makes this comparison particularly pertinent is that the only way we can compensate our descendants for the materials we are denying them is to leave them with a technology that will enable them to live in reasonable comfort without these materials. The key to such a technology must be cheap and abundant energy. With cheap and abundant energy and a reasonable degree of inventiveness man can find substitutes for nearly anything: virtually unlimited quantities of iron and aluminum for metals, hydrogen for fuels and so on. Without cheap and abundant energy the options are much narrower and must surely lead back to a quite primitive existence. It seems clear that we who are alive today owe our descendants a source of cheap and abundant energy. The only such source we can now guarantee is nuclear fission.

# 16

# The Reprocessing of Nuclear Fuels

## COMMENTARY

**B**ecause the enriched uranium used for nuclear power does not literally burn up as fossil fuels do, there is a different kind of waste, a product that still contains a good deal of uranium as well as fission products built up by transmutation of elements in the metals of the reactor. How we can reprocess these wastes in an effective way is the subject of the article by William Bebbington. Reprocessing allows us to reuse a valuable and expensive fuel and so makes nuclear power less expensive. It also allows us to bank less on future reserves of high-grade uranium ore, reserves that are few and widely dispersed and thus not so easy to discover. It would seem, then, that reprocessing is a natural option for the nuclear industry and the government to take. However, as we have seen in other articles in this book, the choice is not so simple.

Reprocessing recovers the isotopes of plutonium that are generated in reactors. This exceedingly toxic and radioactive heavy metal is a major constituent of atomic bombs. Only a few thousandths of a gram is enough to kill someone. And only 25 kilograms is needed to make a large bomb. It presents a danger, explored in the last two articles in this section, that reprocessing will lead to the proliferation of nuclear weapons. That is not the immediate environmental hazard that may be associated with reprocessing plants, however. Aside from accidents in which critical masses of radioactivity accumulate, leading to excessive exposures of workers at the plant to radiation, there are problems of venting gases such as krypton 85 and waters containing tritium, the radioactive isotope of hydrogen. Because reprocessing plants will have to be associated with large-scale transportation of fission reactor wastes and the reprocessed uranium and plutonium, dangers of transport have to be taken into account.

Much of Bebbington's article is devoted to the chemical engineering methods by which uranium and other fission products can be separated from the spent fuel rods and condensed to small volumes. The technology is at hand for doing this—in fact, we have been doing it for atomic weapons production steadily since World War II—but the industry in the United States has remained relatively undeveloped (although it is moving ahead rapidly in Britain and France). This may be explained in part by the large expense involved and the kind of mixed partnership developed in the nuclear industry between government and private corporations, an arrangement by which the government bears many of the costs of research and development. As the author points out, only one private company has ever been licensed to operate—Nuclear Fuel Services, Inc., of West Valley, New York—and it has been out of business for over six years after only six years of operation at a small scale. The sole effort of private industry left the company unable to show sufficient profit to continue and left the citizens of that part of New York State and the state government a headache of large proportions. The shallowly buried wastes from the West Valley plant are leaking badly, and they must be dug up and transferred. In addition, the entire plant is so radioactive that the surrounding area has had to be quarantined until such time as the plant has been decontaminated, for which no provision was ever made. Not a very promising first experience.

Over the long run, the future of reprocessing will depend ultimately on our reserves of high-quality uranium ore, on the development of the breeder reactor, on the rate of solar energy development, and on the environmental costs of burning fossil fuels such as coal instead of investing in fission reactors. It may well be that we will have to move to this technology if we want the energy; it may also be that we will be able to devise energy alternatives that will make such plants unnecessary.

# The Reprocessing
# of Nuclear Fuels

by William P. Bebbington
*December 1976*

*The economics of fission power would be much improved
if spent fuel were processed to remove fission products
and plutonium and reclaim uranium. The industry
needed for the task does not yet exist in the U.S.*

Nineteen years after the first American nuclear power station went into service at Shippingport, Pa., the U.S. still has no commercial facility licensed to recover plutonium and unburned uranium 235 from the spent fuel of nuclear power reactors. Only one private plant was ever licensed to operate, and it was shut down in 1972 for modifications and enlargement. Its owners, Nuclear Fuel Services, Inc., of West Valley, N.Y., have since withdrawn their application for a license to reopen. Between 1966 and 1972 the plant reprocessed somewhat less than 650 tons of spent fuel. In Barnwell County, S.C., the separation facilities of a $500-million reprocessing plant with a capacity of 1,500 tons per year, owned by Allied-General Nuclear Services, were completed about a year ago. The owners are awaiting a Nuclear Regulatory Commission license, which in turn hinges on Government decisions on waste storage and on rules governing the utilization of recovered plutonium. Britain, France and several other countries reprocess spent fuel from nuclear power reactors in government facilities, but that is not the policy in the U.S. As a result the spent fuel from the nation's 62 operating fission power reactors has been piling up at repository sites. The current inventory is now about 2,500 metric tons.

Unlike coal, the fissionable fuel of a nuclear power reactor cannot be "burned" until all that is left is an essentially worthless and innocuous ash. The fresh fuel for American power reactors usually contains between 2.5 and 3.5 percent of the fissionable isotope uranium 235, having been enriched from the natural value of .7 percent uranium 235 by the gaseous-diffusion process. The remainder of the uranium in the fuel (and in the natural ore) is almost entirely the nonfissionable isotope uranium 238. When the nuclei of uranium 235 fission in the reactor, they give rise to a great variety of radioactive products, many of which act as fission "poisons" by absorbing the neutrons needed to keep the chain reaction going. By the time the uranium-235 content of the fuel has decreased to about 1 percent, the combined effects of depletion and by-product poisoning make it necessary to replace the fuel.

In addition to uranium 235 the spent fuel contains between .7 and 1 percent of plutonium 239, synthesized from uranium 238 by the absorption of a neutron. Plutonium 239 is even more fissionable than uranium 235, and the Federal Government is now deciding whether or not to approve the use of reactor fuel containing a mixture of the two nuclides. The fissionable material recovered from the spent fuel of three reactors is sufficient to fuel a fourth. The economics of the nuclear power industry will be strongly influenced by the decision that will allow or not allow the use of recycled, mixed fuels.

At the moment a reactor is shut down its spent fuel contains some 450 synthetically produced nuclides, including uranium 237 and neptunium 239, which decay into neptunium 237 and plutonium 239. The methods for chemically separating plutonium from uranium and its fission by-products were developed during World War II to provide highly purified plutonium for atomic bombs. Plutonium 239 was separated from the unenriched metallic uranium that served as the fuel of the Manhattan District reactors at Hanford, Wash. The heat from the reactors was discarded in the cooling water, and initially only the plutonium was recovered.

Uranium, neptunium and plutonium are members of the actinide series of elements, whose chemical properties are similar to those of the lanthanide series of rare-earth elements. Some months before Enrico Fermi and his coworkers demonstrated that plutonium could be made by a chain reaction in a uranium pile Glenn T. Seaborg and his colleagues had separated and purified several micrograms of pure plutonium metal that had been created by the bombardment of uranium in cyclotrons. The early studies revealed that plutonium had chemical properties that varied with its oxidation state and that could thus be exploited for separation processes. Those useful properties included the solubility of plutonium phosphates and fluorides in aqueous solutions (compared with the insolubility of the phosphates and fluorides of fission products) and the fact that certain plutonium ions could be extracted with organic solvents.

The fission products are isotopes of elements ranging in atomic number from 30 (zinc) to 66 (dysprosium). Most of them are radioactive, with half-lives that range from less than a second to thousands of years. The fission products are the chief source of the heat and radiation from spent fuel. Only a dozen or so combine intense radiation and long half-life with chemical and physical properties that are troublesome in reprocessing or in the ultimate disposal of wastes.

The first step in the treatment of spent nuclear fuel is to store it for several months in water-filled pools at the nuclear power station. During this period the radioactivity and the evolution of heat decrease by a factor of about 10,000. For example, the radioactivity of iodine 131, which has a half-life of 8.14 days, decreases by a factor of between 3,000 and 30,000. Indeed, iodine 131 is the chief determinant of how long the fuel is allowed to cool: the decay of the volatile element removes it as a problem in reprocessing.

The designers of the chemical separation plants at Hanford recognized that the technological innovations required for conducting chemical operations by remote control behind thick concrete walls were demanding enough without trying to achieve such niceties as the optimization of the process. They chose the simple batch operations that had been developed by Seaborg for working with microgram amounts of plutonium. Briefly, the uranium rods were first dissolved in acid, leaving an aqueous solution in which plutonium ions were extremely dilute. Bismuth and lanthanum were added as "carriers," so that when bismuth phosphate and lanthanum fluoride were subsequently precipitated out, they would carry with them plutonium phosphate and plutonium fluoride in quantities of precipitate large enough to separate. By repeated dissolutions and precipitations, with intervening changes in oxidation state, plutonium was separated from uranium and fission products. Simple tanks were used for the dissolutions and precipitations; centrifuges were used for separating the precipitates.

The processes worked well and safely, without any significant damage to the health of workers or to the environment. Removal of the fission products was efficient, and more than 95 percent of the plutonium was recovered. Operating ca-

pacity so far exceeded expectations that of four chemical-separation buildings planned only three were built and only two were operated. Uranium was not recovered, and the volume of waste was large because of the bismuth phosphate and lanthanum fluoride that had been added. Considering how long it takes to design and construct nuclear power facilities today it seems almost unbelievable that barely two and a half years elapsed between the initial demonstration of the chain-reacting pile on December 2, 1942, and the explosion of the first plutonium bomb on July 16, 1945.

The important legacy of Hanford to the nuclear-fuel-reprocessing industry was the concept of remote operation and maintenance, together with the innovations of engineering design that were needed to implement it. The buildings were long, thick-walled concrete

structures that enclosed the "canyons," or process spaces. The piping was embedded in the walls and ended in connectors precisely located at standard positions on the inside and near the top of the canyons. It was connected to the process equipment by accurately made jumpers that could be installed and removed by cranes that traveled the length of the canyons on rails. The crane operator, protected by heavy shielding and observing his tasks through a periscope, could remove and reinstall any of the equipment by using impact wrenches to manipulate the connectors at the ends of the jumpers. All liquids were transferred either by gravity or by steam-jet ejectors. Ingenious gang valves were developed to ensure that the steam lines were purged with air so that condensation could not suck radioactive solutions out of the shielded spaces.

After the war a major effort was

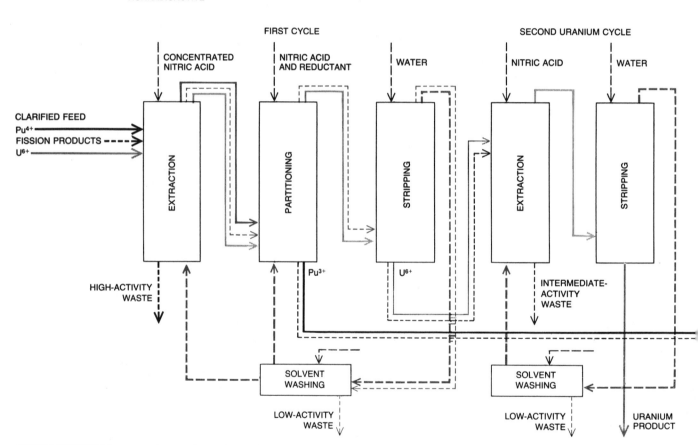

**PUREX PROCESS** for recovering uranium and plutonium from the spent fuel of power reactors employs TBP (tributyl phosphate) dissolved in a kerosenelike hydrocarbon as the separating agent. When uranium and plutonium ions are in a highly electron-deficient state, that is, are highly oxidized, they are more soluble in the TBP-hydrocarbon solution than they are in an aqueous solution. Under the same conditions the hundreds of radioactive by-products created when uranium-235 atoms fission in a reactor are more soluble in a strongly acid aqueous solution than in the organic one. This simplified diagram shows seven vertical columns in which organic and aqueous solutions are forced to travel countercurrently in intimate contact, so that substances more soluble in one solution than in the other can be efficiently separated. The feed mixture entering the first extraction column is the spent fuel in aqueous solution. In addition to the highly radioactive by-products it typically contains about 1 percent of unfis-

sioned uranium 235, more than 90 percent of the nonfissionable isotope uranium 238 and between .5 and 1 percent of mixed plutonium isotopes, primarily plutonium 239 and plutonium 240, the first produced from uranium 238 by the capture of a neutron and the second from plutonium 239 by the capture of another neutron. The uranium ions are in a highly oxidized state, deficient in six electrons ($U^{6+}$); the plutonium ions are deficient in four electrons ($Pu^{4+}$). The aqueous feed enters the first extraction column near the middle; the TBP solvent enters at the bottom. The uranium and plutonium are extracted by the upflowing solvent; the fission products are "scrubbed" out of the solvent by the downflowing aqueous stream of nitric acid and leave from the bottom of the column. The uranium-plutonium mixture passes to the second, or partitioning, column, where the plutonium is "stripped" out of the solvent by countercurrent contact with nitric acid that contains a reductant that reduces the plutonium to

launched to develop technically superior processes that could operate continuously rather than in batches and that could recover both uranium and plutonium with high yields. Solvent extraction received the most attention because it had previously been successfully applied to the purification of uranium. In solvent extraction aqueous and organic solutions flow in opposite directions (countercurrently) through a column or some other kind of mixing chamber that disperses one of the solutions in small droplets through the other. In the solvents that were used hexavalent uranyl ions, $(UO_2)^{++}$, and plutonyl ions, $(PuO_2)^{++}$, together with tetravalent plutonium ions, $Pu^{4+}$ (plutonium atoms from which four electrons have been removed), are soluble, whereas trivalent plutonium ions, $Pu^{3+}$, and fission-product ions are not. Thus the solvent can extract the uranium and plutonium (in

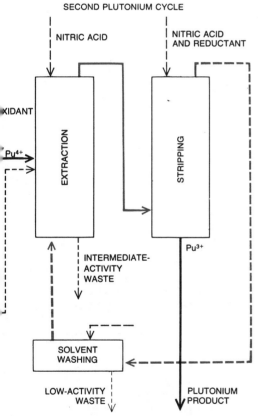

SECOND PLUTONIUM CYCLE

NITRIC ACID

NITRIC ACID AND REDUCTANT

OXIDANT

$Pu^{4+}$

EXTRACTION

STRIPPING

$Pu^{3+}$

INTERMEDIATE-ACTIVITY WASTE

SOLVENT WASHING

LOW-ACTIVITY WASTE

PLUTONIUM PRODUCT

**the 3+ state ($Pu^{3+}$), making it insoluble in the organic solvent. Simultaneously upflowing solvent scrubs the last traces of uranium from the aqueous solution of plutonium, which leaves from the bottom of the partitioning column. In the third, or stripping, column the uranium is removed from the organic solvent by dilute nitric acid. In the second uranium and plutonium cycles the extraction and stripping are repeated separately. In passing through the system, particularly in the first cycle, solvent is somewhat degraded by intense radiation and by chemical attack. Degradation products, along with traces of fission products, are removed from solvent with alkaline solutions.**

its highly oxidized forms) from the aqueous feed solution, which retains most of the fission products. In separating the plutonium from the uranium the plutonium is reduced to the trivalent $Pu^{3+}$, making it insoluble in the solvent, which then contains all the uranium.

This play on oxidation states gave rise to the name Redox for the first solvent-extraction process to be applied on a large scale. The Redox process, with Hexone (methyl isobutyl ketone) as the organic solvent, was put into operation at Hanford in 1951. Later processes with other solvents exploited the same oxidation-reduction cycle. To force the highly oxidized ions of uranium and plutonium into the solvent high concentrations of nitrate ions are needed. In most chemical processing nitric acid is used to supply nitrate ions. Since the Redox solvent Hexone is decomposed by high concentrations of nitric acid, however, aluminum nitrate was used instead. This added greatly to the quantity of highly radioactive waste. Hexone also had the disadvantage of being highly volatile and flammable.

Shortly after the war the British built production reactors and a separation plant at Windscale in Cumbria. As an extraction solvent they chose Butex ($\beta,\beta'$ dibutoxy diethyl ether). Butex is chemically stable in strong nitric acid, making it unnecessary to resort to aluminum nitrate. It is also denser and less volatile than Hexone, but it is more expensive. In the early 1950's, when the U.S. built a major new plant for producing plutonium and the hydrogen isotope tritium on the Savannah River near Aiken, S.C., tributyl phosphate (TBP) was selected for the solvent-extraction process. When TBP is dissolved in a kerosenelike solvent, it is chemically even stabler than Butex, is cheaper than Hexone and gives better separations than either. The TBP, or Purex, process is now used in all reprocessing plants.

The Purex process comprises three cycles of extraction with TBP. Extraction is preceded by a "head end" step in which the spent fuel is dissolved and the solution is clarified, a process that varies with the nature of the fuel and the cladding of the fuel rods. At the Savannah River Plant, where the reactors are fueled with natural uranium metal clad in aluminum, the cladding material is removed by dissolving it in an aqueous solution of sodium hydroxide and sodium nitrate. The uranium oxide elements that fuel all American power reactors are encased in long, slender tubes made either of stainless steel or of the zirconium alloy Zircaloy. Such rods are prepared for processing by chopping the tubes into short sections and dissolving out the oxide ("chop-leach"). (Chemical and electrochemical dissolution of the oxide fuel rods has been demonstrated, but it calls for process equipment made of alloys that are highly resistant to cor-

rosion and adds to the volume of liquid wastes.) The solutions from the head-end dissolvers are usually centrifuged to remove finely divided solids that would interfere with the solvent extraction. A substance such as manganese dioxide is sometimes precipitated to help clarify the solution and carry down some of the fission products.

When the separated uranium and plutonium streams emerge from the Purex process, they contain only about a millionth as much radioactivity due to fission products as the feed material did. At this low level of radioactivity the products in the two streams can be purified further and converted into the preferred final forms by fairly conventional chemical operations with relatively little radiation shielding. Evaporation, ion exchange, adsorption, precipitation and calcination have all been employed at one time or another. In the Government plants plutonium is reduced to the metallic form needed for weapons. If plutonium is ever used as fuel in nuclear power plants, plutonium oxide would be the preferred form, as is uranium oxide ($U_3O_8$). If the uranium is to be returned to the gaseous-diffusion plants for reenrichment, it is converted into uranium hexafluoride ($UF_6$), which is a gas at room temperature. Largely because of the differences between fuel forms two different practices have been adopted with regard to wastes. The wastes at Hanford and Savannah River are made strongly alkaline; this makes it possible to store them in tanks of carbon steel, which are placed in underground concrete vaults. Power-reactor wastes are concentrated in acid form and thus call for stainless-steel tanks.

The Purex process, with some modification, also lends itself to reprocessing the spent fuels from reactors using highly enriched uranium (such as the reactors of nuclear submarines) in which only traces of plutonium are formed. The chemical processing plant at the Idaho National Engineering Laboratory near Idaho Falls, Idaho, reprocesses the fuels from naval propulsion reactors and from research reactors of various kinds. The Idaho reprocessing plant differs markedly from the units at Hanford and Savannah River in being designed for direct (as opposed to remote) maintenance. The process equipment must be chemically decontaminated inside and out to allow men to enter the cells for repairs and replacements.

The efficiency of the Purex process depends heavily on the design of the solvent-extraction apparatus in which two immiscible liquids, one aqueous and one organic, are brought into intimate contact and then cleanly separated. This is done in an apparatus called a contactor. The simplest apparatus for countercurrent solvent extraction is the packed column, a vertical tube usually fitted with metal or ceramic rings that break up the liquid phases and direct them into tortuous paths through the column. The lighter organic solution flows up through the column as the heavier aqueous solution flows down. In such a column the mixing is not vigorous and the flow rates are low. As a result the column must be very tall to achieve a good separation, which complicates a plant that must be heavily shielded and must avoid the use of pumps. When packed columns were installed for the Butex process at Windscale, the result was a process building 20 stories high (with the fuel dissolver at the top) to allow the radioactive streams to flow downward by gravity.

The effectiveness of the extraction column can be greatly increased and its height can be reduced by "pulsing," so that the phases are drawn back and forth through perforated plates as they pass through the column. The pulsing can be done either by means of a piston or by applying air pressure to an external chamber. Pulsed columns were installed in the Purex plants at Hanford and at Idaho Falls.

One alternative to the extraction column is the "mixer-settler," in which the organic and the aqueous solutions are repeatedly mixed and separated in banks of from 12 to 24 horizontal stages, each consisting of a square mixing chamber at one end and a long settling chamber at the other. The mechanical agitator that mixes the solutions also propels the liquids from stage to stage. The chief drawback of mixer-settlers is the large volume of uranium and plutonium that is held up in liquid inventory. Because of the large holdup the solvent is subject to considerable damage from radiation and chemical activity. Among the advantages of the system are that the contactor can be readily adapted to remote maintenance, as it is at Savannah River, or be remote from the motors that drive the mixers, as it is at Windscale. Mixer-settlers are used in most of the European reprocessing plants.

An improvement on both the extraction column and the mixer-settler is a centrifugal contactor developed at Savannah River. The settling section that accounts for the large holdup of uranium and plutonium in the mixer-settler is replaced by a small centrifugal separator mounted on the same shaft as the mixing vanes. Typically arrayed in groups of six, the centrifugal units are more efficient than the mixer-settler, have only 2 percent of the volume, need only a small fraction of the time to come to a steady state of operation or to be flushed out and cause only about a fifth as much damage to the solvent. A few years ago an 18-stage centrifugal contactor replaced a 24-stage mixer-settler as the extraction contactor in the Savannah River Purex plant.

An axial-flow, multistage centrifugal contactor called the Robatel has recently been developed by a French company, Saint-Gobain Techniques Nouvelles. In this device eight stages are arrayed along the single vertical shaft of the centrifuge bowls. The apparatus has been selected as the extraction contactor for the first Purex cycle of the Barnwell plant of Allied-General Nuclear Services.

The large-scale use of nuclear energy for the generation of electricity got under way in Britain before it did in the U.S. To reprocess the magnesium-alloy-clad uranium-metal fuel from their first power reactors the British chose to modify and expand the plant at Windscale, which had originally been built to separate weapons-grade plutonium. They designed the plant on the principle that the equipment inside the shielded cells where the most highly radioactive material was handled would never be repaired or modified. This no-maintenance principle called for materials and equipment of the highest quality. Reliability was ensured by building two complete primary separation plants, one to serve as a spare. In addition each plant had a complete spare dissolver and a spare first solvent-extraction contactor. The spare primary plant was never needed as such, and it was later modified and increased in capacity. In 1957 it began reprocessing power-reactor fuel. Decontamination and modification of the first plant were then found to be feasible, with the result that the modified original plant served the British nuclear power program until 1964.

In the early 1960's the British designed and built their second-generation reprocessing plant, this time based on

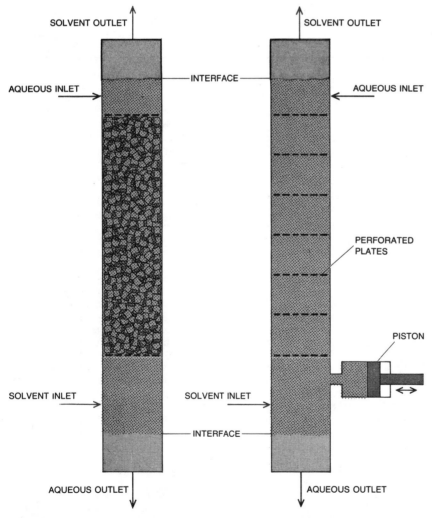

SOLVENT OUTLET

SOLVENT OUTLET

INTERFACE

AQUEOUS INLET

AQUEOUS INLET

PERFORATED PLATES

PISTON

SOLVENT INLET

SOLVENT INLET

INTERFACE

AQUEOUS OUTLET

AQUEOUS OUTLET

**SIMPLE EXTRACTION COLUMNS** were used to provide intimate contact between the solvent and aqueous solutions in the first spent-fuel-reprocessing plants. In the column at the left contact is provided by a packing of randomly oriented ceramic or metal objects, usually in the shape of rings or saddles. The aqueous solution in the column flows downward under the influence of gravity; the lighter-organic solution travels upward. A smaller, more efficient extractor (*right*) can be built if a piston or air pressure is employed to "pulse" the fluid in the column so that two solutions are repeatedly drawn back and forth through tiers of perforated plates.

**WORLD'S LARGEST REPROCESSING PLANT** for recovering uranium and plutonium from the spent fuels of nuclear power reactors is the Windscale plant at Seascale on the west coast of England. The facility was originally built to reprocess uranium from Britain's first plutonium-production reactors, which are barely visible in the distance. The multistory building with the tallest stack is the original plutonium-extraction facility. Its height was needed so that process streams of organic and aqueous solutions could flow countercurrently by gravity through extraction columns. The special railroad cars in the foreground are delivering spent nuclear fuel from power stations operated by the United Kingdom Central Electricity Generating Board. The Windscale plant, operated by British Nuclear Fuels Ltd., a government-owned corporation, can process 2,000 to 2,500 tons of fuel per year, and has processed fuels from several other nations.

**OPERATING FLOOR AT WINDSCALE** supports rows of motors that turn the agitators of "mixer-settlers," multistage horizontal chambers that perform the same function as extraction columns in bringing organic and aqueous solutions into intimate contact (*see illustration on page 188*). The plant operators are shielded by a thick concrete floor from the intense radiation in the mixer-settlers below. All equipment that may require repair or replacement is located above the floor. The mixer-settler cells themselves were designed never to be entered.

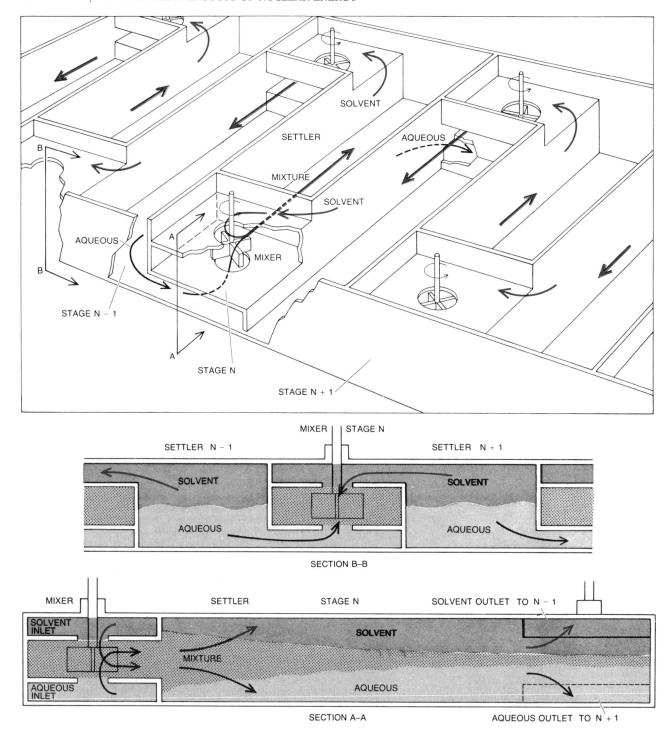

SECTION B–B

SECTION A–A

**MIXER-SETTLERS, in which flow is maintained by paddles rather than by gravity, were first used at Savannah River Plant in the U.S.** Aqueous and solvent solutions flow countercurrently through horizontal "stages." Each stage consists of mixing chamber and settling one.

Purex solvent instead of Butex. With a capacity to reprocess 2,000 to 2,500 metric tons of fuel per year, the new plant is the largest of its kind in the world. The no-maintenance principle was again followed. In 1969 a chop-leach dissolving facility was added as a head end to handle uranium oxide fuel (clad in either stainless steel or Zircaloy) that had been subjected to much longer "burnup" (exposure in the reactor) than earlier uranium-metal fuel rods and that as a result had a higher content of fission

products. Chop-leach dissolving is followed by one cycle of Butex extraction to bring the fission-product content of the oxide fuel into line with that of the uranium-metal feed to the main plant.

There is also a small reprocessing plant in northern Scotland for the spent, highly enriched uranium fuel from the adjacent Dounreay reactor and from materials-testing reactors. At Dounreay the fuel cycle is completed under conditions that anticipate the more stringent requirements of later generations of

commercial power reactors. Enriched-uranium fuel assemblies that have been irradiated to high burnup are reprocessed after short cooling times and are refabricated into new fuel elements.

The Windscale reprocessing plants (and the Dounreay operations as well) are now a part of British Nuclear Fuels Ltd., an independent (albeit government-owned) corporation that provides complete fuel-cycle services and has reprocessed spent nuclear fuels from other countries, including West Germany,

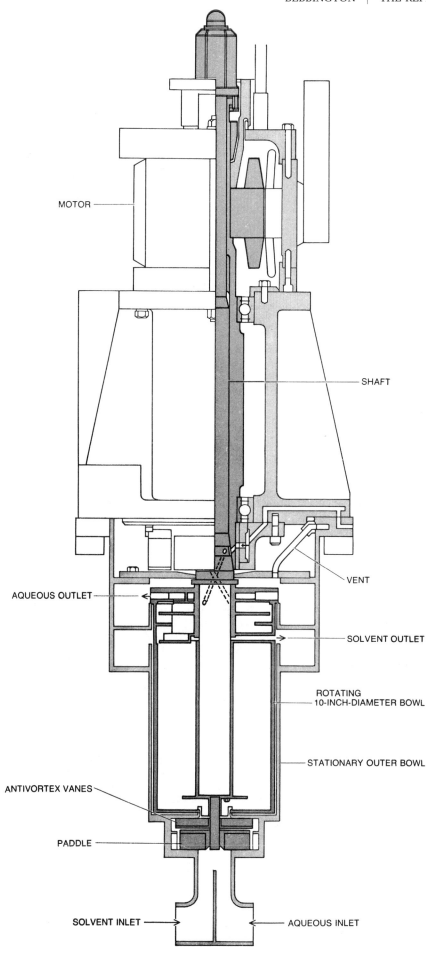

MOTOR

SHAFT

VENT

AQUEOUS OUTLET

SOLVENT OUTLET

ROTATING
10-INCH-DIAMETER BOWL

STATIONARY OUTER BOWL

ANTIVORTEX VANES

PADDLE

SOLVENT INLET

AQUEOUS INLET

Italy, Japan, Spain and Sweden. It is a member of United Reprocessors GmbH, a joint Anglo-French-German company set up to coordinate requirements and operations in Europe.

In the U.S. the Atomic Energy Commission, now merged into the Energy Research and Development Administration (ERDA), supported nuclear power by research and development in national laboratories, constructed demonstration reactors (such as the one at Shippingport, which was built in collaboration with public utilities) and stored (and in a few instances reprocessed) spent fuels from those reactors. The AEC did not, however, take the responsibility for either fuel fabrication or fuel reprocessing. The same policy continues under ERDA. Only the enrichment of uranium and the ultimate disposal of highly radioactive wastes are Government responsibilities.

Interest in the reprocessing of nuclear fuels developed among the suppliers of nuclear power equipment who felt the need to assure their customers of a closed fuel cycle, the chemical companies that had the necessary technological skill and background, and the oil companies that hoped to expand their operations into other energy sources. Several ventures into reprocessing emerged. The first, Nuclear Fuel Services (originally a subsidiary of W. R. Grace & Co. but now owned jointly by the Getty Oil Company and the Skelly Oil Company), designed and constructed a plant with a capacity of 300 tons of spent fuel per year on a site owned by the state of New York in West Valley, N.Y. After six years of operation the plant was shut down in 1972 for a planned expansion to 750 tons per year, for the correction of some deficiencies in the process, for the improvement of environmental-protection features and for the installation of waste facilities needed to meet new regulatory requirements. The plant used the Purex process in pulsed columns. Fuel was prepared for processing by chop-leach. The chop-leach equipment could be maintained or replaced remotely; the Purex-process cells were maintained directly. At last reports, however, the estimated cost of the modifications had risen from $15 million to $600 million, and Nuclear Fuel Services had withdrawn its application to the Nuclear Regulatory Commission for permission to reopen the plant.

**CENTRIFUGAL CONTACTOR for mixing and separating solvent and aqueous phases was developed at the Savannah River laboratory of the Energy Research and Development Administration. Role of settling chamber in mixer-settler is taken over by a bowl on same shaft as mixing paddle. Drive motor, with its frame and bearings, is remotely replaceable.**

The General Electric Company had meanwhile become convinced that relatively small reprocessing plants might be built to serve a group of power reactors within a short shipping radius. General Electric designed and built such a plant, the Midwest Fuel Recovery Plant at Morris, Ill., near the Dresden nuclear power station of the Commonwealth Edison Company. With a capacity of 300 tons per year, the Morris plant embodied major departures from the typical Purex-TBP process, with the aim of minimizing the contribution of reprocessing costs to the cost of nuclear power. The General Electric Aquafluor process involved TBP solvent extraction for the separation of uranium and plutonium from most of the fission products, ion exchange for separating uranium and plutonium from each other, and fluidized beds for the calcination of uranyl nitrate to the oxide ($UO_3$) and for the conversion of the oxide to the hexafluoride ($UF_6$).

Instead of the usual second solvent-extraction cycle for the uranium, General Electric incorporated a separation step that exploited differences in volatility for separating the fluorides of the fission products from the $UF_6$. This step reduced costs and eliminated some liquid waste, but it entailed the remote handling of radioactive powders. In the course of testing the plant equipment with nonradioactive feeds it was concluded that the problems of handling fine radioactive solids were far greater than had been anticipated and would preclude successful operation of the plant. It now seems that the plant cannot be modified economically to avoid such difficulties and meet the current requirements of the Nuclear Regulatory Commission.

In 1968 the Allied Chemical Corporation announced plans to build a 1,500-ton-per-year fuel-reprocessing plant on land in the Barnwell County industrial park, adjacent to (originally part of) the site of the Government's Savannah River Plant. Allied Chemical was joined by the General Atomic Company, jointly owned by the Gulf Oil Corporation and the Royal Dutch/Shell Group of Companies, as co-owner of Allied-General Nuclear Services, the operator of the Barnwell facility. Apart from its proximity, the Barnwell plant is independent of the Savannah River Plant. Construction at Barnwell was begun in 1971, and the originally planned facilities are now complete. They provide for receiving and storing fuel, chop-leach dissolving, Purex separations, storage of high-activity wastes and plutonium nitrate product, and the conversion of uranyl nitrate product into uranium hexafluoride.

Design and construction at Barnwell of "tail end" facilities for the solidification of the waste for shipment to a Fed-

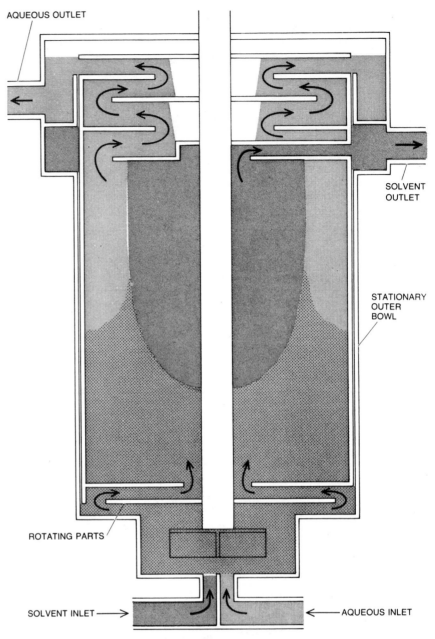

FLOW PATH IN A CENTRIFUGAL CONTACTOR is depicted schematically. After thorough mixing the organic and aqueous solutions travel upward into a rotating bowl where they are separated centrifugally. Heavier aqueous solution is thrown to outside of bowl; lighter organic solution is driven inward. Baffles at top of bowl direct two solutions to separate ports.

eral repository and for the conversion of plutonium nitrate to solid plutonium oxide await decisions by the Nuclear Regulatory Commission and ERDA on the specifications and destinations of those materials. So far Allied-General Nuclear Services has invested some $250 million in the Barnwell plant (more than three times the original expectation); the waste and plutonium facilities are expected to cost another $250 million. Half a billion dollars may seem like a large investment for a single reprocessing plant, but in the overall economics of nuclear power the outlay represents less than 1.5 percent of the value of the 50 to 60 nuclear power reactors

whose spent fuel the Barnwell plant can reprocess.

In the Allied-General Nuclear Services separations facility the spent fuel will be chopped into short lengths by a shearing device that was conceived by its engineers and designed and built by Saint-Gobain Techniques Nouvelles. The uranium oxide pellets will be dissolved continuously from the cladding hulls in a series of vessels where fresh acid leaches the last traces of fuel from a batch of hulls. Solid particles are removed from the solution by centrifugation. There are two innovations in the Purex system: the first extraction contactor is the Saint-Gobain centrifugal unit I described above, and the separation of plutonium is achieved by reducing the plutonium electrolytically in an "electropulse" column, a development of the Allied-General Nuclear Services technical staff. The other contactors are also pulsed columns. Equipment that is subject to mechanical or electrical failure or to unusually corrosive conditions can be replaced remotely; the rest of the equipment is designed for direct maintenance.

Exxon Nuclear is a supplier of uranium and of reactor fuel assemblies and is actively interested in the rest of the fuel cycle, including enrichment and reprocessing. Earlier this year Exxon announced plans to build a 1,500-ton-per-year reprocessing plant on land that is now part of the ERDA site at Oak Ridge, Tenn. The company is awaiting a construction permit from the Nuclear Regulatory Commission. Although other companies have from time to time expressed interest in fuel reprocessing, no other commitments have been made.

One industry executive has summed up the current situation by saying: "At this moment the nuclear-fuel cycle does not exist." In the U.S., at least, this is true; even the design and construction of modified and new facilities are at a standstill pending the resolution of environmental and regulatory impasses.

Hearings on the recycling of plutonium as an oxide mixed with uranium are just getting under way, and waste handling is in limbo until the final disposal site and specifications are decided. Even receipt and storage of spent fuel at Barnwell awaits license hearings that are only now about to begin. The separations facility is ready and could be operated, with interim storage of waste and plutonium in solutions, but this too awaits completion of environmental and safety appraisals and subsequent license hearings. There is doubt about whether the plant will be cleared for start-up before the end of the decade.

The situation abroad is strikingly different. Both the British and the French have relied on military production facilities to process spent uranium from the first or second generation of power reactors, which used metallic fuel rather than oxide. The construction of additional facilities to reprocess uranium oxide fuel from the newer light-water (as opposed to gas-cooled) reactors has fallen behind schedule, but not seriously. The Windscale head-end facility for oxide fuel operated from 1970 to 1973,

**MULTISTAGE CONTACTOR called the Robatel has been developed by the French firm Saint-Gobain Techniques Nouvelles. The rotating bowl of this centrifugal machine has a diameter of 80 centimeters, which is about three times diameter of the bowl in the Savannah River unit. The path through one stage of Robatel is shown on opposite page.**

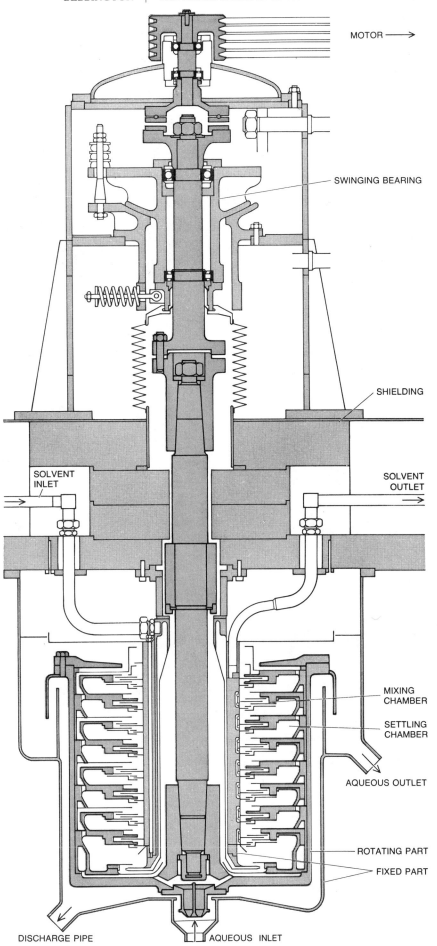

when it was shut down after a small release of radioactivity that led to a comprehensive review of the processing of highly irradiated oxide fuels. The British have now decided not to modify or rebuild the head-end facility and are planning to put up two more oxide-reprocessing plants with a capacity of 1,500 metric tons per year each, to be completed during the 1980's.

The original French reprocessing plant at Marcoule, with a capacity of processing 1,000 tons of uranium metal per year, has been running since 1958. A second plant of the same capacity went into operation at La Hague in 1967. A head-end facility able to handle about 800 tons of oxide fuel per year was recently added to the La Hague plant. The French are now proposing to build two more complete oxide-processing facilities at La Hague, each with a capacity of 800 tons per year, the first to be ready by 1984 and the second by 1986.

In West Germany a group of four chemical and nuclear engineering companies, which has been operating a small demonstration reprocessing plant, is now selecting a site for a plant with a 1,500-ton-per-year capacity that is expected to be operating by the late 1980's. The overall scheduling of European reprocessing facilities has been guided since 1971 by United Reprocessors, a consortium of British, French and West German enterprises. Its goal is to provide an integrated reprocessing capacity of about 20,000 tons per year by the early 1980's. There are small demonstration plants in Japan and India. Brazil and Pakistan have recently negotiated respectively with West Germany and France for the purchase of full-scale plants. Japan has also announced plans to build a large plant.

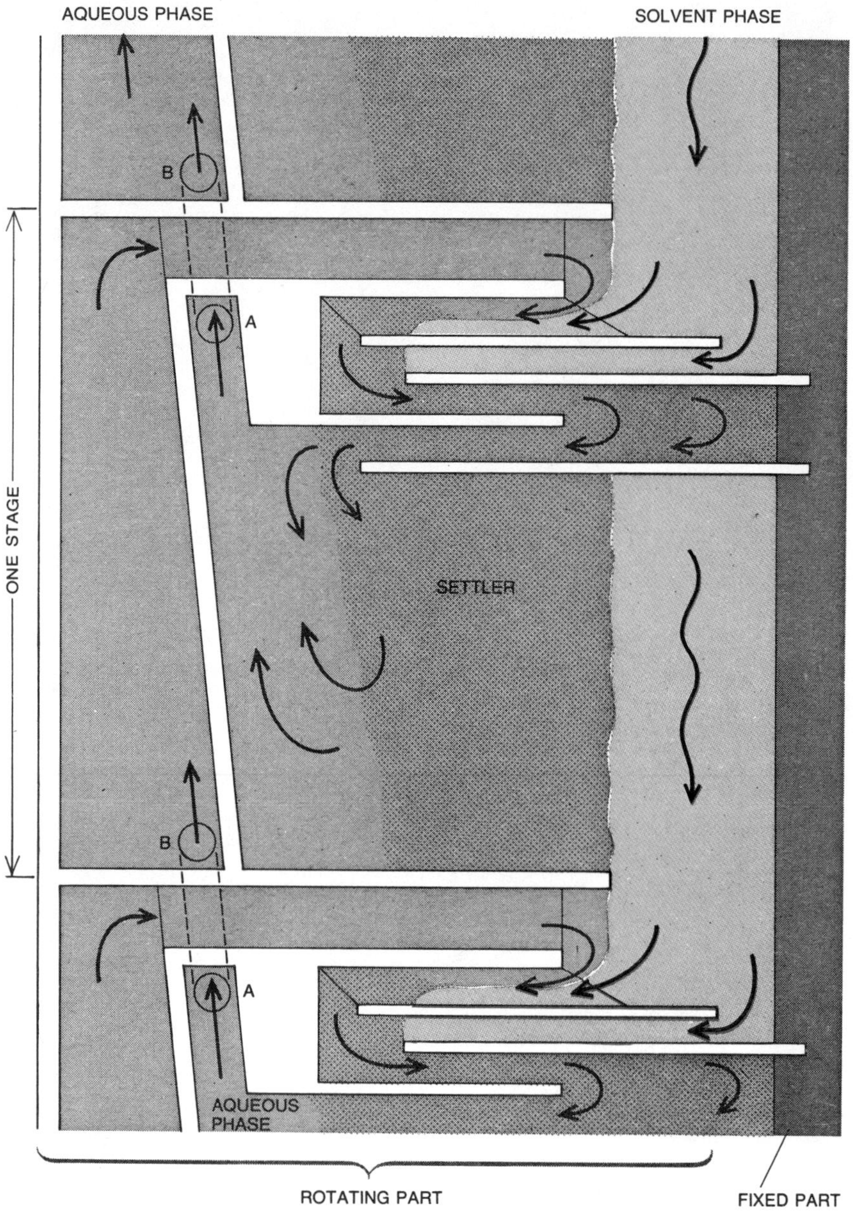

How can the U.S. nuclear power industry continue to operate without the reprocessing of its spent fuels? For the present there is enough uranium-enrichment capacity to allow once-through operation of existing nuclear power reactors, partly because the expansion of nuclear power facilities has been greatly retarded as a result of the economic slump, high construction costs and licensing delays. The volume of spent nuclear fuel accumulated per year is still manageable; in 1977 about 1,100 tons will be discharged, and its storage for long periods is simple and safe. The high-integrity, corrosion-resistant cladding is more than adequate to contain the fuel in the high-purity water of the storage basins. The capacity of the storage basins is being taxed, however, and modifications are being made to increase the size of some of them. The storage basin at Morris is in service, and the one at Barnwell has been completed.

Once-through operation of nuclear power reactors and the increasing investment in spent-fuel inventory add

AQUEOUS PHASE    SOLVENT PHASE

B

A

ONE STAGE

SETTLER

B

A

AQUEOUS PHASE

ROTATING PART    FIXED PART

**FLOW SCHEME IN THE ROBATEL** provides for eight stages of mixing and settling arranged one above the other. The schematic diagram shows the flow through a single stage. Briefly, the organic solution, traveling downward on the inside of the rotating bowl, is repeatedly mixed with the aqueous solution, which is conducted upward through a series of ports and baffles. Flow of organic solution is readily followed from diagram. At each stage aqueous solution leaves settler through ports labeled *A* and reappears in stage above through ports labeled *B*.

substantially to the cost of electric power from the nuclear plants, perhaps as much as 20 percent. These costs must ultimately be covered by the consumer. Even more important, the spent fuel constitutes a high-grade energy resource that must ultimately be "mined." The fuel cycle needs to be closed so that the technologies for reactor-fuel fabrication and for reprocessing can remain in step with reactor technology and meet their mutual requirements. It is particularly desirable that the commercial reprocessors have experienced staffs and demonstrated processes before they are called on to take up the more demanding task of reprocessing plutonium fuels

from breeder reactors and other advanced systems with high burnup rates and perhaps shorter cooling periods.

The U.S. has now had more than three decades of highly successful experience in reprocessing reactor fuels to extract hundreds of tons of plutonium, with no proof that these activities have done any significant harm to man or his environment. In spite of this experience critics of nuclear power point to such hazards as possible leaks from existing liquid-storage tanks containing highly radioactive wastes, the long life of highly radioactive wastes under any storage procedure and the harm that could be done by the routine discharge of effluents with

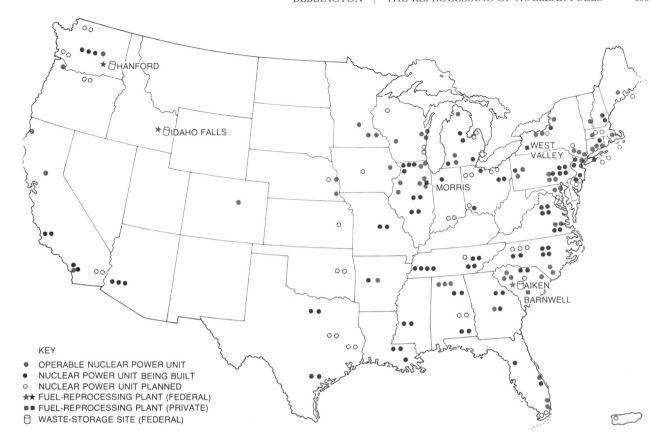

KEY

- ● OPERABLE NUCLEAR POWER UNIT
- ● NUCLEAR POWER UNIT BEING BUILT
- ○ NUCLEAR POWER UNIT PLANNED
- ★★ FUEL-REPROCESSING PLANT (FEDERAL)
- ■■ FUEL-REPROCESSING PLANT (PRIVATE)
- ⬠ WASTE-STORAGE SITE (FEDERAL)

**SIXTY-TWO FISSION POWER REACTORS** are now licensed to operate in the U.S. at 44 sites. Another 72 reactors are under construction and 61 more are in the planning stage. The operating plants have a total capacity of 44,650 megawatts, which represents just over 8 percent of the total U.S. electric-generating capacity. The 72 reactors under construction will add another 75,500 megawatts of capacity. Only one privately owned spent-fuel-reprocessing plant is substantially finished and awaiting a license to operate: the $500-million plant of Allied-General Nuclear Services in Barnwell, S.C. Two other reprocessing plants (*black squares*) have been constructed, one by the

General Electric Company at Morris, Ill., the other by Nuclear Fuel Services, Inc., at West Valley, N.Y., but their owners have no present plans to put them into operation. The Federal Government has three major fuel-reprocessing facilities: one at Hanford, Wash. (now shut down), one on the Savannah River near Aiken, S.C., and one at Idaho Falls, Idaho. At these three sites the U.S. has also stored some 75 million gallons of radioactive wastes, the residues from more than 30 years of processing spent fuels, chiefly for extraction of plutonium. Fuel from power reactors is stored in pools adjacent to power plants and at reprocessing plants, including those at Morris and West Valley.

**CHEMICAL REPROCESSING "CANYON,"** 800 feet long, at the Government's Savannah River Plant is one of two parallel remote-maintenance facilities. All piping and equipment can be removed and replaced by an operator riding in a heavily shielded crane that travels

length of canyon on rails visible on facing walls. Pipe sections are balanced so that they hang level when they are lifted by crane. Connectors are operated by wrenches manipulated from crane. Reactors at plant were designed primarily to produce plutonium and tritium.

# 17

# The Proliferation of Nuclear Weapons

## COMMENTARY

If part of the cost of expanding nuclear power, especially if we reprocess nuclear spent fuel and develop the breeder reactor, is the possibility of nuclear weapons proliferation, we need to evaluate that prospect as part of the whole system. In this article, William Epstein discusses the international politics of nuclear proliferation and the chances for containing the spread of nuclear weapons to a great many nations. The article was written shortly after India had exploded its first nuclear device, presumably a "peaceful" version rather than a bomb. That device was made from reprocessed nuclear fuel. Today the danger of proliferation remains even more ominous because of the many armed conflicts in the world in 1979—those in Southeast Asia, in the Mideast, and in Latin America. The issue of nuclear weapons is related to the continuing disarmament negotiations between the two major nuclear powers, the United States and the Soviet Union—the SALT talks that have been going on since 1969. When this article was written, the SALT agreements made at Vladivostok in 1974 had recently been concluded. In mid-1979 we were awaiting senatorial confirmation of the SALT II agreement and resumption of further talks and an extension of the SALT agreements. In spite of all these agreements, there seems to be no real diminution of the arms race between the two superpowers.

This is the backdrop of the nonnuclear powers' desire to become full members of the "nuclear club." The relation between nuclear power and nuclear proliferation is clear. The way any country can join the nuclear club is to get reactors and then develop reprocessing plants that will allow them to separate the plutonium needed for a nuclear device, presumably for "peaceful" uses in engineering works. It seems eminently reasonable for all but the poorest and least developed countries to develop nuclear capacity in the name of energy production. Once the reactors are in place, producing the plutonium, all it takes is a few years and a few tens of millions of dollars to build a reprocessing plant that will produce enough plutonium for two or three bombs per year. As Epstein sees it, the lack of trust in the big powers by the smaller ones and the insecurity of many of those countries who feel threatened by their neighbors will always operate to push them into producing nuclear bombs. And the lack of any serious restraint in the nuclear arms race by the superpowers does not help.

For these reasons, President Carter announced his decision not to advance reprocessing in this country and has urged other technologically advanced countries, France and Germany, for instance, to show similar restraint, a position for which they have shown no enthusiasm. There is a growing nuclear reactor export industry, and those countries that have small reserves of fossil fuels need energy from somewhere in the face of rising costs of oil and gas.

There are possible solutions. For example, it is possible to monitor reactors to see that there is no diversion of plutonium for weapons production, but in the face of the major powers' refusal to countenance any such interference with their sovereignty and the India experience, it is unlikely that this will succeed. Epstein points out other ways by which nuclear proliferation can be controlled. Compared to the threat of nuclear war, the other environmental costs of reactors may pale to insignificance.

# The Proliferation of Nuclear Weapons

by William Epstein
*April 1975*

*Unless the major nuclear powers begin to live up to their obligations under the Nonproliferation Treaty, it seems likely that a large number of near-nuclear countries will emulate India and join the "nuclear club"*

Next month, five years after the entry into force of the Treaty on the Nonproliferation of Nuclear Weapons, the representatives of the 84 nations that are party to the agreement will meet in Geneva in fulfillment of a pledge "to review the operation of this Treaty with a view to assuring that the purposes of the Preamble and the provisions of the Treaty are being realized." How well has the Nonproliferation Treaty worked toward the accomplishment of its stated goals? It is hard to escape the conclusion that it has failed in almost every important respect.

The magnitude of this failure was emphasized last May by India's successful underground test explosion of a "peaceful" nuclear device. Now that India, a poor, underdeveloped country, has joined the other five nuclear powers in demonstrating its potential for making nuclear weapons, one can hardly expect that membership in what once seemed to be an exclusive "nuclear club" can be held to six.

The roots of the failure of this arms-control effort, however, go deeper. The preamble and the provisions of the Nonproliferation Treaty call for, among other things, the discontinuance of all nuclear-weapons tests, the cessation of the nuclear-arms race, the enactment of effective measures in the direction of nuclear disarmament and the commitment of the nuclear powers to make available the benefits of the peaceful applications of nuclear technology (including non-military nuclear explosives) to all parties to the treaty. Nothing seems clearer than that the major nuclear powers—in particular the U.S. and the U.S.S.R., both of whom (unlike India) signed and ratified the treaty—have failed to live up to those obligations. How has this situation come about? And what can be done at this late stage to prevent things from getting even worse?

Let us begin by considering what the Indian nuclear explosion means, both in terms of the proliferation of nuclear weapons and in terms of the structure of international relations. First of all, it is important to realize that there is no essential technological difference between a nuclear explosive intended for peaceful purposes and one intended for waging war. The same device that blew a hole in the earth under the Rajasthan desert and left a large crater on the surface could just as well wipe out a city and its inhabitants. Indeed, the explosive yield of the Indian device, estimated to be equivalent to from 15 to 20 kilotons of TNT, was of the same order as the yield of the bombs that destroyed Hiroshima and Nagasaki. The main difference was in the ostensible purpose of the explosion. Indian government officials have repeatedly declared that their explosion was for peaceful purposes only and that India has no intention of developing nuclear weapons. Intention is a subjective matter based on a unilateral decision, however, and as such it can be changed at will, with or without notice. Thus in the absence of any binding legal commitment there is nothing to prevent the Indian government from changing its mind whenever it wants to. Even if one fully accepts the Indian declaration of intention to use nuclear explosions exclusively for peaceful purposes, the plain fact is that India's nuclear devices can also be used as nuclear weapons whenever India so decides. Other powers can only regard India's peaceful nuclear devices as nuclear weapons. Henceforth, in spite of repeated protestations by the Indian government, India must be regarded by other powers as being not only a nuclear power but also a nuclear-weapons power. This perception will be regarded as all the more valid in view of the fact that a public-opinion poll taken in India soon after the explosion showed that two-thirds of the Indian people favored India's making nuclear weapons.

The Indian test explosion has also shown the way for other nations to "go nuclear" under the guise of testing devices for peaceful purposes. Any one of the potential nuclear powers that has not become a party to the Nonproliferation Treaty can emulate India's example. Even countries that are party to the treaty retain this option, since the text of the treaty provides that any party can withdraw on three months' notice.

It is much easier for a government to assuage both domestic and international opinion by proclaiming its intention to conduct nuclear explosions solely for peaceful purposes than to say outright that it intends to make nuclear weapons. Nuclear weapons are, after all, still regarded with abhorrence as weapons of mass destruction. All the first five nuclear-weapons states have declared that they produced nuclear weapons solely for defense and not for aggression. One can now look forward to a new chapter in the nuclear story, where countries that want to become nuclear-weapons states, for whatever reason, would first go through the stage of producing nuclear devices for "peaceful" purposes. This cosmetic façade would be sufficient to enable a moderately advanced nation over a period of time to produce a wide range of nuclear warheads.

The Indian leaders insist that they broke no law, treaty or agreement in conducting the Rajasthan test, and they are right. The Partial Test-Ban Treaty of 1963, to which India is a party, bans tests in the atmosphere, in outer space and underwater, but it does not ban them underground. The only restriction on underground tests is against those that vent and carry radioactive debris beyond the territory of the country where the test is held. Several tests conducted by both the U.S. and the U.S.S.R. have vented and carried radioactive debris beyond their borders, but these were regarded as mere "technical violations" of the treaty since they were accidental in the sense that no violation was intended or expected. It would appear, however, that there was no violation, technical or otherwise, as a result of the Indian test.

The Nonproliferation Treaty is the only international instrument that bans the explosion of nuclear devices for peaceful purposes by states that do not have nuclear weapons. The transfer or acquisition of "nuclear weapons or other nuclear explosive devices" is specifically banned for non-nuclear-weapons states by Article II of the treaty. Peaceful nuclear explosions, however, to be conducted only by nuclear-weapons states under an appropriate international regime for the benefit of non-nuclear-weapons states, are expressly envisioned by both the preamble and Article V of the treaty. India is in any case not a party to the Nonproliferation Treaty. In fact, both during and after the negotiation and conclusion of the treaty, India publicly announced its opposition to the accord as discriminatory and unfair, and declared that it reserved the right to conduct its own nuclear explosions for peaceful purposes. Hence India cannot be accused of any breach of either the letter or the spirit of the Nonproliferation Treaty.

On the other hand, India is a party to and an active participant in the work of the International Atomic Energy Agency (IAEA) in Vienna. The statute of that agency, which went into force in 1957, specifically bans the use of atomic energy "in such a way as to further any military purpose" but positively encourages "the development and practical application of atomic energy for peaceful purposes." A number of United Nations and IAEA conferences from 1958 to 1971 held out high hopes for the potential benefits that would be obtained from nonmilitary nuclear explosions. These benefits may be largely illusory or downright mythical, but there can be no doubt that over the years nuclear and non-nuclear powers alike were dazzled by the glittering prize that could be theirs when nonmilitary nuclear explosions became

CRATER formed by India's underground nuclear explosion on May 18, 1974, appears in this aerial photograph released by the Indian Department of Atomic Energy. The test was conducted "for peaceful purposes" at a site in the Rajasthan desert east of New Delhi. The yield of the device was between 15 and 20 kilotons, approximately the same as the yield of the Hiroshima bomb.

feasible. Although the nuclear-weapons states are apparently becoming increasingly disenchanted by their failure to achieve any important technical or economic objectives after investing years of effort and hundreds of millions of dollars in testing nonmilitary nuclear explosives, the poorer nations of the world seem to regard such devices as the key that could help them to unlock the door to great industrial and engineering undertakings at little cost. As recently as July, 1974, in the Threshold Test-Ban Treaty signed by Secretary Brezhnev and President Nixon in Moscow, specific provision is made for entering into a new bilateral agreement for the exchange of data about nonmilitary nuclear explosions at the earliest possible time. Thus India can hardly be criticized for wanting to achieve what was not prohibited for it by any international treaty or agreement and what was given the specific blessing of a number of international treaties and studies.

Regardless of what one may think of India's tactics and behavior, and convinced as one may be that India will eventually turn its peaceful nuclear devices into nuclear weapons, its declared intention to use these devices exclusively for peaceful purposes cannot be disproved. One can only regret that the nation of Gandhi and Nehru (who first proposed the end of nuclear testing in 1954) may be responsible for undermining efforts to prevent the proliferation of nuclear weapons. One might also be allowed to doubt the wisdom—in terms of India's own ultimate political, economic and military interests—of its having decided to go nuclear.

Public reactions to the Indian explosion have been rather few and mixed. Not a word of criticism has been heard from the two Asian nuclear powers, China and the U.S.S.R. China has attacked the Nonproliferation Treaty from its inception as a device by the two superpowers to maintain their nuclear hegemony and to dominate the non-nuclear states. The Chinese have for many years in effect advocated the proliferation of nuclear weapons as a means whereby the underdeveloped countries of the "Third World" could protect themselves from nuclear threats and blackmail by the nuclear superpowers. In any event it is unlikely that India can become a threat to China in the foreseeable future, even if India decides to become a nuclear-weapons power. Nevertheless, in view of India's close relations with the U.S.S.R. and the fact that India was clearly the strongest military power in southern Asia even before last May, China can hardly regard India's growing nuclear power with equanimity. In the context of Chi-

**CURRENT STATUS OF NONPROLIFERATION TREATY is depicted on this world map. The 84 nations that are full parties to the** agreement are shown in dark gray. The 22 nations that have signed the treaty but have not yet ratified it, and hence are not bound by

nese and Indian relations with other Asian countries and the Third World, and in particular with Pakistan, with whom China has close and friendly relations, the political implications of the Indian explosion are of greater importance than the military ones. Moreover, if Taiwan, which is a party to the Nonproliferation Treaty, should be encouraged by the Indian example to withdraw from the treaty and go nuclear, this would pose some new and difficult problems for China. It is also difficult to believe that China would be completely unconcerned if South Korea, Indonesia, Iran or Australia were also to go nuclear. The official silence from Peking, which is itself conducting tests in the atmosphere, may therefore mean only that China has not yet worked out its final position with respect to the Indian explosion or is biding its time pending a clarification of Third World opinion.

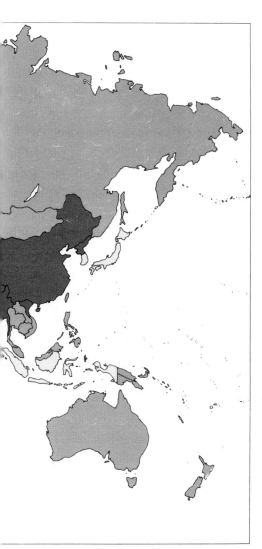

its provisions, are in light gray. The 38 nonsignatories (among them India) are in color.

On the other hand, the U.S.S.R., which together with the U.S. was the chief protagonist of the Nonproliferation Treaty, must surely find the Indian action disquieting. Although the U.S.S.R. too has not uttered a single official word of complaint, Russian diplomats and arms-control experts have privately indicated their unhappiness. It could hardly be otherwise. It may be that a nuclear India that continues to be friendly to the U.S.S.R. provides some benefits or leverage for the U.S.S.R. with respect to China, but any such possible advantage would be far outweighed if India's action should lead to the further erosion of the Nonproliferation Treaty and to the spread of nuclear-weapons capability to other states, particularly those around the periphery of the U.S.S.R.

France, which is also conducting tests in the atmosphere, has made no official statement, although the chairman of the French Atomic Energy Commission sent a congratulatory message to the chairman of the Indian Atomic Energy Commission. The French position is anomalous. France is not a party to the Nonproliferation Treaty, but it has announced from the start that it will behave exactly as if it were a party. Nevertheless, France is busy selling nuclear reactors to a number of countries, and although these deals are subject to IAEA safeguards, as far as is known they do not bar peaceful nuclear explosions.

Great Britain, which has also been a strong supporter of the Nonproliferation Treaty, was at first strongly critical of the Indian explosion. After the initial criticism, however, little has been heard from the British, who have themselves been criticized for resuming underground testing in June, 1974, when they set off an explosion (in the U.S.) for the first time since 1965.

The U.S. was at first rather cautious in its official reaction to the Indian explosion. It did reiterate its views to the Indian government that peaceful and military nuclear explosive devices are indistinguishable, but it seems to wish to avoid any public dispute with India. Privately it has sought a commitment that plutonium produced from nuclear fuel supplied by the U.S. would not be used for any kind of explosion. Failing to receive adequate assurances, the U.S. delayed the delivery of enriched uranium to fuel the Tarapur reactor, which was built with American technical and financial assistance. At the moment it appears that India will give the necessary assurances and that the U.S. will continue supplying uranium to India.

As was to be expected, Pakistan, which signed but never ratified the 1963 Partial Test-Ban Treaty and which has not signed the Nonproliferation Treaty, immediately protested in every possible forum against the Indian explosion and called for a halt to further tests. Pakistan also announced that it would acquire a similar nuclear capability. It has proposed that the UN General Assembly discuss the creation of a nuclear-free zone in South Asia; the proposal (which India rejected) must be regarded as a tactical political move intended to make clear to the world where the blame lies.

Apart from Pakistan, only Canada, Japan and Sweden, all of which have the capability of undertaking nuclear explosions, have taken a strong public stand against the Indian test. Canada cut off all further nuclear cooperation with India almost immediately, and all three countries in statements in their capitals, in the Geneva disarmament conference, in messages transmitted to the Indian government and in the UN General Assembly deplored the Indian explosion and its possible adverse effects on international efforts to prevent the proliferation of nuclear weapons. Australia and the Netherlands have also criticized the Indian test.

As for the nonaligned and underdeveloped countries, while saying little in public, they have in large part welcomed the Indian test as a technological achievement demonstrating that even a poor country can accomplish the sophisticated task of successfully exploding an underground nuclear device, which had for a decade been the exclusive preserve of the five great powers. Yugoslavia, one of the leaders of the nonaligned countries, congratulated India on its technological achievement. Nigeria said that the Indian action was not surprising in view of the lack of progress by the nuclear powers in stopping underground nuclear tests and the nuclear-arms race.

Without the wide support of the non-nuclear-weapons states of the Third World, the Nonproliferation Treaty would never have received the overwhelming commendation of the UN General Assembly. Most of them have no significant nuclear programs and are in no position to go nuclear for several decades to come. In 1968 these countries entered into a tacit alliance with the nuclear powers, because it seemed clear that the further "horizontal" spread of nuclear weapons to the near-nuclear countries, nearly all of which were developed countries, was not in the interest of either group. The Third World countries as a group, however, were never greatly impressed by the Nonproliferation Treaty.

Many of those who decided to support the treaty did so in the dual expectation that the nuclear-weapons powers would halt the "vertical" proliferation of nuclear weapons (their further sophistication, development and deployment) and would also make available to the underdeveloped countries the benefits of the peaceful uses of nuclear energy, including nonmilitary nuclear explosions. These countries have become disillusioned by the failure of the nuclear powers to halt the nuclear-arms race and by the paucity of the benefits received from the peaceful applications of nuclear energy. They are impressed by the achievements of China and India, and some of the more advanced among them are much more receptive now to the argument, illusory though it is, that nuclear weapons are "equalizers" that would better enable them to withstand the unspoken threats of the nuclear-weapons states and promote their own security and economic development. In fact, some of the Third World countries seem to be increasingly inclined to accept the idea that the acquisition of nuclear-weapons capability by some of the near-nuclear powers would place greater restraints on the monopoly position and freedom of action of the nuclear-weapons states, and that this could bring some advantages to the Third World as a whole. At the UN General Assembly in the fall of 1974

apart from the six countries mentioned above there was practically no criticism of the Indian explosion (and none from any Third World country except Pakistan). In short, India has apparently succeeded in becoming a nuclear power with remarkably little adverse reaction.

Why did India go nuclear? To be sure, India had throughout the negotiation of the Nonproliferation Treaty and after its conclusion denounced the treaty as a discriminatory instrument and had repeatedly announced that it reserved the right to conduct its own nuclear explosions for peaceful purposes. That, however, is not the whole story.

India was obviously greatly concerned by the Chinese nuclear explosion of October 16, 1964. On December 4 of that year Prime Minister Lal Bahadur Shastri, discussing the Chinese nuclear bomb, stated that all non-nuclear countries needed a guarantee by the existing nuclear powers against nuclear attack. He added that it would be "very wise" for the nuclear powers "to give serious thought to this aspect of the problem."

In May, 1965, the Indian ambassador to the UN, Birendra Narayan Chakravarty, told the Disarmament Commission that an "integrated solution" was required to solve the problem of the spread of nuclear weapons. He said: "It is no use telling countries, some of which may be even more advanced in nuclear technology than China, that they should enter into a treaty which would stipulate

only that they must not acquire or produce these weapons. Again it is no use telling them that their security will be safeguarded by one or another of the existing nuclear powers. Such an assurance has to be really dependable. Unless the nuclear powers...undertake from now on not to produce any nuclear weapons or vehicles for weapons delivery and, in addition, agree to reduce their existing stockpile of nuclear weapons, there is no way of doing away with proliferation."

In July of the same year the Indian ambassador to the Geneva disarmament conference, Vishnuprasad Chunilal Trivedi, said that the "essential" requirement for a "rational and acceptable" treaty on nonproliferation was "tangible progress toward disarmament, including a comprehensive test-ban treaty, a complete freeze on production of nuclear weapons and means of delivery as well as a substantial reduction in the existing stocks." He added that the institution of international controls on peaceful nuclear reactors and nuclear power stations, while leaving free the vast weapon-producing facilities of the nuclear powers, was "like an attempt to maintain law and order in a society by placing all its law-abiding citizens in custody while leaving its law-breaking elements free to roam the streets."

On April 27, 1967, the Indian External Affairs Minister, Mahomedali Currim Chagla, criticized the draft nonproliferation treaty as "discriminatory" because, among other things, it sought to

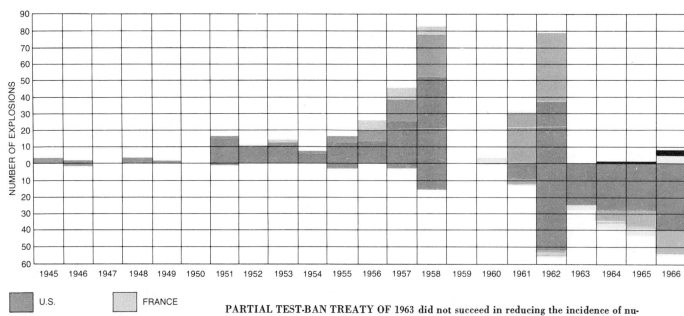

PARTIAL TEST-BAN TREATY OF 1963 did not succeed in reducing the incidence of nuclear-test explosions; it merely drove most tests underground, as is shown in this chart. The bars indicate the total number of known nuclear explosions conducted each year from 1945 through 1974. Bars above the baseline represent explosions in the atmosphere; bars below the baseline count underground (and a few underwater) tests. The data were compiled mostly by the Stockholm International Peace Research Institute (SIPRI) on the basis of of-

maintain the monopoly of the nuclear powers. Only the non-nuclear powers would be prevented from conducting underground explosions for peaceful nuclear research. He added that India was in a "peculiar position" because it was a nonaligned country not under the "nuclear umbrella" of any nuclear country, because it was far advanced in nuclear research and because it was under the "continuing threat and menace" of China, which had become a nuclear power. If India was not to explode a bomb, it must have a "credible guarantee" of its security.

For several years India sought effective guarantees of its security by the nuclear powers, but its efforts were in vain. Failing to obtain any adequate direct security assurances, India shifted its emphasis to the indirect approach by insisting that all the nuclear powers stop testing and manufacturing nuclear weapons and start reducing their nuclear arsenals. When this approach also seemed likely to fail, India began stressing its right and need to conduct its own peaceful nuclear explosions for economic development.

At this late stage one can only speculate that India might not have gone ahead so soon, if at all, with the explosion of its own nuclear device if it had been offered adequate guarantees of its security, and that it might have been willing to accept the protection of a joint American-Russian nuclear umbrella, as Japan seemed content to accept an American one. Unfortunately that possibility was never put to any real test. In fact, none of the main demands in India's "integrated" approach were met.

Are there any benefits to be gained from peaceful nuclear explosions? Ever since the discovery of nuclear fission high hopes have been held out for the potential blessings that would be conferred on mankind by the peaceful uses of nuclear energy and technology. At first attention was devoted to the benefits from power reactors and from the use of radioactive isotopes in science, medicine, industry and agriculture. It was only after the U.S. Atomic Energy Commission launched its "Plowshare" program in the late 1950's that interest developed in peaceful nuclear explosions. At that time great engineering projects were visualized: the digging of canals, harbors and so forth. Those ideas were soon discarded by the U.S. when the dangers of radioactivity from cratering explosions became apparent. Interest then turned to the idea of fracturing oil-bearing or gas-bearing rock by underground nuclear explosions in order to stimulate the flow of oil and gas; the idea of blasting underground cavities for their storage was also promoted, as was the idea of leaching minerals, such as copper ore, by such means. None of the American underground explosions has been successful in achieving any of these goals. It has become apparent that to succeed in fracturing rock to produce substantial quantities of oil and gas not one explosion or two but hundreds or even thousands would be required. Such operations would be extremely costly as well as hazardous, and no practical way of dealing with the radioactive by-products has yet been discovered.

Curiously enough, as American nuclear experts began to lose interest in the peaceful uses of underground explosions and to doubt whether they had any practical end that could not be achieved as well or better by ordinary high explosives or by other conventional means, their Russian counterparts began to show greater interest in them. They spoke of achieving the same goals as the Americans had at an earlier stage and added some new ideas of their own. In the past few years they have suggested diverting water flowing to the Arctic Ocean by means of a canal to the Volga River and thence to the Caspian Sea. This would require from 250 to 400 cratering explosions, with all the hazards attending the release of huge amounts of radioactivity. The U.S.S.R. was successful in throwing up a dam to create a lake and in putting out, by means of underground ex-

plosions, two runaway gas-well fires that had been out of control for more than a year, but here too it is not clear that the jobs could not have been done better with high explosives. Apparently the U.S.S.R. has been no more successful than the U.S. in increasing the flow of oil and gas or in the extraction of minerals by means of nuclear explosions.

Within the past year there has been increasing evidence that the U.S.S.R. is also becoming disillusioned by its inability to fulfill the expectations it once had for the benefits from peaceful nuclear explosions. Although it was the U.S.S.R. that insisted on the inclusion in last year's Threshold Test-Ban Treaty of the article providing for an agreement governing such tests, in private Russian scientists have been stating quite freely their opposition to nonmilitary nuclear explosions because of their harmful rather than beneficial potential.

Some American experts hold the view that there never was a good case for peaceful nuclear explosions, and that the idea was fostered and publicized in the U.S. by the very scientists who wished to promote the military rather than the peaceful applications of nuclear energy; in other words, that the campaign on behalf of peaceful nuclear explosions was conducted as a stratagem, somewhat similar to the campaign for "clean" nuclear weapons, to prevent or circumvent any agreement to ban or halt underground nuclear-weapons tests.

Be that as it may, those who were promoting the potential benefits of nuclear explosions were most successful in promoting their ideas. Three international conferences on the Peaceful Uses of Atomic Energy sponsored by the UN and the IAEA in 1958, 1964 and 1971 stressed the importance of nonmilitary nuclear explosions and the encouraging prospects for them. The same conclusions were drawn by an international group of experts convened by the UN Secretary-General in 1969 at the request of the non-nuclear-weapons states that were interested in an impartial report on the possible peaceful uses of nuclear energy. These conclusions and results were again confirmed by three international panels of experts (mostly American and Russian) convened by the IAEA in 1969, 1970 and 1971. Thus it is not surprising that the underdeveloped countries hold out such high hopes for the potential benefits they will receive from nonmilitary nuclear explosions, or that India has now revived the old arguments.

Nevertheless, in the past two years the evidence from the tests conducted by both the U.S. and the U.S.S.R. leads to

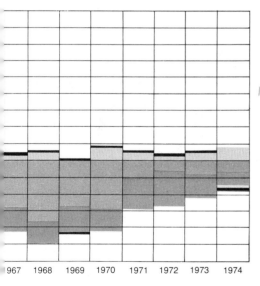

1967  1968  1969  1970  1971  1972  1973  1974

ficial announcements and other sources. The figures do not include several dozen secret tests conducted by the U.S. and the U.S.S.R. France and China are not party to the Partial Test-Ban Treaty and hence are not legally prohibited from testing in the atmosphere.

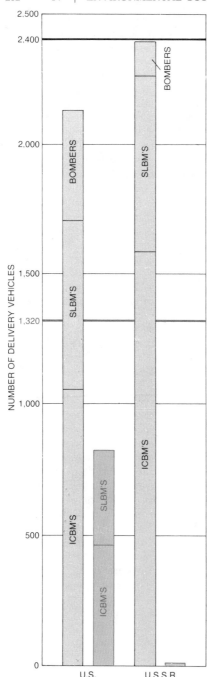

CEILINGS imposed on the numbers of the strategic nuclear weapons of the two super-powers as a result of their Vladivostok "understanding" of November, 1974, are clearly higher than either country's present strength. Gray bars indicate the total number of strategic delivery vehicles deployed at present by each side; the bars are broken down into land-based intercontinental ballistic missiles (ICBM's), submarine-launched ballistic missiles (SLBM's) and heavy bombers. Colored bars indicate number of missiles equipped with multiple independently targetable re-entry vehicles (MIRV's). The Russians have just begun to install MIRV's on some of their land-based missiles. By the terms of the Vladivostok agreement, which runs until 1985, each side is allowed to have no more than 2,400 strategic delivery vehicles, of which 1,320 can be armed with MIRV's.

more doubts than answers, from both the technical point of view and the economic. If the potential benefits elude the highly industrialized and technically sophisticated nuclear-weapons powers, they would seem to be even more remote and more questionable for a country that is still in the developing stage with respect to both industry and nuclear technology. This is an additional reason why many experts look with suspicion on the Indian test as a public peaceful cloak for a private military purpose.

No other question in the field of arms control and disarmament has been the subject of so much study and discussion as the question of stopping nuclear-weapons tests. Ever since Prime Minister Nehru called for a halt to such tests in 1954 the subject has been at or near the top of the disarmament agenda.

By the Partial Test-Ban Treaty of 1963 the nuclear powers undertook to seek "to achieve the discontinuance of all test explosions of nuclear weapons for all time" and expressed their determination "to continue negotiations to this end." That commitment was repeated in the Nonproliferation Treaty. One measure of its implementation can be found in a comparison of nuclear-weapons tests before and after the signing of the Partial Test-Ban Treaty [see illustration on preceding two pages].

After the signing of the Partial Test-Ban Treaty there were in fact no serious discussions between the two main nuclear powers on an underground-test ban for more than a decade, in spite of many resolutions adopted by the UN General Assembly every year calling for a comprehensive test ban. The non-nuclear powers appear to regard an underground-test ban as a litmus test of the seriousness of the intentions of the two superpowers to stop the nuclear-arms race. Although such a halt would not by itself end the further technological improvement of nuclear weapons, it would be an important step in that direction. There is an increasing conviction among the nations of the world that a ban on underground tests is the single most important measure, and certainly the most feasible one in the near future, toward halting the nuclear-arms race. They also seem to regard an underground-test ban by the U.S. and the U.S.S.R. as possibly having a beneficial effect on persuading China and France to curb and ultimately halt their testing. It would certainly put the superpowers in a better moral position to urge the non-nuclear countries that are capable of going nuclear to resist the temptation to do so.

The Threshold Test-Ban Treaty agreed to by the U.S. and the U.S.S.R. in Moscow last year allows the parties to continue unrestricted underground tests of whatever size they wish until March 31, 1976; thereafter they will limit weapon tests to 150 kilotons each, which is about 10 times larger than the yield of the bomb that was dropped on Hiroshima and which exceeds in size all but a few of the tests conducted in recent years [see illustration on pages 204 and 205]. No limitation whatsoever was put on underground explosions for peaceful purposes. This is not just a cosmetic agreement; it is a mockery of a test-ban treaty. Indeed, it may be harmful to the cause of nuclear nonproliferation. It will not help to curb the qualitative improvement, testing and development of new nuclear weapons. Therefore it will not serve to halt the nuclear-arms race. And it will not alleviate the concerns or satisfy the demands of the non-nuclear powers or provide any cogent reason for them to forbear from testing.

The delayed threshold ban has led some interested non-nuclear powers to conclude that once again they were being misled by the nuclear superpowers and that there was no early prospect of any real action to stop the nuclear-arms race. The same can be said of the strategic-arms-limitation talks (SALT). On the day of the signing of the Nonproliferation Treaty (July 1, 1968) it was announced that the U.S. and the U.S.S.R. would begin bilateral discussions on the "limitation and reduction of both offensive and defensive strategic-nuclear-weapon delivery systems." The SALT meetings did not begin until November, 1969. In May, 1972, the U.S. and the U.S.S.R. at the summit meeting in Moscow signed the Treaty on the Limitation of Anti-Ballistic-Missile Systems and also an Interim Agreement on Certain Measures with Respect to the Limitation of Strategic Offensive Arms. Under the ABM treaty each of the parties agreed to deploy no more than 100 ABM launchers and 100 missiles at each of two launch sites in both countries. They also agreed to certain limitations on their ABM radars, but modernization and replacement of ABM systems was allowed. Under the Interim Agreement on Offensive Arms, which has a duration of five years, the U.S. is entitled to increase the number of its nuclear submarines from 41 to 44 with 710 nuclear missiles, and the U.S.S.R. is entitled to build up to 62 submarines carrying 950 nuclear missiles; the U.S. can also retain 1,000 land-based intercontinental missiles and the U.S.S.R. can retain 1,410. No limitation was placed on installing multiple independently targetable reentry vehicles (MIRV's) on either sea-based or land-based missiles.

Last year's Summit III meeting in Moscow also did little to halt or reverse the nuclear-arms race. The two parties agreed to restrict their ABM's to only one site each instead of the two allowed under the 1972 agreement. (The new agreement is practically without significance, since neither party intended to build a second site anyway.) There was complete failure to reach any agreement to limit offensive strategic weapons.

The Vladivostok understanding of November, 1974, was hailed as a "breakthrough" that put a "cap" on the strategic-arms race. It incorporated the interim agreement and fixed a ceiling on the number of all strategic nuclear weapons until December 31, 1985, on the basis of equality between the two superpowers. Each side is allowed to have 2,400 strategic delivery vehicles, including land-based intercontinental ballistic missiles (ICBM's), submarine-launched ballistic missiles (SLBM's) and heavy bombers. Of that number 1,320 may be armed with MIRV's. The agreement was said to establish ceilings well below the levels that otherwise could be expected in 10 years. The ceilings established, however, are clearly higher than the levels each side has at the present time, and even higher than those envisioned for 1977 under the interim agreement.

The ceiling of 1,320 MIRV's is also much higher than either country's present strength. The U.S., for example, has announced that it intends to fit 550 land-based Minutemen with three warheads and 496 Poseidon missiles with from 10 to 14 warheads, for a total of 1,046 missiles with multiple warheads. At present it has about 800 multiple-warhead missiles. The ceiling of 1,320 therefore represents not only a higher level than the U.S. now has but also a higher level than it apparently had ever planned to have.

Meanwhile the U.S.S.R. has tested and is beginning to deploy its MIRV's. It has also developed several new missiles with multiple warheads. It has not announced how many of its land-based or sea-based missiles it intends to equip with multiple warheads, but 1,320 obviously represents a high and costly ceiling that will take several years to reach.

The Vladivostok agreement put no limit on either the number of warheads that can be carried by each missile or on the size of the warheads. Since it is generally believed the Russian warheads are bigger than the American ones, there

will be pressures for the U.S. to increase the size or number of its warheads. The agreement also puts no limitation on the modernization of missiles by improving their accuracy and maneuverability.

In December of last year Secretary of Defense Schlesinger said that he foresaw a need for larger and restructured strategic forces for the U.S. as a result of the Vladivostok agreement, including 12 in-

stead of 10 of the giant Trident submarines (which together would carry 288 missiles, each with 14 warheads, for a total of 4,032 warheads), larger intercontinental missiles with MIRV's and the new B-1 bomber. This program, he said, would call for "some upward adjustment" in the strategic-arms budget.

It is clear that the "limitation" envisioned by the Vladivostok agreement,

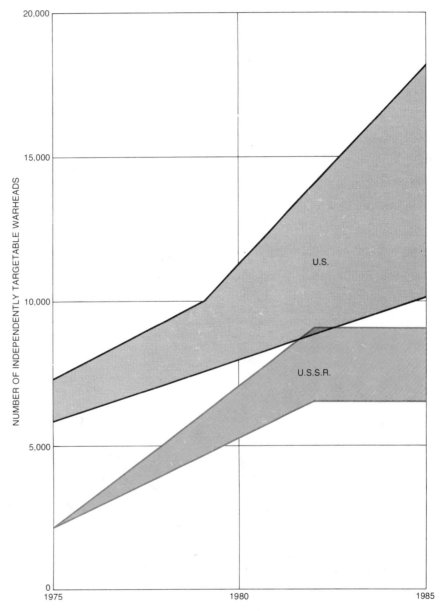

**POSSIBLE FUTURE LEVELS** of independently targetable strategic nuclear warheads allowed under the Vladivostok accords are estimated conservatively in this graph, which is based on material that appeared originally in *Arms Control Today*, a publication of the Arms Control Association. U.S. warheads are represented in gray, Russian warheads in color. The graph reflects the results of current strategic-weapons programs and projects these programs through 1985 on the assumption that they will be revised in order to build force levels up to the Vladivostok ceilings. Shaded areas suggest range of options. Not included in the projections are future U.S. bomber levels, the possible deployment on both sides of strategic cruise missiles, possible increases in the number of MIRVed warheads per missile or changes in present Defense Department estimates of the likely MIRV capabilities of the new Russian ICBM's. Multiple warheads that are not independently targetable are counted on the basis of one warhead per missile. The graph does not take into account the thousands of medium-range nuclear weapons deployed by both sides in Europe.

although it will put an eventual cap on the number of strategic nuclear weapons, allows an expansion in both the quantitative nuclear-arms race and the qualitative one. Since no limit is fixed for the number and size of warheads on the 1,320 missiles with multiple warheads or of nuclear arms carried in bombers, each of the two superpowers can emplace 20,000 or more strategic nuclear warheads under the agreement. This immense "overkill" capacity can be measured by the estimate made about a year ago that the U.S. at that time had enough strategic weapons to destroy 36 times all 218 Russian cities with a population of more than 100,000.

One of the reasons given for maintaining such an unconscionably high overkill capacity is the "counterforce" argument. According to that argument, strategic nuclear arms should not be programmed primarily for the task of knocking out cities and their populations but rather should be aimed at military targets such as missile silos, ammunition dumps, nuclear bases and so on. For that purpose two or more warheads are needed for each target; in addition enough arms must be kept in reserve for a second strike against the other side's cities in case it launches a large-scale first strike. What this argument conveniently overlooks is that a nuclear exchange of such magnitude would poison most of the inhabitants of the Northern Hemisphere with radioactive fallout. In either case, whether a nuclear exchange involved cities or nuclear targets, it would constitute a form of international suicide.

In addition to MIRV's the U.S. is currently developing a new maneuverable missile called MARV, and there is talk in both the U.S. and the U.S.S.R. of building mobile intercontinental missiles, even though the U.S. announced at the time of SALT I that it would regard the building of such weapons as being contrary to the spirit of the SALT I agreements. The U.S. is also proceeding to develop a shorter-range (1,500-mile) cruise missile that could be launched from aircraft, submarines or surface vessels. Further international negotiation may be needed to decide whether or not these missiles will be considered strategic weapons.

The SALT agreements, in short, may have been a diplomatic success in that they tend to stabilize mutual deterrence between the two superpowers, at least for the present, on the basis of each side's retaining a second-strike capability, but they have not served to achieve a cessation or any real limitation of the nuclear-arms race. In fact, many critics of SALT's lack of achievement say that these negotiations have only served to replace the quantitative arms race with an even more dangerous qualitative one. It seems that the agreements already concluded, and indeed those now being negotiated, are designed not to halt or reverse the arms race but rather to institutionalize and regulate it. They can, in fact, be regarded as blueprints for the continuation of the nuclear-arms race by the two superpowers.

The picture that emerges from these agreements is hardly likely to reassure the other nations of the world, nuclear as well as non-nuclear, that the arms race is being brought under control or that their security is being enhanced. The failure of the SALT negotiations to produce any real limitation or reduction of offensive strategic nuclear weapons, and the expansion of the arms race that will result from the Vladivostok agreement, will only serve to confirm the fears of the non-nuclear states that the nuclear powers are unwilling or unable to halt the nuclear-arms race.

The continuing credibility and viability of the Nonproliferation Treaty was in question even before India exploded its nuclear device. The failure of the nuclear superpowers to live up to their commitments under that treaty is likely to give added force to the arguments of those in the near-nuclear countries who, for a variety of reasons, also want to go nuclear. Some of the criticisms voiced by India were echoed by Japan when the text of the Nonproliferation Treaty was approved in 1968. The Japanese ambassador to the nonproliferation talks, Senjin Tsuruoka, warned: "Unless the nuclear-weapons states keep their part of the bargain ... the treaty will lose its moral basis." And when the treaty went into force in 1970 Prime Minister Wilson of Great Britain said: "We know that

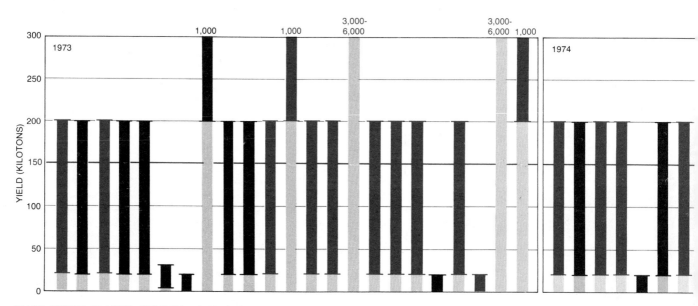

MOST UNDERGROUND NUCLEAR TESTS conducted by the U.S. and the U.S.S.R. in recent years have had yields well within the limit of 150 kilotons set in last June's Threshold Test-Ban Agreement. These bars, black for U.S. explosions and solid color for Russian ones, are based on data released by the U.S. Energy, Resources and Development Agency (formerly the Atomic Energy Commission), which announces yields only in terms of very broad ranges. Independent seismic evidence, obtained by the Research Institute of the Swedish National Defense, suggests that the yields of the great majority of tests in the announced range of 20

there are two forms of proliferation, vertical as well as horizontal. The countries... which are now undertaking never to possess [nuclear weapons] have the right to expect that the nuclear-weapons states will fulfill their part of the bargain."

Talk of the "nth-country problem" had gone out of fashion during the decade that had passed since China exploded its first nuclear device in 1964. After all, it was argued, France (which went nuclear in 1960) and China were great powers, if not as great as the two superpowers, then at least in a class with Great Britain. In any case, all five—and only these five—were permanent members of the Security Council and, as such, were given a special status under the UN Charter. Japan and West Germany were also great powers, but they were special cases as defeated enemy powers in World War II. Canada, Italy and Sweden were highly developed near-nuclear countries that could easily go nuclear, but they had no desire to do so if the nuclear club was confined to five members, and no need to do so since, with the exception of Sweden, they were protected by the American "nuclear umbrella." As for the rest of the world, although there were several countries with the potential of going nuclear, such as India and Israel, it was asserted that they were either too poor or too small and that they faced no serious immediate threat from their neighbors, such as might impel them to undertake an intensive program to become a nuclear-weapons state.

Surprisingly, it was the nonaligned non-nuclear states that had first proposed the nonproliferation of nuclear weapons: Ireland in 1958, followed by Sweden in 1961 and India in 1962. The U.S. and the U.S.S.R. were at first reluctant but finally came to see that it was even more in the interests of the nuclear powers to prevent the spread of nuclear weapons to additional countries. The idea took hold in the 1960's and finally culminated in the compact between the nuclear and the non-nuclear powers that was formalized in the Nonproliferation Treaty. The non-nuclear-weapons states agreed not to acquire or manufacture nuclear weapons or other nuclear explosive devices in exchange for the promise on the part of the nuclear-weapons powers to assist them in exploiting the peaceful uses of nuclear energy and to end the nuclear-arms race. A number of potential nuclear powers did not sign the treaty, including India, Pakistan, Israel, Spain, South Africa, Argentina and Brazil. Among the stated reasons for their not signing were considerations of security, the discriminatory nature of the treaty and the desire or need to develop their own capability in the field of peaceful uses of nuclear technology, including nonmilitary nuclear explosions.

Nevertheless, in the heady atmosphere of 1968, when because of the tacit alliance between the nuclear-weapons states and the least developed of the non-nuclear-weapons states the treaty was commended by the UN General Assembly by an overwhelming vote, it was felt that the danger of proliferation had been put to rest. It appeared that the momentum of a tidal wave of signatures would carry along some of the reluctant non-nuclear-weapons states and that the others would not dare to flout the opinion of the vast majority of the nations of the world. France announced that although it would not sign the treaty, it would behave exactly as though it had done so, and China was considered as comparatively unimportant and isolated. (China, although publicly supporting the idea of proliferation to Third World countries, is in fact the only nuclear power that has not provided any kind of nuclear assistance, military or peaceful, to other countries.) The U.S.S.R. was pleased that West Germany and all the North Atlantic Treaty Organization countries had agreed to sign the treaty. With the announcement, when the treaty was opened for signature on July 1, 1968, that the U.S.S.R. and the U.S.

had agreed to begin the SALT negotiations, it was felt that the world was finally on the right road toward control of the nuclear-arms race.

Within four years of the entry into force of the Nonproliferation Treaty those high hopes had all but vanished. Moreover, they had vanished in spite of the settlement of the Berlin problem, the admission of China and the two Germanys to the UN, the withdrawal of American forces from Vietnam, the 1972 SALT agreements and the beginnings of a détente between the U.S. and the U.S.S.R.

The developing non-nuclear-weapons states on the whole felt that they had been cheated. They had received little in the way of assistance in exploiting the peaceful uses of nuclear energy, particularly in the area they were most interested in: nuclear reactors for the production of power. On the other hand, some of the more advanced countries (such as Italy, Japan and West Germany) that were not parties to the agreement seemed to have been treated better by the nuclear powers in this respect even though it was contrary to the terms of the Nonproliferation Treaty. Moreover, no negotiation had been started to set up an international regime to make peaceful nuclear explosions available to non-nuclear-weapons states, as was pledged by the treaty. Most disappointing of all, the nuclear-arms race was going full speed ahead. France and China continued to test in the atmosphere; the U.S. and the U.S.S.R. had not halted underground tests (on the contrary, they were conducting them at a greater rate than ever before); the Sea-Bed Treaty and the SALT agreements seemed to have been arranged more for cosmetic purposes than as real arms-control measures. On any showing, in spite of the pledges in the Nonproliferation Treaty, the arms race was proceeding apace, particularly in its technological and qualitative aspects, and the gap between the nuclear and the non-nuclear powers was steadily widening.

In addition the so-called security assurances to the non-nuclear-weapons states in the declarations of the nuclear-weapons states in the Security Council in June, 1968, had lost what little meaning they had ever had. With China having the power of veto, action by the Security Council to implement the assurances seemed at best doubtful.

Under the circumstances it was not surprising that even before the Indian nuclear explosion the Nonproliferation Treaty had lost a great deal of its force. The pent-up frustrations of a number of

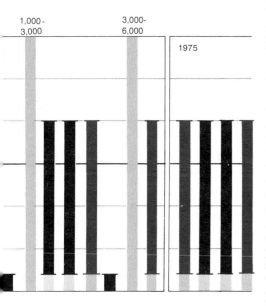

1,000 - 3,000      3,000 - 6,000

1975

to 200 kilotons are toward the lower end of that range. The 150-kiloton restriction is not scheduled to go into effect until next year. Moreover, "peaceful" explosions may be excluded altogether from the final agreement.

non-nuclear-weapons powers may have found a psychological release in India's having breached the walls of the exclusive big-power club.

The Indian explosion also came at a time when there had been a sudden upsurge of interest in nuclear power as a source of energy. The energy crisis and the quadrupling of the price of oil have stimulated the search for alternative sources of energy and have made nuclear power much more economically attractive than it was before. There now appears to be a kind of commercial competition among a number of countries in the Western world to sell reactors, fissionable material and nuclear equipment. Sales to Argentina, Egypt, India, Indonesia, Iran, Israel and South Korea are merely the most publicized ones.

It may take a year or two for another country to explode a nuclear device, and several years for some of the other potential nuclear powers to do so, but there are about a dozen countries that can, if they choose, go nuclear over the next five years, and another dozen can do so over the following five years. Although few of these countries have their own chemical-separation plants for reprocessing the spent fuel from reactors into fissionable plutonium, such plants can be built without much difficulty. It has been estimated that a reprocessing plant capable of producing enough plutonium for two or three explosive devices a year could be built in a year by any reasonably advanced country at a cost of a few million dollars. Even if the cost has been grossly underestimated, it is clear that

the amount of money involved is not large. Moreover, a French company stands ready to sell complete plutonium-reprocessing plants.

There would seem to be a kind of "domino theory" that is more applicable to countries going nuclear than to countries falling prey to a foreign ideology. Whether it is regarded as the $n$th-country problem or as a kind of chain reaction, each time a country goes nuclear it increases the incentives or pressures for its neighbors and other similarly situated countries to do so. Few doubted that once the U.S.S.R. had joined the U.S. as a member of the nuclear club all the other great powers would follow suit. As long as there was a "firebreak" between the big powers, which are permanent members of the Security

NUCLEAR REACTORS currently in operation or under construction in 48 of the 106 member states of the International Atomic Energy Agency (IAEA) are indicated on this world map. The numbers shown include both power reactors and research reactors; they are derived from the 1974 edition of *Power and Research Re-* *actors in Member States,* published by the IAEA. In principle weapons-grade material (either plutonium or uranium) can be diverted from the fuel cycle of any fission reactor. The Nonproliferation Treaty provides that the parties agree to accept the safeguard procedures set up by the IAEA to prevent the "diversion of

Council, and all other powers there was a chance of holding the line against the further horizontal proliferation of nuclear weapons. Once a middle-sized or smaller power joins the nuclear club, however, there is little reason for other middle-sized or smaller powers to refrain from joining.

The countries that have not signed the Nonproliferation Treaty are the most likely candidates to go nuclear. They refrained from signing the treaty precisely because for one reason or another they wanted to keep their options open. The fact that India has now dared to go nuclear, with overwhelming domestic approval and comparatively little international criticism, may well encourage other countries to do so, or at the very least weaken those elements in such countries

nuclear energy from peaceful uses to nuclear weapons or other explosive devices." The IAEA safeguards apply to all fissionable materials and all peaceful nuclear activities. China does not participate in the IAEA.

that oppose their going nuclear. The delays in ratification by countries that have signed the treaty but have not yet become parties to it is an indication of their desire to move slowly in this field. Each of these countries has its eye on the others, and what any one will do may depend on what others do. No country wants to be placed in a position of perceived inferiority to others. If one other country should go nuclear, it would be difficult to keep the dam from bursting. Even those countries that had ratified the Nonproliferation Treaty could withdraw on three months' notice. As one country after another went nuclear, it would not take long for some parties to give notice of their withdrawal. That would mark the inglorious end of the attempt to prevent the spread of nuclear weapons.

If this rather gloomy scenario is acted out, the prospect for world survival itself becomes rather gloomy. A serious problem arises from the fact that at least some of the new nuclear powers may not have the resources or the time to build sophisticated second-strike deterrent forces. They may opt for a small nuclear striking force that would provide them with local military superiority or with a deterrent against attack by a neighbor. The ultimate result will probably reduce rather than increase their security, as may well turn out to be the case with India if Pakistan, Indonesia or Iran should go nuclear.

The danger is that a small or middle-sized nuclear power involved in an acute crisis might fear that a nuclear neighbor might launch a first strike against it and in order to prevent such an attack might decide to launch a preemptive strike. Since the advantage would lie with whichever country struck first, that would create almost intolerable pressures to be the first to take action and could set off a nuclear war no one wants. Apart from the danger of the outbreak of such nuclear war by design, there is the more likely possibility of its happening as the result of accident, miscalculation, misinterpretation of orders, blackmail or sheer madness.

There are real dangers of such an "accidental" war even between the great nuclear powers, but the dangers are becoming less because of "hot line" communication links, better command and control, and the evolution of détente. In a world of nuclear first-strike powers the dangers become infinitely greater. If one could work out all the permutations and combinations of the possible ways in which such a war could begin, the

probability of its beginning sooner or later would become almost a certainty. That a local or regional war could take place without involving the great nuclear powers is quite doubtful.

Prime Minister Gandhi has assured Pakistan and the world of "the peaceful nature and the economic purposes of this experiment" and has stated that "India is willing to share her nuclear technology with Pakistan in the same way that she is willing to share it with other countries, provided proper conditions for understanding and trust are created." One can only speculate whether or not such sharing would extend to the design of nuclear explosive devices either by agreement with Pakistan or by participation in a regional or a global international regime for the conduct of peaceful nuclear explosions under safeguarded conditions.

If India is sincere in its intention to use nuclear explosive devices solely for nonmilitary purposes, it should be prepared to convert this unilateral statement of intention into a binding legal commitment by treaty or otherwise on a bilateral, regional or global basis. It is likely that India would insist that any commitment it undertakes be universal and not selective or discriminatory.

One can certainly conceive of an international regime for the conduct of nonmilitary nuclear explosions, whereby all parties, including nuclear-weapons powers, would agree not to conduct such explosions themselves; they would instead be undertaken either by some international authority composed of nuclear powers or by some designated nuclear powers, and only after the project in question had been examined and approved by some international body. The parties would all have to pledge never to use such explosives for military purposes. It might well be in the interest of all the nuclear powers to agree to undertake any approved project free of charge; the costs are in any event quite small (from \$150,000 to \$600,000 per explosion). If they were free, it might provide some inducement to underdeveloped countries not to seek to acquire their own capability.

The Nonproliferation Treaty already commits the parties to create such an international regime and provides that the potential benefits of such explosives "will be made available to non-nuclear-weapons states party to the Treaty on a nondiscriminatory basis and that the charge to such parties for the explosive devices used will be as low as possible and exclude any charge for research and development." Because of opposition to the Nonproliferation Treaty, it might be better if the international regime were set up by the UN outside the framework of the treaty.

Although such an international regime would appear to be technically and le-gally feasible, it is far from clear that it would be politically acceptable either to the nuclear powers or to those non-nuclear states that might want to acquire their own explosive capability. Never-theless, the idea is worth exploring.

An immediate step that might be un-dertaken would be to have a moratorium on all nonmilitary explosions by all pow-ers, pending the examination of the idea of an international regime for such ex-plosions. If the nuclear-weapons states would agree to such a moratorium, even if only for a fixed period of time, it might be possible to obtain the agreement of India and of all the other potential nu-

# CANDIDATES FOR THE NUCLEAR CLUB

Of the countries that have not signed the Nonproliferation Trea-ty the most obvious candidate to join the second-rank club of nuclear powers is **Pakistan**, which has an-nounced its intention to keep abreast of India. Pakistan, like India, has a nuclear power reactor supplied by Canada, fueled by enriched uranium. Unless Pakistan is helped by China or some other power, however, it may take sev-eral years before it acquires a plutoni-um-reprocessing plant and is ready to undertake testing. It is noteworthy that Pakistan is not a party to either the 1963 Partial Test-Ban Treaty or the Nonpro-liferation Treaty and therefore need have no legal inhibitions about testing in the atmosphere.

**Argentina,** like Pakistan, is not a party to the Partial Test-Ban Treaty or the Nonproliferation Treaty. In addition to having several nuclear reactors (under IAEA safeguards) Argentina is one of the few countries that have a plutonium-reprocessing plant. Thus Argentina is in a position to produce its own plu-tonium and to explode a nuclear device whenever it so decides. Argentina has also recently entered into a nuclear-co-operation agreement with India. If Ar-gentina goes nuclear, **Brazil**, which has always upheld its right to conduct peace-ful nuclear explosions and which regards itself as an emerging great power, will not be far behind. **Chile** also might de-cide that it too has to go nuclear.

**South Africa**, in addition to having several nuclear reactors (under IAEA safeguards), is one of the largest ura-nium-producing countries. Moreover, South Africa has announced that it has a new secret process for enriching uranium, in which case it can explode a uranium device without waiting to acquire a plutonium device. The vice-president of the South African Atomic Energy Board stated after the Indian explosion that South Africa has the ca-pability of making a bomb and is more advanced in nuclear technology than India. He stressed that South Africa would use its available uranium and nuclear technology only for peaceful purposes (whatever that may now mean). Apart from military reasons, South Africa may have an additional in-centive to go nuclear. If it has in fact invented a new process for enriching uranium, it will want to find markets for the sale of its enriched material. It has recently entered into an agreement pro-viding for the sale of uranium to France, and it may want to explode a peaceful uranium device of its own to demon-strate the effectiveness of its enrichment process and the quality of its product.

**Israel** has repeatedly stated that it "will not be the first country to introduce nuclear weapons into the Middle East," a rather cryptic statement. Most experts believe that all that Israel needs to make an atomic bomb is to turn the last screw. The French-supplied reactor at Dimona, which is not subject to IAEA safeguards, has since 1964 had the capacity to pro-duce enough plutonium to manufacture one bomb a year. It is not known, how-ever, whether Israel has a plutonium-re-processing plant. Although Israel does have a grave security problem, many observers believe that it has a tacit agreement with the U.S. not to go nu-clear, in exchange for an American com-mitment to provide all the conventional armaments that Israel may need to de-fend itself against Arab attack. Never-theless, it is generally believed that Israel may have several untested nuclear weapons that it might use in an extreme situation if the survival of its cities and people were in serious jeopardy. In De-cember, 1974, President Katzir stated concerning nuclear weapons: "If we need them, we will have them." As long as the present uneasy truce continues, there is no reason for Israel to go nu-clear, but if the negotiations should break down or an acute threat should suddenly arise, it is possible that Israel might wish to demonstrate its nuclear capability by exploding a nuclear device for peaceful purposes. The Indian test explosion will certainly make it easier for those in Israel who support such action to argue in favor of such a test.

**Egypt** has signed the Nonproliferation Treaty but has not ratified it and has announced that it will not do so unless Israel does. Egypt is far behind Israel in nuclear technology, and stories have circulated in the diplomatic world for some years that Egypt has asked India and other countries to help it acquire nu-clear weapons or nuclear-weapons capa-bility (without success). The agreement last June by President Nixon to provide two 600-megawatt nuclear power reac-tors, one to Egypt and one to Israel, has raised serious questions. Such a reactor could produce enough plutonium to make more than 10 medium-sized nu-clear bombs a year. No matter what safeguards are written into the agree-ment, including placing the reactor un-der IAEA safeguards and returning the spent fuel to the U.S. for reprocessing, it is always possible for a country wanting to do so to evade its commitments or abrogate the agreement. In answer to those who oppose the supply or sale of nuclear reactors to Egypt and Israel, American officials say that if the U.S. does not go ahead, then France or some other country will do so and will prob-ably not insist on safeguards as strict as those the U.S. would require. Because of Israel's opposition to placing all its fis-sionable material under international or American safeguards and inspection, the future of the agreement to supply reac-tors to Egypt and Israel is unclear. In any case Egypt is arranging to obtain a large power reactor from France.

**Spain** has not signed the Nonprolifer-ation Treaty and has drawn attention to its discriminatory character and to Spain's security situation. Spain is the only large country in western Europe that is not a member of the North At-lantic Treaty Organization, although it does have various defense agreements with the U.S. It also has uranium re-

clear powers while the question was being studied. India cannot be too comfortable at the thought of her neighbors going nuclear, and the other potential nuclear powers would have little to lose by agreeing to the delay. Once again, however, as in all nuclear matters, the nuclear-weapons states would have to lead the way. It would clearly be in their interest to do so.

During the moratorium, or independently of it, it might be useful if another international group of experts were convened by the UN to consider all aspects of nonmilitary nuclear explosives. It is becoming clear that such devices are unlikely to bring the benefits that were hoped for. The first underground explosion was not detonated until 1957, and it is barely a decade since the exploration of the practical possibilities was undertaken. Here again nothing would be lost by allowing a year's delay for a more thorough study of the entire question.

---

sources, several nuclear reactors and a pilot plutonium-reprocessing plant, which would enable it to acquire a nuclear capability if it so chooses.

In the category of countries that have signed the Nonproliferation Treaty but not ratified it, the main countries are all potential nuclear powers. They include the technologically advanced Euratom countries: **West Germany, Italy, the Netherlands** and **Belgium,** all of which have several nuclear reactors. In addition there are plutonium-reprocessing plants in West Germany, Italy and Belgium. West Germany and the Netherlands are also partners with Great Britain in centrifuge plants for enriching uranium. West Germany is bound by a 1954 treaty not to manufacture nuclear weapons on its territory. All the Euratom countries have signed safeguard agreements with the IAEA, and West Germany, the Netherlands and Belgium have obtained approval from their parliaments to ratify the Nonproliferation Treaty. Italy, however, is reluctant to complete the process of ratification, and the entire matter is therefore in abeyance. Italy's reluctance seems to be linked to fears that other less advanced Mediterranean countries, such as Israel, Egypt or Spain, may go nuclear. It is questionable whether the other Euratom countries could or would go ahead with ratification without Italy. **Switzerland,** which is also advanced in nuclear technology, appears to be holding up its ratification of the treaty until the Euratom countries ratify it.

**Japan** not only has a highly developed nuclear technology but also has a plutonium-reprocessing plant. It can thus go nuclear whenever it chooses. Public opinion in Japan is overwhelmingly opposed to all forms of nuclear tests and weaponry, and Foreign Minister Toshio Kimura announced in September, 1974, at the UN General Assembly that Japan was preparing to ratify the Nonproliferation Treaty. Nevertheless, there is a small but growing tendency in Japan to delay ratification until the future of the Nonproliferation Treaty is clarified, and this tendency seems to have been strengthened by the Indian explosion. It is unlikely that Japan will deposit its instrument of ratification until it is satisfied that the Euratom countries will also do so. Rather surprisingly, some Chinese nuclear experts have privately urged Japan to go nuclear.

**South Korea,** although not as advanced technologically as Japan and the Euratom countries, does have two research reactors in operation and two power reactors under construction. Security problems are a major consideration for South Korea, but its ultimate decision whether or not to go nuclear will probably depend on what other countries do, particularly in that part of the world.

**Indonesia** also has a research reactor and appears to be in the process of acquiring some power reactors, which should not be difficult in the light of that nation's rapidly growing oil revenues. Following the Indian explosion there were public statements predicting that Indonesia would go nuclear or calling for it to go nuclear. It is not likely to do so, however, for several years.

Among the potential nuclear powers that are party to the Nonproliferation Treaty, **Canada** and **Sweden** are examples of countries that have had the capability for a number of years to go nuclear but have unilaterally decided that it is not in their interest to do so. Other countries with a highly developed nuclear technology are **Taiwan, Australia** and **Norway,** probably in that order. Taiwan also has a pilot plutonium-reprocessing plant and thus can quite easily exercise the nuclear option if it chooses, particularly if it regards its security as being in jeopardy. **Iran,** which now has a research reactor, is somewhat farther down the line, but it has recently embarked on a program to acquire 12 large power reactors and has entered into agreements with France, West Germany and the U.S. to obtain several power reactors. In addition Iran has an agreement with the U.S. whereby the U.S. will undertake enrichment work with Iranian uranium. Iran is also participating in the construction of a large uranium-enrichment plant in France. With its rapidly increasing wealth from oil, Iran can readily acquire a potential nuclear capability, and there are some elements in the country that are urging it to do so.

Apart from Israel, Egypt and Iran no other Middle East country has any potential nuclear capability at present. Nevertheless, the combination of the unstable political situation in that part of the world, the Arab-Israeli conflict and the vast wealth that is being accumulated by the oil-rich countries of the area would seem to make the Middle East an area of particular concern. There have already been press reports of countries in the region being interested in buying or otherwise acquiring nuclear weapons or nuclear-weapons capability. The Indian explosion will certainly not damp any such ideas; it might even tend to encourage them. Apart from action by governments of states in the region there is a growing danger that terrorists will try to steal a nuclear weapon or fissionable material for either blackmail or ransom. That danger will, of course, increase over the years as nuclear power reactors, fissionable materials and nuclear technology proliferate in the area and in the world at large. The world has not been conspicuously successful up to now in dealing with Arab hijacking and blackmail involving less dangerous weapons.

All the Warsaw Pact allies of the U.S.S.R. have been assisted by the Russians in the building of research reactors, and nearly all of them have power reactors in operation or under construction. **East Germany** and **Czechoslovakia** are the most advanced technologically. All of them are party to the Nonproliferation Treaty. It is clearly in the interest of the U.S.S.R. that none of them should acquire any nuclear explosive capability, and they are not likely to do so as long as the Nonproliferation Treaty remains an effective treaty and retains any legal or moral force.

Another idea that merits careful consideration is the possibility of establishing nuclear-free zones in different regions of the world. Among the lessons to be drawn from the creation of a nuclear-free zone in Latin America (by the Treaty of Tlatelolco, signed in 1967) is that the idea must have the sympathetic general support of all the important countries in the area. It is useless to think that a country can be maneuvered by political gamesmanship into agreeing to a treaty unless that country perceives the treaty as being in its own interest. It is also axiomatic that even if a country is a party to a treaty, it will not remain a party if it considers that events have caused the treaty to be contrary to its most important interests.

Finally, it has been suggested that the countries that export fissionable materials should form a "suppliers' club" and agree to supply nuclear materials and

equipment only to those countries that would agree not to undertake nuclear explosions of any kind, to place all their nuclear facilities under IAEA safeguards and to return all spent fuel to the supplier countries for reprocessing. Such measures would, of course, be useful, but like any embargo they would be fully effective only if all supplier countries agreed to abide strictly by the rules.

In August, 1974, the U.S. joined other important supplier nations in a public undertaking contained in letters to the IAEA stating that it would not provide fissionable material or nuclear equipment to any non-nuclear-weapons state unless the material and equipment were subject to safeguards under an agreement with the IAEA. Some important supplier states, such as France and South Africa, have not, however, joined in the undertaking. Moreover, the agreement applies only to future supplies and

does not affect previously supplied material. Even the regulations promulgated by Canada last December, which provide the strictest safeguards imposed by any supplier country, can be evaded by countries that build their own small reactors and plutonium-reprocessing plants, since most countries have at least low-grade uranium resources.

Unless the safeguards govern all nuclear activities (as is required by the Nonproliferation Treaty) and not merely current and future transfers of material and equipment, opportunities for evasion will remain. Moreover, it would seem to be highly discriminatory if any non-nuclear powers that are not party to the treaty could acquire nuclear materials, equipment or technology under less stringent conditions than parties to the treaty. In fact, if the non-nuclear powers that are not parties are subject to safeguards less strict than those required

**POTENTIAL FOR NUCLEAR PROLIFERATION** is represented graphically on this world map. The six current members of the nuclear club are shown in gray. The eight near-nuclear countries (that is, those with the capability of making nuclear weapons in a comparatively short time, given the political decision to do so) are in the darkest color. The countries that would require a somewhat

of the powers that are parties, that would provide an inducement to avoid becoming a party.

One would have thought that, given the prospect of the further proliferation of nuclear weapons, the nuclear powers, which have the most to lose, would be galvanized into some kind of action in an attempt to prevent the emergence of a world of nuclear powers, but such is not the case. There is no evidence that the nuclear powers have any understanding of the seriousness of the situation. If they do have any such understanding, they have shown no urgency in attempting to cope with the situation.

There have been three sessions during the past year of a preparatory committee for the holding of next month's review conference in Geneva. In the course of these preparations the nuclear-weapons

powers have given no indication that they have learned any lessons from the Indian explosion or that they have any intention of abiding by their commitments under the treaty. They of course want to see as many nations as possible become parties to the Nonproliferation Treaty, and they have attempted to put pressure on the Euratom countries and Japan to ratify the treaty before the review conference. It seems that the only other measures contemplated by them are to tighten the safeguard provisions of the treaty in order to ensure that in the future no fissionable material can be diverted to nuclear explosions of any kind, whether peaceful or military, by a nonnuclear state.

These objectives are commendable in themselves, but they hardly approach the requirements of the situation in the world today. The situation is that more and more countries will go nuclear unless it can be clearly demonstrated to them that it is in their interest not to do so. Sanctions in the way of withholding nuclear assistance are hardly likely to be effective against the newly rich oil-exporting countries in a situation where the nuclear powers and other supplier states are competing to sell nuclear reactors, materials and equipment to them. Nor are they likely to be more effective against the poor countries that are determined to close the gap between themselves and the rich countries and that see nuclear technology as one of the ways of closing it. Countries that are determined to evade controls will find ways to evade them. With China encouraging them to be more activist, and with the example of India as evidence that the wishes of the big powers can be flouted with impunity, they may attempt to exploit their sheer numerical majorities to engage in confrontations with the rich countries in order to extract concessions from them.

The longer-term goal of the underdeveloped countries is to readjust the balance between themselves and the developed countries, which means a more equitable sharing of the world's wealth. A shorter-term goal is to acquire nuclear capability either as a step toward attaining their longer-term goal or as a means of their using nuclear threats or blackmail to achieve political and economic gains, somewhat in the way that the oil-producing countries have used oil as a weapon.

Both the longer-term and shorter-term goals are still distant. The immediate preoccupations of the non-nuclear countries are their security and their economic and political situation. A decisive role with respect to the future of the con-

cept of nonproliferation of nuclear weapons will be played by a handful of near-nuclear powers that have not signed the Nonproliferation Treaty. Whether or not these countries proceed to exercise the nuclear option within the next few years will depend in large part on the international climate of opinion. The Indian test explosion has undoubtedly weakened the entire principle of nonproliferation, but the situation may not be entirely hopeless. Domestic considerations and a country's perception of its security requirements, its role and status in the world and its aspirations for future economic development through the application of nuclear energy (whether rightly or wrongly held) will determine whether or not it decides to go nuclear. A most important element in these considerations will be the actions of the great powers, in particular the two superpowers. The standard of international behavior they set, particularly in the field of nuclear-arms control, is bound to have a great and perhaps decisive influence on the actions of the non-nuclear powers. The two superpowers must take the lead. They are the ones that must replace the ethic of the arms race by the ethic of arms control.

The U.S. and the U.S.S.R. must accept the burden of changing the world attitude toward nuclear weapons. Only they can halt and reverse the vertical proliferation of nuclear weapons, which is a necessary condition to preventing their horizontal proliferation. If they continue to militarize the world with both nuclear and conventional weapons, they can hardly expect that other countries will refrain from acquiring such weapons. They have the responsibility of establishing the illegitimacy of the nuclear-arms race and the legitimacy of nuclear restraint and arms control.

If it becomes clear at next month's review conference that the nuclear-weapons states are prepared to live up to the obligations they undertook in the Nonproliferation Treaty, then there is a chance that the treaty can be strengthened and reviewed. This is probably the last chance for the prevention of an uncontrolled nuclear-arms race. There is no guarantee, even if the nuclear-weapons states avail themselves of this last chance, that they would be successful in halting the trend toward proliferation. If they do not make a credible attempt to do so now, however, it would seem to be inevitable that other non-nuclear countries will follow the lead of India. We shall then all have to learn to live as best we can in a world full of nuclear powers.

longer time to acquire a nuclear-weapons capability are represented in lighter shades of color: the lighter, the longer the time.

# 18

# Nuclear Power, Nuclear Weapons and International Stability

## COMMENTARY

The final article in this section, by David Rose and Richard Lester, considers not only the risk of nuclear fuel reprocessing and a future plutonium economy, but the hazards in the present policy of avoiding reprocessing and slowing down research on the breeder reactor. The authors point out that we cannot and do not control other nations' behavior with respect to these decisions; they may well be influenced by our actions to embark themselves on the very policy we wish to discourage.

In choosing our present policy, Rose and Lester say, we may have underestimated the future costs to a viable nuclear power economy. Questions about the continuing health of the U.S. nuclear industry in the face of increasing fears of nuclear power safety and rising costs are real. We might find ourselves in the position, some 20 years from now, of having to import modern reactors, ones safe to operate and with minimal dangers of accidents, because the U.S. industry was allowed to die. If this argument had been followed with respect to coal, which in 1947 was being elbowed out as a major fuel in favor of oil and gas, we would have been forced to subsidize use of coal as well as research and development for new uses and mechanisms of utilization. Instead, we allowed the industry to become almost moribund, and only now is it being revived. Even with this 30-year neglect, the coal industry has shown a remarkable capacity to recover, plan for future expansions, and quickly train new cadres of technical people to run the industry.

Rose and Lester raise serious questions about the extent to which our policy will drive energy-poor nations to the breeder economy for reasons of costs and availability. At the same time, we can ponder whether our refusal to participate in reprocessing will actually discourage other countries from developing the capacity to make nuclear weapons. As the authors point out, there are several routes open to countries to do this even without breeders or reprocessing capabilities, and predicting the behavior of nations in questions of nuclear peace or war is not the most precise of activities. Rose and Lester do not say what *will* happen; they simply ask us to consider that these things *might* happen. The whole matter, however, cannot be argued without respect to the general question of arms control, for in the absence of any workable restraint on both of the big powers, and the complete lack of any restraint on selling all sorts of arms to smaller powers, we cannot count on the restriction of nuclear arms to only those countries that now have them.

In any case, we need to set up some machinery for international cooperation on the questions raised in this article. It is not only global environmental problems that cannot be tackled by one country alone. Equally in question now is what we always thought was our sovereign right—how we decide matters of peace and war, economic development, and the prosperity of our county.

# Nuclear Power, Nuclear Weapons and International Stability

by David J. Rose and Richard K. Lester
*April 1978*

*Irresolution over domestic energy policy and the role of nuclear power may act to undermine current U.S. efforts to control the proliferation of nuclear weapons*

A year ago this month the Carter Administration put before Congress a comprehensive national energy plan that included as one of its key components a revision of this country's long-standing policy on the development of civilian nuclear power. The proposed change, which would have the effect of curtailing certain aspects of the U.S. nuclear-power program and of placing new restrictions on the export of nuclear materials, equipment and services, was based explicitly on the assumption that there is a positive correlation between the worldwide spread of nuclear-power plants and their associated technology on the one hand, and the proliferation of nuclear weapons and the risk of nuclear war on the other. This point of view has become the topic of a lively debate; at the periphery of opinion some see nuclear war lurking behind every reactor on foreign soil, whereas others argue that the connection between civilian nuclear power and nuclear-weapons proliferation is vanishingly small.

We shall advance here the heretical proposition that the supposed correlation may go the other way, and that the recent actions and statements of the U.S. Government have taken little account of this possibility. In brief, it seems to us that if the U.S. were to forgo the option of expanding its nuclear-energy supply, the global scarcity of usable energy resources would force other countries to opt even more vigorously for nuclear power, and moreover to do so in ways that would tend to be internationally destabilizing. Thus actions taken with the earnest intent of strengthening world security would ultimately

weaken it. We believe further that any policy that seeks to divide the world into nuclear "have" and "have not" nations by attempting to lock up the assets of nuclear technology will lead to neither a just nor a sustainable world society but to the inverse. In any event the technology itself probably cannot be effectively contained. We believe that the dangers of nuclear proliferation can be eliminated only by building a society that sees no advantage in having nuclear weapons in the first place. Accordingly we view the problem of the proliferation of nuclear weapons as an important issue not just in the context of nuclear power but in a larger context.

Fundamental tensions exist between the energy objectives and the nonproliferation objectives of U.S. policy, and on a different plane between the respective consequences of measures designed to achieve their primary effect either domestically or internationally. In what follows we shall analyze the complex set of interrelated issues that bear on the entire question of nuclear power and world security.

The most important of the new nuclear measures announced by the Administration last April were that the U.S. would defer indefinitely the reprocessing of spent nuclear fuel from domestic nuclear-power plants to recover and recycle plutonium and unused fissionable uranium, and that it would try to persuade other nations to follow its lead. Legislation submitted to Congress demonstrated the Administration's intention to restrict exports related to the nuclear-fuel cycle and to prevent the retransfer of exported U.S. nuclear tech-

nology to third parties. (A modified version of the Administration's nonproliferation bill has since then been approved by Congress.) Along with these restrictions the U.S. capacity to enrich uranium to standards suitable for use in conventional light-water (as opposed to heavy-water) reactors was to be increased to help meet the growing world demand for this service.

On the domestic front the regulatory requirements for installing light-water reactors were to be streamlined. The Administration also proposed a substantial slowdown of the U.S. program to develop a liquid-metal-cooled fast breeder reactor, a type of nuclear-power plant designed to create and consume fissionable plutonium out of the vast store of ordinary, nonfissionable uranium in the earth's crust. Specifically, the Clinch River breeder reactor, which was to have been built in Tennessee at a cost of some $2 billion, was scheduled for cancellation. The operation of breeder reactors requires reprocessing the nuclear fuel periodically, so that the retreat from fuel reprocessing and the deemphasis of breeder-reactor development complement each other. (Unfortunately the Clinch River reactor has become a focal point of the debate for both the critics and the proponents of nuclear power. The situation is doubly unfortunate because on the one hand that particular program was technologically and institutionally vulnerable and on the other the stopping of it has not helped resolve the deeper issues we discuss.)

The U.S. was also to redirect its nuclear research and development programs to place more emphasis on alternative fuel cycles and reactor designs that might offer reduced access to material suitable for use in nuclear weapons. This initiative has been carried into the world arena with the establishment of an international program to evaluate alternative technical and institutional strategies for the nuclear-fuel cycle.

In the months since the Administration's program was announced it has provoked much discussion within the U.S. and throughout the world. It has dissatisfied both critics and supporters of the U.S. nuclear-power program, and (partly because of the way it was presented) it has generated concern in many foreign capitals. Some of this country's partners in the development of nuclear power feel that they were not consulted adequately during the genesis of the new policy, and that policy communications, at least initially, have been clumsy and insensitive. Deeper-rooted anxieties underlie this irritation, however, since fuel enriched in the U.S. and reactors manufactured by U.S. companies still play significant roles in many national nuclear-power programs, and the effects of U.S. nuclear policies are widely felt.

What was the motivation behind the Administration's new nuclear policy and the related Congressional actions? Several possibilities come to mind. The first is simply that the Administration means what it says, namely that its goal is to increase international stability by taking actions thought to inhibit the proliferation of nuclear weapons. It would do so by reducing the availability of nuclear materials and technology helpful to a weapons program, even though the same materials

and technology had hitherto been commonly assumed to be a part of civilian power programs.

Another possibility is that both the Administration and Congress are undecided as to whether the collapse of the U.S. nuclear industry is desirable. This indecision contributes to the Government's apparent inability to formulate a coherent nuclear-energy strategy.

It is also possible that the Administration announced its policy in sympathetic response to the critics of nuclear power but expects that the policy will not work, and that after this demonstration of good faith a new, more pragmatic program will be unveiled at an appropriate time. One danger in such a tactic is that the Administration might delay its denouement too long. The reaction to an Administration generally perceived to be resigned to the demise of nuclear power in the U.S., or even actively to desire it, might develop its own irreversible momentum.

It may also be that the Administration, frustrated by the diplomatic rigidity of world discussions about international security and arms limitation, is casting about for some new approaches. Such approaches are to be found; we hope that this article is an example. These four general motivations are not mutually inconsistent, and the Government could shift its priorities among them as the consequences of its actions unfold.

Various circumstances created the context in which the Administration formulated its national energy program and in which its set of nuclear-energy and nuclear-nonproliferation

goals were to be pursued. The first circumstance was the urgent need to reduce the growing outflow of U.S. funds, currently running at more than $40 billion per year, to pay for imported petroleum. Such an expenditure, although not liable to bankrupt the country, was inconceivable as recently as 1973. Furthermore, the situation suggested excessive dependence on the policies of the principal oil-supplying nations. The increasing dependence on oil imports was (and is) seen as probably the major contributor to the U.S. energy problem.

The second circumstance was the presence of vast coal deposits in the U.S., amounting to perhaps 10 times the entire domestic oil and gas resource. Only 19 percent of the U.S. energy supply comes from the 650 million tons of coal currently mined each year. Estimates of the amount of coal recoverable at current prices with current technology range from 200 to 600 billion tons; thus even if coal production were to be tripled, the minimum estimate amounts to a 100-year supply. Moreover, the total amount of coal in the U.S. might be as much as 3,000 billion tons recoverable eventually at increased cost—a quarter of the earth's known reserves. Besides coal, an energy resource equivalent to perhaps 1,000 billion tons of coal resides in the oil-shale deposits in the vicinity of northwestern Colorado. Technological advances would surely make many of these resources available later, it was thought. In no absolute sense is the U.S. "running out of energy." Thus arose the goal of increasing coal production rapidly, to several times the present rate by the year 2000. In this

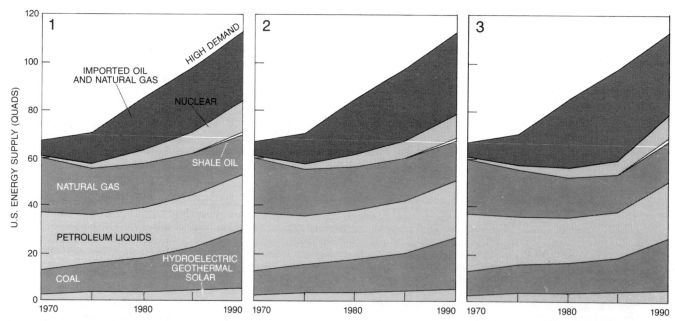

**ALTERNATIVE U.S. ENERGY PROJECTIONS through 1990 are outlined in the set of graphs beginning on these two pages. The graphs represent 12 possible demand-and-supply scenarios constructed by the staff of the Congressional Research Service on the basis of different assumptions about economic growth rates, energy prices, the elas-** ticity of energy demand and the constraints on various energy supplies. The tables from which the graphs were drawn were compiled in the course of a two-year study conducted at the request of several committees of Congress responsible for dealing with energy-related issues; the data appeared originally in *Project Interdependence: U.S.*

way the U.S. could reduce its dependence on imported petroleum, and perhaps also afford a more leisurely nuclear program.

The third circumstance was that energy conservation began to be taken seriously. Many studies under way between 1975 and 1977 showed not only that substantial increases in energy efficiency were possible but also that much energy was being wasted. Energy conservation had received significant recognition but little actual support during the previous Administrations, and Congress had not been overactive compared with what could have been done.

Several arguments had been marshaled against conservation, the main one being that economic activity and energy use were closely bound; hence restricting energy use would probably exacerbate a recession or cause one. In the short term energy and economic activity are indeed closely bound, because machines use energy, and they cannot be replaced overnight. By replacing more energy-intensive machines at the end of their life span with more energy-frugal ones, however, the energy demand could be cut in a matter of decades by 1 or 2 percent per year from what would have been otherwise forecast. With an economic growth rate of 3 or 4 percent per year, energy use might then grow at only half that rate; by the year 2000 the gross national product would have almost tripled, and the energy used per unit of economic output would decline to about 60 percent of its present value. Even so, domestic energy use would have increased by a factor of approximately 1.6, through the diligent exploi-

tation of coal, solar power, light-water reactors and perhaps other technologies. (These numbers are meant only to indicate what many energy planners thought would be possible.)

The fourth major circumstance relates to several aspects of nuclear power itself. First, the U.S. industrial capacity to make light-water reactors is large—perhaps too large. A substantial part of this capacity would be needed to produce some of the base-load electric-generating plants, leaving coal for other electric plants and many other uses. Second, the nuclear-power industry, beleaguered by critics of many persuasions and by a Nuclear Regulatory Commission that it had come to regard as increasingly demanding, also needed some organizational relief. Thus arose the goal of simplifying procedures for fulfilling siting and other licensing requirements. The light-water-reactor industry was to be encouraged by these activities, and electric utilities would be encouraged to "go nuclear" by building light-water reactors wherever such plants were economically attractive.

The fifth circumstance relates to the uranium resources, particularly in the U.S., with which to fuel all those light-water reactors. Each reactor that produces 1,000 megawatts of electric power requires about 5,500 tons of uranium (in the form of uranium oxide) to operate during an expected 30-year life span. The Administration knew that the equivalent of about 680,000 tons of uranium oxide had been located in deposits in the U.S. with characteristics that would make economic recovery possible with current technology, together

with an additional 140,000 tons that will be available between now and the end of the century as a by-product of other mineral-extraction operations. It also estimated that roughly another three million tons would be found when it was necessary and that this amount could be produced at a cost of $50 per pound or less. All this uranium would fuel about 700 reactors for their full life span or an even larger number if a full lifetime commitment of fuel were not made for each plant when it began operation.

Considering also that nuclear-power stations take 10 years or more to build and that orders would increase gradually, the Administration judged that adequate nuclear fuel would be available to last several decades into the next century. All this could be done without reprocessing spent fuel from the reactors. Besides, a number of studies had shown that the recycling of uranium and plutonium in the current generation of light-water reactors would at best be only marginally attractive economically and could in fact result in higher fuel-cycle costs than a "once through" fuel cycle.

This brings us to the sixth circumstance: the Administration's concern about the connection between the technology of nuclear-fuel reprocessing and the development of a nuclear-weapons capability. The past few years have brought increasing doubt about the ability of international safeguards to function satisfactorily in a "plutonium economy," that is, one in which large amounts of plutonium would be present at various stages of the fuel cycle in comparatively extractable form. The objective of international safeguards is

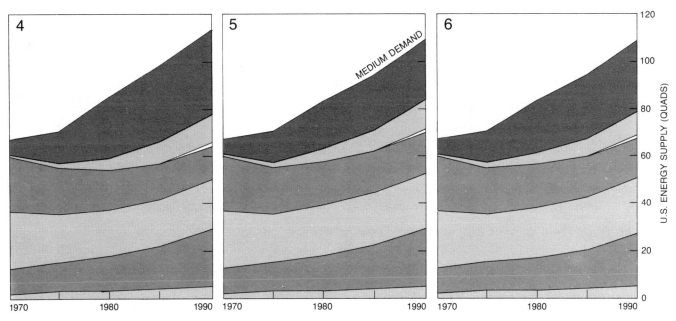

and World Energy Outlook Through 1990, a 939-page report published in November by the U.S. Government Printing Office. The first six scenarios in the set, depicted in the graphs on these two pages, are characterized as follows: high demand, high coal and nuclear supply (1); high demand, medium supply (2); high demand, low supply (3); high demand, low oil and gas supply, high coal and nuclear supply (4); medium demand, high coal and nuclear supply (5); medium demand, medium supply, also referred to in the study as the "base case" (6). All figures are given in "quads": quadrillions ($10^{15}$) of British thermal units. The graphs are continued on the next two pages.

to detect the theft or diversion of nuclear material by nations early enough for diplomatic or other international countermeasures to achieve their objective before the material can be made into an explosive. It was argued, however, that plutonium that had been recovered by spent-fuel reprocessing and then recycled could be turned into an explosive so rapidly after national diversion of the recycled fuel that the ability of the safeguards system to work adequately would be fatally undermined, even if the loss of material were detected. International safeguards do not prevent diversion; they deter it through the threat of timely detection. If plutonium were adopted as a commercial fuel, the deterrence effect of safeguards would be lost. In addition, the presence of plutonium would increase the risks of nuclear terrorism, and there were unresolved questions about the effectiveness of the predominantly national safeguards that would be introduced to deal with this threat.

If, on the other hand, there were no reprocessing, there would be no plutonium either to fuel breeder reactors or to make plutonium-based nuclear weapons; a nation that did not reprocess the fuel from its nuclear-power reactors could not then imperceptibly slip into the position of having a nuclear-weapons capability, and it could not in some temporary passion easily pervert a civilian nuclear-power program. Either it would have to extract almost pure fissionable uranium 235 from natural uranium, an activity that is associated with nuclear weapons and not at all with conventional light-water or heavy-water re-

actors, or it would have to flagrantly set about reprocessing used reactor fuel to extract plutonium. Furthermore, both of these activities are widely thought to be beyond the present capability of any subnational group acting clandestinely.

If the U.S. was mainly worried about the international proliferation of nuclear weapons, why then did it stop the domestic reprocessing of nuclear fuel? The best answer seems to be that in order to argue its case persuasively, it would have, so to speak, to come to court with clean hands.

To be sure, breeder reactors would be delayed, perhaps indefinitely if some better prospect such as economic central-station solar power or controlled fusion came along. Clearly the latter options were to be encouraged. Meanwhile even the U.S. breeder program was to benefit because there would be time to explore a more varied set of technological options, both conceptually and through experiments on a modest scale. Far from being canceled, the breeder program would take on a needed diversity; perhaps more nearly proliferation-proof fuel cycles could be found.

Many doubts about the public acceptability of nuclear power had built up, and the new goals would surely be seen as being responsive to those doubts: no plutonium, no reprocessing, no breeder reactor in this century and so forth. Meanwhile little public concern had yet arisen over the social, environmental or health hazards of coal, the energy-supply option the Administration planned to promote most vigorously.

The Administration's perception of

this complex issue can be analyzed with the aid of a sequential logic diagram, which is useful in clarifying some of the main proliferation-related trains of thought and their impact on international security [*see illustration on pages 222 and 223*]. Two main paths appear in the diagram. First, there is a horizontal decision path that could be followed by a nation (let us call it *Y*) that does not now possess the nuclear technologies in question. The central questions affecting international stability are whether or not nation *Y* decides to develop a general capability with respect to nuclear weapons and, once it has decided to do so, how long it would take to acquire that capability. The second path consists of several vertically arranged inputs to *Y*'s decisions. The U.S. sees the capability to reprocess nuclear fuel as a stimulant to weapons proliferation because *Y* would then have a source of weapons-grade fissionable material; such accessibility might be instrumental in a decision by *Y* to acquire nuclear weapons, and in any case once the decision had been made the reprocessing capability would help *Y* to move toward the right in the diagram: toward the weapons themselves.

The sequential arrangement of events depicted here is too simple. A decision to acquire nuclear weapons might be a prolonged process, and it could be made in parallel with (or could even follow) the acquisition of some of the technological components of a civilian nuclear-power program, which would also be useful for the development of a weapons system. For example, that would be the case with a commercial reprocessing

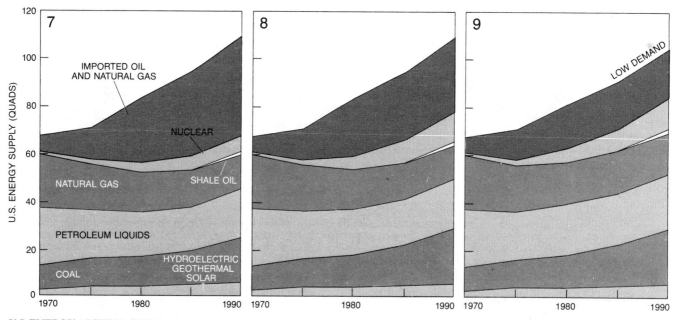

U.S. ENERGY ALTERNATIVES are continued on these two pages. The characterizations of the six remaining scenarios in the Congressional Research Service study are as follows: medium demand, low supply (*7*); medium demand, low oil and gas supply, high coal and nuclear supply (*8*); low demand, high coal and nuclear supply (*9*); low demand, medium supply (*10*); low demand, low supply (*11*); low demand, low oil and gas supply, high coal and nuclear supply (*12*). The authors of the *Project Interdependence* report point out that even with a low energy-demand projection coupled with high coal use, an expanded nuclear-power capacity, an increase of about 50

plant, assuming that in its normal operating procedure it produces plutonium separated partially or completely from the other constituents of irradiated fuel. Such a reprocessing plant would therefore be ambiguously perceived by observers, even if that were not the intention of a peaceful nation Y. The Administration saw that by blocking the connection at the top of the figure a substantial barrier would be erected against Y's either sidling consciously or sliding unconsciously into a technological competence applicable to the manufacture of weapons.

Of course, the Administration realized that other routes exist whereby Y could obtain fissionable material suitable for weapons. First, it might import the necessary technology from elsewhere, but for some time the U.S. has been actively attempting to close those routes by seeking to persuade the other major suppliers of nuclear materials and equipment (through bilateral channels and in the multilateral forum of the London Suppliers Group of nuclear exporting nations) to exercise restraint in the transfer of "sensitive" items that might offer increased access to weapons-grade material.

All the other routes involve a conscious decision by nation Y and a substantial effort on its part. It could develop its own civilian fuel-reprocessing technology, fully intending peaceful uses only, then have it subverted later after a change of attitude on the part of its government. Alternatively, it could attempt the production of weapons-grade plutonium in research reactors (as India did for its 1974 nuclear explosion)

or in a small clandestine reactor, in either case recovering the plutonium from the irradiated fuel in a small reprocessing plant built expressly for the purpose, a task much easier (and cheaper) than the development of the technology and the construction of the plants for commercial reprocessing. Still another alternative could involve diverting irradiated commercial fuel to a clandestine reprocessing plant from a temporary storage facility, where it might have been awaiting either commercial reprocessing or, in the case of a once-through fuel cycle, ultimate disposal.

Rather than work with plutonium from spent fuel Y might attempt to extract the fissionable isotope uranium 235 either from natural uranium (which contains less than 1 percent U-235) or from the low-enriched uranium used for power-reactor fuel (about 3 percent U-235), concentrating it to, say, 90 percent. For this approach there are several candidate technologies at various stages of development. For the past 25 years practically all enrichment, either for power-reactor purposes or for the production of weapons-grade uranium, has been carried out in the huge gaseous-diffusion plants of the U.S. and the U.S.S.R. Gaseous-diffusion plants do not need to be built on such a heroic scale, however; furthermore, other enrichment technologies now challenge the dominant position of gaseous diffusion. Ultracentrifuge enrichment is being actively developed in several countries and is on the verge of commercialization in some of them. It requires less power than gaseous diffusion and has other advantages as well. These factors,

together with the greater operational flexibility of centrifuge plants, suggest that this technology would offer a smoother path to weapons material, either with a plant built specifically for that purpose or through a facility built initially to fulfill civilian nuclear-power needs. It would be much easier to carry out the adjustments necessary to convert a gas-centrifuge plant from a low-enriched product to a high-enriched military-grade one than it would to similarly convert a gaseous-diffusion plant; alternatively a small string of centrifuges can be used over and over again progressively to enrich single batches of uranium.

Other enrichment technologies that are gaining in importance include the aerodynamic, or nozzle, approach, variations of which are being developed concurrently in West Germany and South Africa, and the laser technique for isotope separation, which is also being pursued in several countries. A pilot aerodynamic-enrichment plant in South Africa may have already been used to produce enough weapons-grade uranium for one or more explosive devices. Furthermore, although work on laser enrichment has so far been limited to laboratory research, enough information has been made available to suggest that the technique might ultimately provide a cheaper and more flexible route than any other enrichment process. All the known methods, at whatever stage of development, require sophisticated technology but nothing that is beyond the capability of many of the more advanced developing nations.

Turning to seemingly more bizarre ac-

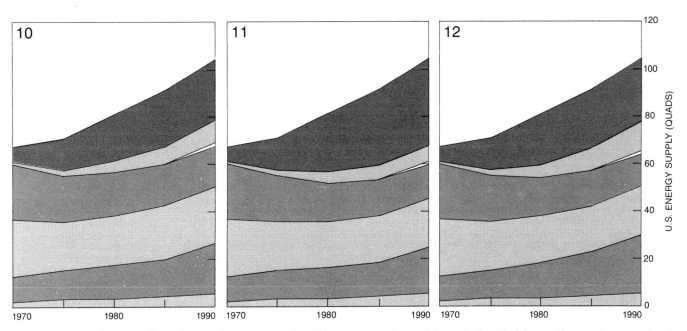

percent in additions to domestic natural-gas reserves and a 100 percent increase in additions to domestic oil reserves compared with the preceding decade (*scenario No. 9*) the U.S. would still have to import close to 20 quads of energy by 1985, equivalent to almost nine million barrels of crude oil per day. On the other hand, if the rate of eco-

nomic growth is greater than the 3.5 annual increase in gross national product projected in the base case and all areas of domestic energy supply turn out to be less productive than expected (*scenario No. 3*), the U.S. could be importing 17.7 million barrels of crude oil per day in 1985. The role of imported oil as a "swing" fuel (*color*) is evident.

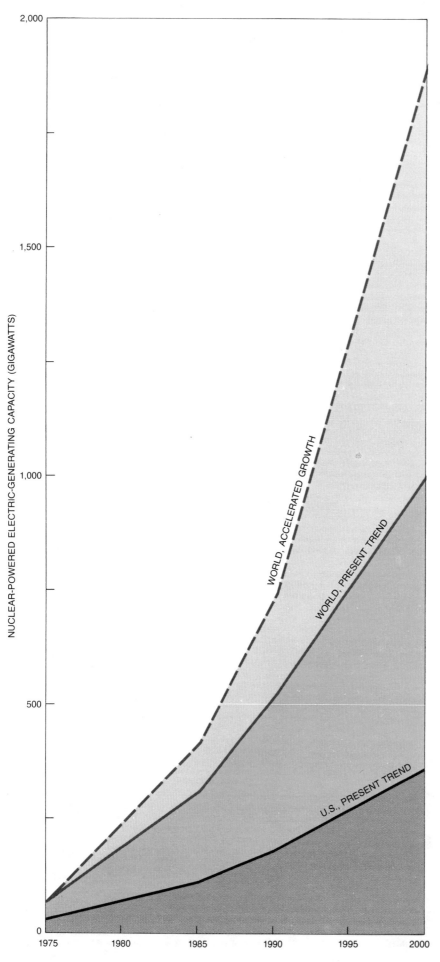

tivities, country *Y* might employ agents to steal material from abroad or buy it in a black market, an open market or an intermediate "gray" market. It could receive such material as a gift or a loan from another government. It might steal an assembled weapon or even be given one. None of these activities can be excluded, and some may be more likely to occur than those we described above.

A really effective barrier to weapons proliferation would involve blocking all the lines marked with a black bar in the diagram. That is impossible, but the U.S. is only trying to make weapons proliferation substantially more difficult. Combining technological denial with an assortment of incentives related to the supply of enrichment services for light-water-reactor fuel (to be used by *Y* under tightly specified conditions) would, the Administration thought, significantly increase international stability.

Several other decision paths of a different nature exist, on which the U.S. Government has only an indirect influence; the principal ones are marked with gray bars. Why does *Y* decide to acquire a weapons capability in the first place? Why does it actually build nuclear bombs? Why might it use them? The answers to such questions depend on many things, and a long-term policy not to proceed at any one of these decision points makes all the technological elaborations irrelevant. The converse, however, is not necessarily true. As we implied when we were discussing reprocessing plants, a decision to proceed might be heavily influenced by the technological capability in place at that time.

When the U.S. policy described here is viewed from other countries or other domestic vantage points, it looks quite different. The main line of devel-

POTENTIAL TRENDS in the growth of nuclear power are shown through the end of the century for both the U.S. and the world (excluding China, the U.S.S.R. and the other countries of Eastern Europe). For the world the lower estimate is based on present trends in energy utilization and supply, including delays in the construction of new nuclear reactors, and assumes a continuation of these trends. The "accelerated growth" estimate assumes that the goals of ambitious nuclear programs will be met and that the world will return to higher rates of energy growth. The "present trend" estimate must be regarded as the more realistic of the two and may itself be too high. The data for these curves were obtained from a recent joint report by the nuclear-energy agency of the Organization for Economic Cooperation and Development (OECD) and the International Atomic Energy Agency (IAEA). U.S. projection is based on recent estimates by the Department of Energy. All such estimates must be viewed with caution, the authors point out, in view of the many uncertainties discussed in their article.

opment—in particular decisions by nation $Y$—can best be discussed in relation to a second diagram, which is similar to the first but starts with a U.S. decision to act restrictively and includes several additional logic paths. To understand its full significance we must start farther back, with the electric-power sector.

The U.S. electric-power industry abhors uncertainty about the future, for several reasons. One is the long time needed to construct new facilities (10 years is typical) and long expected life of these facilities (40 years, say). The industry also needs a stable fuel supply and is required by law to provide reliable service. In this regulated industry justifiable costs can be charged to the consumer. The present program of the Administration increases uncertainty about the future of nuclear power for several reasons. First, the decision against reprocessing spent fuel has raised fears, not yet completely alleviated by the Federal Government, that the electric utilities may in practice be left holding the spent fuel for a long time (for example by long-drawn-out court challenges to the Environmental Impact Statement for a Federal spent-fuel storage facility), a very unappealing prospect to them.

In addition, conflicting Federal opinions about the acceptability of nuclear power make the electric utilities both suspicious of Government motivations and better targets for anti-nuclear-power groups. Many electric utilities also fear that the Nuclear Regulatory Commission will order expensive, and in their view capricious, retroactive modifications to existing nuclear plants, in spite of current efforts to modify the Commission's legislative foundation. Many experts, concerned at the inherent uncertainty associated with the four-million-ton estimate for U.S. uranium resources that could ultimately be made available, feel that a "prudent planning estimate" for the purpose of setting nuclear-power policy should be appreciably lower. A National Academy of Sciences resource-evaluation group recently estimated that 1.8 million tons is all that is likely to be mined in the U.S. by the year 2010 at a cost of $30 per pound or less, even with a Government policy of maximum stimulation.

Furthermore, doubts have been expressed as to whether the U.S. uranium-supply industry, itself troubled by uncertainty about the size of the market for its product, will be prepared to invest in exploration, mining and ore-processing-plant construction at levels that will be sufficient to fuel a growing number of nuclear-power plants. Part of the uncertainty permeating the electric-utility sector stems from concern over the availability of nuclear-fuel supplies, so that the problem exhibits circular characteristics; it is also aggravated by the fact that the strength of the uranium supply industry's commitment to keeping power reactors adequately fueled is less than the utilities might find desirable. For example, it has been estimated that within a few years petroleum companies will own about 40 percent of all U.S. ore-processing capacity and as much as 50 percent of low-cost U.S. uranium resources. In short, the uranium suppliers do not constitute an industry "captive" to the electric-power sector. (Indeed, increasing corporate diversification in the various energy supply industries has led to the suggestion that the reverse might be true.) As a result uncertainty arising from the Administration's program may be compounded, unwittingly or otherwise. Similarly, each U.S. manufacturer of nuclear reactors has 75 percent or more of its business elsewhere (for example in other power systems), and the nuclear business is not essential to it. In a period of rising costs, large-scale cancellations of orders and excess production capacity, the business appears less than inviting.

The last point is worth further comment. The U.S. manufacturers of light-water reactors could turn out between 20 and 30 nuclear-power systems a year. The Administration has estimated that full implementation of its national energy policy would lead to an installed nuclear electric capacity of more than 300,000 megawatts by the year 2000. With 50,000 megawatts already installed, and a further 25,000 megawatts scheduled for completion by 1980, there would be, on the average, a dozen or so reactor systems completed each year for the last 20 years of the century, a situation that implies a large-scale restructuring of the reactor-manufacturing industry sooner or later.

Compounding these difficulties, the electric-utility sector suffers the additional one of raising enough capital. One cause is the host of uncertainties we have described. Another involves the general flight during recent inflationary times from long-term investment; the rate of economic return from the regulated utility industry has become unattractive, a circumstance that also affects other generating plants, particularly those that burn coal.

The upshot of all this is the paradoxical situation that although the existing nuclear reactors run pretty well and deliver economical electric power in many parts of the country, the nuclear industry in the U.S. may nonetheless be close to collapse. The proximate cause is a movement by the electric-utility industry and manufacturers away from nuclear power as they attempt to reduce their own institutional uncertainty, but deeper causes drive these changes and are coupled with the Administration's attitude toward nuclear power. This train of thought points toward the second possible motivation mentioned above: that the Administration, through internal indecision, is incapable of acting to prevent the nuclear industry from collapsing. The indications, however, are ambiguous.

What then is the U.S. electric-utility sector likely to do? The conventional option is coal, with the Administration's apparently enthusiastic backing. Oil and natural gas are expensive and in such uncertain supply that the Administration has submitted legislation prohibiting all new power plants from burning them, with only limited environmental and economic exceptions. Other legislative provisions would, through taxation and prohibitive clauses, encourage utilities not to burn oil and gas in existing facilities and to convert them to coal.

But what if the coal cannot be mined, transported and burned in time, and in socially accepted ways? Even before the Administration announced its national energy policy widespread doubts had grown about the wisdom, or even the possibility, of increasing coal production very quickly. In particular, can a goal of increasing coal production from its current level of 650 million tons per year to a projected total of 1.25 billion tons per year by 1985 actually be achieved? Industrial problems associated with such an expansion, land-use problems, states' policies and obstacles created by the Administration's environmental policy for coal have all been repeatedly raised as evidence to suggest that there will be hesitation on both the supply and demand sides of the coal industry. Even coal transportation, which currently accounts for about 30 percent of the U.S. rail tonnage, will be difficult for the disheveled railroad industry.

The environmental problems with coal appear to grow with time and increased understanding. The comparatively large amounts of disturbed land, the chemically and biologically active complex molecules present in coal and produced by the burning of it, and the ubiquitous nature of these effects create difficulties at local and national levels. On a global scale potentially the most serious long-range environmental impacts resulting from the large-scale burning of coal (or indeed of any fossil fuel) may arise from the effects of the increased concentration of carbon dioxide in the atmosphere. At this stage the problem is not well understood, and the potential contribution of planned U.S. coal-burning activities is therefore also shrouded with uncertainty. Nevertheless, in this problem area and others the prognosis looks more serious as more information accumulates. The U.S. electric-utility sector, generally aware of these difficulties, looks on coal with increasing anxiety.

Irresolution about nuclear power, increasingly apparent difficulty with coal, a partial ban against oil and a half-hearted attitude toward energy conservation make an impossible combination; something has to give. If the electric-utility industry waits a few years for public debate to resolve these issues, the concomitant pressure for rapid and comparatively pollution-free installations will drive it toward oil-burning plants. That would be doubly disastrous, because the conversion of some transportation, industrial, commercial and domestic systems from oil to efficiently used electric power, based on coal or nuclear fuels, is seen as a way of reducing oil imports. If the electric utilities are unable or unwilling to provide the means for this substitution, oil consumption will continue to exceed Administration targets.

Thus imported oil may once again fill the role the Administration has sought to prevent it from playing: the "swing" fuel that satisfies increased energy demands. Reinforcing this trend is the present concentration on increasing domestic production, which will have the effect of keeping up oil-based activities that must surely in the next decade or two be fed by imports.

The international importance of President Carter's attempts to reduce oil imports, and the dangers implicit in failing to do so, cannot be overemphasized. Today the U.S. imports nearly half of its immense consumption of 17 million barrels a day, an amount equal to almost a quarter of all internationally traded oil. A reduction to the Administration's stated import target of less than seven million barrels a day by 1985 from levels that would otherwise be reached if present trends are allowed to continue unabated would save annually an amount of crude greater than the current oil imports of Japan or half those of Western Europe. If the target is not met and the U.S. imports increase, the competitive pressures for oil, particularly Middle East oil, may reach dangerous proportions even without another politically motivated interruption in supplies. No other nation in the world (with the possible exception of Saudi Arabia, with its vast potential production capacity and its role of "swing" producer) can exert such an influence on the world's energy outlook through its domestic policies.

After this analysis, we can now enter the logic diagram on pages 224 and 225 at the point where the U.S. states its nuclear-policy position and then explore the international consequences.

All the foregoing trains of thought have been quite apparent to both developed and developing nations. Japan and most of the advanced industrial nations of Europe have meager coal or oil supplies themselves, relatively speaking; even North Sea oil harvested at the maximum planned capacity will supply only about 20 percent of Western Europe's needs. Thus all those countries, facing their own difficulties and the distinct possibility of a continuingly gluttonous

U.S., see an increased incentive to push ahead with their own nuclear programs, including reprocessing and breeder reactors. Further encouragement to do so seems to be arising from an unintended source. Along with the U.S., Australia (currently not a uranium producer but potentially one of the world's two or three major exporters of uranium within the next few years) and Canada (the world's biggest uranium exporter) have also recently imposed stringent proliferation-related controls on their exports. In all three cases these controls include the requirement that consent must be obtained from the exporting nation before any of the fuel can be reprocessed. In at least one case deliveries of fuel have been delayed pending agreement to these and other conditions by importing nations. Although the controls have been implemented with the intention of creating a more rigorous nonproliferation regime, for the uranium-deficient, fuel-supply-sensitive Japanese and Europeans such manifestations of external political involvement in their domestic fuel-cycle operations, together with the unsettling prospect of further mercurial behavior by their suppliers in the future, may ultimately act to increase the vigor with which these nations set about reducing their dependence on fuel imports by the use of plutonium and breeder reactors. According to statements of intent from many of them, that is already happening.

What will leaders in developing countries see? They will see a rich U.S. liable to forgo nuclear power, in spite of what it might say about preserving light-water reactors. They will see increased short-term pressure on the world's supply of oil, inevitably resulting in shortages and still higher prices. They will see pessimistic projections for world petroleum and gas resources that will allow neither continued profligate use by the industrialized nations nor any chance for their own countries to follow a development path anything like that followed by their predecessors. They will see an offer of nuclear-fuel supplies that binds them to the goodwill of the U.S. and other developed countries for even limited nuclear assistance. (The recent suggestion of an international nuclear-fuel bank is a partial response to this point.) They will see the growing appearance of a world divided into an oligopoly of developed states that turns into an oligarchy as nuclear power becomes more important throughout the world, and a coterie of less developed nations that must fall farther and farther behind. (This latter impression becomes reinforced by U.S. actions that treat certain of its industrialized trading partners as "exceptions" in view of their continued insistence on the need for reprocessing and breeder reactors in their countries without delay.) And they will see little promise of help from the U.S. to

become truly independent in terms of nuclear power.

The inevitable result will be increasing distrust of the U.S. and a growing sensation of unwanted dependence. Both developed and developing nations share these feelings of insecurity. Considering only uranium enrichment as an example, would a U.S. offer of more enrichment services suggest an extension of U.S. market control of enrichment supply, which in turn would suggest increased dependence on U.S. whims? Troubled in large part by the somewhat fickle nature of the decision-making process governing U.S. exports, the out-

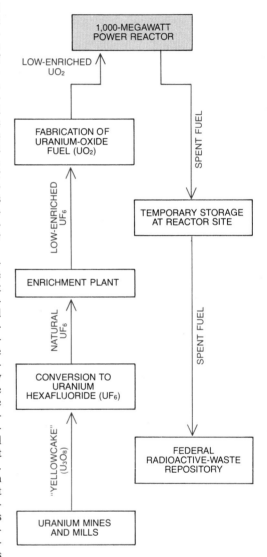

THREE NUCLEAR-FUEL CYCLES suitable with conventional light-water reactors are shown in these simplified diagrams, adapted from a recent report to the American Physical Society by its study group on nuclear-fuel cycles and waste management. In the prevailing "once through" approach (left) the spent-fuel rods, which still contain an appreciable amount of fissionable isotopes (principally "unburned" uranium 235 and plutonium 239 produced by the transmutation of the urani-

side world, including the less developed countries, sees more incentive to set up its own enrichment programs and to go nuclear with or without U.S. assistance.

Both developed and developing countries also share other reactions. Among both groups, for example, there are suspicions that the U.S. program is really designed to improve the sagging fortunes of U.S. nuclear exports: either to increase the attractiveness of U.S. lightwater reactors or to curb the global movement toward plutonium and the breeder reactor until U.S. technology in these areas has caught up with capabilities in Western Europe. It has also been

pointed out that the exemplary nature of the U.S. decision to defer indefinitely the reprocessing of its own commercial power-reactor fuel was compromised from the outset by the fact that fuel reprocessing in connection with the U.S. weapons program would continue as before. Related comments address the entire network of U.S. weapons-manufacturing activities and deployed weapons, suggesting that the scale and wide distribution of this system presents a more attractive target to would-be proliferators than a commercial plutonium fuel cycle would. Furthermore, some observers have speculated that the sub-

sequent decision to use gas-centrifuge technology for the next increment of U.S. enrichment capacity rather than a more proliferation-resistant gaseous-diffusion plant compounds the already present inconsistencies.

To be sure, some of these reactions are mere rhetorical flourishes; nevertheless, they may still have wide-ranging international reverberations. Moreover, many of the reactions are contradictory. How can a rich U.S. liable to forgo nuclear power also be attempting to increase its share of nuclear exports? How can one explain the fact that some of the nations where complaints about the in-

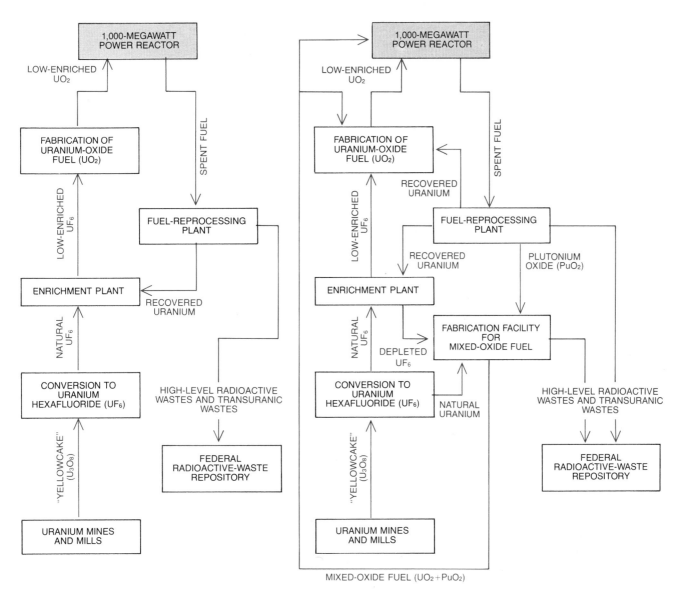

MIXED-OXIDE FUEL (UO₂ + PuO₂)

um-238 nuclei in the fuel are disposed of without reprocessing; disposition of the spent fuel can in principle be either temporary or permanent. In the uranium-recycle option (*center*) the spent fuel is reprocessed to recover only the residual uranium, which can then be enriched in the fissionable isotope U-235 or used as it is to replace some of the virgin natural uranium in the fabrication of new fuel assemblies. In the uranium-and-plutonium-recycle option (*right*) the spent fuel is reprocessed to separate both uranium and plutonium from the wastes. The recovered plutonium can then be combined with uranium having a very low concentration of U-235, in effect substituting the plutonium for some of the U-235 in the normally low-

enriched fuel. Useful mixed-oxide fuels can be made by combining plutonium with uranium derived from a number of different sources, including the normal low-enriched uranium product from an isotope-separation plant, the uranium recovered from spent fuel or the depleted "tails" from a uranium-enrichment plant. It has been estimated that with both uranium and plutonium recycling the industrial operations required to supply enriched uranium could be reduced by about 20 percent in the year 2000 compared with what they would be for either the uranium-recycle or no-recycle options. This saving would of course require the introduction of the costly and complicated fuel-reprocessing and mixed-oxide fuel-fabrication operations.

consistency of U.S. policies toward domestic and military reprocessing have been heard are also those that rely most heavily on the presence of the U.S. nuclear deterrent for their defense? Such contradictions, however, do no more than mirror the ambiguities and contradictions we have recognized in the U.S. policy, as it attempts to strengthen the barriers between peaceful and violent uses of nuclear energy and simultaneously wrestles with an immense and growing demand for energy, both domestic and international.

The Nonproliferation Treaty, to which more than 100 nations are now parties, embodies an internationally negotiated agreement on the framework in which the energy v. proliferation enigma should be resolved. In it the non-nuclear-weapons states party to the treaty undertake not to develop or otherwise acquire any form of nuclear explosive and to accept international safeguards on all peaceful nuclear activities. In return for this commitment the right of all parties to the treaty to develop and use nuclear energy for peaceful purposes is affirmed, as is the right to participate in exchanges of equipment, materials and technology for the peaceful use of nuclear energy.

The restrictive export policies of the U.S. (and of other major nuclear suppliers) are viewed in many parts of the world as extending the inequalities that have always been inherent in the Nonproliferation Treaty between nuclear-weapons states and non-nuclear-weapons states. The new expression of these inequalities is the attempt to influence criteria for the international distribution of certain "sensitive" peaceful technologies, particularly reprocessing. Implied in this policy is a redrawing of the line separating peaceful uses of nuclear energy from violent ones, and therefore a redefinition of proliferation. Traditionally the latter had been defined as the acquisition of nuclear weapons. Now, however, the new U.S. position is being interpreted as an attempt to redefine proliferation as the capability of acquiring nuclear weapons. Had this always been the case, it is argued, negotiating the Nonproliferation Treaty would have been impossible in the first place.

We make no attempt to determine whether in fact the U.S. would be failing to comply with its international legal

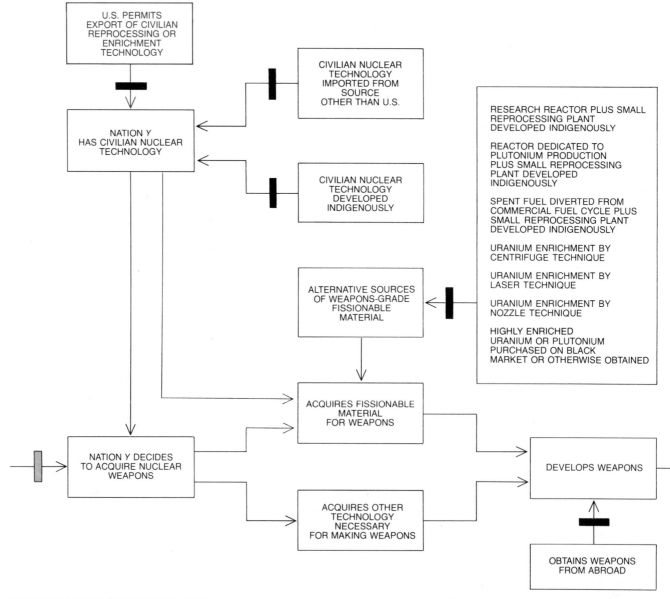

**NUCLEAR-PROLIFERATION SCENARIO** currently perceived as being worrisome by the U.S. Government is illustrated in the form of this sequential logic diagram. The main horizontal decision path shows the series of steps that could be followed by a non-nuclear-weapons nation, designated *Y*, to acquire nuclear weapons and to use them. The vertical paths show several possible inputs to *Y*'s decision. For example, the U.S. sees the acquisition of a nuclear-fuel-reprocessing capability as a stimulant to weapons proliferation. Accordingly

obligations as a party to the Nonproliferation Treaty by implementing its proposed export criteria. We do observe, however, that the loss of confidence in the effectiveness of international safeguards that has taken place in the U.S. is reflected in many non-nuclear states by a corresponding loss of confidence in the ability of the Nonproliferation Treaty to provide an acceptable legal framework for the international distribution of peaceful and military applications of nuclear energy. In such circumstances the fabric of the global nonproliferation regime is inevitably weakened.

All the considerations we have discussed here show up as destabilizing routes in our second proliferation scenario. Not only does country $Y$ find logical incentives to install domestic nuclear-fuel facilities, but also it perceives a world more fragmented and less secure. Feeling less secure itself, it naturally imagines others feeling the same way and hence it must increase its own security unilaterally. Escalation of uncertainty leads to escalation of international instability; a program originally intended by the U.S. to decrease the dangers of nuclear proliferation inadvertently has the opposite effect. Meanwhile the U.S. isolates itself from the mainstream of world nuclear policy, and its ability to favorably affect that policy diminishes.

More caveats and auxiliary views remain to be displayed. None of this analysis is meant to overstate the role of nuclear power in solving the world's energy problems. That mistake has been made too many times before. Some of the problems currently facing the nuclear-power industry in non-Communist developed countries can probably best be understood in terms of a backlash against earlier technological overoptimism. For the majority of the less developed countries nuclear-generated electricity cannot play a significant part in meeting energy requirements for a long time. Costs have risen alarmingly, and besides, the type and scale of the energy supplied by currently available nuclear-power stations seem less compatible with the energy-demand structure in many of these countries than the output of other energy-supply systems.

Moreover, in some developing countries where nuclear power is intended to play a major role the overall development targets frequently appear overambitious and unlikely to be realized. Fears have been expressed that nuclear-power technology could critically exacerbate rivalries among the various political, industrial and technocratic elites and increase the gap between such elites and the remainder of the population. Until now suppliers have not discernibly modified any "hard sell" policies because they might ultimately contribute to domestic political instabilities with unpredictable international consequences, and it is unlikely that such self-restraint will be shown in the future. The point here is not, of course, that the industrialized supplier nations should decide what is good for the development of the poorer countries and impose export restrictions accordingly but that nuclear technology may be "sensitive" for many reasons other than the increased access to weapons-grade material it may provide.

We conclude, therefore, that the conventionally defended analyses have been inadequate. The various original motivations virtually disappeared from our discussion, and rightly so; they were more nearly goals than real policies. Both are necessary; to neglect the hard work of developing policy causes much trouble because then the original vision, however high-minded, is washed away by a sea of events, and only consequences remain.

What to do? In answering this question we have had to assume that many other issues related to nuclear power can be resolved. To us the three largest of those issues seem to be reactor safety, the management of nuclear wastes and the prevention of subnational nuclear felonies. Although we have not dealt with these matters, we realize their gravity. Our analysis and recommendations would be irrelevant, however, only if both the U.S. and almost all other countries opted out of nuclear power. Nuclear power might disappear in the U.S., but neither present reactors nor breeders will go away in many other places. If the activities of Western Europe and Japan are unconvincing, one need only consider the U.S.S.R. and its Eastern European allies; they also develop nuclear power, with the most sensitive activities being reserved to the U.S.S.R. The U.S. must stop acting from time to time as though nuclear power was about to go away, or as though its disappearance would have little consequence.

The Administration has begun to discuss some of the necessary changes: for example a gradual shift to a more flexible policy, more emphasis on providing an assured nuclear-fuel supply and a suggestion to set up an international storage facility for spent fuel. Owing to significant reductions in projected overall energy demand and particularly in forecasts of installed nuclear capacity, the next few years seem to us a period of grace, perhaps overperceived in the U.S. and underperceived abroad, during which fundamental repairs can be made to the fabric of nuclear goals and policies. The period may be a decade, but it can hardly be much longer, being limited by the consequences of the inexorable pressure on other energy resources. The time is technically long enough to develop variations in the current fuel cycle, perhaps long enough to devise a brand-new one and even reactors and other facilities to use the fuel, but such activity would require far firmer decisions and much prompter (and more expensive) implementation than we have seen. Both the preparation of fissionable fuel from new or reprocessed material (the "front end" of the fuel cycle) and the reprocessing of spent fuel must be carefully considered, not just the latter. As we have said, we consider the front end of the fuel cycle, the enrichment of natural uranium for example, to be a sensitive proliferation issue. The exis-

tence of about 200 power reactors around the world working on the present fuel cycle must also be considered, and the opportunities for technological innovation that might be applied to them are limited.

All these things make large demands on one decade or a little more. So do institutional accommodations among nations, not only with respect to the currently developed nuclear-fuel cycles but also to many other things. Time is short, whether for technological modification or for international institution-building. Whatever the outcome of the former, the latter is an indispensable part of efforts to deal with the problems of nuclear-weapons proliferation and energy scarcity. Although the Administration's proposals have created many problems, they have succeeded in injecting a new sense of urgency into the situation. It is essential that this asset not be allowed to evaporate.

Regarding present fuel cycles and other matters directly related to nuclear power in the next decade or two we have five main recommendations to offer:

1. Nuclear power should be kept alive in the U.S. at least as a long-term "insurance" option, and that means not only the continued development of light-water reactors but also progress toward de-

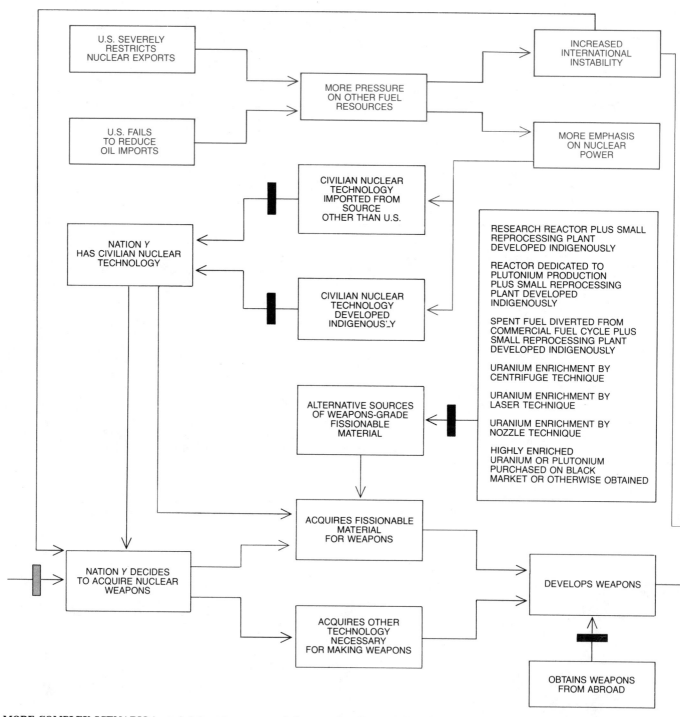

**MORE COMPLEX SCENARIO** is needed to portray more realistically the likely effects of an overly restrictive U.S. nuclear-export policy on the entire problem of international stability and the proliferation of nuclear weapons. The main decision path followed by nation *Y* toward the acquisition of a nuclear-weapons capability is the same as it is in the preceding diagram, as are a number of other elements in the diagram. In this case, however, the vertical inputs to *Y*'s decisions start with the new U.S. restrictions on nuclear exports,

veloping a viable breeder reactor. Central-station solar power and controlled fusion are only long-term possibilities, oil is only a short-term source of energy and we have little faith in coal for the long term.

2. To reduce uncertainty for the U.S. electric-utility industry and others the Federal Government should take several steps. First, it should reaffirm that the reprocessing of spent nuclear fuel is being delayed but not abandoned. Second, the Federal Government should assure the electric utilities of a review of national policy on reprocessing as the debate about it matures, and certainly within five years; that would include an assessment of the projected uranium supply, which would draw on the current national uranium-resource evaluation and other programs. Third, the complexity and prolixity of the licensing process for nuclear-power plants should be eased by making it more difficult for license applications to be recycled again and again to the Nuclear Regulatory Commission. The nuclear licensing bill currently under consideration appears to be facing formidable obstacles at several stages of the legislative process, and in any case it seems to address these issues only partially in its present form. Finally, the Federal Government should take on the entire burden of managing spent fuel, and guarantee to take responsibility for the fuel reasonably soon after its discharge from power reactors. That includes spent-fuel reprocessing, if and when a decision comes to do it. No other sector has an adequately long time perspective to plan and operate the appropriate facilities. In particular, the chemical industry, on which the task might otherwise be expected to fall, traditionally expects a payback on investment in a very few years, and therefore discounts far-future profits too much to match the long-term nature of the tasks, particularly waste handling and storage.

3. The U.S. should offer to explore with other nations the costs and benefits to the international community of completing the reprocessing plant now sitting idle at Barnwell, S.C., and operating it as an international facility. The principal objectives of such a project would be to gain experience with commercial reprocessing technology, to assess the effectiveness of international safeguards and to demonstrate the institutional viability of international cooperation in the provision of fuel-cycle services.

4. Efforts to increase the security of the international supply of uranium and enrichment services should be intensified. Domestically, differences among the various branches of the Government should not be allowed to interfere with the pivotal task of reestablishing the U.S. as a reliable supplier of enriched uranium fuel.

5. In all these activities we note the need for an international agency. We see none better prepared than the International Atomic Energy Agency (IAEA), and we believe it should be greatly strengthened so that it can continuously inspect sensitive facilities. The answer does not, however, lie in the mere strengthening or even proliferation of agencies. For example, restrictions on the export of appropriate nuclear systems may undermine the Nonproliferation Treaty, and the IAEA can do nothing about it.

Beyond all these issues we see others seeming to stand out in the distance. First, it is noteworthy that the diagrams we have drawn differ from the conventionally discussed diagrams of causes and effects. Our discussion has been almost entirely international, as befits the problem. The U.S. approach has been too self-centered, insufficiently sensitive to the problems of other nations and lacking in awareness of its own potentially disruptive character.

Near the beginning of this discussion we mentioned that the Administration has attempted to breathe new life into the larger issues presented by nuclear weapons. If governments and people are so concerned with the risks of future proliferation, how much more should they worry about the huge numbers of nuclear weapons already deployed? One who lives on the edge of an abyss should not squander his effort avoiding small ditches. The real threat of nuclear weapons is seen once again, more clearly than before, in the illuminating perspective provided by the juxtaposition of thousands of existing megatons on the one hand and a few hypothetical kilotons on the other.

This brings us to the more general question of international peace and stability. In the worldwide search for routes to a juster and more sustainable society it has become clear to many observers that a peace in which the world is divided ever more rigorously into haves and have-nots is neither just nor likely to be very sustainable, whether the basis for division is social, economic or (as here) seemingly technological. Such a division not only defeats itself in the long run; even worse, it is wrong.

We propose that the real long-term solution both to the nuclear-power problem and to the larger problems of international instability lies not in fostering division but in its opposite: mutually cooperative international interdependence. Since nations must depend on one another, they lose more by going separately than by staying in partnership. Our analysis shows that this partnership must include the developing countries, since many of them, if they are excluded, are capable of upsetting the international order through the acquisition of nuclear weapons and other acts.

All of this will not be easy, but other approaches have yielded nothing but unstable arms escalation. The partnership should logically involve food, health care and many other sectors where the U.S. can make valuable contributions. Only in that way will we have a chance of answering constructively the question that can no longer be put aside: Why do people want to make nuclear weapons in the first place?

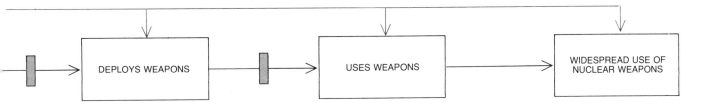

coupled with the failure of the U.S. to reduce significantly its imports of crude oil. Several additional logic paths, shown in color, represent the possible sequence of events that could result in added incentives for nation Y not only to push ahead with its own civilian nuclear-power program, including uranium-enrichment technology, spent-fuel reprocessing plants and breeder reactors, but also perhaps to respond to increased international instability arising out of growing competition for energy resources by joining the nuclear-weapons "club."

# BIBLIOGRAPHIES

# I ENERGY: THE SOCIETAL SETTING

## 1. World Resources and the World Middle Class

RESOURCES AND MAN: A STUDY AND RECOMMENDATIONS. Committee on Resources and Man of the Division of Earth Sciences, National Academy of Sciences—National Research Council. W. H. Freeman and Company, 1969.

MAN AND THE ECOSPHERE: READINGS FROM SCIENTIFIC AMERICAN. W. H. Freeman and Company, 1971.

ECONOMICS OF THE ENVIRONMENT: SELECTED READINGS. Edited by Robert Dorfman and Nancy S. Dorfman. W. W. Norton and Company, Inc., 1972.

THE HUMAN POPULATION: A SCIENTIFIC AMERICAN BOOK. W. H. Freeman and Company, 1974.

## 2. World Oil Production

PETROLEUM RESOURCES: HOW MUCH OIL AND WHERE. John D. Moody and Robert E. Geiger in *Technology Review,* pages 38–45: March/April, 1975.

ENERGY: GLOBAL PROSPECTS 1985–2000. Workshop on Alternative Energy Strategies. McGraw-Hill Book Company, 1977.

ENERGY SUPPLY TO THE YEAR 2000: GLOBAL AND NA-TIONAL STUDIES. Workshop on Alternative Energy Strategies. The MIT Press, June, 1977.

## 3. World Coal Production

ENERGY: GLOBAL PROSPECTS 1985–2000. Workshop on Alternative Energy Strategies. McGraw-Hill Book Company, 1977.

ENERGY SUPPLY TO THE YEAR 2000: GLOBAL AND NA-TIONAL STUDIES. Workshop on Alternative Energy Strategies. The MIT Press, 1977.

SURVEY OF ENERGY RESOURCES 1976. World Energy Conference. United States National Committee of the World Energy Conference. 1977.

## 4. Energy Policy in the U.S.

THE NATIONAL ENERGY OUTLOOK. Shell Oil Company, Houston, March, 1973.

ENERGY RESEARCH AND DEVELOPMENT: REPORT OF THE TASK FORCE ON ENERGY OF THE SUBCOMMITTEE ON SCIENCE, RESEARCH, AND DEVELOPMENT, DECEMBER, 1972. Committee on Science and Astronautics, U.S. House of Representatives. U.S. Government Printing Office, 1973.

# II ENERGY SOURCES: WHAT LIES IN THE FUTURE?

## 5. Oil and Gas from Coal

CLEAN FUELS FROM COAL: SYMPOSIUM PAPERS, PRESENTED SEPTEMBER 10–14, 1973, CHICAGO, ILLINOIS. Institute of Gas Technology, December, 1973.

PROCEEDINGS OF SIXTH SYNTHETIC PIPELINE GAS SYM-POSIUM: CHICAGO, ILLINOIS, OCTOBER 28–30, 1974. American Gas Association, 1974.

FEDERAL ENERGY ADMINISTRATION PROJECT INDEPEN-DENCE BLUEPRINT FINAL TASK FORCE REPORT.

Prepared by the Interagency Task Force on Synthetic Fuels from Coal, under the direction of the U.S. Department of the Interior. U.S. Government Printing Office, November, 1974.

FISCHER-TROPSCH PLANT DESIGN CRITERIA: PRESENTED AT 68TH ANNUAL MEETING OF AMERICAN INSTITUTE OF CHEMICAL ENGINEERS, LOS ANGELES, NOVEMBER 19, 1975. J. B. O'Hara, A. Bela, N. E. Jentz and S. K. Khaderi. The Ralph M. Parsons Company, 1975.

OIL/GAS PLANT DESIGN CRITERIA: PRESENTED AT 68TH ANNUAL MEETING OF AMERICAN INSTITUTE OF CHEMICAL ENGINEERS, LOS ANGELES, NOVEMBER 19, 1975. J. B. O'Hara, G. H. Hervey, S. M. Fass and E. A. Mills. The Ralph M. Parsons Company, 1975.

## 6. The Gasification of Coal

CHEMISTRY OF COAL UTILIZATION: SUPPLEMENTARY VOLUME. Edited by H. H. Lowry. John Wiley & Sons, Inc., 1963.

EVALUATION OF COAL GASIFICATION TECHNOLOGY: PART 1–PIPELINE QUALITY GAS. R & D REPORT No. 74, Interim Report No. 1. Office of Coal Research of the U.S. Department of the Interior, April, 1973.

## 7. The Necessity of Fission Power

THE NUCLEAR CONTROVERY. Ralph E. Lapp. Fact Systems/Reddy Kilowatt, Inc., 1974.

PROJECT INDEPENDENCE REPORT. Federal Energy Administration. U.S. Government Printing Office, 1974.

WASH-1400, REACTOR SAFETY STUDY: AN ASSESSMENT OF ACCIDENT RISKS IN U.S. COMMERCIAL NUCLEAR POWER PLANTS. U.S. Government Printing Office, 1975.

ERDA-48. Energy Research and Development Agency. U.S. Government Printing Office, 1975.

AMERICA'S ENERGY FUTURE. Ralph E. Lapp. Fact Systems/Reddy Kilowatt, Inc., in press.

ENVIRONMENTAL HAZARDS IN HIGH-LEVEL RADIOACTIVE WASTE DISPOSAL. Bernard Cohen in *Reviews of Modern Physics*, in press.

## 8. Natural-Uranium Heavy-Water Reactors

PROCEEDINGS OF THE JOINT CNA-AECL SYMPOSIUM ON NUCLEAR ENERGY. Atomic Energy of Canada Limited, Ottawa, 1974.

THE STANDARDIZED CANDU 600. G. L. Brooks. Atomic Energy of Canada Limited, Ottawa, 1974.

NUCLEAR POWER IN CANADA: QUESTIONS AND ANSWERS. Canadian Nuclear Association, Toronto, 1975.

PERFORMANCE OF CANDU COMMERCIAL UNITS. L. W. Woodhead. Ontario Hydro, 1975.

## 9. Superphénix: A Full-Scale Breeder Reactor

FAST BREEDER REACTORS. Glenn T. Seaborg and Justin L. Bloom in *Scientific American*, Vol. 223, No. 5, pages 13–21; November, 1970.

THE NECESSITY OF FISSION POWER. H. A. Bethe in *Scientific American*, Vol. 234. No. 1, pages 21–31; January, 1976.

THE BREEDER: WHEN AND WHY. *EPRI Journal.* Vol. 1, No. 2; March, 1976.

# III   ENVIRONMENTAL COSTS OF FOSSIL FUELS

## 10. The Carbon Dioxide Question

THE CARBON CYCLE. Bert Bolin in *Scientific American*, Vol. 223, No. 3, pages 124–132; September, 1970.

BROOKHAVEN SYMPOSIA IN BIOLOGY No.: CARBON AND THE BIOSPHERE. Edited by George M. Woodwell and E. V. Pecan. U.S. Atomic Energy Commission, Division of Technical Information. Oak Ridge, Tenn., 1973.

PRIMARY PRODUCTION OF INLAND AQUATIC ECOSYSTEMS. Gene E. Likens in *Primary Productivity of the Biosphere*, edited by H. Lieth and Robert H. Whittaker. Springer-Verlag, 1975.

## 11. Nighttime Images of the Earth from Space

MISSION TO EARTH: LANDSAT VIEWS THE WORLD. Nicholas M. Short, Paul D. Lowman, Jr., Stanley C. Freden and William A. Finch. NASA SP-360. U.S. Government Printing Office, 1976.

## 12. The Importation of Liquefied Natural Gas

SAFETY WITH CRYOGENIC FLUIDS. Michael G. Zabetakis. Plenum Press, Inc., 1967.

LIQUID NATURAL GAS. Noel de Nevers in *Scientific American*, Vol. 217, No. 4; October, 1967.

LNG INFORMATION BOOK, 1973. Prepared by the LNG Information Book Task Group of the Liquefied Natural Gas Committee. American Gas Association, 1973.

LIQUEFIED NATURAL GAS. W. L. Lom, John Wiley & Sons, 1974.

TECHNOLOGY AND CURRENT PRACTICES FOR PROCESSING, TRANSFERRING, AND STORING LIQUEFIED NATURAL GAS. Arthur D. Little, Inc., for the Office of Pipeline Safety, 1974.

LIQUEFIED NATURAL GASES: VIEWS AND PRACTICES, POLICY AND SAFETY. U.S. Coast Guard, 1976.

## 13. Pelagic Tar

PETROLEUM LUMPS ON THE SURFACE OF THE SEA. Michael H. Horn, John M. Teal and Richard H. Backus in *Science*, Vol. 168, No. 3928, pages 245–246; April 10, 1970.

OIL POLLUTION AND MARINE ECOLOGY. A. Nelson-Smith. Plenum Press, 1973.

PELAGIC TAR FROM BERMUDA AND THE SARGASSO SEA. James N. Butler, Byron F. Morris and Jeremy Sass.

Special Publication No. 10, Bermuda Biological Station for Research, 1973.

THE ENVIRONMENTAL FATE OF STRANDED CRUDE OIL. M. Blumer, M. Ehrhardt and J. H. Jones in *Deep-Sea Research*, Vol. 20, No. 3, pages 239–259; March, 1973.

## 14. The Strip-Mining of Western Coal

LEASED AND LOST: A STUDY OF PUBLIC AND INDIAN COAL LEASING IN THE WEST. Council on Economic Priorities in *Economic Priorities Report*, Vol. 5, No. 2; 1974.

PROJECT INDEPENDENCE. Federal Energy Administration. U.S. Government Printing Office, 1974.

REHABILITATION POTENTIAL OF WESTERN COAL LANDS. National Academy of Sciences and National Academy of Engineering. Ballinger Publishing Co., 1974.

EFFECTS OF COAL DEVELOPMENT IN THE NORTHERN GREAT PLAINS. Northern Great Plains Resource Program. Denver Federal Center, 1975.

RESULTS OF A STUDY OF OVERBURDEN HANDLING TECHNIQUES AND RECLAMATION PRACTICES AT WESTERN U.S. SURFACE COAL MINES. U.S. Bureau of Mines, 1975.

SURFACE MINING CONTROL AND RECLAMATION ACT OF 1975. U.S. House of Representatives, Committee on Interior and Insular Affairs. U.S. Government Printing Office, 1975.

# IV ENVIRONMENTAL COSTS OF NUCLEAR ENERGY

## 15. The Disposal of Radioactive Wastes from Fission Reactors

HIGH-LEVEL RADIOACTIVE WASTE MANAGEMENT ALTERNATIVES. Edited by K. J. Schneider and A. M. Platt. Battelle Memorial Institute. Pacific Northwest Laboratories, 1974.

ALTERNATIVE PROCESSES FOR MANAGING EXISTING COMMERCIAL HIGH LEVEL RADIOACTIVE WASTES. Nuclear Regulatory Commission Report NUREG-0043, 1976.

ALTERNATIVES FOR MANAGING WASTES FROM REACTORS AND POST-FISSION OPERATIONS IN THE LWR FUEL CYCLE. Division of Nuclear Fuel Cycle and Production. Energy Research and Development Administration Report ERDA-76-43, 1976.

ENVIRONMENTAL SURVEY OF THE REPROCESSING AND WASTE MANAGEMENT PORTIONS OF THE LWR FUEL CYCLE. Nuclear Regulatory Commission Report NUREG-0116, 1976.

HIGH-LEVEL RADIOACTIVE WASTE FROM LIGHT-WATER REACTORS. Bernard L. Cohen in *Reviews of Modern Physics*. Vol. 49, No. 1, pages 1–20; January, 1977.

## 16 The Reprocessing of Nuclear Fuels

NUCLEAR CHEMICAL ENGINEERING. Manson Benedict and Thomas H. Pigford. McGraw-Hill Book Company, 1957.

ENGINEERING FOR NUCLEAR FUEL REPROCESSING. Justin T. Long. Gordon and Breach Science Publishers, Inc., 1968.

ENVIRONMENT EFFECT OF A COMPLEX NUCLEAR FA-

CILITY. W. P. Bebbington in *Chemical Engineering Progress*, Vol. 70, No. 3, pages 85–86;March, 1974.

REPROCESSING—WHAT WENT WRONG? Simon Rippon in *Nuclear Engineering International*, Vol. 21, No. 239, pages 21–31; February, 1976.

## 17.  The Proliferation of Nuclear Weapons

THE CONTROL OF PROLIFERATION: THE 1968 TREATY IN HINDSIGHT AND FORECAST. Elizabeth Young in *Adelphi Papers*, No. 56; April, 1969.

NUCLEAR PROLIFERATION: PROSPECTS FOR CONTROL. Edited by Bennett Boskey and Mason Willrich. Dunellen Publishing Co., 1970.

THE POLITICS OF NUCLEAR PROLIFERATION. George H. Quester. The Johns Hopkins University Press, 1973.

NUCLEAR PROLIFERATION PROBLEMS. Stockholm International Peace Research Institute. The MIT Press, 1974.

NPT: PARADOXES AND PROBLEMS. Arms Control Association, Washington, D.C., 1975.

## 18.  Nuclear Power, Nuclear Weapons and International Stability

MOVING TOWARD LIFE IN A NUCLEAR ARMED CROWD? Albert Wohlstetter, Thomas A. Brown, Gregory Jones, David McGarvey, Henry Rowen, Vincent Taylor and Roberta Wohlstetter. Pan Heuristics, April 22, 1976.

NUCLEAR POWER ISSUES AND CHOICES. Nuclear Energy Policy Study Group. Ballinger Publishing Company, 1977.

THE NATIONAL ENERGY PLAN. Executive Office of the President: Energy Policy and Planning. Government Printing Office, April 29, 1977.

NUCLEAR PROLIFERATION AND SAFEGUARDS. Office of Technology Assessment, Congress of the United States, June, 1977.

# INDEX